Terrorism and Homeland Security

Terrorism and Homeland Security

Thinking Strategically About Policy

Edited by

Paul R. Viotti
Michael A. Opheim
Nicholas Bowen

 CRC Press
Taylor & Francis Group
Boca Raton   London   New York

CRC Press is an imprint of the
Taylor & Francis Group, an **informa** business

CRC Press
Taylor & Francis Group
6000 Broken Sound Parkway NW, Suite 300
Boca Raton, FL 33487-2742

© 2008 by Taylor & Francis Group, LLC
CRC Press is an imprint of Taylor & Francis Group, an Informa business

No claim to original U.S. Government works
Printed in the United States of America on acid-free paper
10 9 8 7 6 5 4 3 2 1

International Standard Book Number-13: 978-1-4200-7773-5 (Softcover)

Library of Congress Cataloging-in-Publication Data

Viotti, Paul R.
    Terrorism and homeland security : thinking strategically about policy/author/
editor(s) Paul Viotti, Michael Opheim, and Nicholas Bowen.
        p. cm.
    Includes bibliographical references and index.
    ISBN 978-1-4200-7773-5 (alk. paper)
    1. Terrorism--United States--Prevention. 2. Terrorism--Government
policy--United States. 3. Weapons of mass destruction--Government
policy--United States. 4. Internal security--United States. 5. Civil defense--United
States. I. Opheim, Michael, 1968- II. Bowen, Nicholas, 1979- III. Title.

HV6432.V56 2008
363.325'15610973--dc22   2007050385

Visit the Taylor & Francis Web site at
http://www.taylorandfrancis.com

and the CRC Press Web site at
http://www.crcpress.com

Dedication

This volume is dedicated to the late Fred A. Sondermann, professor at Colorado College (1953-78) and co-founder of the International Studies Association, whose summer seminars on national security in the 1970s inspired a generation of policy makers and academics—a commitment to policy-oriented scholarship reflected directly in the work of contributors to this volume. Fred urged us to explore the international and domestic aspects of security that still challenge us in the twenty-first century.

Contents

SECTION 2   TERRORISM, HOMELAND SECURITY, AND WEAPONS OF MASS DESTRUCTION (WMD)

Foreword

More than a year before the fatal attacks on September 11, the National War College in Washington, D.C. and the University of Denver sponsored several workshops, lectures and seminars on the subject of terrorist threats to the United States. Participants included civilian and military officials at the federal, state and local levels as well as academic specialists and policy analysts hosted by the Denver Council on Foreign Relations. Two interrelated issues received special attention: weapons of mass destruction/disruption (nuclear, radiological, biological, chemical and cybernetic) and the special threat posed by anti-western Islamic militants, most notably al-Qaeda. For those in attendance, the audacity of the attacks in Washington and New York City came as no surprise. While tactical details could not be predicted, a major strategic attack was clearly anticipated.

Fearing the worst, the attendees outlined various dimensions and nuances of the terrorist threat after which they turned to the question of how to deal with it. This quickly led to an enumeration of several significant problems that needed to be urgently addressed, particularly the absence of an overarching strategy, the role of intelligence, the principal instruments for dealing with terrorism, international requirements, new laws and policies, root causes of violence and the special matter of military force. Vigorous ensuing discussions gave birth to the articulation of nine principles of counter-terrorism that were outlined and used at America's preeminent institution for the study of national security strategy, The National War College. Most of the Washington-Denver Counter-terrorism Principles would emerge, albeit in a slow and piecemeal manner, after September 11.

In abbreviated form, the Washington-Denver principles were:

1. Think strategically and holistically at the national level;
2. Know your enemy by recognizing the primacy and centrality of intelligence;
3. Place primary emphasis on law enforcement and the judicial system;
4. Assure coordination within and among intelligence and law enforcement agencies at all levels of government;
5. Emphasize international cooperation;
6. Avoid laws and policies that undermine basic political values and principles;

7. Devise relevant and potentially effective social, economic and political policies and programs to address underlying causes of terrorism;
8. Define carefully the role of the military in deterring terrorism, compelling its termination and managing its effects; and
9. Craft the legislation and institutional reforms necessary for coping with terrorism in the twenty-first century. For example, broaden the definition of cooperation ("jointness") among military services to include all government agencies dealing with terrorism.

While these nine principles are now widely accepted, their implementation is an unfinished and at times muddled work. Accordingly, the publication of Terrorism and Homeland Security comes at a crucial moment in our history. The hourglass has run down on procrastination in the face of ever increasing threats. Readers of this volume will not only understand how we stand with respect to the principles and what remains to be done, but they will also benefit from the new ideas and insights presented by an impressive array of specialists.

As an added bonus, there is no one better suited to lead this undertaking than Professor Paul R. Viotti, an educator who has long been recognized for his excellence in teaching and forward-looking thinking. The same creativity and leadership that he formerly brought to the task of defining the terrorist threat to the United States and the principles that should frame the response are called for more than ever. Thankfully, that call has been answered with this thoughtful work.

Bard E. O'Neill
Professor of National Security Strategy
The National War College
Washington, D.C.

Preface

The American homeland is still not secure from terrorist attack, notwithstanding enormous sums already allocated to this purpose. What passes as strategy is often a list of objectives with vague references to marshalling national resources and support drawn from other countries. Strategy for homeland security is at best piecemeal, tackling parts of the problem without linking these elements together into a more coherent whole. The resulting fragmentation of this vital national effort—the absence of a comprehensive, coherent strategy to deal with the terrorist threat to homeland security—leads to misdirection and waste of national resources.

It is to this absence of strategy to deal effectively with the terrorist threat that the chapters in this volume have been written. We do not pretend to present a fully developed homeland security strategy for dealing with terrorist threats. The aim here is modest. It is only to identify the domestic and external elements that need to be addressed in developing such a strategy. A comprehensive strategy specifies objectives, identifies human and material resources that need to be allocated to these purposes, links the "away game" well beyond U.S. shores to the domestic agenda of things that need to be done in the "home game," and seeks allies and coalition partners in a multilateral quest to secure homelands from terrorist threats.

No strategy, however well developed and carefully implemented, can ever provide perfect security from any threat. At the same time, the perfect need not stand as an obstacle to the good. Strategy that effectively ties domestic and external resources to specified objectives can reduce substantially the level of threat that otherwise would be faced. It must also be dynamic—open to modifications as circumstances change.

Governments take steps to provide increased security by increasing intelligence and law-enforcement measures that tend to compromise individual privacy, due process, and other rights and liberties. A central objective in any homeland security strategy, then, is to sustain civil liberties and human rights so essential to life in democratic societies. Put another way, the difficult strategic challenge is to optimize security subject to the constraint of minimizing infringement on rights and liberties.

In Part 1, seven of our authors address in five chapters the central problem of developing strategy for homeland security. Four other members of our team take up terrorist threats in two chapters in Part 2 on the strategic challenge of nuclear, biological, chemical, and radiological weapons of mass destruction (WMD). Finally, in Part 3, six contributors in five chapters on strategy go beyond WMD to the broader context of safeguarding society and its infrastructure not only from terrorists, but also natural disasters. Finally, two of our coeditors step back from the project and draw some preliminary conclusions in this stage of what has become an ongoing project.

Indeed, the project began in January 2000 at a conference on homeland defense hosted at the National War College by Professor Bard O'Neill. Professors Joseph Szyliowicz and Paul Viotti brought this back to the center of the homeland where the Denver Council on Foreign Relations (DCFR) and the Institute on Globalization and Security (IGLOS) at the University of Denver agreed to host a series of three workshops on homeland security beginning in the spring of 2000 and completed a year later. Well prior to 9/11, citizen participants in these workshops even anticipated that terrorists might use airplanes as a high-explosive device against buildings, an inference drawn from an earlier, failed effort to hijack an Air France plane in Paris and fly it into the Eiffel Tower. These workshops have continued since 9/11 to take up transportation, immigration, and other homeland security challenges.

The team of policy-oriented scholars who have contributed to this volume initially came together from the United States and Canada at an August 2004 seminar in honor of the late Colorado College political science professor, Fred A. Sondermann, held at the University of Denver's Graduate School of International Studies and cosponsored by IGLOS, DCFR, and the Army War College. A principal finding in a consensus report identified the absence of an effective strategy to guide policy makers tasked with making and implementing decisions on homeland security, and resulted in an agreement to write the chapters in this volume. Our purpose is limited here to identifying the problem and elements that would be part of a comprehensive strategy in the hope of advancing not only the policy-related academic discourse, but also to assist in some way those we and our fellow citizens put in authority to make decisions so essential to securing the homeland.

Acknowledgment

This volume owes much to support for a number of seminars and workshops on terrorism and homeland security held by the Institute on Globalization and Security (IGLOS) and the Denver Council on Foreign Relations (DenverCFR.org), both located administratively at the University of Denver's Graduate School of International Studies.

Contributors

The Editors

Paul R. Viotti serves as executive director of the Institute on Globalization & Security (IGLOS) and is a professor at the Graduate School of International Studies (GSIS), University of Denver. Among his recent publications are *International Relations and World Politics*, *International Relations Theory*, and *American Foreign Policy and National Security: A Documentary Record*.

Michael Opheim is a fellow at the Institute on Globalization and Security (IGLOS) at the University of Denver. His current research deals with the peaceful and violent ramifications of state dissolution in Eastern Europe. He also teaches at Metropolitan State College in Denver.

Nicholas Bowen is a fellow at the Institute on Globalization and Security (IGLOS) at the University of Denver. His current research interests include: the study of revolution, U.S. foreign policy and the Middle East. He has published articles in the *International Affairs Review* and for the *Danish Institute for International Studies*.

Other Authors

Timothy W. Crawford is a political science professor at Boston College. He is the author of *Pivotal Deterrence: Third Party Statecraft and the Pursuit of Peace*, winner of the 2003 Edgar S. Furniss book award, and co-editor of *Gambling on Humanitarian Intervention: Moral Hazard, Rebellion, and Civil War*.

Alexander C. Diener is a geography professor at Pepperdine University. He is the author of *Homeland Conceptions and Ethnic Integration among Kazakhstan's Ger-*

mans and Koreans (2004) and *One Homeland or Two?: Nationalization and Transnationalization of the Mongolia's Kazakhs* (forthcoming). He is currently editing a book on international border issues and has written articles for *Geopolitics, Geography Compass, Europe-Asia Studies, Nationalities Papers, The International Journal of Central Asian Studies,* and *Eurasian Geography and Economics.*

Robert H. Dorff is research professor of National Security Affairs in the Strategic Studies Institute, U.S. Army War College where earlier he was chair, Department of National Security and Strategy. He also has served as senior advisor on Democracy, Governance and Civilian Military Relations at Creative Associates International, Inc. and as executive director, Institute of Political Leadership (Raleigh, NC). Among his numerous publications are "Managing National Security in the Information and Terrorism Age," *The Forum* (July 2006), "Failed States After 9/11: What Did We Know and What Have We Learned?" *International Studies Perspectives* (February 2005), and *The Search for Security: A U.S. Grand Strategy for the Twenty-First Century* (Praeger, 2003).

David Goldfischer, a professor at the Graduate School of International Studies (GSIS), University of Denver, directs the Institute on Globalization and Security (IGLOS). In this capacity he has developed and expanded substantially the university's programs in international and homeland security. Among his publications are *Nuclear Deterrence and Global Security in Transition; The Best Defense: Policy Alternatives for U.S. Nuclear Security from the 1950s to the 1990s;* and "Prospects for a New World Order" in *Paradigms in Transition: Globalization, Security, and the Nation-State* (2004).

Kevin King is a research analyst and consultant to the energy sector and government agencies. He specializes in issues relating to the oil and natural gas industries, with an emphasis upon U.S. national energy policy, energy security strategy, and renewable energy resources.

Veronica M. Kitchen is assistant professor of political science at the University of Waterloo, Ontario. Her research focuses on transatlantic relations and international security, including transatlantic and North American co-operation on civil security and counter-terrorism. Her publications include 'Smarter Co-operation in Canadian-American Relations?' in the *International Journal* (Summer 2004); and 'From Rhetoric to Reality: Canada, the United States and the Ottawa Process to Ban Landmines,' in the *International Journal* (Winter 2001-2002), winner of the Canadian Institute for International Affairs's Marvin Gelber Essay Prize.

Jeffrey A. Larsen is a senior policy analyst with Science Applications International Corporation in Colorado Springs, Colorado, president of Larsen Consulting Group, and an adjunct professor in international studies at the University of Denver. He was NATO's 2005-06 Manfred Wörner Fellow, and currently serves as president of the International Security and Arms Control Section of the American Political Science Association Recent publications include *NATO's Nuclear Future, Nuclear Transformation: The New U.S. Nuclear Doctrine, Historical Dictionary of Arms Control and Disarmament*, and *Comparative U.S.-Israeli Homeland Security*.

Gregory J. Moore is an assistant professor of political science and East Asian Studies at Eckerd College, St. Petersburg, Florida. He has also served as assistant director of the Center for China-United States Relations at the University of Denver, and he received his doctorate from the University of Denver's Graduate School of International Studies. He has written numerous articles, essays and book chapters on international relations, Chinese foreign policy and East Asian politics and international relations, and is currently working on a book on Sino-American relations.

Greg Moser is executive director of Homeland Security Programs at the Graduate School of International Studies, University of Denver. He has also taught at the Joint Military IntelligenceTraining Center, Defense Intelligence Agency, and has supported homeland security program development and delivery for the Naval Post Graduate School. Prior to assuming his current position, he served as Emergency Management Planning, Training and Exercise coordinator for Jefferson County, Colorado, and before that (1999-2003) he served in the Colorado Office of Emergency Management where he established the state's terrorism preparedness program and supported a broad range of all-hazards prevention, response and recovery-related activities. As an intelligence officer in the U.S. Air Force (1979-99), Greg was a central player in a wide range of military, humanitarian, and diplomatic operations worldwide.

Terrence O' Sullivan is a postdoctoral research associate at the University of Southern California Homeland Security Center for Risk and Economic Analysis of Terrorism Events (CREATE). His background is in international political economy, globalization, and security studies. Current research includes analysis of global and domestic policy related to terrorism and weapons of mass destruction risk, catastrophic infectivesearch deals with the development of sustainable transportation systems and transportation security. Relevant to this volume are the chapters he wrote 'Aviation Security: Promise or Reality?' in *Homeland Security and Terrorism* (2006); 'International Transportation Security' in J.F.Plant, Editor, *Handbook of Transportation Policy and Administration* (2007); and 'Transportation Security and Global Terrorism' in the Proceedings of the Istanbul Conference on Democracy and Global Security (2005).

Brent J. Talbot is a professor of military strategic studies at the US Air Force Academy. His most recent publications include "Gambling with History: The Making of a Democratic Iraq" in *Air and Space Power Chronicles, 2004*, and "Just War in

Iraq? Arab Radical and Reformist Perspectives" in *Wielding the Sword While Proclaiming Peace.*

Jeremy Tamsett is a research analyst at the Center for Terrorism and Intelligence Studies in San Jose, California. His primary interests and fields of expertise are homeland security policy and risk intelligence. He has written several articles for journals and trade associations, and has given interviews as an expert consultant on nuclear and radiological terrorism. He is the editor of *Jihadists and Weapons of Mass Destruction: A Growing Threat*, forthcoming.

Fred L. Wehling is a professor and learning innovations coordinator at the Graduate School of International Policy Studies (GSIPS) at the Monterey Institute of International Studies. In addition to teaching courses on world politics, policy analysis, WMD and terrorism, and other topics, Wehling develops online courses and instructional materials and conducts research in nuclear material security and terrorism with nuclear and radiological materials. He is co-author of *The Four Faces of Nuclear Terrorism* (2005) and *World Politics in a New Era*, 3rd ed. (2003) and author of various other books, articles, and reports.

James J. Wirtz is a professor in the Department of National Security Affairs at the U.S. Naval Postgraduate School, Monterey California. He has chaired the Intelligence Studies Section of the International Studies Association and served as president of the International Security and Arms Control Section of the American Political Science Association. Among his most recent publications are *Nuclear Transformation: The New U.S. Nuclear Doctrine* and *Balance of Power: Theory and Practice in the 21ˢᵗ Century.*

Acronyms

ABM	Antiballistic Missile
AEDPA	Antiterrorism and Effective Death Penalty Act
AIS	Automatic Identification System
AOPA	Aircraft Owners and Pilots Association
APEC	Asia-Pacific Economic Cooperation
ASEAN	Association of Southeast Asian Nations
BT	Bioterrorism
CBP	Customs and Border Protection
CBRNE	Chemical, Biological, Radiological, Nuclear and Explosive
CDC	Center for Disease Control and Prevention
CI	Critical Infrastructure
CIA	Central Intelligence Agency
CIDO	Catastrophic Infectious Disease Outbreak
CI/KR	Critical Infrastructure/Key Resources
CMS	Consequence Management Subgroup
COMINT	Communications Intelligence
CONPLAN	Concept of Operations Plan
CPR	Cardiopulmonary resuscitation
CRCPD	Conference of Radiation Control Program Directors
CRT	CASH Transaction Report
CSI	Container Security Initiative
C-TPAT	Customs-Trade Partnership Against Terrorism
CTC	Counter-Terrorism Committee
CTTF	Counter-Terrorism Task Force
DBT	Design Basis Threat
DHHS	Department of Health and Human Services
DHS	Department of Homeland Security
DNDO	Domestic Nuclear Detection Office
DNI	Director of National Intelligence
DOC	Department of Commerce
DoD	Department of Defense

DOE	Department of Energy
DOI	Department of the Interior
DOJ	Department of Justice
DOT	Department of Transportation
DSM	Demand Side Management
EIA	Energy Information Administration
EMS	Emergency Medical Services
EPA	Environmental Protection Agency
EU	European Union
EURATOM	European Atomic Energy Community
EUROPOL	European Union Police Office
FAST	Free and Secure Trade
FBI	Federal Bureau of Investigation
FCDA	Federal Civil Defense Administration
FDA	Food and Drug Administration
FEMA	Federal Emergency Management Agency
FERC	Federal Energy Regulatory Commission
FRAMC	Federal Radiological Assessment and Monitoring Center
FRERP	Federal Radiological Emergency Response Plan
FRP	Federal Response Plan
FRPCC	Federal Radiological Policy Coordinating Committee
FSRS	Federal Security Reserve System
G&T	Office of Grants and Training
GAO	Government Accountability Office
GDP	Gross Domestic Product
GTRI	Global Threat Reduction Initiative
HAZMAT	Hazardous Materials
HD	Homeland Defense
HEU	Highly Enriched Uranium
HLS	Homeland Security
HMX	Cyclotetramethylene-tetranitramine (high explosive)
HPAI	Highly Pathogenic Avian Influenza (also called H5N1)
HS	Homeland Security
HS/DEC	Homeland Security/Defense Education Consortium
HSDP	Homeland Security Presidential Directive
HUMINT	Human Intelligence
IAEA	International Atomic Energy Agency
IBET	Integrated Border Enforcement Team
IC	Intelligence Community
ICAO	International Civil Aviation Organization
IEA	International Energy Agency
IEEPA	International Economic Emergency Powers Act
IG	Inspector General

IMAAC	Interagency Modeling and Atmospheric Assessment Center
IMO	International Maritime Organization
IND	Improvised Nuclear Device
INS	Immigration and Naturalization Service
LEU	Low Enriched Uranium
LNG	Liquefied Natural Gas
MAD	Mutual Assured Destruction
MDC	Metropolitan Detention Center
MIC	Methylisocyanate
MOU	Memorandum of Understanding
MTSA	Maritime Transportation Security Act
NAFTA	North American Free Trade Agreement
NARUC	National Association of Regulatory Utility Commissioners
NCEP	National Commission on Energy Policy
NCP	National Contingency Plan
NCTC	National Counterterrorism Center
NERC	North American Electric Reliability Council
NEXUS	Northern Border Crossing System
NGO	Non-governmental Organization
NIE	National Intelligence Estimate
NIMS	National Incident Management System
NNSA	National Nuclear Security Administration
NORAD	North American Aerospace Defense Command
NPS	National Pharmaceutical Stockpile
NRC	Nuclear Regulatory Commission
NRP	National Response Plan
NSC	National Security Council
NSS	National Security Strategy
NYPD	New York City Police Department
ODP	Office for Domestic Preparedness
OECD	Organisation for Economic Co-operation and Development
OHS	Office of Homeland Security
OPEC	Organization of the Petroleum Exporting Countries
OSC	Operation Safe Commerce
OSI	Orphan Source Initiative
OSR	Offsite Source Recovery
OTA	Office of Technology Assessment
PAG	Protective Action Guide
PAL	Permissive Action Link
PBX	Plastic Bonded Explosive
PDD	Presidential Decision Directive
PLO	Palestine Liberation Organization
POE	Port of Entry

PSI	Proliferation Security Initiative
R&D	Research and Development
RAC	Regional Assistance Committee
RDD	Radiological Dispersal Device
RDX	Cyclotrimethylenetrinitramine (plastic explosive)
RED	Radiation Emission Device
SAFF	Safing, arming, fusing and firing procedures
SAR	Suspicious Activities Report
SARA	Superfund Amendment and Reauthorization Act
SARS	Severe Acute Respiratory Syndrome
SARS-CoV	Severe Acute Respiratory Syndrome Corona Virus
SCADA	Supervisory Control and Data Acquisition
SENTRI	Secure Electronic Network for Travelers Rapid Inspection
SIGNINT	Signals Intelligence
SNS	Strategic National Stockpile
SPR	Strategic Petroleum Reserve
STAR	Secure Trade in the APEC Region
TIA	Terrorist Information Awareness (system)
TOPOFF3	Top Officials 3
TSA	Transportation Security Administration
TTIC	Terrorist Threat Integration Center
TWEA	Trading with the Enemy Act
UN	United Nations
USAID	United States Agency for International Development
USA PATRIOT ACT	The Uniting and Strengthening America by Providing Appropriate Tools Required to Intercept and Obstruct Terrorism Act
VFWs	Veterans of Foreign Wars
VWPP	Visa Waiver Pilot Program
WHO	World Health Organization
WMD	Weapons of Mass Destruction
WTO	World Trade Organization

SECTION 1

The National Security Challenge: Developing Strategy for Terrorism and Homeland Security

Chapter 1

Toward a Comprehensive Strategy for Terrorism and Homeland Security

Paul R. Viotti

Setting the stage for the chapters that follow, the author laments the absence of a coherent strategy—one that would be both comprehensive and dynamic—to guide policy makers tasked with securing the homeland. A causal analysis of terrorism as a tactic—one form of political violence in a set of choices made by the leadership and conducted by the organizational elements of various groups, movements, or insurgencies—brings us to root causes that lie in the grievances that motivate and sustain popular support for such actions. A comprehensive strategy, then, is necessarily broad in scope. Part of the strategic effort, of course, takes the familiar form of preventive and defensive measures—relying on intelligence for early warning and to assist law-enforcement agents to arrest those planning attacks or otherwise blunting their efforts; establishing detection devices and mechanisms in public places, in transit and at airports, seaports, and other transportation terminals; planning for damage limitation not only of transportation, but also of telecommunications, energy, water and food supply networks, and other critical infrastructure; and organizing, training, and equipping first responders and others at federal, state, and local levels for effective consequence management.

Beyond these and other domestic measures—the "home game" designed to deal with the terrorist threat on the effects side, a comprehensive strategy also addresses the causal side, which typically shifts one's strategic focus abroad to the "away game"—how grievances (whether real or imagined, just or unjust) in a population lead to the formation of (and help sustain) groups, movements, or insurgencies. These entities typically have purposes or objectives with identifiable leadership, ideological, and organizational elements. Given this understanding, we face a set of strategic questions about what is to be done on the causal side: (1) What can or should be done about grievances? (2) Is there any value to be found in communicating with the leaderships of these entities either directly or through third parties? (3) Are there effective ways to counter the ideological appeals or material benefit they offer their followers? (4) How feasible is it—what capabilities exist—to attack these operatives or effectively disrupt their organizations and activities? (5) Before we act, can we make a realistic net assessment of whether measures under consideration likely will weaken or reduce the threat posed—the intended consequence—or, conversely, whether such measures likely will backfire or be counterproductive—strengthening these groups, movements, or insurgencies and thus undermining the antiterrorism effort? The answers to such questions likely will vary over time, which underscores why any effective homeland security strategy also must be dynamic—responsive to changes in circumstances.

Finally, in democratic societies, strategies for homeland security try to minimize adverse impacts on civil liberties and other human rights that are challenged by domestic intelligence gathering and law-enforcement measures. More than just assuring physical security, a comprehensive homeland security strategy also seeks to secure the liberties and rights the people hold dear.

Homeland security strategy—the focal point of the chapters in this volume—is in the broadest understanding a response to threats of all kinds, although the focus in the United States since 9/11 primarily has been on the real-and-present dangers of terrorist attacks. The authors in this volume are responding to what they see as strategic deficiencies in thinking about homeland security—the apparent absence of coherent strategy, not to mention one that is comprehensive, dynamic, and an effective guide policy makers can use for dealing with terrorist or other threats to the homeland. The central question contributors to this volume undertake is the strategic quest—an exploration of factors central to the formulation and implementation of a comprehensive and dynamic homeland security strategy responsive to changes in threats posed to the United States. Terrorism as a form of political violence is the principal threat we consider in this volume, although we also take account of natural disasters that inform consideration of all hazards (or all consequences) regardless of whether the causes are human or due to natural phenomena.

At the federal level the domestic aspects of securing the United States are the primary domain of the Department of Homeland Security (DHS) and military and related intelligence "turf" is reserved for the Department of Defense (DoD), to include the Defense Intelligence and National Security Agencies (DIA and NSA) and the Army and Air National Guard when called into national service. We need not be confined here, however, by a bureaucratic definition of homeland security as if it were limited only to the domestic turf of the U.S. DHS, the Federal Emergency Management Agency (FEMA), the Coast Guard, and other DHS component agencies. Nor need homeland defense as a term be reserved to the operations of the U.S. DoD at home and abroad. These bureaucratic definitions reflect an important division of labor between two cabinet departments, but omit the roles played by other federal agencies or cabinet departments—for example, the Central Intelligence Agency (CIA), the Federal Bureau of Investigation (FBI), the departments of State and Treasury—not to mention an array of state and local police and emergency-management agencies that include first responders.

Setting these bureaucratic understandings aside, in this volume we take a broad, strategic view of homeland security—a focus on the ways and means of securing the homeland from terrorism or other threats and natural disasters. The "home game" and the "away game" necessarily come together in any comprehensive strategy that includes both domestic and external courses of action. As a practical matter, then, the distinction between homeland security and homeland defense that serves bureaucratic purposes is less important analytically to the strategist. Although in common parlance the two terms often are used interchangeably, the former (a broader term) may be seen typically as encompassing the latter. In this regard, we adopt homeland security in its broadest meaning—providing safety from threats to the nation by taking steps toward this end both at home and abroad.

We define *terror* as the rational or purposive use of the "irrational"—fear or other intimidating effects on people—in an effort to accomplish political or other purposes.[1] We are most concerned here with terrorism when it takes the form of politically motivated violence that threatens the homeland. As such, terror may be produced by purposive use of violence, but populations may also be terrorized by other, nonviolent means. Soviet show-trial purges conducted in the 1930s under Stalin, for example, spread fear not only among communist party members, but also within the population as a whole. The "knock on the door" by the police and the arrests that followed (whether in the Soviet Union or Nazi Germany) sent strong messages designed to scare people into compliance with the expectations or mandates of party or regime—state terror in oppressive, but not necessarily violent, form.

Lest we run the risk that virtually all forms of political violence be regarded incorrectly as terrorism or the work of terrorists, we need to differentiate terror analytically from other forms of political violence—guerrilla warfare (typically hit-and-run tactics), insurrection or popular uprising (as in the Palestinian Intifada) that usually becomes violent, sectarian, or intercommunal (as in tribal, clan, national, or ethnic) strife, civil war between competing parties for control of the state, and combat between regular military units. Unless we limit the meaning of terror by differentiating it from these other forms of violence, terror can be construed to mean virtually everything. If the term terror comes to mean so many things, in practice it means little or nothing. Our aim here, by contrast, is to preserve the analytical meaning of terror or terrorism. Indeed, if terror is a principal threat to the security of the homeland, then we need to be clear about what we are addressing.

Even as we limit the term terror as a tactic—one form of political violence differentiated analytically from other forms, we do not see it as limited to use by or against civilians or nongovernmental groups, movements, or insurgencies.[2] If the aim is to intimidate or cause fear in one's adversary—governmental or nongovernmental—we are in the domain of terrorism whether perpetrated by or against the state. By defining the term this way, we depart from those who see terrorism as directed or limited only to civilian populations. When violence is directed toward military or other governmental personnel with the intent to cause fear or intimidation, we may speak of it as terror.

Intent matters. People may suffer intimidation or be fearful, particularly when they find themselves in or near combat operations, but this does not in itself constitute the use of terror. If nearby aerial or other bombardment rattles one's windows, one may be terrorized even though the perpetrators of this violence were merely attacking legitimate military targets. Only if the use of violence is part of a plan or design to foment fear or create intimidating effects on a people may we refer to it as a terrorist tactic.

Indeed, one has to be careful not to confuse other forms of violence with terrorism. Just because soldiers on both sides may experience the intimidating effects of the use of force in combat, this does not make combat a terrorist incident unless intimidation was the effect intended by one side or the other. Military actions are usually intended to destroy or substantially weaken an enemy's war-making capability. Such actions become terrorist incidents only when the intent is to intimidate, cause fear, or terrorize an adversary.

We return, then, to our basic definition of terrorism—the rational or purposive use of the "irrational"—fear or other intimidating effects on a people—in an effort to accomplish political or other purposes. Although most terrorist acts are politically motivated, in some cases other nonpolitical causes may be served by this intentional use of fear. One can argue, for example, that the 1995 sarin gas attack by Aum Shinrikyo in the subway in Tokyo was politically motivated against the Japanese government, local police, or other government officials, but another nonpolitical motive may be found in the extreme religious beliefs of this cult that defined itself by the term *supreme truth.*

Although the precise motive or motives for the attack remain in dispute, the incident reminds us that the threat of terrorism is not confined to external sources, but may well be caused by domestic actors responding to grievances of one kind or another and intending to terrorize their victims. Indeed, in the same year as these sarin attacks in Japan, the United States experienced a massive domestic terrorist bombing attack on the Federal Building in Oklahoma City. Perpetrated by three American citizens directly involved in the conspiracy, the attacks killed 168 people and injured more than 800 others. The conspirators allegedly were motivated by revenge for violent government actions taken in 1992 against a white separatist group at Ruby Ridge in northern Idaho in 1992 and in 1993 against the "Branch Davidian" religious cult near Waco, Texas. Apart from massive deaths, physical harm to survivors, and destruction of a building, it was the intent to terrorize government employees, their families, and the general population that constituted this as a domestic terrorist incident.

In developing strategy for homeland security in relation to terrorist threats, we certainly look for domestic remedies as in providing better intelligence and early warning of attacks, maintaining detection in transit and at airports and other transportation nodes or terminals, and developing and exercising plans for damage limitation and consequence management conducted by well equipped and trained first responders. We do not confine ourselves, however, to domestic remedies—the "home game." We also look abroad to find effective ways of dealing with the source of terrorist threats, taking into account the grievances that lead to the formation of groups, movements, or insurgencies that adopt violent tactics to advance their causes—the "away game." Thus, coping with terrorism at home and abroad is essential to securing and defending the homeland. An effective strategy for homeland security, then, incorporates approaches to reducing the threat of terrorism by taking actions both domestically and externally.

We make no pretense here to present a fully developed homeland-security strategy applicable to the United States or other countries. What the essays in this volume do collectively, however, is to identify the elements we see as essential to developing a comprehensive and dynamic strategy for homeland security. Although our primary focus in this volume is on the United States, we see these understandings of homeland-security strategy as also having application to the strategic discourse pursued in other countries. Finally, we place homeland security as a small but essential component within a broader context of national-security or grand strategies that are well beyond the scope of our more modest effort in this volume.

To construct a strategic blueprint for homeland security we need first to identify the causes for terrorist and other forms of political violence. Typically, these lie in the grievances a population may hold against the target toward which a terrorist group directs its violent actions. Put another way, the interests of those using political violence matter if we are to understand why they resort to terrorism or some other form of political violence.

Identifying the groups, movements, or insurgencies drawn from this population is the next step, specifying their links to each other and to the popular support each enjoys. Crucial to both strategists and policy makers is access to reliable intelligence estimates—accurate data and realistic assessments of these movements or groups, their leaderships, ideologies, and organizational structures and processes. Understanding what strategy or strategies these groups, movements, or insurgencies may be pursuing is essential to designing effective counterstrategies. One needs to specify the purposes or objectives these movements or groups are pursuing, the capabilities or means they possess, and the methods or tactics they apply to the objectives they seek to achieve.

Some entities may be relatively isolated, whereas others are more broadly based movements with sufficient popular support to be called insurgencies. Methods or tactics may include various forms of nonviolent political actions as well as one or more of the following: insurrections or popular uprisings that may become violent, calculated acts of violence intended to produce terror in target populations, irregular or guerrilla warfare tactics, civil war or, when a group, movement, or insurgency enjoys state support, violence may rise to the level of regular or interstate warfare.

Strategizing is not about a "war on terror" or any particular tactic or method. It is instead directed toward the groups, movements, or insurgencies responsible for violent actions, as well as the grievances in the populations on which their support rests. One can focus on reducing popular grievances causally related to those choosing violent activities. In some instances, communicating with the leadership or emissaries of these groups, movements, or insurgencies directly (or through third parties) may be part of an effective counterstrategy; in other instances the effort is to capture or remove the leaders or other violent actors in these movements or groups or to find ways to disrupt their organizations and activities. A most important caveat, however, is the necessity of making a realistic net assessment of measures under consideration—whether they likely will weaken or reduce the threat posed (the intended consequence) or, conversely, whether such measures likely will backfire or be counterproductive—strengthening these groups, movements, or insurgencies and thus undermining the antiterrorism effort (an adverse albeit unintended consequence).

Finally, effective counterstrategies employ intelligence and other detection measures for early warning or, if possible, prevention of violent actions—intelligence that assists law-enforcement agents arresting those planning attacks or otherwise blunting their efforts. Also essential is advance planning both to limit damage to transportation, telecommunications, energy, water and food supply networks, and other critical infrastructure and to manage consequences—employing well trained and equipped first responders and other officials at federal, state, and local levels. In democratic societies, strategies for homeland security try to minimize adverse impacts on civil liberties and other human rights that are challenged by domestic intelligence gathering and law-enforcement measures. More than just assuring physical security, a comprehensive homeland security strategy also seeks to secure the liberties and rights the people hold dear.

Strategy and the Strategic Discourse

We start this strategic discourse with important definitions and distinctions. By *strategy* we mean the ways or modalities by which we link capabilities or means we have or can generate to the ends, purposes, or objectives we seek. In doing so we are best served when we have a causal understanding of what is at issue—the relations among the factors or variables we identify as central to the problem. Strategizing is a highly rational, analytic process, but one fraught with significant challenges.

Clausewitz understood fully the problem of uncertainty with which strategists and policymakers must grapple. Even the most developed strategies and strategic plans still encounter the obstacles or real-world *friction* when put into action.[3] In combat one also encounters enormous uncertainties as circumstances change so rapidly that one may not be aware of essential details about what is happening—the *fog* of war.[4] Testing strategies and the plans that one derives from them by conducting exercises is one remedy for uncovering errors and identifying what needs to be corrected. Maintaining strategic discourse as an open process that welcomes both logical and empirical critique of existing strategies and strategic plans is another way to reduce the likelihood of errors that can thwart the attainment of objectives or, in the case of homeland security, result in catastrophic consequences.

A careful reading of Clausewitz leads one to conclude how important humility is as a tempering factor in strategic discourse. The strategist needs always to be aware that there may be flaws in the causal analysis, not to mention data problems—seeking an accurate take on the relevant facts. The aim is at once not just to be *comprehensive*—including all relevant factors in the strategic analysis, but also *parsimonious*—excluding unnecessary or tangential factors that obscure the strategic view of how to apply means or capabilities to increase the likelihood of goal attainment. Given uncertainties in causal analysis, data problems, and the reality of changing circumstances, effective strategizing necessarily is a *dynamic* process—a willingness to make necessary changes in strategy even as events unfold. Although one may long for greater certainty, strategists (as with other theorists) deal effectively with reality when informed by what James Rosenau calls a "high tolerance for ambiguity."[5]

Uncertainties are also a part of the strategist's continuous quest to match means to ends. Serious, perhaps devastating, consequences result when capabilities fall short of what we need to reach the objectives we have set. The obvious, but difficult (and often painful) remedy for mismatch between means and ends is to enhance the former, to trim or scale back the latter, or both to expand capabilities and to alter objectives until the two coincide. Failure to attend to strategic mismatch—trying to do more with less—more often than not is a prescription for defeat.

Indeed, the strategist has to be careful not to overestimate what a given (or enhanced) set of capabilities realistically can achieve. To pursue (or continue to pursue) a course of action when capabilities are known to be on the short side is effectively to gamble that somehow one has underestimated strategically what it takes to reach objectives. Strategists and the policy makers they inform ought not take such unnecessary risks. It is better not to undertake a course of action in the first place if one is either *unable* or *unwilling* to match or surpass the level of capabilities required. This is certainly the case when one is considering the use of force. As Clausewitz counseled, one ought to be careful about taking the first step into war without considering where the (subsequent or) last steps are likely to lead.[6]

Terrorism and other Forms of Political Violence

Terrorist attacks are best understood as calculated events perpetrated most effectively by adversaries who seek strategically to attain particular objectives by such means. Indeed, as noted above, *terrorism* is the rational use of the "irrational" or intimidating effects of nonviolent or violent actions—the latter including use of explosive devices, assassinations, or other destructive means for political or other purposes. Again, it is this *intent* to use violence or other means for their intimidating effects that makes a particular *act* a terrorist one. Both act and intent matter if we are correctly to apply the term *terrorism*. Terrorism is a *tactic* that can be used in conjunction with other forms of political violence, but it still stands as a separate category.

Effective strategizing on the ways and means for dealing with groups, movements, or insurgencies that use terrorist or other forms of political violence requires analytical clarity. As discussed above, if we do not draw this analytical distinction all forms of violence suddenly become terrorist incidents. Put another way, we need not focus on the perpetrators of all forms of violence because doing so unnecessarily complicates the formulation of an effective strategy for dealing with those who engage primarily in terrorist activities.

Calling such engagement a "war on terror" is an unfortunate misnomer. Whatever its value for public relations purposes, such terminology leads us away from focus on the groups, movements, or insurgencies that employ terrorist tactics. Indeed, uncritical use of such terms may reflect the shallow depth of strategic thought underlying policies pursued. One does not wage war against a tactic; one wages war against those who use such tactics. Efforts are taken to undermine their domestic and external bases of support—populations as well as states or non-state actors. This is not a trivial distinction or *legerdemain* designed to score debating points. Effective strategizing for homeland security requires focus on the causes and producers of the terrorist effect, not just the effect itself.

Policy on homeland security should flow from strategy that is both comprehensive and dynamic. Without guidance from strategic thought, policy typically becomes little more than incrementalism without clear objectives—in effect reacting to current events instead of charting a logical, coherent course of action to achieve national goals. Muddling through without strategy or direction may come at great human and financial cost, whether engaging in war abroad or taking actions domestically to prevent or manage the consequences of political violence.

Intelligence, Law Enforcement, Civil Liberties, and Human Rights

Intelligence is a core part of the strategic design—knowing about the leadership, organization, and composition of followers, their popular support base, the sources of external support, and the ideologies, strategies, locations, and operations of the groups, movements, or insurgencies employing terrorist and other forms of political violence. Early warning of terrorist events and other actions from signals intelligence or human-source reporting can be decisive in successful prevention efforts. Collection of such intelligence from external sources is well established and generally accepted.

On the other hand, the expansion of domestic surveillance does pose a civil liberties challenge, particularly to privacy rights. If not reduced, much less eliminated, such intrusions are managed when subject to effective legislative oversight; judicial review is another check as in the issuance of warrants that conform to specified criteria allowing law enforcement or domestic intelligence collection actions by government agencies. Executive authorities are prone to claim, however, that mechanisms for such management are problematic, particularly given the large flow of timely information deemed essential to providing the adequate warning they need to prevent incidents of political violence from occurring.

Shortly after the 9/11 attack, Congress broadened executive law-enforcement and domestic-surveillance authority by passage of the Patriot Act, an amended version of which subsequently has been renewed. Feeding the domestic civil liberties-homeland security debate are such disclosures as entry by law-enforcement officials into private residences or offices without warrants (so-called "sneak-and-peak" inspections); requests for library, business, and other records; collection of data on financial transfers; and widespread use of signals intelligence—intercepting, monitoring, or tracking domestic communications without warrants or other statutory authority. Massive government collection of information—dubbed by some as "total information awareness"—goes well beyond customary practice. For its part, Congress has been slow to curb expansive use of executive authority for homeland security purposes.

We are left with the question of where should we strike the classic balance between liberty (to include privacy) on the one hand and security through domestic surveillance and law-enforcement intrusions on the other. Some pretend that there is no necessary conflict between liberty and provisions for security, but our experience tells us otherwise. Moreover, what assurances are there that law-enforcement and intelligence mechanisms will afford equal treatment to all groups, not categorizing certain national, ethnic, or religious groups of citizens as inherently suspect?

Whatever may be the justification for legally sanctioned infringements on civil liberties in the short-term interest of providing security, there is no similar rationale for unequal treatment of people in society. Racial, ethnic, or religious "profiling" not only singles out individuals unfairly, but also tends to mislead, divert, and thus waste law-enforcement and intelligence-collection resources from targets toward which strategically they would better be directed.

Security (which can itself be considered a human right) is as vital in society as is protection of civil liberties and other human rights. The strategist necessarily incorporates these considerations as a constraining criterion in any society that places value not only on security, but also on other rights or liberties. Any strategy for homeland security thus takes these liberties and rights into explicit consideration, minimizing adverse impacts on any of them.

Figure 1.1 depicts in simplified form the classic political understanding that the more police and law enforcement (or intelligence gathering) for purposes of order or security, the less liberty citizens will enjoy in a particular society. The downward sloping line shown in the graph is the locus of points in which liberty and order or security are maximized in a given society. The inverse relation between the two variables is readily apparent. As one moves from point A to point B, one increases order or security by the quantity shown between points O1 and O2 on the x-axis, but decreases liberty by the quantity shown between points L1 and L2 on the y-axis. If law-enforcement and other security measures taken in a period of national peril effectively drive the liberty-order trade-off nominally from Point A to Point B, the strategic challenge is somehow to keep such infringements on liberty from becoming permanent intrusions. Moving back up the curve to Point A or above is the obvious objective for those who value civil liberties.

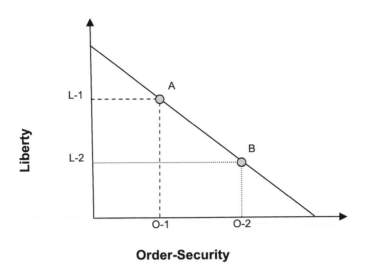

Order-Security

Figure 1.1   Opportunity costs: trade-offs between liberty and order or security. Note that both the slope and straightness of the line in this figure are only for illustrative purposes. A steeper slope would indicate a larger opportunity cost for liberty as each additional "unit" of order or security comes at a higher liberty price; a more gradual slope would indicate a lesser liberty price for increased order or security. The actual trade-off between liberty and order or security may be curvilinear. Moreover, the curve may also vary within a society if intelligence gathering and law-enforcement measures are not applied equally to people of all classes, ethnicities, or other identities. Finally, the line or curve is a statement of maximum liberty and order or security for a society at a given point in time; the society may well be operating at some point below the line—a suboptimal point in which both security and order are less than what they could be.

Causal Understandings Related to Formulating Homeland Security Strategy

Strategy on homeland security has tended in practice to focus on the last part of the causal chain—how to maximize warning so as to prevent or thwart a terrorist attack and, if an attack occurs, how to manage consequences and limit or mitigate damages to lives and property. These are obviously important parts of a comprehensive strategy, but strategy for homeland security ought to begin on the other end of the causal chain—addressing what causes or induces groups, movements, or insurgencies to form and then what leads them to foment terrorist acts. Identifying populations that support the groups, movements, or insurgencies prone to use terrorism and other forms of political violence is where strategizing about homeland security should begin. Figure 1.2 depicts a causal understanding of the sources of

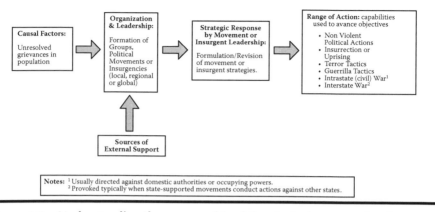

Notes: [1] Usually directed against domestic authorities or occupying powers.
[2] Provoked typically when state-supported movements conduct actions against other states.

Figure 1.2   Understanding the causes of (and the strategic approach taken by) political movements or insurgencies. Effective counterstrategies depend on a comprehensive and dynamic understanding of popular grievances as an underlying causal factor, as well as movement or insurgent strategies and tactics subject to change.

terrorism and other forms of political violence that can be used in the development of counterstrategy directed against those groups, movements, or insurgencies that threaten homeland security.

Societal Grievances as a Cause of Terrorism and Other Forms of Political Violence

One focal point is to attend to interests—the grievances, real or imagined, just or unjust that motivate the formation of these groups, movements, or insurgencies that employ political violence as a means to accomplish their goals. The strategist understands that violence is a political phenomenon typically grounded in social or societal grievances. As such, various forms of political violence are means intended to achieve objectives consistent with the interests of those employing such tactics. The remedy (or set of remedies) is to be found in a political approach to a political phenomenon of which military action is at most only a part.

Dealing with or accommodating grievances and thus undermining the popular support base of those employing political violence is, of course, a most difficult, often very frustrating task to undertake. Quite apart from "winning hearts and minds" in an aggrieved population—a rather high, perhaps impossible bar to reach, one can take strategically a more modest approach of doing what one realistically can accomplish—or at least avoiding measures that make matters worse.

An important part of any strategy intended to serve homeland security is working directly with (not dictating to) the political and other leaders in Afghanistan,

Pakistan, Iraq, Lebanon, or any society beset by political violence (or from which groups, movements, or insurgencies using political violence operate). Such efforts should be directed not just toward incumbents in national and local government offices, but also to the leaders of tribes, clans, and other relevant communities in a particular country. By contrast, arbitrary actions, prison abuses, draconian interrogation techniques, and torture of prisoners or detainees undermine moral authority and produce or accentuate grievances directed against the United States or any other country using such means.

The brutality associated with intracity warfare—the seemingly impossible task of sparing noncombatants even when one tries—is also a major grievance producer that tends to advantage one's adversaries. By no means can military force in such circumstances be seen as a precise instrument that can be employed as if it were a scalpel in the hands of a surgeon. Indeed, military force is a rather blunt instrument at best that if used, particularly against targets in urban areas, likely will produce collateral death and destruction that further aggrieves a population and thus strengthens one's adversaries. Those who justify such tactics as shows of strength that local people allegedly will "respect" miss the larger, adverse implications of such policies.

By contrast, progress on the large issues can reduce popular support for those prone to use political violence. For example, gains in the prolonged peace process in Northern Ireland have met with some success in reducing political violence, as have efforts in the Basque region of northwest Spain. In these cases, diplomacy and more localized social efforts are an important part of conflict management, if not full resolution of conflict.

In the Middle East this strategic approach requires genuine and unrelenting work on the multiple dimensions of Arab (particularly Palestinian)-Israeli and Iranian-Israeli conflicts, notwithstanding numerous setbacks and the enormous frustrations that can lead to abandonment of such efforts. Although diplomats have an instrumental purpose and role to play, enhanced U.S. and other foreign military presence is a grievance that feeds popular support for groups, movements, and insurgencies prone to use political violence. Security conditions may require strong military presence of foreign forces (and some local governments may request it as essential to defending or maintaining their regimes), but any strategy needs to take full account of the downside risks associated with such deployments. In this regard, use of sufficiently manned and properly equipped multilateral forces under UN or other international organization auspices are generally more acceptable to local populations, thus tending to reduce to some degree the downside risks to the forces of particular countries.

Perhaps the most difficult cause of grievances to address is the impact of globalization that challenges traditional societies and their leaders. Advances in transportation and telecommunications technologies have enabled external intrusions on long-established traditions and practices. Beyond whatever benefits they may bring, outsiders are sometimes portrayed as exploiting labor and fouling the local environment. Most threatening of all to local leaders, of course, are the liberal-izing or democratic ideas outsiders bring to the people in these countries, which are seen as legitimizing challenges to existing authorities. The ways and means of avoiding unnecessary intrusions are extraordinarily difficult to implement, particu-larly given genuine external concerns with human rights. Making matters worse is when these intrusions are celebrated by outside countries as advancing democracy or liberal values, but are understood locally as poorly disguised attempts at external dominance.

Groups, Movements, or Insurgencies Using Political Violence

Another strategic focal point is on the groups, movements, or insurgencies that use one or more forms of political violence: (1) insurrections or uprisings that likely will become violent, (2) terror tactics (high explosives, assassinations, or other actions intended to intimidate people), (3) guerrilla (typically hit-and-run) tactics against government authorities or occupying forces, (4) intrastate or civil wars directed against these domestic authorities or occupying powers, and (5) interstate wars provoked when state-supported movements or insurgencies conduct actions against other states. We need to understand that groups, movements, or insurgencies likely are led by strategists in their own right (or leaders informed by strategists) who rationally choose to employ one or another of these tactics as part of their own strategies.

Empathetic analysis of an enemy and its strategy is essential if counterstrategies are to have any chance of being effective. In this regard, it is important to under-score that *empathetic* is not *sympathetic* analysis. Putting oneself in the shoes of a rational adversary, particularly if one despises the ways and means of this adversary, is not easy to do. But how else are we to anticipate what such an adversary is likely to do? How are we to craft effective counterstrategies if we do not recognize the rationality and strategic orientation of adversaries bent on using terrorism or other forms of political violence?

One can, of course, target the leadership and participants in these groups, move-ments, or insurgencies while seeking to avoid or minimize harm to the populations from which they are drawn. Indeed, grievances in a population are typically rein-forced or enhanced when military or police actions are directed against or inadver-tently hurt people who may be supportive of but are not direct participants in the groups, movements, or insurgencies responsible for taking violent actions. Unfor-tunately, limiting countermeasures to leaders and direct participants is extraordi-narily difficult, which raises serious strategic questions about the efficacy of such measures. One has to weigh very carefully the ways, means, and often unintended effects of military and police measures that exacerbate or multiply grievances or disaffection in a population upon which these groups, movements, or insurgencies so heavily depend. It can hardly be considered wise to pursue such tactics without discrimination when the net effect is to strengthen not weaken one's opponent.

Circumstances or opportunities may arise for direct or indirect (through third parties), usually clandestine, communications if not with the high command, then perhaps with the leaders of at least some of the groups linked to the movements or insurgencies at issue. In the popular mind one does not deal with unsavory elements, but strategists and those who make or implement policy ought not be so constrained. If one is thinking and acting strategically, one does not rule out this option without careful consideration of both its merits and possible hazards. It may be possible, for example, to draw some groups away and thus weaken to some degree a network prone to engage in terrorist acts.

Finally, our strategic focus shifts to what can be done in advance not only to provide early warning that hopefully can foil a planned attack, but also to limit damages and manage consequences when attacks occur. Timely intelligence and detection mechanisms in transit and at airports, seaports, and other transportation nodes, as well as in telecommunications, energy, water and food supply networks, and other critical infrastructure are essential if we are to prevent violent acts from occurring. A dynamic, comprehensive strategy for dealing with the terrorist threat to homeland security thus takes account of both cause and effect at home and abroad and is open to modification as circumstances change.

Endnotes

1. I owe this definition to discussions with Bard O'Neill, National War College, that date from the 1970s. He now defines terrorism as "the threat or use of physical coercion, primarily against noncombatants, especially civilians, to create fear in order to achieve various political objectives." We not only agree that terrorism is directed primarily against civilians (though not exclusively, as some would have it), but also that it may take either violent or nonviolent form albeit as "physical coercion" (O'Neill) or, as referenced in this article to show trials and police actions designed to scare or "terrorize" people—mechanisms of societal control. See Bard E. O'Neill, Insurgency and Terrorism: From Revolution to Apocalypse, 2nd ed. (Washington, DC: Potomac Books, 2005), 33.

2. O'Neill defines insurgency "as a struggle between a nonruling group and the ruling authorities in which the nonruling group consciously uses political resources ... and violence to destroy, reformulate, or sustain the basis of legitimacy of one or more aspects of politics" (ibid., p. 15).

3. For an excellent compilation and translation of Clausewitz, On War and Sun Tzu, The Art of Warfare, see Ralph Peters, The Book of War (New York: Random House, Modern Library, 2000). Reference to friction in war is in Book I, chs. 7 and 8, pp. 321–325.

4. Ibid., Book II, ch. 2, Section 24, p. 344.

5. James N. Rosenau, "Thinking Theory Thoroughly," in International Relations Theory, 3rd ed., ed. Paul R. Viotti and Mark V. Kauppi (Upper Saddle River, NJ: Prentice Hall, 1987, 1999), 34. The original source for this article is Rosenau's The Scientific Study of Foreign Policy, rev. ed. (London: Frances Pinter, 1980), pp. 19–31.
6. Clausewitz in Peters, Book VIII, ch. 3, p. 908.

Chapter 2

The Search for National and Homeland Security

An Integrated Grand Strategy

Robert H. Dorff

The United States lacks a reasonably clear and meaningful grand strategy that would effectively integrate the requirements for both national and homeland security. Moreover, the author also concludes that the ability to implement that strategy through the appropriate application of the proper elements of power has been seriously hampered. In developing his argument, Dorff defines strategy in terms of three core concepts–ends, ways, and means. In this regard his treatment of the elements of strategy complements and expands upon the discussion in Chapter 1. He focuses our attention on the strategic challenges faced by both the Clinton and Bush administrations, finding response-driven, ad hoc policies to counterterrorism and homeland security, neither of which is integrated as part of a true grand strategy. In this regard, emphasis has been more on military actions instead of a much-needed comprehensive strategic approach that incorporates all instruments of policy.

The global security environment is a complex variety of potential threats emanating from an even wider array of actors. Confronting those threats and dealing effectively with them comprise the core challenges for security policy and strategy. The profound transformation of the security environment that accompanied the end of the Cold War and the subsequent dissolution of the Soviet Union called into question many of the assumptions that guided U.S. national security policy and strategy for more than half of the last century. And the tragic events of September 11, 2001 placed the stark reality of that transformation squarely in front of us. Yet even for the casual observer of contemporary international security affairs, it is apparent that U.S. security policy and strategy have not fully adjusted to this fundamentally transformed environment in which security of the homeland has become an urgent, even greater national priority than before.

That is not to say that the United States has remained idle during more than a decade and a half since the end of the Cold War. From the decisions that led up to the Gulf War in 1990 to 1991 to the ongoing Balkan crises and the "war on terrorism" in Afghanistan and now in Iraq, there has been no paucity of responses to international security challenges. By almost any measure, the instruments of U.S. security policy and strategy, especially the military, are employed more today than at any time in post-World War II history. But the problem goes well beyond meeting wartime obligations, transforming the military, employing other instruments of national power, or even increasing the defense budget. The real underlying problem is, in fact, the absence of a reasonably clear and meaningful grand strategy for dealing with the contemporary security environment, one that would effectively integrate the requirements for both national and homeland security. And even when we have come close to having that overarching strategy, our ability as a country to implement that strategy through the appropriate application of the proper elements of power has been seriously hampered by some critical problems that we must address if we are to be successful in the future.

For the purposes of our analysis we can focus on the two most recent U.S. presidents—Bill Clinton and George W. Bush—and their attempts to address this overarching security challenge.[1] Because each won re-election to a second term, these two presidents and their administrations span virtually all of the post-Gulf War I period (at the time of this writing). So we will limit this relatively brief assessment of U.S. national security strategy to these two presidents. We begin this chapter with an examination of the basic elements of strategy. We then turn to a general consideration of strategy formulation before addressing an assessment of how (and even whether) U.S. national security strategy has evolved from the time Bill Clinton first took office in January 1993 to roughly June 2007, nearing the final year of the George W. Bush presidency. Finally, we conclude with some observations about the necessity for generating an integrated grand strategy that addresses both national and homeland security, and some of the challenges we face in our efforts to do so.

The Basic Elements of Strategy

In simple terms strategy is the calculated relationship among ends, ways, and means. *Ends* are the objectives or goals sought. *Means* are the resources available to pursue the objectives. And *ways* are the concepts or methods for how one organizes and applies the resources. Each of these components suggests a related question. What (*ends*) do we want to pursue? With what (*means*) will we pursue them? And how (in what *ways*) will we pursue them?

In addition to these three core concepts—ends, ways, and means—we must also understand some essential principles of strategy. First, when it comes to strategy, ends clearly matter. They matter because strategy is meaningful only in terms of the objectives sought. One does not simply "do" strategy; one decides on and pursues objectives strategically. One can evaluate the success or failure of a strategy only in terms of how it fared in the pursuit of those objectives. Second, selecting the proper objective is more important than selecting the proper way in which to use the means. This is much like the difference between efficiency and effectiveness, with efficiency defined as "doing things right" and effectiveness defined as "doing the right things." Whereas most of us would like to be both effective and efficient and whereas both are important to overall success, in the end effectiveness is more important. Why? Because spending our time very efficiently doing the wrong things will not lead to success. Doing the right things only half as efficiently will still get us further down the road toward the desired objective. But if you get the ends wrong, it is quite simply impossible to get the strategy right. If the ends are wrong, no amount of tinkering with the ways and means will fix the strategy.[2]

At the same time, however, simply getting the ends right does not in and of itself guarantee success. That is because another important principle of strategy is at work: the relationship between the ends sought and the means applied is critical. If one envisions the national means as consisting of the core elements of national power—military, political/diplomatic, economic, and informational—then the problem becomes one of matching the best tools (constructed from these elements of power) to apply toward the particular end. And in the complex world of grand strategy at the highest levels, this almost always implies that we need to find a complicated, integrated combination of multiple tools to apply in a synchronized and coordinated way. As we will observe shortly, the unnecessarily restricted application of a single tool or set of tools (say, for example, using only the military element of power) or the misapplication of tools (again, for example, employing only military tools in an effort to address what is, say, fundamentally an economic objective), generally reflects an inability or unwillingness to address this need for complex yet integrated strategic approaches to complex problems. Moreover, this principle also illustrates the intrinsic importance of correctly identifying the nature of the problem one is addressing; one cannot possibly construct the proper ends, means, or ways in the face of an incorrect prior understanding of the problem. The core challenges in formulating an effective security strategy are to identify correctly where we need to go, what means we have to get there, and how best to use those means to get there as effectively and efficiently as possible.

Where is it we generally "want to go" in terms of national security policy? The answer lies in the concept of "interests." Historically we have most often thought of these interests as "national interests." Typically we express these broad interests as general goals or ambitions, such as protecting and promoting our way of life with our institutions and values intact. From these broad interests we can then derive a much more specific set of objectives. So, for example, promoting and sustaining economic prosperity as a general interest can lead to the derivative objective of maintaining access to oil, or protecting the flow of goods and services.

National security strategy or grand strategy is a country's broadest approach to the pursuit of its national objectives in the international system. The essential point is that a country chooses objectives based on its interests and values and how they are affected, threatened, or challenged in the international system. The means to pursue those objectives fall into four broad categories, the "elements of national power." Those elements, noted above, are political or diplomatic, informational, military, and economic.[3] How a country generates, organizes, and applies those elements of national power together comprise the "ways" of its national security or grand strategy. An abbreviated example of U.S. strategy during the Cold War can help illustrate the key concepts in a more practical way.

The U.S. cold war grand strategy is most often referred to as "containment," a name derived from the core objective, which was to contain communism (or prevent its spread). The cold war strategy of containment developed along the lines suggested by George Kennan in his "long telegram" from Moscow: "The main element of any United States policy toward the Soviet Union must be that of a long-term, patient but firm and vigilant containment of Russian expansive tendencies."[4] Kennan saw both offensive and defensive dimensions in the strategy. The defensive objective was to prevent any expansion of the political, economic, and military influence and physical presence of the Soviet Union. The offensive objective, generally overlooked in many discussions of containment, was the promotion of stable democracies and market economies; the idea was that healthy market democracies would prevent the spread of communist ideology and influence by denying the opportunity for it to spread.[5] As the strategy evolved, and especially as one looks back on it, we can see the different elements of power as they were applied in an integrated, coordinated strategic effort: The political/diplomatic element in the form of the Truman Doctrine, the military in alliances such as NATO and the forward deployment of U.S. troops stationed abroad, the economic in the Marshall Plan, and the informational in efforts such as Voice of America and Radio Free Europe.

Over time, according to the views of some historians and analysts, the strategy of containment grew to rely ever more heavily on the military element.[6] While this did not completely supplant the employment of other elements of power, U.S. resources did shift over time and by the 1980s this had resulted in a large increase of those at the disposal of the Pentagon relative to those available for the State Department and USAID, for example. We highlight this shift here not to criticize the Pentagon, but to point out that by the time the cold war ended, and a new set of threats, challenges, and opportunities emerged as part of a transforming strategic environment, the U.S. toolbox was in relative terms heavily filled with military instruments and much less so with instruments derived from the other three elements of power. Moreover, the resources reflected the way in which our national security policymaking structures were organized and how we thought about and constructed national security strategy.[7] Having an organizational structure evolve over time in the cold war context, and developing certain "habits" for the kinds of means we preferred to employ in certain ways against known and somewhat "comfortable threats," all left the United States in a very difficult position from which to see and grasp the changing security environment that was emerging. And perhaps arguably, that same historical vestige has hindered our efforts to come to grips strategically with the post-9/11 security environment.

There is considerably more one can say about strategy generally, but the discussion of these basic elements should be sufficient for the arguments made here. The purpose is to provide an underlying foundation from which we can then assess the strategic context within which the search for national and homeland security takes place, and to offer some observations about the challenges to strategic success. Understanding these key concepts of strategy and strategy formulation is essential in order to place the specific challenges of national and homeland security in an appropriate strategic context. Only then can we approach the problem on a less *ad hoc* basis in an attempt to devise a more integrated and ultimately effective national strategy for homeland security. A final note in terms of the general principles of strategy is that, although strategy and strategic thinking do incorporate strong elements of rationality, strategy is anything but rigid and linear. Precisely because one is adapting to changing circumstances, as well as decisions and actions taken by other actors, some of whom may wish to do us great harm, sound strategy must always include and incorporate flexibility. Planning is an important component of strategy, but strategy should never be confused with "a plan" or a blueprint to be rigidly followed.

Post-Gulf War I: Tracing U.S. Grand Strategy

The 1991 National Security Strategy (NSS) was the last formal statement of U.S. national security policy and strategy produced by the Bush administration. Looking back on the Clinton presidency and its approach to national security, it appears that its formally articulated strategy did not depart significantly from the core elements of the 1991 document. As I have argued elsewhere, however, that does not mean "that the two presidents pursued the same goals and objectives nor did so in the same ways."[8] Having very similar statements of security policy and strategy does not necessarily lead inevitably to similar behavior, in no small measure because the circumstances that presidents and their national security teams must respond to will be different. Those all-important circumstances necessarily can and almost always do lead to very different decisions and policy choices. The new and less traditional crises that confronted Clinton—notably in the Balkans and in Somalia initially—were very different from the much more traditional invasion of Kuwait by Saddam Hussein. And the means for addressing them, as well as the ways of applying those means—also reflected the transforming security environment. But the United States under Clinton adapted at best very slowly and perhaps very ineffectively at the strategic level. And the result tended to be a series of ad hoc crisis responses.[9]

Eight years later, and given the campaign rhetoric of the 2000 presidential election, one would have logically expected a significant change in formally articulated U.S. security strategy. After all, candidate Bush argued strongly against "nation-building" and for bringing the troops back home. National security advisor-to-be Condoleezza Rice wrote that a redefined set of vital national interests would drive U.S. national security policy and strategy, with a focus on priorities such as rebuilding our military power, managing relations with China and Russia, and confronting rogue regimes.[10] Yet once again, events and circumstances had a way of trumping campaign promises and strategic slogans. In this case, the Bush administration had produced no formal national security strategy statements prior to the attacks of September 11, 2001. In fact, the administration produced a new Quadrennial Defense Review on September 30, 2001, prior to releasing a new national security strategy, something that some analysts found more than a little disconcerting in that a defense strategy should be based on the national security objectives it is designed to support.[11] By the time the Bush security team did produce formal statements of U.S. strategy they were heavily driven by the events and individual issues confronting the country. Nowhere was this more apparent than in the release of the National Strategy for Homeland Security in July 2002, two months before the 2002 National Security Strategy (released in September). The 2002 NSS called for the preemptive use of military power against hostile states and terrorist groups seeking weapons of mass destruction (WMD), U.S. global military primacy, multilateralism when possible and unilateralism when necessary, and a commitment to spreading democracy and human rights around the world. All of these strategic pillars were very much in line with traditional U.S. strategic thought, though perhaps the formal statements dealing with preemption and primacy appeared to be departures in that they had previously remained largely unstated and arguably implicit. And the 2002 NSS was subsequently followed in February 2003 by individual national strategy documents on critical infrastructure protection and combating terrorism, joining homeland security in that category of separate, individual national strategies.

By mid-2007 the Bush administration was trying to hold together public and congressional support for the war in Iraq and the objective of promoting democracy abroad. As much as his predecessor, President Bush's approach to a series of crises was seemingly held together more by the "ad hockery" he had campaigned against than the consistent pursuit of clear strategic objectives through the systematic, integrated application of all elements of power toward them. In the end, there is little argument disputing that the Bush and Clinton administrations have chosen very different approaches to the crises they faced. But the reliance on military force and the inability to organize and apply other elements of power effectively and in coordination with that military power continue to characterize U.S. national security strategy. The main point is this: The formal statements of U.S. security policy and strategy, as evidenced in the annual NSS documents, have changed rather little in the past decade even in the face of enormous changes in the global security environment. One result of this has been an inability on the part of the United States to formulate consistent and effective responses to the kinds of threats and challenges it confronts. Moreover, the fits and starts that have characterized U.S. efforts to address homeland security requirements further highlight the challenges we face and the persistent problems we still encounter in adapting to a new strategic environment with a more comprehensive grand strategic approach. We turn now to a consideration of those challenges and problems, the central arguments of this chapter.

Homeland Security and National Security

Some have argued that the attacks of September 11, 2001 transformed the strategic landscape and ushered in a fundamentally new era in U.S. national security policy and strategy. Others, including this author, have taken a somewhat different perspective, arguing instead that the attacks reflected less of a transformation than a clarification of a strategic environment that had been transforming since even before the cold war ended and the Soviet Union dissolved.[12] Regardless of the position one takes on this general issue, the post-9/11 period did introduce a new term to the everyday security lexicon: homeland security. Given the peculiar historical experience of the United States—and especially its relative geopolitical isolation from the world—our national security strategy has rarely had to deal with direct threats to the homeland. Whereas other countries might not use a term such as homeland security because there would be no concept of national security without security of the homeland, U.S. national security culture developed in such a way that relatively little attention was paid to the vulnerability of the homeland. The single most important departure from this kind of thinking, of course, occurred during the height of the cold war as the United States was confronted by the threat of Soviet intercontinental ballistic missiles (ICBMs). And even then, the strategic concept Americans developed—Mutual Assured Destruction or MAD—conceived of protecting the homeland by a kind of shared homeland vulnerability.

In any case, the attacks of September 11, 2001 ushered in an era of strategic thought in which the focus on protecting the homeland would come to occupy a prominent if not preeminent position in national security strategy. And counterterrorism became the lynchpin on which almost all of our national security strategy was based. Our focus shifted almost immediately to protecting the homeland from future terrorist attacks through a combination of external measures (fighting terrorism abroad) and internal measures (taking steps to secure our borders and denying terrorists future opportunities to strike at home). Initially with the creation of a special office for Homeland Security, and then with the legislation that created a Department of Homeland Security (DHS), the president and Congress formalized the new strategic focus and ensured that no discussion of national security strategy would exclude the homeland dimension. Because of the multidimensional nature of the concept, and its external and internal dimensions, the organizational approach that was chosen included combining some twenty-four already existing agencies into a single new department, DHS. While combining functions as diverse as border patrol and emergency management in a single mega-agency appeared at least questionable to some observers and analysts, a host of factors (some perhaps strategic and others more logically domestic and political) combined to push this so-called "strategic reform" through to completion. But for all of the time and effort given to this "single largest reform" of the U.S. national security organizational apparatus since the National Security Act of 1947, relatively little attention and debate were focused on the strategic-level logic of the reorganization. And in fact, some critics argued that the decision simply to combine the existing agencies reflected less a focus on strategic thought than a bureaucratic "fix" that protected the different agencies and their domestic constituencies. Some wondered aloud whether domestic politics had again trumped national security strategy.

Sadly, and perhaps ironically, it took an act of nature and not another conscious act of terrorists to bring this fundamental gap in strategic thought into focus. When Hurricane Katrina hit New Orleans in August 2005, little attention had been paid to how the Federal Emergency Management Agency (FEMA) would function in its new organizational home as a part of the DHS. In fact, what exercising of the diverse emergency management capabilities that had been conducted prior to that disaster had been done largely in the context of responses to terrorist attacks modeled after those of September 11, 2001. Whether or not a DHS could effectively organize, plan, and execute the kind of complex strategic, operational, and tactical responses necessitated by such a natural disaster, including the communication and coordination across the various levels of government from national to local, and the nearly mind-boggling number of different agencies, had received almost no serious attention. Despite rhetoric to the contrary, our national security strategy was focused almost exclusively on rooting out and eliminating terrorists at home and abroad, and only secondarily on consequence management at home. And sadly, the focus on natural disasters was seriously ignored, with the likely underlying assumption being that we had dealt with such disasters before and there was nothing in the national security reorganization to suggest that they would not be handled successfully in the same ways in the future. While there were a number of compounding factors that made Hurricane Katrina different from almost all of its predecessor natural disasters, post-Katrina studies and congressional hearings revealed the extent to which the national security reorganization and the new focus on homeland security created serious gaps in our overall strategic ability to organize, plan, and execute such complex contingency operations.[13]

Our purpose here is not to dwell on the disasters that ensued after Katrina made landfall on August 29, 2005, nor to place blame on any individuals or agencies. Plenty of that has occurred over the past two years. Instead, we wish to draw attention to the national security strategy implications of the Katrina experience and what it suggests about the place of homeland security in our new national security strategy thinking. There are several overall lessons that stem from our experiences with Katrina and our ongoing struggles against terrorism, and all of them bring us back to our earlier discussion of strategy. First, we must properly identify our general strategic objectives. Failing to do so will prevent us from translating those broad strategic ends into the kinds of operational objectives we must be able to achieve. Simply put, protecting the homeland is not solely a matter of addressing terrorism (whether at home or abroad). When we choose to combine the different kinds of threats (manmade and natural) and our possible responses to them in a single concept of homeland security, we must think more broadly at the strategic level about what this entails for our strategic ends. Second, just because certain capabilities exist that can be applied toward both kinds of threats (in this case consequence management for emergencies), it does not necessarily follow that they can be used in the same ways. Understanding what capabilities we need (the means) and how we can best employ them (the ways) is a function of tying those ways and means to the accomplishment of specific ends. The relation between the tools and how they are used to meet the objectives one wishes to accomplish is critical. Assuming a kind of universal or general application of tools to "generic" ends will more likely than not lead to strategic failure.

Third, nowhere is this issue of relating specific ends to specific ways and means more critical than in how we are organized to devise and implement strategy. Adding homeland security to our national security strategy lexicon may in fact be the absolutely proper thing to do in confronting the twenty-first century strategic environment. The attacks in 2001 suggest strongly that it was high time for the United States to do so. And the vulnerabilities and shortcomings those attacks revealed in areas such as cross-agency communication, interoperability, data-sharing, intelligence gathering and sharing, and so on, speak volumes about the need to organize properly to conduct twenty-first century national security strategy. And yet the events that followed the "attack" by Hurricane Katrina suggest the initial reorganization was prompted by and reflected a near preoccupation with only one kind of homeland security threat—the premeditated actions of highly motivated individuals and groups to do harm. In the debates that ensued, and the organizational decisions that grew out of them, the United States has tried once again to reorganize for conducting homeland security. But have we given all the careful strategic-level thought and attention to what the best organizational structure is for addressing not just the emergency management dimension of homeland security but its counterterrorism dimension as well? Although much was learned at great cost from the Katrina experiences, one must wonder today whether elevating FEMA to a special role within DHS is not yet another case of "preparing to fight the last war." If the next DHS challenge—and by that we mean the next national security challenge—is not a natural disaster but a terrorist-induced one, will the extra-organizational role now assigned to FEMA cause the United States to be overly prepared for another Katrina and under-prepared for the actual event we face? If we are not willing to incorporate all of the dimensions of homeland security into national security strategic thought, including how we are organized, what capabilities we will need, and how we will employ them, then we would do well to reconsider the assumption that natural and manmade "threats" should be housed together.[14]

Conclusion

We began this chapter with the observations that the United States lacks "a reasonably clear and meaningful grand strategy … that would effectively integrate the requirements for both national and homeland security," and that the ability "to implement that strategy through the appropriate application of the proper elements of power has been seriously hampered." Simply put, the problem is that as Americans responded to the attacks of September 11 and as the country reoriented the military element of power toward a "global war on terrorism," the United States created its own concept of homeland security and devised a military strategy of counterterrorism without simultaneously building them into a unifying and integrating grand strategy. Although published documents such as the various national strategies and the two National Security Strategies (2002 and 2006) spoke to "strategy," none represented a genuine departure from prior national security policy statements, and none effectively rose to the level of a new national security or grand strategy for the twenty-first century. The concepts of homeland security and counterterrorism remained somewhat separate from a true grand strategy. As a consequence, counterterrorism efforts have tended to be rather one-dimensional, focusing very heavily on the use of military force, and homeland security efforts similarly one-dimensional, focusing heavily on the terrorist sources of the threats. In both cases this has led to strategic shortcomings, in the first case by limiting our efforts to integrate all of the elements of power in a more comprehensive approach to counterterrorism, and in the second case by initially downplaying the natural disaster dimension of homeland security. The strategic consequences of these shortcomings is that U.S. national security policy continues to display the kind of ad hoc, crisis management that has characterized it since the early years following the end of the cold war.

Relative continuity in our strategic approach is the underlying theme that cuts across several administrations. This is also not surprising, given the enormous constraints that act on the processes and the players who articulate, shape, and ultimately produce the documents and create the organizations responsible for that approach. The formal statements of U.S. security policy and strategy, as evidenced in the annual National Security Strategy documents, have changed rather little in the past decade and a half, even in the face of enormous changes in the global security environment. And as a consequence the United States remains handicapped at the strategic level in formulating the overarching grand strategy to drive our decision making, and in our abilities to develop the appropriate means and apply them in the most effective ways to accomplish the large ends that are fundamental in grand strategy. It is not so much that we lack options, although there admittedly appear to be more bad options than good ones.[15] It is more fundamentally a lack of strategy and an integrated application of all the elements of power that tend to limit U.S. ability to succeed.

As noted earlier, a grand strategy is not a perfectly rational and completely comprehensive "plan" for how a country will respond to every challenge and counter every threat. Given the nature of strategy, it must allow for significant flexibility and adaptation as one adjusts to the shifts in the strategic environment and the choices and actions made by other actors in that environment. Consequently, simply having a grand strategy does not remove the uncertainty and dynamism inherent in any strategic engagement, particularly those involving cunning and ruthless enemies such as we face today. But the absence of grand strategic thinking as an organizing principle for helping shape the specific decisions we make and responses we choose almost always ensures the perpetuation of the kind of ad hoc actions referred to earlier. And this in turn leads not only to a greater risk of inconsistency and conflicting choices and actions, but also to the very dangerous potential misuse and waste of precious resources. Without a reasonably clear and consistent overall strategy, any country is likely to respond to the *crises du jour* and expend valuable resources in the wrong ways for the wrong ends, ultimately resulting in strategic failure.

The security environment we confront today is highly fluid, and it contains ambiguous threats and challenges, and a diverse set of actors that include traditional tyrannical regimes, failed and failing states, non-state terrorist and criminal actors, and even natural disasters, all with the potential for generating strategic-level consequences for the United States and its citizens. The search for national security and homeland security, whether one considers these concepts separate and distinct or simply one part of a broader conception of national security, must be included in a twenty-first century integrated grand strategy. Anything less will cause the United States to bear unnecessary risk in potentially unidentified ways.

Endnotes

1. President George H. W. Bush certainly oversaw the formal end of the Cold War, and the early signs of the difficult challenges that lay ahead were already on the horizon as the first Gulf War concluded and the problems in the Balkans and Africa emerged. But the actual formulation of a U.S. grand strategy for addressing the post-Cold War world fell first to his immediate successor and then to his son.

2. That said, of course, we should also not lose sight of just how important the relationship among these components of the strategy is. We will return to the key issue of the proper selection of means and ways in our subsequent assessment of the problems the United States faces in achieving an integrated grand strategy that includes homeland security.

3. The U.S. government and, especially, the U.S. military generally apply the acronym of DIME when referring to these elements of power.

4. George F. Kennan, "The Sources of Soviet Conduct," reprinted in Foreign Affairs 65, no. 4 (Spring 1987): 852–868. Quote p. 861.

5. As then Secretary of State George Marshall observed in 1947: "Our policy is directed not against any country or doctrine, but against hunger, poverty, desperation and chaos. Its purpose should be the revival of a working economy in the world so as to permit the emergence of political and social conditions in which free institutions can exist." The Marshall Plan Speech, 5 June 1947. Available online at http://www.cnn.com/SPECIALS/cold.war/episodes/03/documents/marshall.plan/. Quoted in David Rothkopf, Running the World: The Inside Story of the National Security Council and the Architects of American Power (New York: Public Affairs, 2006): 41–42.

6. Douglas T. Stuart, "Ministry of Fear: The 1947 National Security Act in Historical and Institutional Context." International Studies Perspectives 4-3 (2003): 293–313.

7. Robert H. Dorff, "Failed States After 9/11: What Did We Know and What Have We Learned?" International Studies Perspectives 6, no. 1 (February 2005): 20–34.

8. Robert H. Dorff, "Current U.S. National Security Strategy and Policy," in The Search for Security: A U.S. Grand Strategy for the Twenty-First Century, ed. Max G. Manwaring, Edwin G. Corr, and Robert H. Dorff (Westport, CT: Praeger, 2003). Cited in Endnote No. 2, 30.

9. Ibid. 27–28.

10. Condoleezza Rice, "Promoting the National Interest," Foreign Affairs 79, no 1 (January/February 2000): 45–62.

11. This could have been a result of the political pressures to "do something" in the aftermath of the 9/11 attacks, but it could also reflect the traditional weight and priority being given to the military element of power. Although this is certainly understandable in the context of the previously unthinkable acts of terror leveled against the United States, it also suggests that the lack of balance in the toolbox was already quite evident.

12. See the series of articles in The National Interest (2002), no. 69. See also Dorff, "Failed States."

13. See, for example, the various Congressional Reports, including House Report 109-377 and the supplemental House Report 109-396. HR 109-377 concludes: "If 9/11 was a failure of imagination, then Katrina was a failure of initiative. It was a failure of leadership."

14. We specifically and consciously choose in this chapter not to take a position on the issues of whether both the natural and manmade threat components of homeland security should be combined in a single DHS, or whether a DHS is in fact the best way to incorporate the concept of homeland security into our national security strategy. Subsequent chapters in this book will address those issues and some will make specific recommendations. What we do recommend here is that homeland security must be a core concept in how we think about our national security strategy, and that strategic-level thinking must in turn drive the decisions about how we are organized. Elsewhere I have argued that the United States needs to conduct a complete national security strategy review that would lead to a comprehensive "National Security Act for the 21st Century." See Robert H. Dorff, "Managing National Security in the Information and Terrorism Age," The Forum 4, no. 1 (July 2006): http://www.bepress.com/forum/vol4/iss1/art4/, and Robert H. Dorff, "Strategy, Grand Strategy, and the Search for Security," in Manwaring, Corr and Dorff, 127–140.

15. See Richard L. Millett, "Vague Threats and Concrete Dangers: The Global Security Environment at the Start of the Twenty-First Century," in The Search for Security: A U.S. Grand Strategy for the Twenty-First Century, ed. Max G. Manwaring, Edwin G. Corr, and Robert H. Dorff, 3–19 (Westport, CT: Praeger, 2003).

Chapter 3

Assured Vulnerability
Homeland Security and the Cold War Legacy of Defenselessness

David Goldfischer

The author focuses on how an offense-oriented strategic culture in the United States continues to impede development of strategy for homeland security. The period from 1812 until World War II and the Cold War in which the United States did not face substantial external threat to the homeland left an historical legacy in which both domestic preparations and defense orientations remain underdeveloped. Even early Cold War efforts in the 1950s and 1960s on civil as well as antibomber and antimissile defenses foundered as the nation put its strategic focus in the 1970s and 1980s almost entirely on the offense—a condition the author describes as "mutual, assured vulnerability" vis-à-vis the Soviet Union. In the post-Cold War (and now post-9/11) period, efforts to secure the homeland are still an uphill battle in the absence of a strategic culture with greater defense orientation to complement

a deeply embedded emphasis on offense. Education
of professionals in homeland security should thus go
well beyond training in the mechanics of what is to be
done to include strategic thinking that gives defense its
proper place alongside offensive consideration.

The response to Hurricane Katrina, which struck the Gulf Coast on August 29, 2005, made it clear that U.S. efforts post-9/11 to augment homeland security had floundered. As the crisis unfolded and during subsequent weeks and months, scorn was heaped on an assortment of individuals and government agencies. Some held the president and his homeland security director responsible, while others pointed to the seeming ineptitude of the head of the Federal Emergency Management Agency (FEMA). Still others insisted the governor of Louisiana or the mayor of New Orleans was primarily at fault for failures of planning, breakdowns in communication, and a lack of resources or their misallocation. Assigning blame was driven largely by one's preferred theory of federalism. Many pundits in Washington insisted that homeland security (or at least emergency preparedness and response) was basically a local affair, while others happily pointed their fingers at the federal government.

It was conceivable, of course, that Katrina would prove to be a threshold event, finally generating the sense of urgency necessary to launch a serious national effort at homeland security. That thought was expressed in the foreword of the official report on the lessons of Katrina submitted to President Bush, which stated: "We hope that this Report marks the beginning of a truly transformational state of preparedness throughout all levels of our Nation."[1] Unfortunately, that sentiment only faintly echoed the impassioned sense of national resolve experienced in the wake of 9/11. It was sobering to note that several years had already gone by without anything remotely approaching a transformation of national preparedness.[2] If the shock of the destruction of the World Trade Center and the attack on the capital had failed to inspire a serious national commitment to homeland security, why should we have expected Katrina to provide the decisive "wake-up" call?

The central argument of this chapter is that an important reason for the U.S. failure to launch a "truly transformational" homeland security effort, despite 9/11 and Hurricane Katrina, lies in the historical context that has shaped our views of national defense. In that sense, the overall weakness of the defensive side of the national response to 9/11 has more fundamental causes than any particular set of decisions made by individual policymakers of varying levels of competency. Only by coming to grips with the historical record that culminated in almost complete national defenselessness long before 9/11 can we both gain a realistic sense of the obstacles to progress in homeland security and understand how best to overcome them, thus being better prepared for future terrorist attacks. To contribute to that effort, this chapter examines the historical roots of U.S. vulnerability to attack, assesses our post-9/11 progress in overcoming that legacy, and briefly considers how that effort might be accelerated.

The Roots of Vulnerability

In the middle of the twentieth century, the United States experienced a profound shift in its strategic environment from the long-term absence of any need for homeland defense—a period stretching from the War of 1812 until the 1940s, when attacks on Hawaii and threats to the Pacific Coast in World War II were followed by the onset of the Cold War and Soviet acquisition of nuclear weapons. The nuclear competition with the U.S.S.R. that followed made defense (in the traditional sense of physically protecting the American population in the event of an enemy attack) seemingly impossible. Faced with the quixotic nature of hopes to defend against the Russian nuclear arsenal, many policymakers took refuge in the belief that the threat of U.S. nuclear retaliation would reliably and permanently deter attack, making defense simply unnecessary.

New concerns about U.S. vulnerability arose in the post-Cold War (and pre-9/11) period, resulting in increased support for developing defenses against missile attack—an important but narrow aspiration long dear to the political right. This preoccupation only underscored the complete absence of a coherent national strategy for addressing the spectrum of plausible attacks on the U.S. homeland. Indeed, long-time observers of nuclear policy could recognize that the revival of support for missile defense preceding (and in a sense eclipsed by) 9/11, represented only the latest manifestation of an episodic debate that had waxed and waned since the 1960s—a debate in which even supporters of missile defense produced very little serious analysis of what a meaningful effort at "homeland security" would entail.

In short, from the emergence of the first sustained threat against the United States in the early years of the Cold War until 2001, U.S. leaders never undertook significant measures to overcome the condition of "assured vulnerability," whether by minimizing offensive threats through pursuing serious arms control and disarmament, progressively augmenting the spectrum of defensive capabilities, or combining both of these approaches.

The outcome of a series of domestic power struggles among proponents of various contending nuclear doctrines was twofold. First, the aim of the substantial buildup of strategic nuclear (and later of general-purpose or conventional) forces was to provide sufficient *offensive* power to destroy any enemy (indeed, as the offensive buildup proceeded enough firepower was produced to destroy all human civilization). Second, the focus on offense was marked by the absence of any meaningful effort to limit damage to the American population. Put another way, there was no development of a viable homeland security strategy, much less one accompanied by the necessary military or civil capabilities to achieve such a domestic defense. Minimal efforts in the 1950s and 1960s to provide for bomber, missile, and civil defenses were subsequently downgraded or abandoned completely. Indeed, the national preoccupation with offense for more than a half century of the nuclear age left behind a legacy of institutions, doctrines, and beliefs that greatly impeded U.S. adjustment to the new defensive challenge posed by the attacks on 9/11.

Before evaluating the Cold War-era origins of this neglect of defense, it may be useful at least briefly to note what homeland security (or homeland defense) means. These terms have attracted a great deal of contentious discussion, especially regarding the distinction between *homeland security* and *homeland defense*. It was not until after 9/11 that both terms entered mainstream policy discourse. "Defense" in this context refers primarily to the measures a state takes to protect what lies within its borders (i.e., its people along with the physical and institutional foundations of human sustenance and society as a whole). Capabilities are purely defensive to the extent they are useless until an enemy has launched an attack—that is, they have no capacity themselves to launch an attack against others.[3]

In the language of cold war strategy, defenses could be divided into "active" and "passive." Active defenses comprise weapons systems that spring into action in order to shoot down the enemy's offensive forces (e.g., bombers or missiles) as they approach their targets. Passive defenses are measures such as radar detection designed to give warning or, as with civil defense, to cope with the consequences of an attack. Civil defense—the pre-9/11 term that is a direct antecedent of the phrase "homeland security"—is directed toward the protection of people and society as a whole (as opposed to the defense of a country's military forces).

The imposition of these terms *homeland security* and *homeland defense* and especially the difficult if not impossible effort to distinguish neatly between them have set back efforts to think clearly about requirements for defending society. We may well have been better off had we stuck with *civil defense*—the older (and more precise) term of art that captures our main concerns when we speak of securing the homeland.

Be that as it may, we use *homeland security* here to refer to the spectrum of purely defensive measures—both active and passive, though its main concern is with civil defense. After all, the issues of "defense" that have filled the media since 9/11 have generally focused on preparedness and emergency response to disasters caused either by terrorists or by nature. Moreover, because they involve all levels of government as well as non-governmental organizations (often grassroots organizations staffed by volunteers), the robustness of these societal defenses is a good barometer of the depth and intensity of the national commitment to homeland security.[4]

The Cold War Neglect of Homeland Security

As noted above, the United States went from a long period in which homeland security was unnecessary to a Cold War, nucleus arms competition in which defense seemed desperately necessary, but almost certainly hopeless, and possibly even dangerous to attempt.[5] Given this historical context, we turn now to a brief discussion on the evolution of thinking about homeland security during the cold war.

In Britain, Germany, and Japan, the bombing of cities in World War II made civil defense a central activity. By contrast, in the United States it had become clear by late 1943 that there would be no attack on U.S. cities, and people were already talking about abolishing the wartime "Office of Civilian Defense."[6] Feeble efforts by the enemy (such as Japan's release of 9,000 balloons carrying incendiary bombs into the winds blowing across the Pacific Ocean toward the U.S. west coast) were insufficient to inspire substantial civil defense preparations by the United States outside of immediate coastal areas.[7]

Why didn't the United States choose to learn and apply the civil defense lessons adopted by its allies and enemies during World War II? One purpose of the post-war Strategic Bombing Survey, aside from evaluating the damage U.S. and British bombers had inflicted, was to assess the effectiveness of various civil defense measures in limiting that damage. An obvious lesson of World War II was that the era of strategic bombing had arrived, and it might have been equally obvious that future enemies of the United States would achieve the range to attack the American shoreline and within the interior of the country. In fact, the report of the Strategic Bombing Survey in 1945 called for a national civil defense program designed to make it impossible for any "single or small group of successful attacks" to "paralyze the national organism"—that is, it called for a serious long-term augmentation of what we now call homeland security.[8]

That report was the first of a long series of government-sponsored studies of homeland security requirements over the decades stretching ahead to 9/11—which would be either entirely ignored, or which would set in motion brief frenzies of ultimately useless activity. Far more typical of official policy in the aftermath of World War II was to ignore the implications of strategic bombing (let alone nuclear attack) for national preparedness. For example, according to the 1950 "Blue Book" on Civil Defense produced by the National Security Resources Board, "the basic operating responsibility for civil defense is the individual and his local government." Indeed, the family was cited as the "basis for organized self-protection."[9]

But this was also the period of the Berlin blockade in 1948, the first Soviet nuclear test and the fall of China to communist forces both in 1949, and the invasion of South Korea by the communist north in 1950. If those events did not guarantee greater attention to homeland security, they at least ensured that defense policy would become a central issue for U.S. policymakers. Although President Truman made a gesture toward homeland security by introducing the Civil Defense Act, creating the Federal Civil Defense Administration, the real policy debate over what one day would be called "homeland security" (but was then called "continental defense") occurred during the first year of the Eisenhower administration.[10]

For one side in that debate, the prospect of war against a nuclear adversary made it obvious that a major federal program combining active and passive defenses was critically needed. This was the message conveyed by such studies of civil defense as "Project Charles" and "Project East River." The message received strongest endorsement in the 1952 Report of the Panel of Consultants on Disarmament, chaired by the "father of the atom bomb," J. Robert Oppenheimer, and also including future CIA Director Allen Dulles. (The Report's secretary was the future influential National Security Council advisor, McGeorge Bundy.)

In the heated political environment of the early Cold War, however, the recommendations of these studies were extremely controversial. The problem was most dramatically evident in the report of Oppenheimer's disarmament panel. That report emphasized what in retrospect would seem two obvious points: first, that in the face of an adversary capable of a nuclear buildup the United States needed a "continental defense"; second, that in order for U.S. active and passive defense measures to have any prospect of ensuring the wartime survival and recovery of the American people, they would have to be accompanied by Soviet restraint in the development and deployment of nuclear weapons and the means to deliver them. Put another way, the success of "homeland security" would depend on arms control agreements with the Soviet Union, agreements in which *both* superpowers would greatly limit their offensive striking power.

That reasoning infuriated a political coalition in the United States for whom the exploitation of American offensive nuclear power was seen as the essential centerpiece of U.S. national security policy. These advocates of atomic airpower included fiscal conservatives (who saw the atom bomb as providing "more bang for the buck" than conventional forces), Cold War hawks (who wanted to maximize—and perhaps carry out—the U.S. nuclear threat against the Communist world), and the Air Force, whose new Strategic Air Command (SAC) was promoting nuclear bombers as both necessary and sufficient for the victory of the United States over the Soviet Union.

From the vantage point of these groups, the homeland security advocates' call for a "mutual foreswearing of strategic air warfare" was at best foolhardy, at worst evidence of a communist plot. Then classified Air Force documents revealed the fear of the Air Force leadership that if the American public knew the reality of the danger posed by the emerging Soviet nuclear threat, they would have heeded the advocates of homeland security. The result would be a "fortress America," in which the public would demand that the United States pursue its own safety domestically rather than develop the offensive capability to obliterate the population of the Soviet Union.

The first period of serious advocacy of homeland security ended in 1953 when a group of airpower supporters accused Oppenheimer of being a Soviet spy and succeeded in having him banned as an advisor to the United States government. Their victory in the struggle for policy was confirmed in the January 1954 "massive retaliation" speech by Secretary of State John Foster Dulles, which presented the doctrine that the United States would protect itself, Western Europe, and other allies chiefly through the threat of nuclear attacks.

Ironically, the very success of the airpower advocates in crushing supporters of continental defense now helped improve prospects for serious homeland security measures. Now that there was no fear that defensive preparations would be linked to offensive disarmament, the need for defenses as a component of war-fighting became apparent. After all, the credibility of launching a massive nuclear attack against an enemy capable of retaliation would require defensive measures to minimize the impact of such retaliation.

Other events also conspired to make it impossible to continue a policy of nearly complete defenselessness. One was the 1954 Bikini Atoll Test by the United States of the new thermonuclear weapon (the "H-bomb"). As a result of that blast, 7,000 square miles of the Pacific Ocean were covered with fallout sufficient to cause death or serious injury, making it impossible to continue assuring the American public that nothing more need be done to build up defenses to protect them. Given the fact that the Soviet Union also had the H-bomb and was on the verge of deploying its first generation of intercontinental-range bombers (which it did starting in 1955), thinking began to shift from disparagement of the need for defense by political and military leaders, to frantic calls for massive defensive deployments.[11]

In psychological terms, the succeeding thirty plus years (i.e., until the end of the Cold War) would witness wild swings between hysteria during superpower crises and relative complacency at other times. In terms of defensive measures, a massive anti-aircraft program was pursued in the mid-1950s only to be overtaken by the Soviet launch of Sputnik in 1957—an event that presaged the arrival of the ICBM—the intercontinental-range ballistic missile armed with a nuclear warhead (against which there was literally no defense). While Sputnik demolished the hope that anti-aircraft defenses could protect the American population, it gave rise to a new lobby in support of ballistic missile defenses. That lobby persuaded three presidents (Johnson, Nixon, and especially Reagan) to commit themselves to nationwide deployments of antimissile systems. In the end, the outcome of those passionate debates over ballistic missile defense (the "ABM debates" of the late 1960s and the "Star Wars" debate of the 1980s) were determined by the fact that no defensive weapons system actually existed (or could reliably be anticipated) that could cope with even a fraction of the thousands of nuclear bombs and warheads that the Soviets were capable of launching.

The advent of the missile age in ultimately defeating the claims of those who were maintaining that a combination of offense and defense could enable the United States to win a nuclear war enabled the proponents of an equally unpalatable doctrine—"mutual [or mutually] assured destruction"—to gain apparent control over nuclear policy. Given their absurd combination of calls for a U.S. capability for victory in a nuclear World War III and acknowledgment that "victory" would likely include the elimination of major American cities and the loss of tens of millions of lives, advocates of nuclear war-fighting ultimately were repudiated by the American public; their calls for extensive civil defense efforts as an integral part of a robust nuclear war-fighting strategy producing little more than black humor.

The apparent futility of nuclear war-fighting enhanced receptivity in the 1970s to the argument that the superpowers should accept relations defined by nuclear parity based, as noted above, on bilateral capabilities for "mutual assured destruction" (a doctrine whose unfortunate acronym was "MAD"). From the perspective of MAD advocates, defense was completely unnecessary because the threat of unleashing a holocaust would reliably deter both superpowers from ever launching such an attack. Defenses were also seen from this strategic perspective as being supremely dangerous because if either power tried to protect its people with civil defense measures, active defenses, or both, such actions would provide evidence that could be interpreted by the other power as preparations for starting a nuclear war, perhaps leading that power to preempt. Advocacy of nuclear "war-fighting" doctrines—evidence of some combination of delusion and aggressive designs—was seen as destabilizing deterrence relations between the superpowers with potentially disastrous consequences.

Unfortunately, MAD proponents could also be accused of suffering from dangerous illusions. Another way of characterizing mutual assured destruction, after all, was to note that it called for the "assured vulnerability" of both superpowers' populations. As MAD critic Donald Brennan put it, the doctrine appeared to favor "dead Russians over live Americans."[12] MAD in fact had arguably fatal defects. In the context of the Cold War, it offered no hope if something went wrong with the system—for example, decisions taken by a crazy leader or regime, or a fatal miscalculation at the height of a crisis. It also provided a rationale for nuclear proliferation because it claimed that huge nuclear arsenals could be safe and even necessary to preserve the peace between adversarial states. Also problematic was the fact that MAD was conceptually incompatible with defenses, even against attacks that were serious but short of apocalyptic. It would take 9/11 to reveal that such attacks (whether by non-nuclear means or with weapons of mass destruction) could become a chronic feature of life under conditions of globalization, and the events of that day represented the death knell for thinking premised on "mutual assured vulnerability."

Throughout the Cold War, episodic increases in superpower tensions could be counted on to generate increased attention (however ephemeral) to civil defense. Whenever that occurred, the two contending approaches favored by advocates could be described, as did one official of the Federal Civil Defense Administration (FCDA) in the 1950s, as "duck and cover" versus "run like hell."[13] The former approach began in the Eisenhower years, exemplified by the now notorious FCDA film in which Bert the Turtle showed how schoolchildren could achieve safety against an atomic explosion by hiding under their desks. That was complemented by the distribution of 22 million comic books and 50 million wallet cards, and other corresponding public relations efforts to convey that a nuclear attack was really not that big a deal so long as one was prepared to take effective defensive measures.

In 1956, the FCDA proposed a national blast and fallout shelter program to protect 315 target areas (asking roughly $300 billion in current dollars). That idea lapsed until 1961 when President Kennedy, in the middle of one of the crises over the fate of West Berlin, revived the call for a national shelter program. A brochure on the subject was mailed to every American family, and fallout shelter signs went up at entrances to sturdy looking public buildings throughout U.S. cities. For six months, debate raged over whether families (with government support) should build blast and fallout shelters. The debate ended in December 1961 when the president proposed in a nationwide address that the country concentrate more "on keeping enemy missiles away from our shores, and less on how to keep our neighbors out of our shelters."[14]

The "run like hell" approach began in earnest with the Interstate Highway Act of 1956, which created what was then called the "National Defense Highway System" (culminating in the 41,000 miles of the modern interstate highway system.) The central selling point of this plan, as Eisenhower put it, was that the country's roads were "too small for the flood of traffic of an entire city's people going one way," so that they "would turn into traps of death and destruction during an aerial attack or national disaster."[15] These highways were obviously built for reasons that went beyond civil defense; they were a means of encouraging the national transition to a "car culture," a transition that would provide a huge economic boost to a range of industries. Nevertheless, it is fair to say that the construction of the interstates is one legacy of the Cold War that actually contributed to long-term civil defense efforts, facilitating evacuations, and making it feasible for industrial development to be more dispersed than otherwise.

The black humor potential of the "run like hell" approach was not fully revealed until the years of the Reagan presidency, the final round of the Cold War that began with the president's calls for a U.S. capability to "prevail in a protracted nuclear war." In 1982, the president asked FEMA (which had been created in 1979 to centralize federal management of natural disasters) to plan for the relocation of 150 million Americans from around 400 high-risk areas to about 2,000 host areas at least 50 miles away. New York, among other cities, refused to work with FEMA. In the hypothesized context of early warning of an all-out Soviet nuclear strike (i.e., involving more than 10,000 nuclear bombs and warheads), the thought of managing the evacuation of eight million New Yorkers, combined with the image of host communities calmly waiting to care for them, was simply too bizarre to be taken seriously. FEMA continued working on protecting critical infrastructure and responding to attacks, including terrorist attacks, but substantial funding for their effort ended in 1988, as the Cold War waned.[16]

When the Cold War ended, the initial victors in the longstanding "war-fighting versus MAD" debate were the supporters of MAD, who seemed truly convinced that the "assured vulnerability" doctrine could now result in permanent arms control agreements among the nuclear powers; however, the erosion of that doctrinal commitment long preceded 9/11. First, the Scud missile attacks by Saddam Hussein against Israel during Desert Storm in 1991, however ineffectual, reminded people that it was easy to imagine why one might want some combination of antimissile systems and civil defense. As the range of missiles held by smaller states increased, this concern became ever more salient. Equally important, the coup against Gorbachev, during which no one knew who had control of the nuclear "button" in the Soviet Union, followed by the Soviet breakup, seemed to suggest that certain levels of global instability made MAD a very risky proposition. In the months preceding 9/11, the Bush administration had begun forcefully moving toward ending the 1972 ABM Treaty, the U.S.-Soviet agreement that had precluded militarily significant defenses against missiles. 9/11, aside from ending meaningful political support for MAD, ironically also showed that missile defense, at least for the near term, was hardly the most important component of a national homeland security policy.

To sum up the Cold War-era legacy, once the superpowers fell into the trap of focusing on building up their nuclear offenses, homeland security became an impossible dream. In a major cost study of U.S. nuclear weapons-related programs (from 1940 to 1996), the authors concluded that only about 16 percent of the nearly $6 trillion spent was on defensive measures (which included anti-aircraft, antisubmarine, antimissile, and civil defense). Out of the roughly $940 billion spent on defending against the bomb, only $19 billion was spent on civil defense. In other words, civil defense received roughly 10 percent of the total spent on defensive measures against nuclear attack, and less than one-third of 1 percent of the total spent on nuclear war preparation.[17] Over the same period, Switzerland, with one-fortieth of the U.S. population, spent more on civil defense than did the United States.[18]

In short, nearly one and a half centuries of not needing a defense was followed by a half-century in which—because of the nuclear arms race for which the United States bore significant responsibility—providing an effective defense rapidly became impossible. In large measure as a result of the doctrine of "mutual assured vulnerability" that arose in recognition of that impossibility, serious advocacy of what would become known as "homeland security" was seen as utopian or dangerously provocative (since it implied an effort to escape from the "balance of terror" and achieve victory). The combined result of decades of debate between the unrealistic doctrines of war-fighting and MAD was near paralysis in efforts to plan rationally for homeland security, both during the era preceding 9/11 and in its aftermath.

After 9/11: The Legacy of Neglect

After the first effort to destroy the World Trade Center in 1993, a number of noted experts on national security offered guidelines for a major national effort at preventing and responding to future attacks, as well as conveying that future terrorist incidents were not only inevitable but also likely to be on a far greater scale of destruction.[19] For the reasons described in the preceding section, those warnings and policy prescriptions fell on deaf ears. Even though securing the homeland is essential in this new era characterized by globalization and radical Islamist terrorism, efforts to do so have been impeded by the absence of a supporting defense-oriented culture among political elites, the military, or the general population. Had it existed, an agreed analytical framework for homeland security planning could have facilitated adjustment to radical change in the nature of the threat.

Thus, when 9/11 occurred, what followed was a long period of improvisation, much of which was understandably aimed at addressing the specific vulnerabilities revealed by the attack. The first authoritative effort at designing an overall approach, the July 2002 National Strategy for Homeland Security, provided a familiar set of categories (e.g., intelligence and early warning, border and transportation security, critical infrastructure, etc.) but no overarching vision that could give shape to a cohesive national strategy to guide rationally an efficient allocation of resources.

The chief institutional response to 9/11, of course, was the creation of the Department of Homeland Security (DHS), which began operating in January 2003. While it remains the task of future historians to judge the ultimate impact of DHS, the response to Katrina made the agency's internal chaos—already well known to every informed observer—a matter of grave public concern.

That doesn't mean that there was no evidence of progress or of hope for the future. The United States Northern Command, created in April 2002 and declared fully operational on the second anniversary of 9/11, progressed with a serious sense of mission to assess the role of the military in homeland defense, to coordinate with its Canadian, Mexican, and Caribbean partners, and to work on developing its support function for civil authorities in the event of large-scale disasters. As for DHS, even before Katrina, the replacement of Tom Ridge by Michael Chertoff in February 2005 resulted in a sharper analytical focus on a spectrum of issues facing the agency, as well as prioritization of missions and specific tasks.

Well aware of past problems in coping with homeland-security challenges, Chertoff noted the need to recognize that "lurching from either extreme forms of protection to total complacency … [is] not an appropriate way to build a strategy."[20] As soon as he took office, he began repeating in speech after speech that the general model to be applied would be one of risk management in which assessments of a combination of threat, vulnerability, and consequence would guide decision making on priorities. Although far too little is known about the nature of future threats to allow that model to become a formula offering specific guidance, a commonsensical approach to linking those factors nevertheless led Chertoff to identify some clear priorities (e.g., improving and deploying radiation sensors both at points of entry and within cities, developing command-level communications interoperability within cities and regions, etc.).[21]

The greatest single contribution to framing the debate over homeland security was the July 2004 report of the 9/11 Commission. While future research will deepen review of the vulnerabilities that made 9/11 possible, and while there will be endless debate over its recommendations, the Commission succeeded brilliantly in providing an authoritative structure—within a single volume—for thinking through the challenges of homeland security, coupled with specific guidance that is remarkably thoughtful, especially given that it is the product of a bipartisan committee.

Finally, although the British could take credit for uncovering, in August 2006, the terrorist plot to blow up planes en route from the U.K. to the United States, that event did highlight what is generally an invisible, hard-to-measure dimension of homeland security success: the absence of attacks on the United States in the years immediately following 9/11. On the other hand, in retrospect, the eight years that passed between the first and final attacks on the World Trade Center show that even long lulls in violence within the United States cannot automatically be attributed to successful prevention.

Despite impressive progress, however, the gap between current capabilities and any reasonable standard of national preparedness remains vast. And it is more than the glaring problems in the response to (and recovery from) Katrina that indicate that daunting problems remain. One indicator of deeper problems is the way resources have been geographically distributed, with allocations based largely on political power and standard pork-barrel politics rather than on any reasonable assessment of what constitutes high-risk targets. Another indicator has been the mind-boggling scale of local mismanagement of federal homeland-security money. A third, and perhaps the most revealing, has been the conflation of resentment directed against illegal Hispanic immigrants with homeland security. The involvement of DHS in the political tug-of-war between anti-immigrant politics on the one hand and the alliance between a business community dependent on illegal labor along with liberal supporters of relatively open borders on the other, has shown that the national conception of homeland security itself remains vague and prone to politicization. (Whatever the merits of Mexican border fences and mass arrests of illegal immigrants, such a diversion of homeland-security resources away from efforts to stop terrorists arguably heightens the danger of future attacks.)

Indeed, it is the issue of borders that best illustrates the challenge of moving beyond the Cold War legacy of defenselessness. In one important sense, the advent of long-range airpower, and especially the addition of nuclear bombardment, forever eradicated realistic hopes of reliably preventing attacks within one's borders. If anything, the half-century of Cold War created a legacy in which the idea of a protected border was laughable. (During the debate in the 1980s over President Reagan's call for a population defense against nuclear missiles, former Secretary of Defense Robert McNamara used to joke that even an effective missile defense system would be worthless since the Soviets could simply cross the border from Mexico with nuclear bombs hidden inside bales of marijuana.) Although the consequences of a failure to guard our borders and other points of entry were made dramatically evident on 9/11, the optimal role of border security remains an open question, the answer to which can only be drawn from a strategic perspective on homeland security as a whole.

The origins of civil defense lay in the walled city, which from ancient times until the Middle Ages provided physical protection for its inhabitants. The shift in advantage from defense to offense, starting with the invention of gunpowder in the fourteenth century, meant that the walls of cities could no longer provide safety, and contributed to the consolidation of the larger political unit represented by the modern state.[22] If 9/11 seems to call for some modern state-level resurrection of the walled city, it may well be the case that we have reached a stage, as a result of the forces of globalization, in which reliance on state borders may be becoming as anachronistic as the walls and moats around cities became in modern Europe. Although it is evident that defense has a critical role to play in the security of those who live within the United States (and within other threatened states), it is also true that decisions about allocating roles and resources between offense and defense and within the different components of the defensive mission can only be specified in terms of a strategic conception of the foundations of safety in the globalization era.

Unfortunately, notwithstanding the considerable merits of various improvised responses to 9/11, and however laudable have been some of the early steps toward thinking more rigorously, there is little evidence that we have overcome the cultural and intellectual inertia of historical defenselessness. Multiple future attacks on a scale similar to 9/11 no doubt would alter this traditional lack of commitment to defense. Thus, Israeli defense experts, whose country has managed to preserve a semblance of normal life within the borders of a state under constant terrorist attack (nearly all of which are stopped), sometimes point out that the U.S. failure to transform homeland security is largely the result of not having been attacked enough to force an effective defensive response. Since we obviously wish to avoid that particular path toward wisdom, it is worth briefly considering what has to change. In concluding this chapter, I will describe four interlocking areas in which we can hope for and, perhaps in some cases, help prod progress. The first concerns political leadership, the second addresses the role of defense intellectuals, the third is the realm of cultural change within the community of homeland security professionals, and the last (though hardly the least) concerns the role of education.

The Unfinished Task of Inventing Homeland Security

After the failures surrounding Katrina, and as investigatory journalism documents how, in an evasion of responsibility of historic proportions, the Bush administration invaded Iraq in 2003 without even a rudimentary plan for how to occupy the country,[23] it is apparent that President Bush and his administration were not up to the challenges—offensive and defensive—posed by 9/11. One dimension of that failure of leadership was the administration's reflexive dependence on the U.S. tradition of relying on the offense to resolve its security challenges. Thus, President Bush often offered some version of his assertion that "we will engage enemies in these countries [Iraq and Afghanistan] abroad so we do not have to face them here at home." Similarly, Vice President Cheney insisted that "wars are not won on the defensive. ... [W]e have only one option—and that's to take the fight to the enemy."[24]

Although it is obviously true that offense is a crucial component of the current struggle, the national leadership failed to articulate the limitations (and possible dangers) of an offense-dominant war-fighting strategy. One dimension of the inadequacy of relying on the offense, as Stephen Flynn has pointed out, is that "there is no central front on which al Qaeda and its radical jihadist imitators can be cornered and destroyed." That observation has two implications. First, it suggests why the ultimate defeat of the threat lies outside of the realm either of offense or of defense; that is, victory must ultimately address the reasons why violent religious extremists attract support.

Second, when combined with the extended reach and destructive potential of terrorism under conditions of globalization, it means that in contrast to past United States wars, offense simply cannot substitute for defense. There is thus no alternative to devoting substantial resources toward the development of meaningful defenses. Once those basic aspects of current reality are recognized, it is the inescapable responsibility of leadership to identify realistic standards of defensive preparedness deemed vital for national security, realistically to assess the costs, the time, and the reorientation of national priorities required to reach that level, and to undertake a patient, effective process of communication that aims to persuade (i.e., to inspire) the American public to make the necessary sacrifices and bear the costs.

The fact that a series of U.S. leaders failed that test during the Cold War, alternating empty, short-lived appeals to "duck and cover" with the obsessive construction, decade after decade, of a nuclear arsenal large enough to exterminate all of humankind, has not made it easier for their successors in the post-9/11 era. Leadership will require thinking creatively about future requirements in a radically changed strategic environment, breaking free of a Cold War fixation almost exclusively on the offense that was foolhardy then and irrelevant now. The first U.S. president in the post-9/11 era and his administration failed to meet that challenge.

The Role of Defense Intellectuals

One outcome of the simultaneous advent of the nuclear age and a bipolar world was the emergence of the field of security studies. The leading lights among the first generation to come to grips with that transformed security environment (e.g., Bernard Brodie, George Kennan, Herman Kahn, Glenn Snyder, Thomas Schelling, Albert Wohlstetter, et al.) approached the challenge of their times with a level of strategic vision and analytical rigor that has, so far, not been matched by current thinkers. The issue here is not who was then right or wrong about different aspects of the problems confronting national and international security. The point is that, while there is no current shortage of experts who cogently address important elements of strategy and tactics in the struggle against Islamist extremism, security studies has yet to produce works that fundamentally engage and illuminate the new strategic environment.

If political leadership, as always, will be critical, sound policy will have to rest on a foundation of deeper inquiry into grand strategy than has so far emerged. Topics as diverse as border security, intelligence sharing, nation building, and integration of Muslim communities in the developed (and secular) West, will either be located within some common vision (or debate over persuasive claimants to an integrated vision), or policy will never achieve a sense of coherence and reasonably steady direction. Whatever the virtues of the notion of "containment," it provided an answer to the questions of "security for what and whom?" and "security against what and whom?" In the age of globalization, those questions that touch on ultimate questions of identity and legitimacy have to be re-asked and re-answered.

Developing Defense Orientations Within Homeland-Security Strategic Culture

In his 2004 Strategic Plan for homeland security, then DHS Secretary Tom Ridge offered the following as one of the three guiding principles of his department: "We will blend 22 previously disparate agencies, each with its employees, mission and culture into a single, unified Department whose mission is to secure the homeland." [25] Katrina of course made the lack of common organizational culture within the DHS painfully obvious, even as it simultaneously revealed a number of equally consequential divides: between the military and civilian authorities, between cities and states, and between states and the federal government. At these levels of interaction, cultural divides tend to be largely self-sustaining, despite noble and often capable efforts to enhance integration. Far-reaching and durable integration can only occur when something galvanizes the enormous number of bureaucratic and political fiefdoms that inhabit the realm of "homeland security."

The external force can come in several forms that may be somewhat distinct or mutually reinforcing: (1) recognition of a common threat whose magnitude drives home the aphorism that "we must all hang together or we will all hang separately"; (2) leadership (exemplified in the modern era by Winston Churchill), whose inspirational power makes it seem almost possible to explain heroic national commitment to the common defense in terms of the vision of a single individual; and (3) grassroots activism, in which new organizations, ranging from intensely motivated groups to mass movements, challenge, reform, or replace regimes seen as unrepresentative, or paralyzed by division, or corrupt, or simply out of touch with the demands of the time.

Of those three categories of possibility, it is hard to glean much potential guidance. After all, we all hope to avoid future terrorist attacks, however motivating they might be in overcoming frustrating problems of integration at the level of bureaucratic and electoral politics. And while we all would wish for the sort of future national leader who can offer the commanding vision and practical ideas to build a working consensus among the myriad semiautonomous entities that govern America, the election of such a leader is a matter of good fortune. Finally, it is also hard to imagine how a largely apathetic public (however roused momentarily either by bouts of panic or jokes about using duct tape to protect themselves) can ever inspire a movement that can result in real change when it comes to homeland security.

One way in which a relatively small number of interested individuals has tried to effect change is in the field of education. Education that incorporates the strategic challenges described in this chapter can help to enhance homeland security in numerous ways. At the undergraduate and particularly at the graduate levels, it can raise awareness of the sorts of hurdles identified in the rapidly expanding homeland security literature (drawing as well from such related fields as international relations, human rights, religious studies, and economics). Students carry that education into their professions, hopefully combined with practical training in the nuts and bolts dimensions of preparedness. They bring a broad perspective that resists the "stove pipes" or bureaucratic constraints they are certain to encounter within every agency at every level of government. In the ideal case, students educated in homeland security will emerge as leaders in different levels of government and begin to take practical actions that elevate the sense of common purpose.

One way that process can be expedited is for farsighted homeland security leaders who are conscious of the absence of historical institutions, practices, and beliefs supportive of the common defense, to invest in homeland security education for themselves and their subordinates. Beyond that, they can also hire the new generation of aspiring homeland security professionals who are beginning to emerge from the best programs in the country.

There is now a short post-9/11 history of homeland security education. Within a year, programs began to pop up in diverse places, and the active interest of the first commander of Northern Command, General Ralph Eberhardt, made possible the founding (and funding) to build what is now called the Homeland Security/Defense Education Consortium (HS/DEC). While this is not the place to tell the story of the struggle to educate the present and future community of homeland security professionals, it is worth noting that the tale is complete with both heroes (who have worked hard to develop the programs needed to impart a strategic perspective and the necessary skills) and villains (who have obstructed the endeavor by placing their own struggles for bureaucratic turf or personal control above the national interest). The single largest barrier to progress has been the self-perpetuating chaos of the Department of Homeland Security, which has tended neither to support education for its staff (beyond the training programs born in the disparate agencies that coexist just short of sectarian violence) nor to establish an organized program to identify and hire the potential future leaders emerging out of top homeland security programs around the country. More than anything else, the failure of

DHS to support homeland security education ensures that the acknowledgments we endlessly hear of the need for "vision" and "integration" in the speeches of DHS secretaries will remain empty rhetoric.

In the face of the enormity of the need to advance homeland security more rapidly, more intelligently, and more sustainably than it has progressed in the years since 9/11, support for education may seem an unduly modest (even uninteresting) concept. Yet it is an indispensable albeit incremental source of change, and in a complex world of evolving, increasingly dangerous terrorist threats, it is vital. Thus, more educational endeavors need to be launched and institutionalized—efforts designed to build and improve integrated networks in the United States and between allied states in the war on terror. Since we cannot afford to wait either for more attacks or more capable presidents and administrations, education is the most reliable foundation for the long-term project of reshaping national and organizational cultures so as finally to move homeland security—however saddening its necessity—from the margins to the mainstream of national life.

Endnotes

1. The Federal Response to Hurricane Katrina: Lessons Learned, submitted February 23, 2006. http://www.whitehouse.gov/reports/katrina-lessons-learned/letter.html
2. As Stephen Flynn had noted in September 2004, three full years after 9/11: "The United States is living on borrowed time—and squandering it." "The Neglected Homefront," Foreign Affairs (September/October 2004): 20.
3. For a discussion of the meaning of "offense" and "defense," including the reversal of their traditional meanings by supporters of mutual, assured destruction, see David Goldfischer, "Rethinking the Unthinkable After the Cold War: Toward Long-Term Nuclear Policy Planning," Security Studies 7, no. 4 (summer 1998): 169–171.
4. Support for the combat capabilities associated with homeland security (some of which these days are assigned the narrower label of "homeland defense"), of course also requires a level of popular support, since they are mandated by the president and funded by Congress. The point is that deeper engagement at the local level is more central to civil defense (e.g., shelters, evacuation, emergency assistance, fire-fighting, etc.) than to military programs such as anti-aircraft defenses, antimissile defenses, or Naval and Coast Guard defenses of the coastline). The evident need for, and controversies surrounding, civil-military coordination in homeland security is beyond the scope of this chapter.
5. While there is a long history of domestic terrorism (including assassinations of American presidents), there had never, before the Soviet acquisition of nuclear weapons, been any serious national preoccupation with attacks that could substantially disrupt the social and economic life of the country. (An argument could be made, though, that labor unrest in the late nineteenth and early twentieth century came close.) Though one could also argue that the Civil War made homeland security (for both sides) a critical concern, it makes more sense to set aside that time of two "homelands" from any assessment of U.S. attitudes toward defense.

6. Lawrence J. Vale, The Limits of Civil Defence in the USA, Switzerland, Britain and the Soviet Union: The Evolution of Policies since 1945 (New York: St. Martin's Press, 1987), 58.

7. Stephen I. Schwartz, Ed., Atomic Audit: The Costs and Consequences of U.S. Nuclear Weapons since 1940 (Washington, D.C.: Brookings Institution Press), 271.

8. U.S. Strategic Bombing Survey, The Effects of Atomic Bombs on Hiroshima and Nagasaki (Washington, D.C.: U.S. Government Printing Office, June 30, 1946), p. 38. Cited in Vale, Limits of Civil Defence (n. 5), p. 59.

9. Vale, Limits of Civil Defence.

10. For a detailed discussion, and supporting documentation, of the following description of the debates over "continental defense" during the 1950s, see David Goldfischer, The Best Defense: Policy Alternatives for U.S. Nuclear Security From the 1950s to the 1990s (Ithaca, NY: Cornell University Press, 1993), 79–146.

11. See Vale, Limits of Civil Defence, 61–63.

12. Donald G. Brennan, "The Case for Population Defense," in Why ABM? Policy Issues in the Missile Defense Controversy, ed. Johan J. Holst and William Schneider Jr. (New York: Pergamon Press, 1969).

13. Alan M. Winkler, "A 40-Year History of Civil Defense," Bulletin of the Atomic Scientists 40 (June/July 1984). See also Bruce Watson, "We Couldn't Run, So We Hoped We Could Hide," Smithsonian (April 1994): 50.

14. For a discussion of the shaping of public attitudes toward civil defense during the 1960s, see Goldfischer, The Best Defense, 208–215).

15. Mark H. Rose, Interstate: Express Highway Politics, 1939–1989, rev. ed. (Knoxville, TN: University of Tennessee Press, 1990), 77–78. Cited in Schwartz, Atomic Audit, 312.

16. These details are drawn from the descriptions of Reagan-era civil defense contained in Schwartz, Atomic Audit, 321–325, and Vale, Limits of Civil Defence, 78–93.

17. Schwartz, Atomic Audit, see Figure 1, opposite p. 1, and Figure 4.1, p. 270.

18. Vale, Limits of Civil Defence, 8.

19. See for example: Richard Betts, "The New Threat of Mass Destruction," Foreign Affairs 77, no. 1 (January/February 1998): 26—41; Ashton Carter, John Deutch, and Philip Zelikow, "Catastrophic Terrorism: Tackling the New Danger," Foreign Affairs (November/December 1998): 80—94; and David Goldfischer, "Rethinking the Unthinkable After the Cold War," 190–192. The most intensive and visible effort by far to forewarn the nation was the Hart-Rudman Commission, co-chaired by former Senators Gary Hart and Warren Rudman. See The Phase 3 Report of the U.S. Commission on National Security/21st Century, Roadmap for National Security: Imperative for Change (Preface and pp. 10–29) http://www.fas.org/irp/threat/nssg.pdf.

20. Remarks by Homeland Security Secretary Michael Chertoff on Protecting the Homeland: Meeting Challenges and Looking Forward, December 14, 2006. http://www.dhs.gov/xnews/speeches/sp_1166137816540.shtm.

21. The 9/11 Commission, in a follow-up to its original report, provided a "report card" (covering various aspects of emergency preparedness and response, transportation security, border security, reforming the institutions of government, and foreign policy), that provides a useful guide to homeland security progress as of December 2005. See Final Report on 9/11 Commission Recommendations, December 5, 2005. http://www.9-11pdp.org/press/2005-12-05_report.pdf.

22. See Vale, Limits of Civil Defence, 14, and George Quester, Offense and Defense in the International System (New York: Wiley, 1977).

23. Among several recent books documenting this tragedy, probably the best is Thomas E. Ricks, Fiasco: The American Military Adventure in Iraq (New York: Penguin Press, 2006).

24. Flynn, "The Neglected Homefront," 21.

25. Securing Our Homeland, U.S. Department of Homeland Security Strategic Plan, 2004. http://www.dhs.gov/xlibrary/assets/DHS_StratPlan_FINAL_spread.pdf.

Chapter 4

Terrorism and Deterrence by Denial

James M. Smith and Brent J. Talbot*

The authors break new, important strategic ground in their application of deterrence by denial of capability (the operational level), opportunity (the tactical level), and objectives sought by groups, movements, or insurgencies considering the use of terrorism as a tactic to advance their cause (the strategic level). The approach flows from a causal analysis of what leads to the use of terrorist tactics in the first place. Strategy implementation calls for pursuing both external or international actions—the "away game" as well as various domestic measures—the "home game." Success comes from efforts to marginalize the terrorist message and deter or preclude attainment of terrorist objectives, thus defeating strategically the group, movement, or insurgency threatening the U.S. homeland.

---

* The views expressed in this chapter are those of the authors and do not necessarily reflect the official policy or position of the Department of the Air Force, the Department of Defense, or the U.S. Government.

53

Conventional wisdom holds that terrorists and terrorism cannot be deterred: terrorists do not fear punishment or death, nor do they possess the territory and population of a state, and they are therefore immune from psychological coercion via threat of retaliation. We argue, however, that deterrence—specifically psychological coercion through denial as opposed to traditional deterrence by punishment—can not only be applied to terrorism, but also can be utilized at the tactical, operational, and strategic levels for an overall coercive effect. In developing this application, the chapter presents terrorism as a dynamic process described by interrelated essential elements and communication flows. It then presents concepts of deterrence as these enter into this dynamic process and disrupt its elements and linkages, thus shaping coercive influences, removing terrorist options, and forcing decisions that alter terrorist plans and actions.

At the base or tactical level the operative coercive mechanism for deterrence of an act of terrorism is *denial of opportunity*, which delinks the terrorist action cadre from its intended victim or victims. At the higher operational level—deterrence of a series of related terrorist actions or a campaign of terror—the mechanism is *denial of capability*, which disrupts organizational recruitment and maintenance, training, access to weapons and sanctuary, communications, finance, and other resources needed to undertake hostile actions. At the highest and most important or strategic level—deterrence of terrorism itself or defeat of the strategy—the mechanism is *denial of objectives*, or marginalization of the terrorist message from both its target population and its support base, leading to ultimate failure.

The chapter concludes with a discussion of how to implement a framework to create these effects, with specific attention to both international perception and influence, and domestic preparation and insulation. A wide range of efforts is required to create the synergistic deterrent effect within and across the tactical, operational, and strategic levels. Cognizant that terrorism is a form of strategic communication, implementation must be informed by the effort to use international effects and influence to shape messages to and among the regional and global terrorist "core" audience and potential supporters, and domestic effects that shape both U.S. government and population reactions to terrorist threats and actions. Only this total, deliberate, and strategic approach can achieve a deterrent effect on this otherwise intractable adversary.

Terrorism as a Dynamic Process

The term "terrorism" is today used to describe a wide range of tactics, campaigns, and strategies of criminal and political violence. This chapter is specifically addressed to terrorism as deliberate violence undertaken for political objectives, with the attainment of these objectives resulting from psychological effects on targets beyond the direct victims of the violence. We look to second- and third-order psychological effects of political violence—an examination that goes well beyond the physical act, weapon, and victim to the larger motivation, preparation, and orchestration of terrorism and the terrorist, as well as to the instrumental creation of fear or terror as the primary lever seeking to cause changes in government policy and action, particularly in driving popular demands on that government for the changes sought. At the same time, the act sends messages to create, deepen, and reinforce support for the terror and the terrorist group among its core audience, and it seeks to engender sympathy and support among wider regional and global audiences to foster its cause and secure both general and tangible support. It is both political violence and psychological communication—sometimes called "propaganda of the deed"—undertaken as asymmetrical warfare against an otherwise superior adversary.[1]

One way to conceptualize terrorism, and to design effective anticipatory and response efforts toward deterrence, is to depict it as a systematic process (a cause to action to effects chain, as depicted horizontally in Figure 4.1). The focal point for much of the terrorism analysis we see is the terrorist act—the terrorist committing a violent act employing some weapon against a selected victim. Although the terrorist, the act, the weapon, and the victim constitute an important tactical level of analysis relevant to responders and to the overall effort to combat terrorism, it is insufficient either to understand fully or to respond effectively to the threat. The process model we develop here adds the operational and organizational underpinnings to the terrorist and his act, and it also includes the essential consequences and audiences terrorized or influenced by such acts.

The operational level of analysis—a focus on cause and organizational response—adds the foundation and structure of terror, from its underlying causes and roots of discontent through the organizing infrastructure of recruitment, training, support, communications, weapons procurement—all that goes into motivating, organizing, preparing, supporting, and sustaining a quasi-military structure and strategy. It also includes focus on the complex psychological and organizational transformation from discontent to violence, or the action link that brings all of those motives and capabilities to the act of terrorist violence.

Terrorism does not end with the act of violence; that is only the beginning. It is the fear generated in the minds of the target audiences—not the victim—that provides the lever through (and only through) which the terrorist organization can hope to attain its objectives. Terrorism is a tool used by the relatively weak to attack a strong adversary, an asymmetrical tool that bypasses adversary strengths and seeks out the soft and vulnerable underbelly of society as the focus of influence. It is this second-order psychological effect on the "target of terror" that is the key to influencing adversary decisions and policies. The terrorist act also is to reinforce and expand the group's influence on and support from its core support base, its broader regional or cultural base, and even the global audience—all "targets of influence."[2]

Terrorism and Deterrence by Denial[3]

Viewing terrorism as an interactive process as briefly outlined above indicates points of attack for an effective strategic response. These components and the dynamics between them define the terrorist group; its critical characteristics; and its operational, tactical, and strategic dimensions. They also point to its relative strengths and weaknesses, indicating potential responses to counter effectively its key strengths and capitalize on its weaknesses. Terrorism can be blunted—its damage prevented, deflected, or limited by tactical response policy elements. And it can be preempted or altered, even ultimately defeated, by strategic countermeasures that target and attack its operational and strategic bases or operational centers. This process context—its essential elements developed and related within an overarching strategic perspective—is at the center of both the terrorist threat and the strategic response to that threat. It provides not only a template for a comprehensive threat assessment, but also a framework for systematic response.

Tactical Level: Deterrence by Denial of Opportunity

The tactical level of deterrence aims at prevention of an act or acts of terrorism. It seeks to delink terrorism from its victim. This can be accomplished by denying either the victim access to the terrorist through protection and hardening or by denying the terrorist access to the victim or weapon through efforts to block entry and obstruct movement. Potential "victims" with high value and high symbolic visibility can be protected through physical means and protective measures. Making it difficult to reach or attack specific victims can cause terrorists to look elsewhere or to change (delay or defer) their decisions to act. Making it difficult to gain entry to the country, to travel with impunity within the vicinity of the priority victim, or to access weapons of choice or their essential components can also have this preventive effect.

Another key point here is that if short-term deterrence fails and an act of terrorism does occur, then the visible effectiveness of the response can have strong and larger-scale deterrent effects toward future acts and continued terrorism. An effective implementation of crisis and consequence management—strength of response, rescue, recovery, and clear leadership within those efforts—will limit the degree of "terror" in the local and national population, blunt the fear, and shorten the period of major psychological impact.

Accurate and timely attribution of the attack to the responsible party or parties and identification of weapons components employed by these terrorists will allow decisive retribution and a clear chain of movement toward effective prosecution of both perpetrators and their weapons suppliers. Rapid recovery followed by both symbolic and substantial reconstruction and reconstitution also will blunt much of the long-term effect. This limits the "terror" outcome and it helps with the stra-

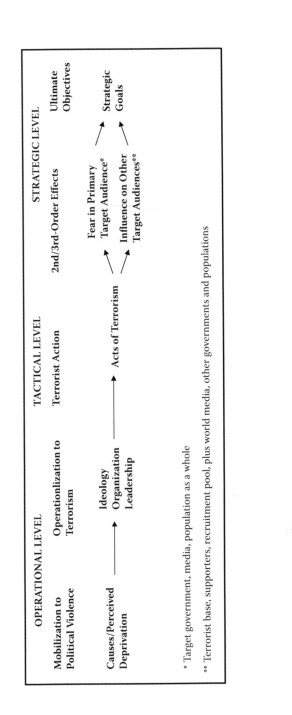

Figure 4.1 Essential process elements, dynamic linkages, and audiences.

tegic preparation of the population for a sustained campaign to combat terrorism, also limiting the likelihood of the terrorist obtaining any favorable effect through future attacks. Less than fully effective deterrence today does not signal total failure; today's attack response can contribute significantly to tomorrow's strengthened deterrent outcomes.

Operational Level: Deterrence by Denial of Capability

Actions that contribute to effective deterrence at the operational level address the organizational and operational process. In organizational terms, the United States can seek to affect the legitimacy and attractiveness of the organization's cause, its ability to recruit members and supporters, and most significantly its process of socialization and mobilization toward violent action. These are often broadly based and long-term counterterrorism efforts.

Shorter-term actions include attempts to disrupt the operational process by removing access to sanctuary and open support, putting and keeping terrorist leadership underground and on the run. Terrorist action can be disrupted by denying access to weaponry—at least its worst forms—training grounds and resources, free movement and associated travel documents, secure communications, and finance.

With effective intelligence and international support, we can sometimes preempt terror preparations and attack. We can interdict these organizational and operational processes, and we can at least limit group capabilities and attack severity. In the end, we seek to isolate the terrorist from support bases and sources of sanctuary, and to limit the ability even to undertake acts of terrorism.

Strategic Level: Deterrence by Denial of Objectives

Strategic deterrence of terrorism is aimed at creating the clear perception in the mind of the terrorist leadership that their goals cannot be achieved by means of a terror campaign against the United States; their strategy cannot succeed, and any action on their part can only leave them exposed to all levels of audience as ineffective, irrelevant, and unworthy of attention or support. This level of deterrent action builds from the tactical and operational levels specifically to limit the psychological vulnerability and to build the psychological strength of the target—in this case the United States public and its government.

Preparing the American target to mute the effects of terrorism is, first, a function of education prior to attack. Fear of the misunderstood magnifies the impact of terrorism, and knowing something about the true weakness and understanding the morally bankrupt foundation of the terrorist cause can provide an effective damper on the generation of "terror." Knowing what is going on across an attack through open and nonsensational information is essential to limiting fear. These effects, along with strong and visible tactical and operational efforts to prevent and respond to terror, will go far toward insulating the target from the full, desired terrorist reaction. Effective prevention, mitigation, and response combine to marginalize and mute the terrorist message. Since the terrorist is already an ineffective, marginal player on the global stage in all other dimensions of power and influence, such a negative impact on his strategic "message" dooms him to failure. Terrorism without "terror" cannot succeed as a political strategy, and failure ultimately will feed on itself, destroying the terrorist cause and effort.

All of these levels and components of terrorism and deterrence are graphically displayed in Figure 4.2. While that depiction only provides the framework for deterring terrorism, the following discussion of implementation gets at the broad, combined, and synergistic effects on the target audiences of terrorism and of the response; the international and domestic audiences, or targets of influence and targets of terror. It is ultimately here that success or failure for the United States or for the terrorist is written.

International Implementation—the "Away Game"

The implementation of the components of a comprehensive, synergistic strategy has to be centered on the international community since the most significant threats to the United States stem from transnational terrorism. This represents the "away game" within the overall effort, focusing on affecting the terrorists before they manifest their threats in the U.S. homeland, and specifically on the "targets of influence" that provide essential support, sanctuary, and sustenance to the terrorists and terrorism. This effort, besides the operational preemption and interdiction actions mentioned above, centers on creating operational and strategic effects to deny terrorist capabilities and attainment of the objectives of terror. The success of our strategy to combat terrorism depends significantly on the image and influence of the United States in the regional and cultural world from which this threat stems.

International implementation efforts must first identify the target population that provides the terrorists with recruits as well as a support base. Second, with the target population in mind, we must develop an influence strategy that marginalizes the terrorist message, which means we must initially define the core message at the strategic level, and then outline appropriate counters against it. This simply boils down to getting out the real truth. Finally, we must also offset the operational-level propaganda efforts of the terrorists that attempt to mask the rationale for U.S. military operations in their region of concern while at the same time distorting the truth behind their own involvement in terror attacks, which attempt to draw implausible parallels to "just causes." Terrorists might even devise conspiracy theories designed to inspire doubt as to who are the real instigators of acts of terror. At the operational level we can also use the media to analyze the results of terrorist

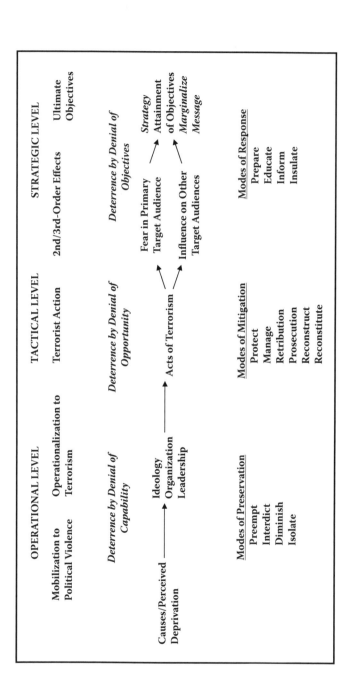

Figure 4.2 Terrorism dynamic process model with deterrence overlay: strategic response based on causal analysis of terrorist threat.

attacks and point out to the targets of influence that often those attacks leave many innocents as victims—including members of the target of influence populations, which if properly publicized, could turn significant numbers of supporters against the attacks.

Identifying and Influencing the Target Population

The primary locus for U.S. strategy in combating terrorism today is found within the Muslim world. As the basis for the rest of this analysis, we will focus on the application of this process model to the Muslim world. Even though Muslims comprise over 1.3 billion members worldwide, Richard Clarke, former terrorist "czar" in the Clinton and early-Bush administrations, subdivides the Muslim population into three concentric circles. The outermost circle comprises all 1.3 billion Muslims worldwide—most being "absorbed in their daily lives with no inclination to terror or extremism." By contrast, the innermost circle is made up of extremist Islamists, perhaps 50,000 to 100,000 radical "jihadists bent on the West's destruction, and against whom hard power is the only viable response." In the middle, however, are millions of Muslims either living in the West or Western-educated who, under the right circumstances, could be persuaded to support terrorism. According to Clarke, this is the group the United States "most urgently needs to cultivate."[4]

From a strategic perspective, influencing this particular group is the best means of cutting support to the core radicals who are unable to sustain a global jihad on their own. The growth of extremist groups like al-Qaeda in terms of both recruitment and popularity depends on developing supporters within this middle group. They are reliant on these supporters for political and economic support as well as safe-haven in states where they are persecuted by the governments, such as Saudi Arabia and Egypt.

Terrorism is not a randomly occurring process, so what could motivate this middle group to support acts of terror? Many scholars recognize that a perceived sense of deprivation provides a strong motive for violence. Pillar identifies two precursors relevant to the surfacing of terrorist groups and those sympathetic to their cause: (1) "political repression and an accompanying lack of self-determination" and (2) the poor "socioeconomic prospects of populations that are, or may become, the breeding stock for terrorists."[5] Related is Rapoport's assessment describing modern terrorism as a "religiously inspired fourth wave" based upon "anti-globalization … tension between the have and have-not nations … the elite and underprivileged. … In an era where reforms occur at a pace much slower than is desired, terrorists … exploit the frustrations of the common people (especially in the Arab world)."[6]

Although conditions of poverty and political repression remain commonplace throughout the Arab and Islamic worlds, as indeed they have existed historically, it is particularly in regions or countries experiencing increased urbanization and the interconnectedness of globalization that populations become aware of their underprivileged status, terror directed against outsiders or oppressors becoming a tool for mobilization. Education is a key difference between those in the middle group enabled politically and the outermost circle of the Muslim masses less prone to engage in political activities. Terrorist groups can exploit awareness brought about by education and subsequent attempts to engage in politics that are repressed by government. Islam becomes a tool for mobilization against the perceived injustices of the state. After all, Islam is a religion calling for an end to injustice, sharing of wealth to help the poor, and reverence for God above the state.

Given its access to education, this media-savvy middle group—the target population—can be influenced to turn its support away from the jihadists who, of course, are themselves increasingly prone to use the same media to advance their cause. Moreover, educational awareness is also prevalent among the Muslim *diaspora*—those who have migrated to countries outside of the Arab and Muslim worlds. In fact, the sense of relative deprivation is perhaps greater between immigrants and native populations, particularly in Europe and North America where Muslims are a minority unable to climb social ladders to the same degree of success. Indeed, the Club de Madrid summit on terrorism held in March 2005 claimed that 80 percent of new recruits to the global jihadist movement are Muslim immigrants or refugees.[7]

If the extremist core is recruited primarily outside the Arab or Muslim states, then it follows that sympathizers are at least as likely to come from immigrant sources. Those outside the Middle East are also more likely to be educated and have surplus resources with which they might support terrorist causes. When one considers that the London, Madrid, and even 9/11 attackers were all Muslim immigrants—or in the more recent cases, those born to immigrants in the West—it follows that radicalism is just as likely to rear its head among Muslim immigrants as among those who remain in the Middle East. This also means that an influence campaign should not limit itself to the Middle East arena, but also focus on global media sources referenced by the Muslim *diaspora*, particularly Muslim sources emanating in Europe and North America.

In sum, an influence campaign against Islamic-inspired terrorism should focus on the middle group identified by Clarke. These educated Muslims, many of whom live outside the Middle East, are deprived politically and economically and are thus the most likely supporters of the global jihad inspired by al-Qaeda actions against the United States. Strategic and operational elements of the influence campaign are spelled out below.

Denial Strategy—Marginalizing the Terrorist Message

A corresponding effort must focus on development of a proper influence strategy to marginalize the terrorist message, which means we must first define the message. In the case of al-Qaeda, its longer-term, overall goal apparently is to bring about a "new world order." Its terror campaign is aimed at the United States and Israel because they make up what it labels the "far-away enemy." This far-away enemy is distinct from the "near enemy"—the corrupt Arab and other Muslim state governments that prevent the implementation of *sharia* (God's law) and whose existence prevents the unification of the *umma* (the Muslim community) under a single *caliphate* (understood to be a divinely inspired government). It is Western governments, particularly the United States, that protect corrupt Muslim governments from overthrow by their own populations.

Al-Qaeda also believes the United States is interested in dominating and subjugating the region (aided by its Zionist client state, Israel) because of its oil resources, and due to a religious divide—God-fearing Muslims versus Godless, materialistic, Westerners—the United States blamed for initiating what Samuel Huntington refers to as a "clash of civilizations." Thus, based upon *fatwas* (religious rulings) and other pronouncements issued in the past by al-Qaeda leaders such as Osama bin Laden and Ayman al-Zawahiri,[8] the far-away enemy must be driven from Muslim lands to save Islam from destruction; the jihadists are to effect the downfall of corrupt governments, ushering in a return of the caliphate.

Countering this al-Qaeda appeal is complicated by the early error by President Bush, alluding to a "crusade" against terrorism that, consistent with Huntington's clash-of-civilizations thesis, was interpreted in the Muslim world as the latest chapter of anti-Muslim efforts—a direct, historical reminder of the European Christian campaign to recapture the Holy Land during the eleventh and twelfth centuries. This slip of the tongue—repeated frequently in Middle East media—set the context in many minds for an adverse interpretation of U.S. actions in the region. It was relatively easy for bin Laden and others to liken U.S. interventions in Afghanistan and Iraq to modern crusades aimed at destroying Islam in those regions.

An influence campaign at the strategic level should refute the al-Qaeda and other terrorist messages directly, attempting at the same time to make the Arab and Muslim worlds well aware of U.S. public and private assistance to Muslims worldwide. This counter-message should also highlight respect for religious practices of Muslims and others within the United States and underscore the freedoms and economic successes enjoyed by American Muslims. The generosity of both public and private American donors to charitable causes should be made known as a counter to the image of America as if it were a corrupt and Godless nation bent only on material gain.

Denial of Capability: Public Diplomacy and Disrupting Recruitment and Retention

Next we turn to a discussion of the means of disrupting terrorists at the operational level. At this level, terrorists fighting the global jihad have distorted the rationale for U.S. involvement in the Middle East. Jihadists paint an image of the United

States bent on making war against Islam in order to control Muslim oil. But this can be countered by comparing U.S. involvement in the first Gulf War—to liberate Kuwait from Iraqi occupation and to defend another Muslim country, Saudi Arabia. In fact, the United States neither took control of Kuwaiti oil, nor did the U.S. forces residing in Saudi Arabia stay in place but, rather, subsequently withdrew from Saudi soil. The message needs to underscore that the U.S. military is not in the Middle East to stay or to occupy territory.

A related operational-level concern is al-Qaeda's attempts to justify each individual attack with its overall rationale for global jihad. Osama bin Laden went to great lengths to legitimize the September 11 suicide hijackings as a logical extension of the Palestinian suicide bombings against Israel, which began in earnest after the failure of the Camp David peace talks during the summer of 2000. By 2001, images of Israeli repression and Palestinian funerals filled Middle Eastern airwaves, which in bin Laden's view provided sufficient legitimacy on the Arab street for his massive suicide attack plan.

Still, a famous *al-Jazeera* television cleric condemned the hijackings by stating that "the anti-Israeli suicide attacks of the Palestinians could be justified as martyrdom ... since they were part of a defensive jihad aimed at reclaiming Palestinian Islamic land that had been usurped by the Jews ... [But, the] September 11 hijackers [were] suicides rather than martyrs, because, contrary to Muslim teachings, they had unduly taken the lives Allah had given them ...the difference ... was that America is not a legitimate target of defensive jihad."[9]

Such condemnations against al-Qaeda's operational justification for September 11 and other attacks needs to be presented repeatedly to audiences to underscore how such terrorist actions are contrary to Islamic teachings, thus countering claims by al-Qaeda to the contrary.[10] If a potential martyr doubts that his actions will lead him to paradise, then he is less likely to carry out his attack. But more importantly, doubts among potential terrorist supporters hurt recruitment and retention necessary to sustain operations.

Still, CIA expert Michael Scheuer asserts that "U.S. public diplomacy cannot negate the impressions formed by real-time video from Palestine, Iraq, and Afghanistan that shows Muslims battling aggressive Western forces, thus validating in their minds bin Laden's claim that the West intends to destroy Islam."[11] Scheuer believes that ultimately it is the radical Islamists who have the upper hand when it comes to control of the Arab media. Be that as it may, the Arab media are not really so monolithic. Western efforts to influence Middle East publics are an uphill contest, but an important one nonetheless.

Another factor often contributing to resistance against condemning known terrorists is the widespread belief in conspiracy theories. Rumors after the September 11 attacks, for example, initially blamed the Israeli *Mossad* (Secret Service) or in some instances even the CIA, for the attacks in New York and Washington, and some even went so far as to claim that e-mail was sent to all Jews working at the World Trade Center informing them to stay home on that tragic date. So why do people cling to conspiracy theories? Johnson reports that "while the idea of a Muslim hero standing up to the United States has appeal, many Muslims remain deeply disturbed by terrorist tactics."[12] They do not want to believe such acts could be carried out in the name of Islam, defiling the very religion the attacks were supposed to defend. Publicizing admissions of responsibility for terrorist actions as well as counterarguments to the conspiracy theories that abound in this region of the world are essential if the West is to have any opportunity at all to counter the claims of terrorist groups.

Domestic Implementation—the "Home Game"

The international or "away game" is critical to the success of the comprehensive effort to deter and defeat terrorism; however, the domestic components of the strategy or "home game" are also critical to achieving the overall synergy that defines success. Terrorism must be attacked before, during, and after it is carried out. The domestic effort is aimed directly at preparing and mitigating impacts on the "target of terror," generating tactical and strategic effects to deny terrorists the opportunity to achieve their objectives. The domestic effort certainly revolves around the actions taken to harden victims against attack, to limit terrorist access to those victims, and to limit access to weapons of choice to carry out attacks. These actions contribute to effective prevention of terrorist attacks. The "home game" equally involves efforts to mitigate the effects of attacks that do take place. And the mitigation, response, and recovery actions during and after a terrorist attack that is not prevented all contribute to longer-term strategic deterrent effects against terrorism.

Educating and Preparing Domestic Publics

Uncertainty and a lack of understanding breed fear, magnify the already negative emotions generated by casualties and destruction of properties—both fueling and deepening the terror that flows from calculated acts of violence. On the other hand, education based on accurate information effectively delivered contributes to mental preparation and "hardening," thus reducing to some degree adverse effects on the mass population. Education of this kind is needed well prior to any terrorist attack if such knowledge and understanding are to serve as a solid foundation for effective crisis communication and management.

Former Speaker of the House Thomas "Tip" O'Neill's dictum on American politics (that "all politics are local") also applies to the most fundamental level of domestic terrorism; all terrorism is local. The effects, the search for useful information by the public in the face of crisis, and the fundamental propensity to experience greater or lesser degrees of fear—the depth and extent of "terror" generated by the incident—are all firmly rooted at the local level. In crises, one's perceptions are reality, and local factors most significantly shape those perceptions of the most directly impacted "target" audience. Even those far removed from the immediate scene can be profoundly influenced by the role of the news media. In essence, "journalists *are* first responders":[13]

> This country isn't ready to deal with a catastrophic terrorist attack, and government preparedness may not be the biggest problem. Indeed, one of the most critical parts of our infrastructure—the nation's news media—doesn't appear near the top of anyone's list of concerns. They should be of utmost concern to those responsible for homeland security.[14]

We need clear, well-designed educational materials to address the technical and human dimensions of the threat, and we need a prepared noninflammatory channel of presentation for those materials in times of crisis. A comprehensive homeland security strategy must capitalize on quality materials and experiences to target localized delivery of education and the information. It must involve establishing cooperative relations with local media outlets. This is not easy, as adversarial relations may exist between government and the media at various levels, but being able to harness the support of the media in extending information during these times of crisis is a critical variable in implementing a successful homeland security strategy.

The implementation of a comprehensive strategy to create deterrent effects requires measures at both international and domestic levels of implementation. These measures do require a strategic guiding hand to ensure comprehensive, complementary implementation and synergistic deterrent effects. This coordination of the effort must remain a central area of emphasis at every level, including leaderships at the pinnacles of power and authority.

Concluding Comments

First, there is no one "magic bullet" that can be used to defeat terrorism. Terrorism aimed at the United States today is a complex, asymmetrical threat. And this threat demands an equally complex, asymmetrical, adaptive, and cumulative response package.

Second, each of the response actions and strategies is individually important. Each element of effective response advances the effort to blunt and defeat terrorism. As stated in the *National Strategy for Combating Terrorism*: "Ours is a strategy of direct and continuous action against terrorist groups, the cumulative effect of which will initially disrupt, over time degrade, and ultimately destroy the terrorist organizations."[15] We agree completely with that strategic response perspective.

Finally, even if all of the actions addressed are implemented immediately, terrorist violence likely would still continue—at least in the short term. Over the longer term, however, the net effect can indeed be a deterrent effect, leading the terrorist leadership, core support base, and regional or ideological community to select other, less violent means of addressing their political, economic, and social grievances.

Endnotes

1. Dan Gressang's presentation "Reconsidering the Functionality of Terrorism: Implications for Security Planning" to the International Studies Association in Chicago, 23 February 2002, spurred the author's development of the strategic communication dimensions added to this model.
2. The terms "target of terror" and "target of influence" are from Donald J. Hanle, Terrorism: The Newest Face of Warfare (Washington, D.C.: Pergamon-Brassey, 1989) as adapted by Troy S. Thomas in Beneath the Surface: Intelligence Preparation of the Battlespace for Counterterrorism (Washington, D.C.: Joint Military Intelligence College, November 2004), 11.
3. The three-tiered construct for deterrence of non-state actors (including terrorism) is a refined development of ideas first expressed in James M. Smith, "A Strategic Response to Terrorism," in After 9/11: Terrorism and Crime in a Globalised World, ed. David A. Charters and Graham F. Walker (Halifax, Nova Scotia: University of New Brunswick Centre for Conflict Studies and Dalhousie University Centre for Foreign Policy Studies, 2005), 259–277.
4. Clarke's categories are outlined in Zachary Shore, "Can the West Win Muslim Hearts and Minds?" Orbis 49 (Summer 2005): 479.
5. Paul R. Pillar, Terrorism and U.S. Foreign Policy (Washington, D.C.: Brookings Institution Press, 2001, updated 2003), 30–31.
6. David Rapoport's arguments are summarized by Audrey Kurth Cronin, "Behind the Curve: Globalization and International Terrorism," International Security 27 (Winter 2002/03): 35.
7. "Addressing the Causes of Terrorism," Volume I, The International Summit on Democracy, Terrorism, and Security, 8–11 March 2005, Club de Madrid, 9.
8. See chapter 3, "Striking at the Faraway Enemy," for further discussion, in Giles Kepel, The War for Muslim Minds (Cambridge: Harvard University Press, 2004), 70–107. Additional references on bin Laden and al-Qaeda include Michael Scheuer, Imperial Hubris (Washington, D.C.: Potomac Books, 2004), see ch. 5; and Yossef Bodansky, Bin Laden: The Man Who Declared War on America (Roseville, CA: Prima Publishing, 2001).
9. Kepel, War for Muslim Minds, 102–103.
10. Too detailed to present in depth here, Patai describes the need among Arabic speakers to repeat and exaggerate threats in order to make them understood, but at the same time repeating the threat also removes the psychological pressure to carry it out, which may also explain why some terrorist threats never come to fruition. See Raphael Patai, The Arab Mind (New York: Charles Scribner's Sons, 1983), 49–65.

11. Scheuer is the noted CIA expert on Osama bin Laden. See Michael Scheuer, "Al-Qaeda's Next Generation: Less Visible and More Lethal," Terrorism Focus 2, no. 18 (October 2005): 3.

12. Jeannie L. Johnson, "Exploiting Weakness in the Far Enemy Ideology," Strategic Sights, IV, 6 (June 2005):2.

13. Randy Atkins, "The News Media Could Be Our Weakest Link," Washington Post, 26 January 2003, B3.

14. Ibid.

15. National Strategy to Combat Terrorism (Washington, D.C.: The White House, February 2003).

Chapter 5

The Importance of Multinational and Transnational Cooperation Strategies for Homeland Security

Veronica M. Kitchen and Gregory J. Moore[1]

The authors underscore the importance of multilateralism in the strategic effort to secure the American homeland. The array of transnational networks and flows we find in globalization has altered the manner and speed with which states and peoples relate to one another. So too has globalization changed the way nations must organize and defend themselves, particularly in the face of an asymmetric threat from non-state actors. Because terrorists form networks, plan globally but act locally, exploit modern business and communications networks to inflict maximum damage, and launch cross-border attacks, this transnational threat requires a complex, transnational response. The authors conclude that strategic and creative thinking about theory and policy are urgently required. This will happen only when we recognize the importance of multinational and transnational cooperation and assure that it permeates all aspects of America's homeland security strategy.

Much as the Second World War woke the United States from the isolationism of the interwar period, the 9/11 terrorist attacks woke the country from the idea that its territory was invulnerable. In the post-9/11 world, it is increasingly apparent that not only is the United States vulnerable to attack, but the nature of the threat is such that the United States can no longer defend itself without help from other countries, even in a task as fundamental as protecting U.S. soil. The threat from terrorism blurs the lines between foreign and domestic policy, rendering old notions of national security obsolete. We argue that the United States can only be secure from terrorist threats when it works with other states to take a multinational and transnational approach to homeland security. A globalized world makes such cooperation imperative and the United States' homeland security strategy cannot merely be multinational. It must also be transnational, operating through networks at all levels of government and stretching to include allies of many stripes. We examine existing examples of U.S. cooperation on homeland security issues not only to show that this is already so to some degree, but also to highlight the pathologies of existing international cooperation to show where improvement is still necessary and possible.

The Bush administration's 2002 National Strategy for Homeland Security outlined nine issue areas for international cooperation: creating smart borders, combating fraudulent travel documents, increasing the security of international shipping containers, intensifying international law enforcement operations, helping foreign nations fight terrorism, expanding the protection of transnational critical infrastructure, amplifying international cooperation on the science and technology of homeland security, improving cooperation in response to attacks, and reviewing obligations to international treaties and law.[2] These are homeland security issues in the sense that they contribute to the protection of Americans on U.S. soil, but undoubtedly cross boundaries in a way that territorial defense has rarely done in the past.

The blurred distinction between domestic and foreign policy responses to terrorism leads us to prefer to discuss homeland security in this chapter in terms of what is commonly known as antiterrorism. We do so because of the distinction that is made between antiterrorism and counterterrorism, antiterrorism referring to *defensive* measures to detect, prevent, and respond to terrorism, whereas counterterrorism involves *offensive* measures toward reaching the same goal.

Thus, while we adopt a definition of homeland security as a coordinated effort to prevent terrorist attacks within the United States, as well as to minimize damage and to maximize recovery from attacks that do occur,[3] for the purposes of this chapter we define antiterrorism more precisely as the coordinated defensive effort to prevent attacks, minimize damage, and maximize recovery. Counterterrorism is not our primary focus here, and though we recognize that the line between counterterrorism and antiterrorism is more of an analytical and organizational convenience than an empirical fact, international cooperation on the counterterror aspects of homeland security has been extensively studied elsewhere,[4] as has U.S. multinational cooperation on activities like targeting known terrorists in their safe areas and countries of origin.[5] Our primary focus here is instead on the antiterror aspects of homeland security, for these have been understudied and homeland security too often conceived of as strictly a domestic affair. This forward defense, or the "away game," as the Pentagon calls it, influences homeland security in a number of ways. Preventing individuals and groups from adopting terrorism as a tactic in the first place is ultimately the most effective way of securing U.S. territory. Preventing terrorists and their weapons from getting close to the United States is also effective: every terrorist apprehended abroad is a terrorist that does not need to be apprehended on the home front. Thus, although counterterrorism and antiterrorism are intimately linked, a closer look at U.S. interests in multinational and transnational cooperation on the antiterror aspects of homeland security is revealing and long overdue.

Homeland Security and Globalization

Globalization has altered the manner and speed at which states and peoples relate to one another. So too has it changed the way nations must organize and defend themselves, particularly in the face of an asymmetric threat from nonstate actors, such as al-Qaeda, which use the forces of globalization against the nations and peoples who benefit from them. Relations along the spectrum from conflict to cooperation occur not just between central governments, or multinationally, but also transnationally, which is to say across borders at nonexecutive levels of government, between subnational governments or government departments, and between private and nongovernmental actors.

International relations scholars have typically concentrated their attention on the foreign relations of central governments, as enacted by foreign ministries and militaries. It has become increasingly apparent that this focus is too narrow because most government ministries, the police, and the military have some level of involvement beyond state borders. Furthermore, governments and entities below the central government also have relations outside the state. This is particularly true in the realm of public safety and civil security, where local and state governments often hold more authority and responsibility than the federal government does. To this must be added public-private partnerships, international organizations such as the United Nations, partnerships between states and provinces across borders, interactions between NGOs and international organizations, and many other relationships. The result probably looks more like 3-D chess than international relations' traditional levels of analysis. In a globalized world, traditional government-to-government cooperation is insufficient and only part of a larger picture.

These transnational networks and flows mean that securing U.S. territory and assets today is far different than it was in previous decades. Not only do the territorial security interests of the United States exist in a virtual space that goes beyond its borders, but actors with intent to harm the United States may seek to use the same networks to achieve their goals. New technologies mean that accounting firms in Bangalore, India, can compete with those in Boston, Massachusetts, and that firms in Shenzhen, China, can supply U.S. computer makers with high-quality, low-cost parts through global supply chains and just-in-time delivery to firms in Toledo, Ohio. Globalization, however, has also increased the possibilities for asymmetric warfare.

Thomas Friedman traces contemporary globalization to several important developments he calls "flatteners."[6] In explaining globalization, or what he calls the "flattening" of the world, Friedman notes that first, the end of the Cold War increased the number of people able to participate in the international capitalist economy. Second, globalization of business, with its focus on out-sourcing, in-sourcing, offshore production, global supply chains, and the horizontal diversification of firms, created a reliance on transnational infrastructure and networks. Third, the Internet reduced the conceptual space between people and between firms, enabling business transactions, the exchange of ideas, and collaboration on common projects like the Linux operating system or Wikipedia. Finally, the exponential growth of information, as well as the digital, personal, and virtual technologies that allow people to access it, has amplified the other factors.[7] This has enabled the United States to enjoy a large measure of prosperity, but it has also ensured a sense of vulnerability.

U.S. soil is less secure in an interconnected world. Like multinational corporations, international terrorist organizations form networks and franchises. Al-Qaeda forms alliances with locally operating groups with compatible aims. Just as global business has taken advantage of advances in technology and communications to create a globalized economy, al-Qaeda did the same to launch a globalized campaign to achieve its political aims. Michael Mandelbaum nicely captures the problem posed by "enemies of the state" in a globalized world:

> Think of Mao at the beginning of the Chinese communist revolution. The Chinese Communists had to hide in caves in northwest China, but they could move around in whatever territory they were able to control. Bin Laden, by contrast, can't show his face, but he can reach every household in the world.[8]

Travel and communications of all sorts, including the Internet, satellite, cellular phones, and closed circuit technology, make it easier for terrorists to travel to and work in their target countries, and easier as well to communicate with each other, and with media outlets, while doing so.[9] These changes have also made the transfer of funds speedier, more convenient, and arguably easier to execute. To achieve their political goals, terrorists use, and sometimes seek to destroy, the same networks that enable globalization.

Reconceptualizing Defensive Homeland Security

Because terrorists form networks, plan globally but act locally, exploit modern business and communications networks to inflict maximum damage, and launch cross-border attacks, this transnational threat requires a complex, transnational response. The contemporary security environment looks as little like the Cold War's mutually assured destruction (MAD) as MAD looked like the Battle of Waterloo. Re-imagining our security environment involves more than just acknowledging the existence of new actors like terrorist cells, firms, NGOs, and international organizations. Scholars towards the end of the Cold War advocated "broadening" and "deepening"[10] the security agenda to encompass more than military threats by taking into account the possible consequences of biological, cyber, or environmental attacks, and to consider protecting individuals, cities, and/or industries. Re-imagining our security environment today requires more than just broadening and deepening; rather, it calls for a new conception of how different parts of the world and different actors are interconnected. International policy cooperation is often described as a regime: "implicit or explicit principles, norms, rules and decision making procedures around which actor expectations converge in a given issue area."[11] But regime theory assumes a unitary conception of actor-ness: governments tend to cooperate with other governments, or possibly with nongovernmental organizations.[12]

Anne-Marie Slaughter's conception of transgovernmentalism illustrates the conceptual shift necessary to think strategically about cooperation in homeland security. We argue that for the United States, thinking strategically about homeland security means that thinking about multinational and transnational cooperation must permeate each of the nine issue areas of the National Strategy for Homeland Security. Such thinking cannot be restricted to the Department of Homeland Security's Office of International Affairs. Slaughter encourages us to think about a state as being made up of its component parts: agencies, judicial systems, legislatures, and bureaucracies. Each of these can make connections with its counterparts abroad, and together they may develop mechanisms for governance in their sectors. They may even delegate authority to a supranational organization. By Slaughter's definition, a network is "a pattern of regular and purposive relations among like government units working across the borders that divide countries from one another and that demarcate the 'domestic' from the 'international' sphere."[13] Together, these networks form the basis for a new kind of disaggregated global governance without global government:

> ... a disaggregated world order would be a world latticed by countless
> government networks. These would include horizontal networks and
> vertical networks; networks for collecting and sharing information of all
> kinds, for policy co-ordination, for enforcement cooperation, for tech-
> nical assistance and training, perhaps ultimately for rule making. They
> would be bilateral, plurilateral, regional, or global. Taken together, they
> would provide the skeleton infrastructure for global governance.[14]

All of this is envisioned without challenging the basic sovereignty of nation-
states as we know them. While Slaughter focuses on the component units of central governments, the idea can be expanded to include subnational governments,
such as states, provinces, and municipalities, and sometimes even their component
parts.[15] Add to these the non-state actors discussed above, and it becomes clear that
complexity is not just on the side of threats and vulnerabilities, but must be on the
side of responses as well.

Not all of these multinational and transnational relations are equal. The United
States has different kinds of cooperation with different kinds of allies. We envisage
the U.S. domestic security environment as a series of concentric circles.[16] First is the
U.S. domestic environment: federal, state, and local governments, with cooperation
between them in both the public and private sectors. The next layer out includes
Canada and Mexico. Cooperation with these two states is by necessity more intense
than with any other states. Some cities and towns straddle borders, and resources
are shared.

If there is a terrorist attack in the United States, it may affect Canada and Mexico
as well, and the converse is also true. The United States shares long borders with
both countries, and relies on Mexican and Canadian officials to help prevent terrorists from gaining access to the continent. There is a long tradition of cooperation in North America, though particularly with Canada, even on security matters.
NORAD monitored North American airspace through the Cold War, and continues to do so today. The three countries are also united in cooperation in the
North American Free Trade Agreement (NAFTA). Shortly after 9/11, the United
States concluded Smart Border Action Plans with Canada and Mexico, specifically
to address the problem of balancing trade and security.

In 2005 Canadian Prime Minister Martin, President Bush, and Mexican President Fox expanded on the Smart Border agreements to sign the Security and Prosperity Partnership, a program envisaging a more comprehensive North American
security strategy, as well as cooperation on health, the environment, and prosperity.[17] Most cooperation among these three countries, however, is transgovernmental
and informal. Officials in each government maintain close personal contact with
their counterparts in Canada and Mexico. States and provinces have an extensive
history of military and police cooperation.

The next level comprises the United States' traditional allies, primarily the European countries, Australia, New Zealand, Israel, and Japan. With this group of countries, long-established personal relationships grease the wheels of cooperation, but geographic noncontiguity means that cooperation on some homeland security issues is less intense than with Canada and Mexico. In Europe, the United States cooperates bilaterally with individual states, especially the United Kingdom,[18] but also with the institutions of the European Union. Cooperation with this group of states is important because they are all democracies sharing democratic values and thus also a common need to balance civil liberties and democratic principles with security imperatives. The United States is also more likely to cooperate with these like-minded and wealthy states in sharing technology, equipment, and research.

The next concentric circle consists of polities such as Singapore[19] and the United Arab Emirates (UAE).[20] Though not liberal democracies, they have been important partners with the United States for years prior to the current campaign against terrorism. Each has a significant history of close cooperation with the United States and plays an important role in current U.S. strategic operations, particularly in terms of naval operations and port access.

Next we have countries that are important allies of the United States in the campaign against extremist elements, but yet are not particularly close on other matters. Countries like Pakistan, Malaysia,[21] the Philippines,[22] and some of the former Soviet republics in Central Asia,[23] among others, fall into this category, though some are certainly closer to the United States than others. Aside from allowing the United States to use facilities for troops, aircraft, or ships, cooperation in these countries might also entail intelligence sharing, military or police training, as well as assistance from the United States to these countries to develop their infrastructure so that terrorists and their weapons do not make it to the United States.

The United States also has agreements with other important partners in the campaign against terrorism who share important interests with the United States and cooperate with it in stopping terrorism, even though they are neither allies nor host to U.S. forces. For example, China and the United States cooperate on a number of antiterrorism measures, and in his January 2002 State of the Union Address, President Bush mentioned two other important partners: "In this moment of opportunity, a common danger is erasing old rivalries. America is working with Russia and China and India, in ways we have never before, to achieve peace and prosperity."[24] Cooperation with this group of states requires a delicate balance. The United States has important trade links with these countries, and attracts immigrants and refugees from them, thus reinforcing the need for cooperation on the antiterror aspects of homeland security. Relations with these countries are sometimes tense. They may even differ in their understandings of who constitutes terrorist groups. For instance, Chinese analysts regularly say that China is also a victim of terrorism, citing bombings committed by members of its Uighur population in Western China, some of whom would like to see an independent East Turkistan there.[25] In this case, Chinese and American analysts agree that the East Turkistan

Independence Movement among the Uighurs has links to al-Qaeda.[26] With states such as China, the United States is "sharing [counterterrorism] information to an unprecedented extent."[27] Yet cooperation with some countries necessarily raises questions of morality: how much cooperation is too much? Questions of the balance between security and morality, like that between liberty and security, occur at all levels of cooperation.

Finally, the outermost concentric circle is the rest of the world. Here, the United States must engage in public diplomacy, maintaining its image abroad and addressing root causes of terrorism.[28] In the U.S. National Strategy for Combating Terrorism,[29] the Bush administration put forward four fundamental goals, sometimes called "the four Ds": (1) defending U.S. citizens and interests at home and abroad; (2) defeating and destroying terrorist organizations; (3) denying sanctuary and support to terrorist organizations; and (4) diminishing the underlying causes of terrorism. Retired General Wayne Downing notes that the United States has had notable success at the first two, partial success with the third, but "little, if any progress in achieving the fourth goal. In fact, perhaps the opposite has occurred."[30] Rather than diminishing the underlying causes of terrorism, the United States now finds itself in a situation wherein Iraq has replaced Afghanistan as the major international training ground for terrorists. A 2006 National Intelligence Estimate (NIE) judged that al-Qaeda continued to pose the greatest single terrorist threat to the United States and its interests abroad, and that the Iraq conflict had become a "cause célèbre" for jihadists, inspiring new terrorists and terrorist leaders.[31] Downing argues that the United States cannot win this "worldwide insurgency" unilaterally, or by using the U.S. military as the lead instrument in the long term, but must cooperate with other governments and win the war of ideas.[32] The U.S. government is slowly acknowledging the importance of this task.[33] Diminishing the causes of terrorism, as the president has suggested by including it in his National Strategy, is something the United States must improve upon, for otherwise the American homeland will not be secure, no matter how well the United States prepares domestically. Winning this "war of ideas" is fundamentally an international task:

> Overall, to incorporate the war of ideas fully into the global counterinsurgency campaign, the Executive Branch must develop a coordinated strategic information strategy prioritizing education and media aimed specifically to discredit extremism, preferably using Arab media outlets, avoiding overt U.S. sponsorship as appropriate. The United States must also develop a sophisticated campaign unique to each country and region. Using domestic arguments has not only been unsuccessful overseas, in many cases it has further alienated and incensed foreigners, especially in third world countries.[34]

As was noted in the introductory chapter to this volume, a comprehensive strategy for homeland security must begin at the beginning of the causal chain by addressing root causes. This task, like other aspects of a comprehensive homeland security strategy, must take into account the networks of international and transnational links described above. Global counterterrorist campaigns must be combined with tactics that attempt to make extremist causes less appealing. The Pentagon has reportedly started to recognize this imperative in its most recent strategy.[35] Some argue that the Bush administration has made some headway in this regard as well by sending under-secretary of state for public diplomacy Karen Hughes to the Middle East and other parts of the Muslim world in 2005 to 2006 in an attempt to boost American relations with Middle Eastern countries;[36] by initiating a USAID program whereby Americans train Muslim teachers in Pakistani madrassahs (Islamic schools) in science, math, civics, and health care; by creating and funding the Al Iraqiya network in Iraq, an organization showing programs such as "Terrorism in the Grip of Justice" (an attempt to depict for the Iraqi people the dark nature of those who commit terrorist acts);[37] and by his efforts at finding a two-state solution to the Palestinian-Israeli crisis in 2008.[38]

Multinational and Transnational Cooperation on Homeland Security

Across the aforementioned concentric circles we currently see cooperation in many realms. Here we outline some of the networks of international and transnational cooperation existing in the areas of justice, civil security and transportation, intelligence sharing, terrorist financing, and finally, cooperation within the United Nations. The examples are not comprehensive, and they should not be taken as an indication that the United States is doing all it can to create an effective, internationally focused homeland policy. In fact, we will outline some of the pathologies of cooperation at the end of the chapter.

Judicial and Law Enforcement Cooperation

Cooperation in matters of justice and law enforcement is most intense in the innermost concentric circles. It typically takes place at a traditional, state-to-state level of diplomacy, often in the context of international law. But, as in other realms, developments in homeland security have prompted some new and interesting international cooperative initiatives involving actors not traditionally concerned with issues of foreign policy.

At the most operational level of cooperation, the United States and Canada have used Integrated Border Enforcement Teams (IBETs) composed of immigration, law enforcement, and customs officials, often operating from shared facilities, to target cross-border crimes.[39] There is a long tradition of this sort of law enforcement cooperation on border issues between Canada and the United States. Certainly, the renewed attention to border issues after 9/11 has highlighted its importance once again, and resulted in the extension of similar programs to Mexico.[40]

Another effect of the new networked approach to homeland security is that such law-enforcement cooperation is not restricted to border issues or contiguous territories. The New York City Police Department (NYPD) has a counterterrorism bureau with liaison officers in major cities around the world, and its Special Intelligence Division has sent NYPD investigators on fact-finding missions to places such as Afghanistan and Egypt. Other police departments return the favor: a special constable of the Toronto Police Department was dispatched to New York as well.[41] After the terrorist attacks on the London Underground system, NYPD liaison officers working in London and other cities worked with their home department to help shape New York's antiterror response.[42] Such initiatives require a foundation of trust and experience, and are thus most often undertaken with the United States' closest allies.

More cooperation across levels occurs between the United States and various regional organizations. An American national liaison officer is posted within Europol, the European Union Police Office. A December 2002 agreement between Europol and the United States to make Europol the first point of contact for exchanges of urgent information was the first cooperative agreement between an external EU partner and an institution of the European Union.[43] Europol opened a liaison office in Washington in 2002, and the FBI sent a liaison to Brussels in 2005.[44] Of course, bilateral cooperation between the United States and individual European countries continues. The European Union's permanent network of judicial authorities, Eurojust, and the United States plan to conclude a formal agreement to govern their interactions, while prosecutors from each side have met to share information on terrorist cases of mutual interest. Moreover, an initiative exists to train American and EU officials on one another's judicial and law-enforcement systems, to better facilitate cooperation and develop strong working relationships.[45] The United States has also signed an "ASEAN-United States of America Joint Declaration for Cooperation to Combat International Terrorism," wherein the United States and countries belonging to the Association of South East Asian States will cooperate on matters of intelligence, information sharing on terrorist financing, counterterrorism, liaison relations between national law enforcement agencies, capacity building through joint training and education and joint operations, as well as providing assistance on matters of transportation and border and immigration control.[46] Also, the United States has encouraged greater cooperation against terrorism with APEC (Asia-Pacific Economic Cooperation), joining with them in forming the Counter-Terrorism Task Force (CTTF) in October 2002. In 2005, the CTTF developed the Counter-Terrorism Action Plans, which provide a checklist of steps taken by APEC economies to fulfill commitments made to the organization's counterterrorism initiatives. APEC has also created the STAR program, Secure

Trade in the APEC Region, focusing on securing Asia-Pacific trade while protecting regional transportation networks.[47]

With states in the outer concentric circles, the United States has shared best practices and training. There are cooperative programs within the DHS's Customs and Border Protection section working mostly with Central and Eastern European and Central Asian countries to exchange personnel. The United States gets access to information on trends of what is crossing borders in these countries; and the quality of border observation and interdiction in these countries is improved by the training their officials receive in the United States. American officials can also learn about problems that are more prevalent in those parts of the world than they are in the United States, such as human trafficking. Such agreements are possible even with countries lacking a cooperative history with the United States, and may help set the foundation for yet more intensive antiterrorism cooperation.

Cooperation in Civil Security and Transportation

Civil security includes the protection of critical infrastructure, the networks and processes described above that support global trade, government, and civil society relations, and ensuring the secure movement of people.[48] This is perhaps the realm with the most complicated networks of antiterrorism cooperation, encompassing local, national, international, and private partnerships.

The example of international cooperation in homeland security that comes most readily to mind is cooperation with Canada and Mexico across common borders. Indeed, the United States has extensive agreements to ensure the secure movement of people and goods across its borders while preserving trade, summarized in the Security and Prosperity Partnership discussed above. Among others, the FAST, or Free and Secure Trade, program emphasizes a risk-based rather than a transactions-based approach to clearing goods across the border. Companies that regularly send freight across the border go through a special certification process that entitles them to use express lanes at the border, and there is an increasing focus on clearing freight away from the border at joint facilities. NEXUS at the northern border and SENTRI at the southern border streamline processing and entry for frequent travelers.[49]

Thinking about civil security and transportation security in terms of ports of entry, or POEs, rather than in terms of border crossings, makes it clear how such cooperation extends to the outer concentric circles. Denying terrorists access to the United States and preventing dangerous materials from entering U.S. territory requires clearing goods as far from the border as possible. The Container Security Initiative (CSI) is Customs and Border Protection's (CBP's) major initiative for securing goods by prescreening, using tamper-resistant containers, targeting containers that pose a risk, instead of inspecting every container, as well as using automated detection technology.[50] The CSI currently operates in nearly forty ports in North America, Europe, Asia, and Africa. U.S. customs officials are posted in ports abroad, while U.S. ports currently host customs officials from Canada, Japan, and even China.[51] Across the world, passengers can be pre-inspected in at least twenty-five airports, effectively pushing the border out from the United States. More generally, however, the United States benefits from high global standards on passports and travel documents, and works with the International Civil Aviation Organization to achieve them.[52]

Civil security cooperation also manifests itself in public-private partnerships, such as the C-TPAT (Customs-Trade Partnership Against Terrorism). Like FAST, it is concerned with expediting the passage of precleared goods, but it is more specifically focused on the security of the supply chain from start to finish. Such programs are advantageous to the government because they transfer some of the burden of extra security to private companies by providing incentives to increase security. C-TPAT's emphasis is on self-policing rather than customs inspection. To the private company, they are advantageous because government certification of the supply chain is an added signal of quality, and because it allows them to ship their goods more efficiently. Importers agree to assess their supply chain security based on CBP guidelines, and to develop and implement a program to increase supply chain security. In return, CBP promises shorter border wait times and fewer inspections, and streamlined accounting procedures.[53] In the private sector, multinational firms using globalized trade networks have an interest in developing their own strategies for "business recovery preparedness" in the event of a terrorist attack.[54] As more and more commerce occurs between parts of the same company located in different countries, is dependent on just-in-time delivery, or has supply chains stretching around the globe, such plans are by necessity international. When incentives to improve security exist privately, or, as in the case of C-TPAT can be created, part of the burden of creating homeland security is removed from the government's shoulders.

At the inner concentric circles, cooperation may be more transnational than international. It will take place between lower levels and branches of government, rather than from executive to executive. For cities that straddle the northern or southern borders of the United States, public safety and emergency preparedness cooperation may entail joint management of shared facilities, and first responders may be adept at working together. Border states and provinces often have memorandums of understanding, or MOUs, pledging assistance in case of an emergency, and have experience doing so in cases of floods, fires, and other natural disasters. Increasingly, state and local authorities are seeing the importance of training across international boundaries, because a great deal of infrastructure is shared across borders. For example, the Pacific Northwest Economic Region, comprising Alaska, Alberta, British Columbia, Idaho, Montana, Oregon, Washington, and Yukon, launched a series of table-top exercises focused on "raising awareness of interconnections among the region's critical infrastructures and resulting vulnerabilities associated with largely physical attacks and disruptions."[55] The third exercise in the series also focused on potential security problems associated with the Vancouver Olympics in 2010. One of the conclusions drawn from a previous exercise was that more study and training needed to be undertaken to understand U.S.-Canadian cross-border disaster response, and to incorporate the lessons learned into bilateral discussions on cooperative activities.[56]

Exercises and simulations in homeland security are now becoming as much a part of multinational security cooperation as joint military exercises have been. Some 15,000 local, state, tribal, federal, private, and international participants have engaged in full-scale simulations of a multisite, large-scale terrorist attack in the United States. In TOPOFF (i.e., top officials) now becoming a semiregular exercise, participants from the United States, Canada, and the United Kingdom worked through all levels of response from the local to the international, including private and media responses.[57] A similar set of exercises, Ardent Sentry, involves Northcom, NORAD, the Canada Command, Public Safety and Emergency Preparedness Canada, several federal and state or provincial agencies in the United States and Canada, and, at least in 2006, the governments of Arizona, Michigan, New Brunswick, and Ontario. Ardent Sentry is designed to test plans for military support to civilian authorities in times of crisis.[58] As DHS has recognized, even chemical and biological attacks in Connecticut and New Jersey require an international response, and DHS is practicing for it.[59]

In a period of increasing globalization cooperation need not be only among contiguous states. Cities everywhere in the world face similar problems and already come together to discuss common solutions. Cooperation among the world's largest cities may not always be directly focused on antiterrorism, but many of the solutions used to address problems such as sustainable urban development will have direct applications in homeland security.[60] Imagine an urban space designed with antiterrorism in mind, built using lessons in earthquake-resistant building design from Tokyo, in safe transportation from Tel Aviv, in emergency response from London, in community policing from New York City, and in the integration of new immigrants from Toronto. The Secure City was on the agenda as one of the major topics of debate for the 2006 World Urban Forum in Vancouver, Canada, truly a network of the global and the local, of international security and human security.[61]

Civil and transportation security in a globalized world is about the security of networks. As these networks are international, crossing boundaries between states, levels of government, and the public and private sectors, securing them must be a multinational and transnational endeavor.

Intelligence Cooperation

Intelligence sharing is one of the most important aspects of homeland security. As stated earlier, if al-Qaeda and other transnational terrorist groups plan globally but act locally, it is imperative to have strong intelligence relations with other countries, both those who are close allies, and those who are allies only on matters of counterterrorism. Martin Rudner estimates that there are about 100 countries that are a part of the intelligence coalition against militant Islamist terrorists, with relations of varying intensity.[62]

The most important set of intelligence relations for the United States is the UK-USA alliance. Comprising traditional allies, the United States, the United Kingdom, Canada, Australia, and New Zealand, it is now about 60 years old. Through this alliance, virtually all signals intelligence, or SIGINT, is shared, along with its source, among the UK-USA countries at "Five Eyes" classification. Communications intelligence, or COMINT, is also shared through the Echelon system. The UK-USA alliance represents the closest possible intelligence cooperation sources, with each of the five members having virtually automatic access to each other's interception facilities without the host nation necessarily knowing what the member is looking for.[63] While being a member of a global alliance with this sort of technical capability probably has disproportionate benefit for its middle power members, there are distinct advantages for the United States as well. For instance, when the NSA's computer system crashed for four days in 2000, SIGINT interception continued uninterrupted and processing was directed to other parts of the Echelon system.[64] Moreover, cooperation with these traditional allies affords the United States a second opinion on data from a country with a different perspective working toward the same goal. Perhaps more important, however, are the benefits the United States obtains from comparative advantages derived from functional or knowledge expertise, location, or sociocultural similarity. The United States and the United Kingdom, for example, work well together because the United States has unsurpassed technical capabilities, but the United Kingdom has maintained a stronger tradition in HUMINT.[65]

Intelligence relations at the outer concentric circle are less intense. Information may be shared without a source, or a summary of the data or the analysis may be passed along. While the United States has strong intelligence relations with the European Union, using EUROPOL as a single point of contact,[66] intelligence relations with partners at the outer concentric circles are more typically bilateral and concentrate on specific issues. The United States cooperates with countries such as Egypt, Jordan, Morocco, Syria, and Pakistan on counterterrorism efforts, working together on joint investigations, interrogations, analysis, and threat assessment.[67] Such relations are useful because of the cultural and geographic affinity these countries have to the militant Islamist groups the United States is trying to penetrate. Such cooperation may reduce some of the pressure on the United States to rebuild its human intelligence capabilities, which former CIA director George Tenet believes may take years.[68]

Financial Cooperation

International financial cooperation is also vital to securing the U.S. homeland. The U.S. government has already passed domestic laws and signed international agreements and regimes that facilitate financial cooperation on fighting international terrorism. Its primary domestic move has been the September 2001 National Money Laundering Strategy, revised in 2002 and very comprehensive and international in its scope.[69] One of the six major goals of the strategy is to strengthen international anti-money-laundering regimes. The U.S. Department of the Treasury has an Office of Terrorism and Financial Intelligence playing an important role here. An important recent example of the Department of the Treasury's invoking such measures was the 2005 to 2007 U.S. sanctions against North Korean financial interests centered on Macau, China's Banco Delta Asia, because of the bank's reputed role in facilitating North Korean money-laundering and counterfeiting activity.[70] The sanctions involved close cooperation with China and other nations, proved to be very effective, and were resolved in June 2007 as a part of the agreement reached between North Korea and the five other members of the Six Party Talks on North Korea's nuclear programs.

The United States has also been engaged in international financial cooperation, such as the G7's and subsequently G8's Financial Action Task Force. Since its inception in 1989 this group has played an instrumental role in coordinating the world's policies on fighting and closing down terrorist money-making and money-laundering operations.[72] International financial organizations such as the Asian Development Bank, in cooperation with APEC, have established a Cooperation Fund for Regional Trade and Financial Security Initiative, designed to help facilitate counterterrorism-related capacity building in the Asia-Pacific, to fight money laundering and the financing of terrorism, and also to help improve seaport and airport security in the region as well. The UN, too, has an International Convention for the Suppression of the Financing of Terrorism with similar aims, as well as the Security Council's Sanctions Committee against Taliban and al-Qaeda operatives. All of these measures are vital for a secure U.S. homeland, and U.S. cooperation on such initiatives should be deepened and expanded with time, as politics and technologies permit and circumstances necessitate.

Homeland Defense Cooperation

What Americans today call homeland defense is the more traditional domain of territorial defense. Because the United States shares land borders with close allies, territorial defense usually falls into the hands of the Air Force and the Coast Guard. After 9/11, the United States reorganized its commands to include North America in Northern Command, an entity working closely with NORAD, or North American Aerospace Defense.

Since the early Cold War, NORAD has monitored and protected North American skies. Integration through NORAD is so complete that, at any time, either an American or a Canadian could be in charge of North America's aerospace defense at its headquarters outside Colorado Springs, Colorado. In fact, on September 11, 2001, it was a Canadian, Lt. General Eric Findley, who was the commanding officer at NORAD's Cheyenne Mountain complex that day. The remarkable effectiveness of this partnership has led to proposals to extend it to land and sea cooperation; in 2002, a binational planning group was established to investigate extending NORAD.[71] In 2006, when NORAD came up for renewal, it was extended permanently, subject to review every four years, or at the request of either country. A maritime warning mission was also added.[72] This is a substantial revision of the premier North American security treaty, one that marks the importance of homeland defense in security cooperation.

The other significant domain for cooperation is the United States' coastlines. In this domain, cooperation extends beyond the U.S. coastlines to all of the concentric circles. The U.S. Coast Guard's mandate for protecting the United States' territorial borders means enhancing transparency to detect, deter, and defeat threats away from American interests and enabling accurate and dynamic decision making, as well as maintaining the freedom of navigation and the efficient flow of commerce.[73] As with border security, the antiterror elements (as well as the counterterror elements) of homeland security in effect get pushed out from the coasts. One such "pushing out" initiative is in the Pacific, with the Regional Maritime Security Initiative, "a partnership of willing nations to enhance capabilities and leverage capacities through unity of effort to identify, monitor, and intercept transnational maritime threats consistent with existing international and domestic laws."[74] Secure waterways in the Asia-Pacific are essential to securing the flow of goods, but also securing the United States from the entry of WMD or other threats. Thus, even the most traditional realm of territorial defense is affected by the structural imperatives of globalization and terrorism, and requires multinational cooperation. In this realm as in others, however, cooperation with allies is not always smooth. In October 2006, the U.S. Coast Guard was forced to suspend live-ammunition drills after protests from the Canadian government, pending the renegotiation of the Rush-Bagot Treaty, prohibiting the use of warships with cannons on the Great Lakes.[75]

Cooperation through the United Nations

The United Nations has taken terrorism seriously, within the limits placed upon it by the UN Charter and the member states, and it is in the interest of the United States to help the UN in its stand against terrorism, and work with the UN as much as possible in both counter- and antiterrorism. The UN has twelve universal instruments or conventions related to terrorism, nine regional instruments, four declarations, and since September 11, 2001, there have been twenty-one Security Council

Resolutions concerning terrorism and the suppression and prevention thereof.[76] Some of the more important UN Security Council (UNSC) Resolutions dealing with terrorism are as follows:

- UNSC Resolution 1368, passed the day after the September 11, 2001, terrorist attacks, which stressed that states have a right to self-defense under the UN Charter and urges all nations to work together to bring the perpetrators of the attacks to justice.
- UNSC Resolution 1373 says all states should take strong antiterrorism measures, including ratifying all twelve antiterrorism conventions and taking specific measures against the financing of terrorism. It also established the Counter-Terrorism Committee.
- UNSC Resolution 1526 supports the work of the UN sanctions regime against al-Qaeda.

In fact, UN Resolution 1368 was seen as giving the United States a green light to invade Afghanistan after diplomatic moves had failed, given the connection between al-Qaeda and September 11 on the one hand, and the Taliban's known policy of harboring members of al-Qaeda on the other. Moreover, UNSC Resolution 1441, the resolution the U.S. government cited as giving legitimacy to its invasion of Iraq in 2003, held that Iraq could face serious consequences if it did not cooperate with UN arms inspectors. The United States argued that it was carrying out enforcement actions under UNSC 1441.

The UN is also one means whereby nations coordinate and carry out the blocking of terrorism financing. The UN has established an International Convention for the Suppression of the Financing of Terrorism, requiring states to criminalize under domestic law the funding of terrorist activities and to search out, seize, and freeze funds slated for use for terrorist purposes. This includes the requirement to extradite or prosecute persons involved with the financing of terrorism and to cooperate with other entities in investigation and prosecution of such suspects. Lastly, states must require their financial institutions to take measures that stop funds from being used for terrorist activities. The Security Council's Sanctions Committee also has such functions as they pertain to those identified as Taliban and al-Qaeda operatives. It is very difficult for the United States or any single nation to organize such a coordinated effort to cut off financing to extremist individuals and groups, but it is something the UN can do through its good offices and member states, and this has the effect of keeping the United States more secure in the long run.

There are a number of additional reasons why the United States should cooperate through the United Nations. First, even considering the right of any nation to self-defense, American action abroad will be considered more legitimate and is often more effective with the support and sanction of the United Nations. When the United States sought support from the UN for its invasion of Iraq in 2002 and 2003, it was this legitimacy and support that U.S. policymakers sought. They did not ultimately achieve this objective, and this cost the United States in terms of international public opinion. Had they received the support of the Security Council and its members, potential financial and military support might have been more forthcoming.

Second, the UN has an important "naming and shaming" function. If a country is condemned by the international community via a UN Security Council Resolution, the General Assembly, the Counter-Terrorism Committee, or any of a number of UN bodies, the weight of international opinion can be very heavy indeed. For years South Africa bore the brunt of UN criticism and it could be argued that the pressure did bear fruit, with the eventual success of sanctions and the end of apartheid. More recently, the United Nations came together in unity for two Security Council resolutions naming and shaming North Korea for its long range missile and nuclear weapons tests and development, as well as endorsing limited sanctions against North Korea. Diplomatic and military pressure on states that sponsor terrorism or proliferate WMD will be more effective, and more legitimate, coming from a group than from a single state, especially when that group includes the target state's peers.

Third, the UN has established a Counter-Terrorism Committee, or CTC as a part of UN Security Council Resolution 1373, all of which requires UN member states to ensure that terrorist groups do not receive funds, haven, or support of any kind from member states. The CTC requires all UN member states to sign the twelve UN antiterror conventions and monitors their progress in this and other anti- and counterterror measures, including the requirement that states report regularly as to their progress. The UN also has a sanctions committee attached to the UN Security Council which keeps a running list of known Taliban and al-Qaeda operatives, and which requires countries to freeze assets of such persons if found in their countries, as well as apprehending them if possible. In terms of international accountability, the sanctions committee and the CTC can act in ways that the United States itself cannot, or at least cannot do legitimately in the eyes of other member states.

In addition, the UN has important information-sharing capabilities and serves as a forum to discuss terrorism and other matters. The UN is a convenient place for officials from various countries to meet and exchange information, particularly if the countries in question are not on good terms. For example, the United States does not have formal diplomatic relations with North Korea, but North Korea has a mission to the UN and so U.S. officials have taken advantage of this to meet quietly with North Korean officials from time to time in New York.[77]

Areas for Improvement

At first glance, the United States seems to have a remarkable record of international cooperation on homeland security. Indeed, the United States has initiated cooperative endeavors either bilaterally, multinationally, transnationally, or in cooperation with private companies in many sectors. But in order to sustain an effective and efficient antiterrorism strategy in cooperation with its partners to bolster the security of its homeland, the United States must ensure that there are incentives for other states to invest in common initiatives. Despite progress in some areas, five problems plague U.S. policies, ultimately making cooperation more difficult in the long run.

1. *Disguised unilateralism.* Some policies couched as multilateral are, in fact, unilateral. For example, the Container Security Initiative is a U.S. policy that other countries must comply with in order to gain access to U.S. markets. Although such a measure may be good for U.S. security, and may spur international changes, allies and partners may resent being coerced into action. Thus, policies should be developed in consultation with allies and within multinational institutions, rather than implemented unilaterally, wherever feasible.

2. *Insufficient reciprocity.* In a similar vein, the preponderance of U.S. power means that it can solicit cooperation from its allies without offering much in return. Again, however, the United States should use its power judiciously, especially with its strongest allies. The United States must offer incentives for cooperation that are perceived by its partners as being attractive and fair, or it will eventually become more difficult to reach beneficial agreements with them. For instance, although intelligence sharing within the UK-USA group is open and extensive, the United States does not always share sources with its other traditional European allies. This reduces the ability of European policymakers to make independent judgments about the data that is shared, and leads many Europeans to feel that the relations are one sided.

3. *Negative externalities.* If one of the interests of the United States in its homeland security is maintaining a moral stance consistent with its traditional values, the United States must pursue such a policy in its international agreements. We discussed the moral dilemmas inherent in cooperation with states with questionable human rights records or different views of what counts as a terrorist group. These moral quandaries and negative externalities are present, however, even at the inner concentric circles. The revelation that the United States has used the practice of rendition, undoubtedly with at least the partial knowledge of its allies, to hold enemy combatants in secret prisons without adhering to the Geneva Conventions, led to outrage among the citizens of the countries involved, as well as in the United States. The broader issue of torture against detainees has become a political liability for the U.S. government, and an issue where counterterrorism policy may affect the ability to gain allies for homeland security policy. Despite an Executive Order of July, 2007 prohibiting "cruel and unusual punishment" and torture against detainees, the treatment of what the government calls "unlawful enemy combatants" remains controversial because it continues to maintain that such enemy pris-

oners captured in the course of the war on terrorism are not covered by the Geneva Conventions. Such counterproductive policies damage the reputation of the United States abroad and make both counterterrorism and antiterrorism strategy more difficult. Besides being in the United States' strategic interests, multinational and transnational cooperation on homeland security is also in the legal and moral interests of the United States. By deepening and expanding its cooperation with other nations for the security of U.S. territory, the United States will be in a better position to help further develop international legal norms, as well as help generate compliance.[78] Since the Second World War, the United States has been an important guarantor of the economic and legal system that has evolved internationally. If the United States is seen as shirking its responsibilities, or worse, if its actions or words are seen as undermining this international economic and legal system, potential chaos could ensue if other nations decide they can do the same. Similarly, moral interests can also accrue strategic benefits when they bring about greater U.S. legitimacy in the eyes of others, greater trust by others in the United States and its policies, and ultimately higher levels of cooperation towards securing vital U.S. interests. Trust, legitimacy, deference, and cooperation are far more likely when an actor acts morally and is perceived by other actors to be doing so. When the United States does not act in accordance with its traditional domestic morals and values and the international treaties to which it is a signatory, it could create an election year backlash for policymakers at home, or a backlash abroad, as was the case with the U.S. treatment of prisoners at the Abu Ghraib prison in Iraq.

4. *Insensitivity to allies' values and/or interests.* When seeking international cooperation, the United States must endeavor to be cognizant of and sensitive to the ways in which its allies' interests and values may be different from its own. For example, data protection remains a controversial issue between the United States and its allies in the European Union, with airlines caught in the middle. The EU has stricter privacy laws than the United States does, and the EU and the United States have had some difficulty coming to agreement on the sharing of passenger name records, namely the lists collected by airlines to allow security checks to be conducted in advance on travelers. After multiple delays, a final agreement reached in mid-2007 reduced the number of data points to be shared, but allows the United States to keep the data for a longer period of time. Similarly, Canadian trust in American good faith was damaged in the wake of the inquiry into the case of Maher Arar, a Canadian of Syrian origin who was deported to Syria and tortured for ten months, despite a lack of evidence that he was involved in terrorist activities. Canadians were outraged, and this was made worse when the U.S. ambassador both refused to cooperate with the Canadian parliament's commission of inquiry and declared that the United States had no regrets about the case.[79] The U.S. government refused to review the case in the United States,

and Arar remained on terrorist watch lists. The idea of multilateralism usually emphasizes a somewhat thicker definition of multinational cooperation, emphasizing content, not simply form. Rather, multilateral cooperation is built around common principles developed independently of the interests of an individual party or the strategic demands of a specific event.[80] While pursuing a multilateral strategy in antiterror homeland security measures may not always be possible or efficient for the United States, it should remain the ideal to strive for. Multilateralism remains the best way of promoting generalized, reciprocated cooperation with countries who share American values.

5. *Inefficient cooperation.* The networked model of antiterrorism cooperation described may result in inefficient cooperation because of duplication, gaps in cooperation, or one actor not knowing what another is doing. For instance, intelligence cooperation and evidence sharing at the level of police departments could duplicate or undermine state-level cooperation. We have previously recommended implementing the principle of centralized control, and decentralized execution as a way of increasing the efficiency or effectiveness of domestic homeland security policy.[81] The same principle can be applied internationally, by combining high-level political attention to a problem, enabling effective overall coordination, with bureaucratic and technical cooperation at lower levels of government.[82] For example, while twin cities at the borders or police departments in cities around the world should be encouraged to undertake independent cooperative measures, some degree of centralized coordination and guidance at the federal government level is desirable to ensure that duplication and dysfunctionality are avoided and synergies of cooperation are captured for the United States more generally.

Concluding Comments

A unilateral strategy for homeland security makes little more sense in ensuring security in a flat, globalized world today than autarky does in ensuring economic development. Because of globalization and the "flattening" of the world, an international focus must permeate all aspects of the strategy. Securing borders is important but insufficient, and securing processes and networks is impossible without multinational and transnational cooperation.

If terrorism becomes nonviable and unattractive as a means toward political ends, the United States will be more secure, and it is for this reason that traditionally "outside-focused" U.S. foreign policy is so important to its traditionally "inside-focused" homeland security in the post-9/11 world. Although it certainly must use its hard power against forces that threaten it,[83] Joseph Nye and others have argued persuasively that the United States has not used its soft power very effectively in the wake of 9/11.[84] In fact, it has gone from a position of having an immense outpouring of sympathy in the days following 9/11 to a position wherein today many abhor U.S. policy, often because of ill will over the intervention in Iraq and the perception that, in Thucydidean fashion, the strong (Americans) do what they can and the weak (everyone else) accept what they must. Yet Americans have both the hard and soft power to do much to shape people's perceptions in other directions.

The United States has been perceived by too much of the rest of the world as more of a bulldozer than a seed planter in terms of paving a way forward in its relations with other members of the international community and in its relations with the Muslim world in particular, while it seeks to deepen its sense of security in the U.S. homeland.[85] The precedents Americans set for international law and norms in the present security environment will have very important implications for U.S. interests of all kinds in the future as it regards international law, norms, conventions, and treaties. The Chinese, the Russians, and others observe American actions and are quick to point out American inconsistencies in domestic security laws or in its policies toward Iraq, toward the WTO, and elsewhere. By cooperating with neighbors, allies, and partners on antiterrorism as well as counterterrorism, Americans must show the world once again that they are team players. We are convinced that in the process U.S. territory will become more secure.

A homeland security strategy for the United States seeks to prevent terrorist attacks, limit damage from them, and coordinate an effective response, where an effective response is the first step in preventing the next attack. This volume argues that homeland security must be planned strategically and that strategy must be comprehensive. To be comprehensive and effective, it must include multinational and transnational elements. U.S. interests make a transnational homeland security strategy a strategic preference, and globalization makes it a structural imperative. As we have shown, existing cooperation in the fields of justice and law enforcement, civil security, intelligence sharing, financial cooperation, homeland defense, and cooperation in the United Nations already defy traditional notions of what international cooperation in securing the U.S. homeland has looked like. Multinational and transnational cooperation on homeland security has been paid little attention by policymakers and scholars, and working out a solution for the extant and potential pathologies of such cooperation requires particular attention. Strategic and creative thinking about theory and policy are urgently required. This will happen only when we recognize the importance and utility of multinational and transnational cooperation and assure that such cooperation permeates all aspects of the United States' homeland security strategy.

Endnotes

1. We wish to thank the other authors in this volume, as well as the participants of the International Relations Research Colloquium at the Free University of Berlin for their helpful comments. We are also grateful to our co-participants in the Sondermann Summer Seminar on Homeland Security at the University of Denver in 2004 for helping to formulate some of the initial ideas from which this chapter arose.

2. The White House, The National Strategy for Homeland Security (Washington, D.C.: Office of Homeland Security, the White House, 2002), xii. http://www.whitehouse. gov/homeland/book/.

3. This definition is based on the following report, which the authors played a part in producing: A. Burgos, T. W. Crawford, A. C. Diener, A. M. Gardner, L. K. Griffith, W. Josiger, V. M. Kitchen, R. S. Lauer, and G. J. Moore, "Homeland Security in a Multinational Context: A New Strategic Vision," a report stemming from the Fred A. Sondermann Summer Seminar, University of Denver and Vail Cascade Resort (August 2004), 2.

4. For example, Tom Lansford, All for One: Terrorism, NATO and the United States (Aldershot, UK: Ashgate, 2002); Bob Woodward, Bush at War (New York: Simon & Schuster, 2002); Ken Booth and Tim Dunne, Worlds in Collision: Terror and the Future of Global Order (New York: Palgrave-MacMillian, 2002); Russell D. Howard and Reid L. Sawyer, eds., Terrorism and Counterterrorism: Understanding the New Security Environment—Readings and Interpretations (Dubuque, IA: McGraw-Hill, 2006).

5. General (Ret.) Wayne A. Downing, "The Global War on Terrorism: Re-Focusing the National Strategy," in Howard and Reid, eds., Terrorism and Counterterrorism; Brig. General (Ret.) Russell D. Howard, "Preemptive Military Doctrine: No Other Choice," in Howard and Reid, eds., Terrorism and Counterterrorism; Steven Simon and Jeff Martini, "Terrorism: Denying Al Qaeda Its Popular Support," The Washington Quarterly (Winter 2004/2005); and Rob de Wijk, "The Limits of Military Power," The Washington Quarterly (Winter 2002).

6. For detailed explanations of his ten flatteners, see Thomas L. Friedman, The World is Flat: A Brief History of the Twenty-First Century (New York: Farrar, Straus and Giroux, 2005), 48–172.

7. Ibid.

8. As cited in Friedman, 436.

9. Of course these same technologies make it easier in some cases for authorities to track their movements, because of the electronic "footprint" that they leave, whether by e-mail addresses or credit card or cell phone usage records.

10. Richard Ullman, "Redefining Security," International Security 8, no. 1 (1983): 129–153.

11. Stephen D. Krasner, International Regimes (Ithaca, NY: Cornell University Press, 1983), 1.

12. See also Robert Keohane and Joseph Nye, Power and Interdependence, 3rd ed. (London: Longman, 2000 [1977]); Jessica Tuchman Mathews, "Power Shift," Foreign Affairs 76 (January/February 1997).

13. Anne-Marie Slaughter, A New World Order (Princeton, NJ: Princeton University Press, 2004) 14.

14. Ibid., 15.

15. For more on cooperation at the domestic level, see Moser, Chapter 9 in this volume.

16. Burgos et al., "Homeland Security," 18.

17. See "Security and Prosperity Partnership of North America" at www.spp.gov (accessed October 17, 2006). This Web site includes annual reports to the North American readers which contain detailed updates on new and ongoing initiatives. For a summary of criticisms of the SPP, see R. Paris, "A Trilateral Mishmash," Globe and Mail, February 26, 2007.

18. The Department of Homeland Security's Office of International Affairs identifies Canada, Mexico, and the United Kingdom as the United States' most important allies on homeland security. See the Office of International Affairs organizational structure page, http://www.dhs.gov/dhspublic/interapp/editorial/editorial_0874.xml (accessed October 10, 2006).

19. The United States has long-term port of call arrangements for its Navy in Singapore "…for maintenance, repairs, supplies, and crew rest and recreation," and regular access to a Republic of Singapore Air Force base as well (www.globalsecurity.org, accessed October 12, 2005).

20. UAE ports host more U.S. Navy ships than any port outside the United States. The UAE provides outstanding support for the U.S. Navy at the ports of Jebel Ali—which is managed by DP World—and Fujairah, and for the U.S. Air Force at al Dhafra Air Base (tankers and surveillance and reconnaissance aircraft). (Web site of the White House [February 2006; http://www.whitehouse.gov/news/releases/2006/02/20060222-10.html, accessed May 31, 2006.)

21. "Malaysian forces regularly conduct joint training with United States counterparts, and the United States routinely enjoys access to Malaysian airfields and ports. Also, Malaysia provides one of the few bases outside the United States for U.S. military jungle-warfare training … 1,500 Malaysian defense personnel have benefited from the U.S.-sponsored IMET (international military education and training) program" (Malaysian Defense Secretary Najib bin Tun Abdul Razak, "U.S.-Malaysia Defense Cooperation: A Solid Success Story," Heritage Foundation Lecture no. 742 [May 3, 2002; http://www.heritage.org/Research/AsiaandthePacific/HL742.cfm]).

22. The United States has had troops in the Philippines since 2002 as a part of a long-term operation to stop Muslim militants there and the United States has a mutual defense treaty with this "special non-NATO ally."

23. The United States has military bases in Kyrgyzstan and Uzbekistan. Secretary of State Condoleezza Rice recently travelled to Kyrgyzstan and secured a long-term lease on the base there, but the United States will close the Uzbek base by year's end.

24. President George W. Bush, State of the Union Speech, January 29, 2002, as reported in Shirley Kan, "US-China Counter-Terrorism Cooperation: Issues for U.S. Policy," Congressional Research Service Report for Congress (December 7, 2004; http://www.fas.org/irp/crs/RS21995.pdf, accessed October 22, 2005).

25. The China Institute of International Studies' (Beijing) Le Rongrong, "China-U.S. Counterterrorism Cooperation," Sandia National Laboratories (http://www.cmc.sandia.gov/links/cmc-papers/regional-us-china-counterterrorism/regional-us-china-counterterrorism.htm, accessed October 22, 2005).

26. There is debate over links between al-Qaeda and the Uighurs' ETIM, but both Chinese and U.S. intelligence sources maintain there have been, as do a number of other sources. See Council on Foreign Relations, "East Turkestan Islamic Movement," CFIR Backgrounder (November 2005, http://www.cfr.org/publication/9179/#2, accessed October 21, 2006); Kenneth George Pereire, "Jihad in China? Rise of the East Turkestan Islamic Movement," IDSS Commentaries 56 (2006) (Singapore: Nanyang Technological University, Institute of Defense and Strategic Studies, International Centre for Political Violence and Terrorism Research, June 22, 2006, http://www.ntu.edu.sg/IDSS/publications/Perspective/IDSS0562006.pdf, accessed October 21, 2006); and Hayder Mili, "Xinjiang: An Emerging Narco-Islamist Corridor?" Jamestown Foundation Terrorism Monitor (April 21, 2005).

27. Assistant Secretary of State James Kelly, December 2002, quoted in Shirley Kan, "U.S.-China Counter-Terrorism Cooperation: Issues for U.S. Policy," Congressional Research Service Report for Congress (December 7, 2004; http://www.fas.org/irp/crs/RS21995.pdf, accessed October 22, 2005).

28. We shall say little here on this subject, for it is covered elsewhere in this volume; see Chapter 4.

29. The White House, U.S. National Strategy for Combating Terrorism (Washington, D.C.: Office of Homeland Security, the White House [February, 2003]), 11–12, http://www.whitehouse.gov/news/releases/2003/02/counter_terrorism/counter_terrorism_strategy.pdf, accessed October 22, 2005.

30. Downing, "Global War," 436–438.

31. "Declassified Key Judgments of the National Intelligence Estimate 'Trends in Global Terrorism: Implications for the United States' dated April 2006," published September 26, 2006, www.odni.gov/press_releases/Declassified_NIE_key_judgements.pdf, accessed September 30, 2006. Former CIA Bin Laden unit head Michael Scheuer has said, "There's no bigger gift we could have given to Osama bin Laden than the invasion of Iraq" (Daniel L. Byman, Michael Scheuer, Anatol Lieven, and W. Patrick Lang, "Iraq, Afghanistan, and the War on 'Terror,'" Middle East Policy [Spring 2005]: 4, as cited in Downing, "Global War," 438).

32. Downing, "Global War," 436–438.

33. Eric Schmitt and Thom Shanker, "Washington Recasts Terror War as 'Struggle,'" International Herald Tribune, July 27, 2005, http://www.iht.com/articles/2005/07/26/news/terror.php, accessed October 23, 2005.

34. Downing, "Global War," 444.

35. Linda Robinson, "Plan of Attack," US News and World Report, August 1, 2005, 26–34.

36. See Glenn Kessler, "Campaign Methods Put to Test in Tour to Boost U.S. Image: Bush Policies Remain Obstacle for Hughes," Washington Post, September 30, 2005, A12; Hassan Bin Yousef Yassin, "Hughes' Visit Beneficial for Americans and for Saudis," Arab News via Al Jazeera, October 9, 2005, http://www.aljazeera.info/Opinion; and Glenn Kessler and Robin Wright, "Hughes to Leave State Department after

Mixed Results in Outreach Post," Washington Post, November 1, 2007, A19, http://www.washingtonpost.com/wp-dyn/content/article/2007/10/31/AR2007103100788.html, accessed January 11, 2008.

37. Downing, "Global," 443.

38. Steven Erlanger and Steven Lee Myers, "Bush Begins Peace Effort Bonded with Olmert," New York Times, January 10, 2008, http://www.nytimes.com/2008/01/10/world/middleeast/10prexy.html?fta=y, accessed January 11, 2008.

39. U.S. Department of Justice Press Release. "Integrated Border Enforcement Teams Now Cover Canada-U.S. Border from Coast to Coast" (November 19, 2003, http://www.usdoj.gov/opa/pr/2003/November/03_ag_640.htm, accessed September 24, 2005).

40. See the edited volume by Peter Andreas and Thomas Biersteker, The Rebordering of North America: Integration and Exclusion in a New Security Context (New York: Routledge, 2003) for details on this cooperation.

41. Stephen Handelmann, "The Longest Beat," Time Canada 160, no. 9 (August 26, 2002); and William Finnegan, "The Terrorism Beat: How Is the NYPD Defending the City?" The New Yorker, July 25, 2005, 58.

42. Raymond R. Kelly (Police Commissioner, NYPD), "NYPD Response to London Bombings" (July 7, 2005, http://www.nyc.gov/html/nypd/html/dcpi/london_bombings.html, accessed September 24, 2005).

43. Dorine Dubois, The Attacks of 11 September: EU-US Co-operation against Terrorism in the Field of Justice and Home Affairs," European Foreign Affairs Review 7, no. 3 (2002): 328.

44. Europol Press Release "Enhanced cooperation with the USA" (April 24, 2006), http://www.europol.eu.int/index.asp?page=news&news=pr060424.htm, accessed October 17, 2006. See also U.S. Department of State Fact Sheet "U.S. Measures Implementing the 2004 US-EU Declaration on Combating Terrorism" (June 17, 2005), www.useu.be/Article.asp?ID=9CC663FP-9652-4015-9505-C786EAB89C72, accessed September 21, 2005.

45. U.S. Department of State Fact Sheet, "U.S. Measures."

46. Association of Southeast Asian Nations, "ASEAN-United States of American Joint Declaration for Cooperation to Combat International Terrorism" (August 1, 2002, http://www.aseansec.org/7424.htm, accessed August 23, 2005).

47. For more, see the Asia-Pacific Economic Cooperation Web site, http://www.apec.org.au/docs/Star_Symposium_Report.doc.

48. For a broader definition, see Amanda J. Dory, "American Civil Security: The U.S. Public and Homeland Security," The Washington Quarterly 27, no. 1 (Winter 2003–2004): 37–52.

49. For details of these programs, see the U.S. Customs and Border Protection Web site, www.cbp.gov. The 2006 Report to Leaders on the Security and Prosperity Partnership also provides a useful summary of initiatives within North America; http://www.spp.gov/2006_report_to_leaders/index.asp?dName=2006_report_to_leaders, accessed October 17, 2006.

50. Information on the CSI is available at http://www.customs.gov/xp/cgov/border_security/international_activities/csi/, accessed September 24, 2005.

51. People's Daily, "China, U.S. Strengthen Anti-terrorism Cooperation in Container Security" (July 30, 2003, http://english.people.com.cn/200307/30/eng20030730_121201.shtml, accessed August 23, 2005).

52. See Mark Salter, "Passports, Mobility and Security: How Smart Can the Border Be?" International Studies Perspectives, 5, no. 1 (2004): 71–91.

53. For further information on C-TPAT, see www.cbp.gov/xp/cgov/import/commercial_enforcement/ctpat/ (Accessed January 30, 2008).

54. For examples of the ways in which business recovery plans are international, see Victoria Hardy and Phil Ross, "International Emergency Planning for Facilities Management," Journal of Facilities Management 2, no. 1 (2003): 7–25.

55. Blue Cascades III Action Planning Meeting Web site, http://pnwer.org/pris/Blue%20cascades%20III.htm, accessed June 1, 2006.

56. Pacific Northwest Economic Region, Blue Cascades II Executive Summary, www.pnwer.org/pris/bluecascades.htm, 7.

57. Department of Homeland Security, "TOPOFF 4 Frequently Asked Questions," www.dhs.gov/xprepresp/training/gc_1179422026237.shtm (Accessed January 30, 2007). "TOPOFF 3 Exercise," http://www.dhs.gov/dhspublic/interapp/editorial/editorial_0588.xml, accessed September 24, 2005.

58. Backgrounder: Exercise Ardent Sentry 2006 (April 28, 2006), www.forces.gc.ca/site/newsroom/view_news_e.asp?id=1915, accessed October 17, 2006.

59. Note Hurricane Katrina in September 2005 tested not just U.S. civil security infrastructure, but also international civil security infrastructure. In addition to the bilateral aid sent directly to the United States, NATO played a role in cocoordinating assistance among member states and providing equipment to transport it to the Gulf Coast. See NATO Press Release, "Statement by the Secretary General on NATO Katrina Support Operation" (September 9, 2005), 110, http://www.nato.int/docu/pr/2005/p05-110e.htm, accessed September 24, 2005.

60. See, for example, the agendas of the Seoul World Mayor's Forum 2005, www.swmf.org and the World Association of Major Metropolises, www.metropolis.org (Accessed September 20, 2005).

61. See Lloyd Axworthy, Arthur L. Fallick, and Kelly Ross, "The Secure City," Vancouver Working Group Discussion Paper for the World Urban Forum (Liu Institute for Global Issues, University of British Columbia, 2005, www.wd.gc.ca/ced/wuf/secure/secure_e.pdf,, accessed September 24, 2005).

62. Martin Rudner, "Hunters and Gatherers: The Intelligence Coalition against Islamic Terrorism," International Journal of Intelligence and Counter Intelligence 17 (2004): 193–230.

63. Ibid., 201.

64. Ibid., 203.

65. See Chris Clough, "Quid Pro Quo: The Challenges of International Strategic Intelligence Cooperation," International Journal of Intelligence and Counter Intelligence 17 (2004): 605; and Rudner, "Hunters and Gatherers," 215.

66. Mirjam Dittrich, Facing the Global Terrorist Threat: A European Response, Working Paper no. 14 (Brussels: European Policy Centre, January 2005).

67. Chris Clough. "Quid Pro Quo," 608; and Rudner, "Hunters and Gatherers," 217.

68. National Commission on Terrorism Attacks Upon the United States (9/11 Commission), 9-11 Commission Report (Washington, D.C.: U.S. Government Printing Office, 2004), 93 (www.9-11commission.gov).

69. See U.S. Department of the Treasury, "National Money Laundering Strategy" (2002; www.treas.gov/offices/enforcement/publications/ml2002.pdf, accessed on November 5, 2005).

70. See John McGlynn, "Banco Delta Asia, North Korea's Frozen Funds and U.S. Undermining of the Six Party Talks: Obstacles to a Solution," Japan Focus (June 9, 2007), http://japanfocus.org/products/topdf/2466, accessed June 11, 2007.

71. For details see Philippe Lagassé, "NORAD, NORTHCOM, and the Binational Planning Group," Canadian American Strategic Review (2003) http://www.sfu.ca/casr/ft-lagasse1.htm, accessed September 24, 2005.

72. NORAD News Release, "US, Canada Strengthen NORAD Agreement" (May 23, 2006), http://www.norad.mil/newsroom/news_releases/2006/052306.htm, accessed June 1, 2006.

73. See the U.S. Coast Guard's Web site on Maritime Domain Awareness (http://www.uscg.mil/mda/, accessed September 24, 2005).

74. See the Regional Maritime Security Initiative Web site (http://www.pacom.mil/rmsi/, accessed September 24, 2005).

75. Jeff Sallot, "U.S. Suspends Gun Drills on Great Lakes," The Globe and Mail, October 17, 2006.

76. For more, see Action by the Security Council (http://www.un.org/terrorism/sc.htm); International Instruments Related to the Prevention and Suppression of International Terrorism (New York: United Nations, 2004); and Jane Boulden and Thomas G. Weiss, eds., Terrorism and the UN: Before and After September 11 (Bloomington, IN: Indiana University Press, 2004).

77. U.S. assistant secretary of state for East Asian and Pacific Affairs Christopher Hill discussed this in 2005 (Reuters Report, "U.S.-North Korea Contacts," The New York Times [October 5, 2005]).

78. John Ikenberry, After Victory (Princeton, NJ: Princeton University Press, 2001).

79. See www.ararcommission.ca for details of the case and testimony; and Jim Brown, "No Regrets, No Apologies About Arar Deportation, Says U.S. Ambassador," Canadian Press (September 18, 2005).

80. See John Ruggie, Multilateralism Matters: The Theory and Praxis of an Institutional Form (New York: Columbia University Press, 1993).

81. Burgos et al., "Homeland Security," 3.

82. See Veronica Kitchen, "Smarter Cooperation in Canada-U.S. Relations?" International Journal 59, no. 3 (Summer 2004): 694–696.

83. It should be recalled that the United States acted with a large and supportive group of allies against Afghanistan after 9/11, had the sympathy and support of much of the world in this action in the wake of 9/11, and could even be said to have acted with a UN mandate given UN Security Council Resolution 1368, passed on September 12, 2001, saying states had a right to defend themselves against terrorist aggression.

84. Joseph S. Nye, Jr., "The Decline of America's Soft Power," Foreign Affairs (May/June 2004).

85. The Pew Global Attitudes Project's most recent surveys showed that numbers of those with positive views of the United States had fallen in most countries since 2005, in some cases significantly (falling from 23 percent to 12 percent in Turkey, 21 percent to 15 percent in Jordan, 38 percent to 30 percent in Indonesia, 52 percent to 43 percent in Russia, and, most significantly, 41 percent to 23 percent in Spain). Pew Global Attitudes Project: Summary of Findings (released 13 June 2006) http://pewglobal.org/reports/pdf/252.pdf, accessed October 18, 2006). In a poll by CNN/USA Today/Gallup conducted in Iraq with Iraqi respondents between March and April of 2005, when asked, "Taking everything into account, do you think the coalition invasion of Iraq has done more harm than good or more good than harm?" 46 percent said "more harm than good," while 33 percent said "more good than harm." In the same poll, when respondents were asked, "Do you think now of Coalition forces mostly as occupiers or mostly as liberators?" 71 percent said occupiers, 19 percent said liberators, and 8 percent said both (USAToday/CNN/Gallup, "Key Findings: Nationwide Survey of 3,500 Iraqis," USA Today (May 20, 2005, http://www.usatoday.com/news/world/iraq/2004-04-28-gallup-iraq-findings.htm).

SECTION 2

Terrorism, Homeland Security, and Weapons of Mass Destruction (WMD)

Chapter 6

WMD Terrorism
New Threats, Revised Responses

Jeffrey A. Larsen and James J. Wirtz

The authors begin with a brief history of terrorism, the modern variants of which they describe as occurring in four waves. Their principal concern, however, is potential access by terrorist groups to weapons of mass destruction, which they discuss in detail. Denying terrorists access to nuclear or other weapons-grade materials is the aim. Approaches under consideration include expanding the existing Nunn-Lugar cooperative threat reduction programs with Russia; signing the Fissile Materials Cutoff Treaty, and developing a plan for ensuring that no new states develop fissile materials—including Iran and North Korea; and eliminating surplus Cold War nuclear weaponry—encouraging Russia to do the same.

The worst potential WMD problem is nuclear terrorism, because it combines the unparalleled destructive power of nuclear weapons with the apocalyptic motivations of terrorists against which deterrence, let alone dissuasion or diplomacy, is likely to be ineffective.

Ashton Carter[1]

By the end of the last century, the threat of mass casualty terrorism had begun to edge its way onto the agendas of defense and law-enforcement agencies. The arrival of the millennium, and the worldwide celebrations that would accompany it, had taken on sinister connotations for many officials. There was a concern that cults, disgruntled individuals, or terrorist organizations might view the dawn of a new century as a signal to take violent action to help prompt the coming of some long awaited utopia. The air was filled with apprehension as many officials believed that the multitudes gathered at various New Year's celebrations might prove to be tempting targets for individuals or organizations bent on violence. The fact that enormous crowds of revelers could be wiped out by a weapon of mass destruction (WMD), a chemical, biological, nuclear, or radiological device, was not lost upon officials. When the millennium passed quietly, a collective sigh of relief could be heard in police and defense ministries around the world.

Evidence exists, however, that terrorists did intend to launch attacks to coincide with the millennium. In December 1999, police in Jordan rounded up an al-Qaeda terrorist cell that was about to strike. Seventy-one drums of "acids" were uncovered in their weapons cache. Closer to home, Ahmed Ressam, who has been linked to al-Qaeda, was arrested on December 19, 1999 while entering Port Angeles, Washington from Canada. Alert border patrol agents discovered high explosives hidden in the trunk of his car. Months later, intelligence analysts determined that Ressam had intended to bomb Los Angeles International Airport on New Year's Day 2000.[2]

The fact that these al-Qaeda operatives were thwarted and that they were primarily armed with high explosives sharpened the debate about the likelihood of mass casualty terrorism, especially involving weapons of mass destruction. Some argued that terrorists would shy away from attacks that produced massive death, injury, and destruction. Agreeing with Brian Jenkins's famous observation that terrorists wanted people watching, not dead, they pointed out that it would be difficult to harness an attack that produced thousands of casualties to achieve some political objective.[3] Such a heinous act would unite potential supporters, opponents, and fence sitters against the terrorists, dooming not only their organization, but also their political goals. They also noted that even though terrorists had come to possess WMDs, such weapons required demanding technical skills and operational savvy if they were to be used to produce large amounts of death and destruction. The Aum Shinrikyo cult, for example, possessed substantial economic and technical resources, yet it failed to use sarin to its optimal effect when it placed the chemical agent on Tokyo subway cars in March 1995.[4] Although they injured 6,000 people in the attack, cult members only managed to kill eleven individuals—a death toll that can easily be exceeded using conventional weapons. For example, more than fifty people died when al-Qaeda sympathizers, using high explosives, attacked the London Underground and bus system in July 2005.[5] Skeptics agreed that mass casualty terrorism involving chemical, biological, nuclear, or radiological weapons was possible, but they asserted that the threat was greatly exaggerated.

By contrast, others focused on the consequences of a terrorist attack involving weapons of mass destruction and how such an attack might change the course of history. They agreed that terrorists generally did not resort to mass casualty terrorism, that it was difficult to use such an event to achieve political objectives, and that significant technical and operational hurdles made it difficult to obtain and employ chemical, biological, nuclear, and radiological weapons. But they also noted that just because an activity had not yet occurred was not a compelling reason to believe that it would not occur in the future. In the minds of these Cassandras, the consequences were too significant not to take seriously the possibility that terrorists might employ WMD.

The September 11, 2001 al-Qaeda suicide attacks on the United States ended the debate about the likelihood of mass casualty terrorism. And the 2004 Madrid train bombings, the Bali tourist bombings in 2002 and 2005, the 2003 bombing of the Marriott Hotel in Jakarta, the 2005 London Underground and Amman hotel bombings, and the George W. Bush administration's revelations about foiled terrorist plots continue to highlight al-Qaeda's interest in launching terrorist attacks intended to produce as many casualties as possible.[6] If they somehow managed to acquire them, would al-Qaeda operatives use chemical, biological, radiological, or nuclear weapons in a terrorist attack? Or does the threat of terrorism involving WMD represent a barrier that will not be crossed in the future? What international actions can government officials take to prevent or deter the use of WMD by terrorists?

To address these questions, this chapter briefly describes the evolution of modern terrorism, exploring how the motivations and targets of terrorists have changed over time. The second section describes the characteristics of chemical, biological, nuclear, and radiological weapons, which are often referred to as WMD because of their potential to cause enormous numbers of casualties or horrendous physical destruction. The third section explores the problem of domestic WMD terrorism from an international perspective by placing the issue within the context of current U.S. national security documents and policies, including the National Security Strategy, the National Strategy to Combat WMD, and the Nuclear Posture Review.

This chapter offers a unique perspective on the WMD terrorist threat by exploring the interaction between foreign and defense policy—counterproliferation, counterforce, preemptive and preventive war, arms control, supplier agreements, export controls, general nonproliferation policy, and new international surveillance agreements, such as the Proliferation Security Initiative—and the domestic threat of terrorism involving nuclear, chemical, biological, or radiological weapons.

The Changing Threat of Modern Terrorism

Although various types of violence have permeated societies throughout history, most scholars link the emergence of modern terrorism, and modern warfare for that matter, to the French Revolution. The Revolution demonstrated that what average people thought and believed mattered, and that war was no longer simply the sport of kings, noblemen, or mercenaries. Indeed, this "first generation warfare," a term popularized by Bill Lind and G. I. Wilson, saw many developments that remain the basis of today's armies and contemporary combined arms operations: an increasingly professional officer corps, volunteers for military service, industrial production, and national zeal.[7] It also saw the use of violence to manipulate elite and public opinion. The Committee of Public Safety, led by Robespierre and his followers, used the guillotine in a Reign of Terror (1793–1794) to gain control of the public bodies of the French Republic. When Robespierre forewarned several of his colleagues that they would soon lose their heads too, members of the Committee became concerned about their own safety and killed him first. But the Reign of Terror allowed 22 people to hold a nation of 27 million hostage, killing at least 40,000 of their countrymen in the process. At its inception, terrorism emerged as the weapon of the weak, used to instill fear in the hearts of a *public* audience to achieve a political objective.[8] It was violence directed as a matter of political strategy against innocent persons.[9]

The First Wave

David Rapoport, one of the world's foremost authorities on political violence, divides the evolution of modern terrorism into four waves that roughly correspond to broad generational change and to the major political issues of their day.[10] The first wave of terrorism emerged near the end of the nineteenth century when rebel and revolutionary movements embraced sensational violence to attack local regimes. The *Narodnaya Volya* (People's Will) movement in Russia, for instance, deliberately violated social and legal norms by targeting civilians in an effort to prompt a government overreaction, which in their view would provoke a revolutionary outburst. Soon various terrorist movements, following in the wake of economic, political, educational, and social advances in Russia and Central Europe, emerged in various countries. Terrorists armed with handguns or dynamite targeted elected officials or royal families to advance the cause of political reform, nationalism, or various ideological movements, such as communism and anarchy. This first wave ended with the assassination of Austrian Archduke Franz Ferdinand, an act that precipitated the outbreak of the First World War. Gavrilo Princip, the Serbian nationalist who pulled the trigger that day, set off a chain reaction that ultimately led to the deaths of millions of people. The death and destruction that swept Europe set several countries back decades in terms of demographics or economic development, illustrating an important fact about terrorism: its effects often are unforeseen and unintended. Nevertheless, the fact that spectacular acts of terrorism can unleash uncontrollable social, political, and military forces has seemed to encourage those who want to use mayhem to achieve their objectives.

The Second Wave

The second wave of terror, prompted by the forces of decolonization, emerged in the aftermath of World War II. Instead of targeting senior officials and government luminaries, these nationalists targeted the instruments of colonial control, such as local officials, police, and military outposts, to confront colonists with the possibility that by occupying some distant land they would be forced to endure never-ending casualties. Terrorist cells were formed in cities and attacks were carried out against prominent urban targets, although these attacks were not necessarily directed at civilians. Second-wave terrorists sometimes provided warning of their attacks to minimize casualties, but mistakes occurred. For example, the Irgun bombing of the King David Hotel in Jerusalem in July 1946 knocked out the center of British mandatory rule in Palestine but also killed 91 people, a death toll that undermined Irgun's credibility among friend and foe alike. The crest of the second wave, however, occurred in Southeast Asia. "People's war," a strategy whereby terrorism is used to rid the countryside of a government's presence, was put to good use by the North Vietnamese and their Viet Cong allies during the Vietnam War to drive the U.S.-supported regime in Saigon from power.[11] The first stage of people's war involved the use of violence against government officials and supporters to demonstrate to the local population that the colonial power was on the wrong side of history. By reducing the government presence in the countryside, the Viet Cong placed themselves in a position where they were able to communicate their own political program to the peasantry. In theory, the Vietnamese version of people's war also ended in a burst of revolutionary terrorism, the so-called general offensive-general uprising, a spontaneous revolt against the government.[12] The second wave produced its own lesson: terrorism can be integrated into a complex political-military strategy that over time might wear down and defeat even the strongest military power. Terrorism was not just the weapon of the weak, it was an *effective* weapon of the weak.

The Vietnamese success against the United States spurred other organizations to use terrorism as a political instrument, although few groups described themselves as terrorists because the term had taken on a pejorative connotation by the 1960s. Many of these organizations, such as the Weather Underground in the United States, the Italian Red Brigades, or the German Red Army Faction, saw themselves as the vanguard for socialist revolution, a view that was welcomed by Soviet officials who looked for every available opportunity to cause trouble for the West.

The Third Wave

The Palestine Liberation Organization (PLO) came to exemplify third-wave terrorism that was inspired by the Viet Cong's struggle against overwhelming odds. Left alone in its fight to regain lost lands following Israel's defeat of the Arabs in the 1967 Six Day War, the PLO's operations had virtually all of the hallmarks of today's Islamic fundamentalists who use terror to advance their cause. Because they lacked access to their own territory, the Palestinians had to create operating and training facilities in countries sympathetic to their plight. They also attacked targets outside the Middle East. Palestinian terrorists struck the Munich Olympics in 1972 and kidnapped OPEC ministers in Vienna in 1975. Because they primarily sought to draw attention to their cause, the PLO and other third-wave groups adopted hostage taking and airplane hijackings as preferred tactics. Third-wave terrorists, however, had to strike a delicate balance. Too little violence would fail to draw attention to their cause, while too much violence would cause a backlash of international outrage as people turned against the perpetrators of what appeared to be senseless acts of violence. Still, there was a gradual escalation in terms of death and destruction produced by terrorism. Tens of people died in the worst terrorist incidents in the 1970s, while hundreds would die in the worst incidents in the 1980s and 1990s.[13] Observers also came to several conclusions about third-wave terrorism. These terrorists appeared to be rational, in the sense they used violence in a calculated way to achieve political objectives. Additionally, terrorists seemed to stick with tried and true operations. Innovation was rare because terrorists often strove to minimize risks in what were inherently demanding operations.[14]

The Fourth Wave

The lessons drawn from the third wave became conventional wisdom as a new generation of fourth-wave terrorists emerged in the aftermath of the Soviet defeat in Afghanistan and the triumph of the Islamic revolution in Iran at the end of the 1970s. Although the Iranian Hostage Crisis demonstrated that Americans were vulnerable to this new type of Islamic terrorism, U.S. policymakers tried to harness the religious forces that motivated Islamic militants in the Cold War by supporting their battle against the Soviets in Afghanistan. Al-Qaeda emerged from the remnants of the mujaheddin forces, especially foreign volunteers, once allied with the United States. Returning from the brutal struggle in Afghanistan, these individuals found it impossible to reintegrate into what they believed were amoral and corrupt societies. Wandering around the Islamic world, they began to gravitate towards Osama bin Laden, a rich Saudi financier who had built a reputation as a logistics and construction expert during the war in Afghanistan. Bin Laden's motivations and rhetoric have evolved over the course of a decade of terrorist activity, but his initial ire seems to have been directed towards what he believed was a hypocritical

Wahabi regime in Saudi Arabia and its strongest backer, the United States government. The U.S. military presence in the Persian Gulf and Saudi Arabia, made necessary by the requirement to maintain sanctions against Baghdad following the first Gulf War, only fueled bin Laden's animosity towards the Saudi royal family and the United States.

Al-Qaeda and other jihadists launched a war against the United States in the 1990s. After the first attack on the World Trade Center in 1993, the Central Intelligence Agency collected information on bin Laden. For its part, the U.S. military strengthened security at its facilities in the Persian Gulf region following the attacks on the Khobar Towers in Saudi Arabia. By 1998, bin Laden had held press conferences calling for attacks against American interests and issued a *fatwa* justifying his actions. In August 1998, al-Qaeda attacked U.S. embassies in Nairobi, Kenya, and Dar Es Salaam, Tanzania. In 2000, after a failed attempt to attack the USS *The Sullivans*, bin Laden's operatives launched a suicide attack against the USS *Cole*, inflicting fifty casualties on the crew and nearly sinking the vessel. Bin Laden was quite vocal about his ambitions, which were repeated in a riveting article published by *Foreign Affairs*.[15]

Since the French Revolution, terrorism has changed its stripes to reflect the outstanding political and social grievances of the day as seen from the viewpoint of the weak. Its targets have been political elites and royalty, government outposts, the international news media, and most recently, the citizens of opposing governments and societies. It seems to be shaped and encouraged by the example of previously triumphant movements, especially campaigns that ultimately proved successful against powerful states. Terrorism also had been distinctly secular and localized until third-wave movements incorporated Islamic fundamentalism into the mix, and the PLO was forced by circumstances to conduct international operations. Over the last several decades, terrorism has become increasingly lethal as transnational organizations use international communication and transportation networks to wreak death and destruction across the globe.

WMD Terrorism

In the aftermath of the September 11, 2001 attacks against the World Trade Center and Pentagon, analysts have devoted considerable effort to assessing al-Qaeda's ability to use chemical, biological, nuclear, or radiological weapons. On the one hand, the international response to Islamic terrorism has hampered al-Qaeda's ability to launch attacks, and networks and cells have been disrupted. Al-Qaeda operations in Iraq also resemble third-wave terrorist attacks in the sense that they are directed at the ability of the U.S.-supported regime in Baghdad to exercise control over the country and to establish democratic institutions. On the other hand, dispassionate assessments of the likelihood that al-Qaeda might launch a terrorist attack using WMD are not reassuring. Lewis Dunn, for instance, notes that al-Qaeda operatives have attempted to acquire chemical and possibly nuclear weapons and that plots have been uncovered involving ricin, cyanide, and radiological weapons.[16] Nevertheless, Dunn also concludes that al-Qaeda has come to rely on explosives as its primary terrorist weapon and the use of chemical, biological, or nuclear weapons would entail significant technological and operational challenges that would require innovation, a course of action that is extraordinarily risky from the terrorists' perspective. He notes, however, that Western officials must act as if al-Qaeda *will* use WMD if they somehow manage to acquire them, but that policymakers should not abandon efforts to deter al-Qaeda's use of WMD. The effectiveness of deterrence, or related efforts to create self-deterrence in the minds of al-Qaeda leaders by highlighting how WMD use will hurt their cause, cannot be ruled out. Audrey Kurth Cronin has reached a similar conclusion that terrorists probably prefer conventional weapons, but that WMD use cannot be ruled out because "terrorism seeks to shock."[17]

Nonetheless, it is the assessment of most analysts, and the U.S. government, that WMD might become increasingly available to terrorists. As a result, the threats emanating from both state and nonstate actors could increase. Chemical and biological weapons are particularly easy to produce by skilled laboratory personnel with a minimum of necessary materials or advanced equipment. This is not a hypothetical threat: coalition forces in Afghanistan uncovered trace amounts of ricin and anthrax at several locations. Evidence captured along with Khalid Shaikh Mohammed in March 2003 also suggests that al-Qaeda was planning an ambitious effort to manufacture anthrax.[18] The Japanese group Aum Shinrikyo released sarin gas on the Tokyo subway system in 1995 and attempted to aerosolize anthrax in a Tokyo neighborhood earlier that year. Attempts were undertaken to release cyanide in the London subways in 2002, and to use ricin in 2003, but British police foiled both plots. Other reports claim that Jordan stopped a plan by al-Qaeda to release a chemical agent in Amman in 2004. A person or group still at large conducted a terror campaign in the United States in 2001, placing powdered anthrax in envelopes and mailing it to key American figures. And the arrest of an al-Qaeda agent in the United States in 2002 broke up a plot to acquire and use a radiological dispersal device (RDD), commonly referred to as a "dirty bomb."[19] Terrorists are dabbling with WMD, although no group has yet employed them with maximum effect.

Nuclear Weapons

Nuclear weapons are extremely difficult to produce because their manufacture requires a large industrial infrastructure. Building a nuclear weapon might be within the realm of possibility, however, if a group was able to get its hands on fissile material such as highly enriched uranium (HEU) or plutonium. The physics and engineering of nuclear weapons are well understood; the challenge lies in creating or obtaining the fissile material. By contrast, an RDD would be much easier to build. An RDD is a conventional bomb wrapped in radioactive material; when detonated, radioactive material is spread by the blast. Unlike the HEU or plutonium needed to make a nuclear weapon, low-level radioactive materials can be used in an RDD, and as Fred Wehling and Jeremy Tamsett note in their chapter, these materials are plentiful in modern societies because they have a myriad of industrial and medical uses in everyday life.

Most observers are not too concerned that terrorist networks will actually build a nuclear weapon. Instead, they worry that terrorists might find a way to procure a weapon through theft or purchase. Nuclear weapons may emerge on the black market, for instance, if they are stolen from the large remaining stocks of Russian nonstrategic nuclear weapons, or from the growing numbers of warheads in the Pakistani and Indian arsenals. Informal, entrepreneurial networks have already emerged in the realm of nuclear technology, materials, and know-how. In 2004, revelations that the Pakistani scientist A. Q. Khan probably provided information about gas-centrifuges used to produce weapons-grade uranium and nuclear bomb designs to North Korea, Iraq, Iran, Libya, and Syria, a revelation that shocked the nonproliferation community.[20] Iran, a designated state sponsor of terrorism, is actively pursuing an indigenous nuclear weapons program. Many observers worry that the Iranian nuclear industry might become a clandestine source of fissile material for terrorists.

Biological Weapons

Biological weapons include bacteria, toxins, and viruses. Modern genetic engineering has already been used by Soviet and Russian scientists to modify naturally occurring diseases by increasing their virulence, resistance to antibiotics, or persistence on the battlefield and to improve their suitability as biological warfare agents.[21] Over a dozen states already possess biological agents. Because they can be manufactured in even run-of-the-mill medical laboratories and would produce a great psychological and political impact, many observers believe that biological agents will eventually be used by terrorists. An effort to use biological weapons to inflict mass casualties, however, would have to overcome several technical and operational barriers. Outbreak of a deadly epidemic would probably hit hardest among populations lacking state-of-the-art public health programs and medical facilities; as a result, terrorists might actually inflict relatively few casualties among targeted populations while killing thousands among their own supporters. Dispersing a biological agent so that it actually causes infection is not an easy task; an agent can be rendered harmless by household disinfectants or even sunlight. The fact that disease outbreaks are commonplace might reduce the psychological impact of a biological weapons attack, especially in parts of the world where reports of illness are unlikely to generate flashy international news coverage. A biological attack may not initially look any different than a flu outbreak, and as a result may not be of use to a terrorist group.

Chemical Weapons

Chemical weapons fall into several categories, depending on the manner in which they cause physical effects: choking, blister, blood, and nerve agents. In addition, there are reports of laboratories moving to develop so-called fourth-generation nerve agents with greater lethality and persistence. At least twenty-five states have chemical weapons or agents, and every advanced state has a large supply of toxic industrial chemicals that could be diverted to terrorist use. Terrorists also might sabotage chemical plants with deadly consequences. The 1984 industrial accident at the Union Carbide plant in Bhopal, India, for example, killed thousands of people exposed to methyl isocyanate (MIC), which acted as a choking agent. At Bhopal, the MIC wafted as a poisonous cloud from the chemical plant, but chemical weapons can be delivered from aircraft, commercially available sprayers, or even household containers. For example, Aum Shinrikyo simply punched holes in plastic bags full of sarin and left them in the Tokyo subway. Chemical weapons, however, are less likely to cause large numbers of casualties than nuclear weapons or biological agents because dangerous amounts of chemical agent actually have to come into contact with individuals to produce injury or death. Large quantities of chemical agent, dispersed in a measured way, also are required to be effective on the battlefield or in a terrorist attack, making this type of weapon hard to move, easy to spot and interdict, and relatively easy to defend against with proper protective clothing.

Chemical, biological, nuclear, and radiological weapons would provide terrorists with different capabilities and pose different operational challenges. Simple chemical weapons are relatively easy to procure, for example, but relatively large quantities of agent, dispersed in the right quantity over the targeted area, are needed to produce mass casualties. By contrast, nuclear weapons pose fewer challenges in terms of use, but they are extremely difficult to manufacture or procure on the black market. Terrorists also have an operational code and history that leads them to prefer certain types of weapons over others. Aum Shinrikyo experimented with biological agents, but chemical weapons were incorporated as part of its belief structure. Al-Qaeda has attempted to launch attacks using lethal chemical or non-contagious biological agents, but it has not yet used a radiological dispersal device or contagious biological agent, weapons it could probably acquire. Al-Qaeda has shown a preference for weapons that blow up in dramatic fashion, thereby garnering the attention of the world media. This implies that bin Laden may be unwilling to launch a chemical or biological attack. The jury is out on whether al-Qaeda would immediately use a nuclear weapon, should it get its hands on one, or save it for some other future political purpose, such as blackmail, deterrence, or to shore up an Islamic Caliphate.[22]

U.S. Responses to the Threat from WMD Terrorism

U.S. foreign and defense policy has slowly responded to the threat posed by terrorism and the emerging possibility that terrorists might try to acquire and employ WMD. The old and new threats posed by terrorism and U.S. strategies in response to these threats are summarized in Figure 6.1.

America's awareness of the need for greater capabilities to counter WMD threats was raised during the 1991 Persian Gulf War, when U.S. military forces were not properly prepared to counter the Iraqi chemical, biological, or nuclear threat, a danger that turned out to be more significant than anticipated. As a result, the Clinton administration launched the counterproliferation initiative, a DoD-centered program to identify and rectify known shortfalls in the nation's ability to meet and defeat WMD threats around the globe. The Clinton administration was primarily concerned with meeting the WMD threat on some future battlefield, although the possibility that terrorists might attempt to acquire and use these weapons was also beginning to influence defense planners in the 1990s.

The Clinton administration focused on reducing and countering WMD threats by launching several types of programs that addressed different aspects of the proliferation threat, something they hoped would have an impact on both state and nonstate actors. Nonproliferation and arms control were designed to prevent or roll back WMD programs. Cooperative threat reduction was an attempt to gain physical control, accounting, and security for the obsolete stockpile of Soviet Cold War weapons. Deterrence would deny the political-military aims of an adversary

	Third-Wave Terrorism	Fourth-Wave Terrorism
Threat Profile	• State sponsored • Local reach, regional cause • Low cost, high visibility targets • Examples: Hezbollah, PLO	• Independently funded, some state support • Global reach, global and regional issues • High cost, high visibility targets • Examples: al-Qaeda
U.S. Response Strategy	• Measured, long term • Theater engagement • Political pressure • Case-by-case action • Selective, surgical response	• Preemption, near- to mid-term • Deploy & deter forward • Coalition warfare • Intelligence, Special Operations, conventional forces • Total war against terrorism, using financial, political, and military instruments

Figure 6.1   Changing terrorist threat profile and U.S. responses.

following WMD use against U.S. forces, allies, or interests. If deterrence failed, passive defenses would allow the United States to sustain operations in a WMD environment, and counterforce capabilities would attempt to destroy an adversary's WMD before it could be used. National and theater missile defenses would defend U.S. and allied forces and populations from ballistic missiles that might be armed with WMD. The Clinton initiatives expanded the capability of the U.S. military to operate on a WMD battlefield, increased U.S. force protection capabilities against terrorists, and improved the ability of U.S. forces to retaliate following a chemical or biological attack.

In addition, in 1995 the Clinton administration released Presidential Decision Directive (PDD) 39, characterizing terrorism as a national security concern as well as a matter for law enforcement. It described four main program areas for dealing with the threat of terrorism: reducing vulnerabilities, deterrence, response, and preventing terrorists from acquiring WMD.[23] This change in perspective regarding terrorism was further codified in May 1998 with PDD 62 and the creation of a "Small Group" within the National Security Council whose mandate was to focus on the terrorism threat.[24]

Responses to Fourth-Wave Terrorism

The fourth wave of terrorism redirected efforts away from the battlefield and toward homeland security and the interdiction of potential terrorist supply networks. The Bush administration arrived in early 2001 with a mandate that led them to develop national security policies that reflected both continuity and change from the Clinton administration's programs. Continuity was found in its comprehensive strategy that mirrored the preceding administration's policies. These included counterproliferation efforts to deter and defend against a threat before it was unleashed, and the requirement to integrate counterproliferation in military transformation and homeland defense. It also included strengthened nonproliferation efforts, including increased emphasis on coalition interdiction, such as the Proliferation Security Initiative, rather than universal, formal initiatives outlawing the possession of or trade in contraband weapons or agents. Continuity was also evidenced by the administration's decision to keep counterterrorism expertise within the National Security Council that President Clinton had set up with PDD 62. In the aftermath of the September 11 attacks, the administration also created the Department of Homeland Security, charged with focusing U.S. domestic efforts on preventing and coping with the consequences of a homeland WMD incident.

The shift in Bush administration policies reflected official beliefs that the threat had changed. WMD was now seen as a weapon of choice for an adversary, rather than a weapon of last resort. This meant that deterrence also had to change to reflect the new reality, and a new paradigm of preemptive measures and preventive war was required in order to block nuclear terrorism. These changes can best be understood in three categories: the global war on terrorism, homeland security, and counterproliferation.[25]

The global war on terrorism, as enunciated by President George W. Bush in his January 2002 State of the Union address, is a U.S.-led effort to seek and destroy terrorist groups while simultaneously addressing the root causes of terrorism. It includes a much-increased effort to gather timely intelligence, disrupt terrorist operations, block financial flows to terrorists, deter states from supporting terrorists, eliminate safe havens for terrorists, and destroy terrorist networks. In this way it blocks nuclear terrorism by eliminating the demand for WMD through the elimination of the groups themselves.

The new emphasis on homeland security is an attempt to use active and passive defenses to prevent and, if necessary, mitigate the consequences of a WMD attack on the United States. Its measures include cooperative international law enforcement and intelligence sharing, domestic customs and border security, federal, state, and local law enforcement, the Nuclear Emergency Search Team, the Chemical and Biological Incident Response Force, incident management, and response and recovery. The Department of Homeland Security and U.S. Northern Command share responsibility for various aspects of these programs.

The third major thrust for blocking terrorist WMD use is found in the more aggressive U.S. policies of counterproliferation and cooperative threat reduction. This includes such aspects as smuggling interdiction, finding stable jobs for former Soviet nuclear scientists, and when necessary, active nonproliferation through the use of offensive military force.

The area of emphasis by the Bush administration that raised the greatest public and international concern is that of preemption and preventive war, although it is difficult to characterize the global war on terror as a preventive war because al-Qaeda and its allies clearly landed the opening blows.[26] According to this policy, when diplomacy and deterrence fail, military action may be required to effect regime change in a country that poses an imminent WMD threat and cannot be deterred. This policy refers primarily to rogue state regimes, but there were obvious implications for terrorist groups, as well. America's willingness to remove the Taliban in Afghanistan and Saddam Hussein in Iraq sent strong signals to the rest of the world that actors with WMD would not be tolerated. Libya, for example, may have heeded that message, giving up its WMD programs and opening its borders to international inspectors in December 2003.

Interdiction is another measure that has been emphasized by the Bush administration. The Proliferation Security Initiative (PSI) is a U.S.-led effort to interdict the transfer of weapons of mass destruction, their delivery systems, and related materials to or from states of proliferation concern. An international body was created in September 2003 to enforce the PSI. Over 70 states now support PSI and its statement of interdiction principles, applying laws already on the books in cooperative and innovative ways. This group has since conducted several successful interceptions of WMD or precursor materials and delivery means on the high seas.

PSI is not a traditional treaty; it is a partnership of like-minded countries acting proactively to enforce national and international laws and deter, disrupt, and prevent state-sponsored WMD and missile proliferation and to interdict clandestine trade by entrepreneurs in materials and equipment related to WMD.

In addition to PSI's efforts on the demand side, there are several multinational organizations that work to establish and enforce supply side controls on the proliferation of nuclear, chemical, or missile technology, materials, and knowledge. These include the Wassenaar Arrangement (a 33-nation group providing export controls on conventional munitions and dual-use goods and technologies), the IAEA Nuclear Supplier's Group (an informal group of 39 states that seeks to control the export of nuclear-related materials and technologies), and the Australia Group (a 32-nation group organized to monitor and control the trade in sensitive materials and technologies useful in the development of chemical and biological weapons). These groups do not necessarily work in concert, but they have overlapping memberships, and serve as an effective corollary to the demand-side groups that deal directly with the proliferant states, such as the International Atomic Energy Agency and its nuclear safeguards programs and ad hoc United Nations committees, such as the UN Special Commission on Iraq.[27] The United States has taken the lead in designating entities and persons engaging in proliferation activities and support, just as it has in tracking and identifying sources of terrorist financing. In June 2005 President Bush signed an Executive Order authorizing the government to freeze assets involved in WMD proliferation.[28]

One of the largest international efforts to date has been the G-8 Global Partnership Against the Spread of Weapons and Materials of Mass Destruction. In 2002 the United States and its global partners committed up to $20 billion ($10 billion from the United States, and $10 billion in matching funds from the other seven members) dedicated to responding to the WMD threat. In addition, there are a number of U.S.-initiated programs dealing not only with Russia and the former Soviet states, but other nations of concern around the world. Examples of these programs include the Global Threat Reduction Initiative to reduce and secure fissile materials worldwide; the Second Line of Defense and Megaports programs to install radiation monitors at major seaports, airports, and border crossings; and "redirection" programs in Libya and Iraq to provide alternative employment for former weapons scientists and engineers.[29]

America's counterforce capabilities have been significantly upgraded in recent years and tested on the battlefields of Kosovo, Afghanistan, and Iraq. At the same time, the 2001 Nuclear Posture Review called for changes to U.S. nuclear forces and policy to make those weapons more relevant to modern threats, thereby enhancing their deterrent capabilities. The new U.S. military strategy, highlighted in the 2001 Quadrennial Defense Review and reiterated in the 2001 Nuclear Posture Review, emphasized a fourfold approach to dealing with threats to U.S. security: assurance, dissuasion, deterrence, and defeat. These concepts have been further enshrined in the 2002 National Security Strategy of the United States, the 2002 National Strategy to Combat Weapons of Mass Destruction, the 2003 National Strategy to Combat Terrorism, and the 2004 National Military Strategy.

The National Strategy to Combat WMD united for the first time all the elements of national power, including diplomacy, intelligence, law enforcement, and the military, into one document reflecting a coherent strategy. It emphasizes the three pillars of U.S. efforts to deal with adversaries armed with WMD: counterproliferation, nonproliferation, and consequence management. Building on those concepts, the national strategy identified four cross-cutting functions that will prove critical to combating WMD: improved intelligence collection and analysis, research and development, bilateral and multilateral cooperation, and tailored strategies against hostile states and terrorists.[30]

Dealing with the Threat By Denying Access to Materials

Graham Allison, a leading expert on WMD proliferation, proposes a simple yet challenging solution to the problem of dealing with WMD terrorism. He focuses on the two types of WMD that have the greatest destructive capability: nuclear and biological weapons. Although in his mind a terrorist group cannot be deterred from using these weapons once they get them, he is equally convinced that preventing them from acquiring a nuclear weapon is simple: control the earth's stockpiles of fissile material and terrorists will not be able to construct or acquire a nuclear weapon. Because these materials do not occur in nature, and have only been created by a handful of states, all that is required is to develop a program to ensure that nuclear proliferation, and hence nuclear terrorism, is stopped at the source. As Senator John Kerry put it during the 2004 presidential election campaign, "No material. No bombs. No nuclear terrorism."[31]

Allison's three steps to achieve this objective are, first, to ensure that all governments securely lock up all their enriched uranium and plutonium so it cannot be seized, sold, or diverted to a terrorist. Second, all states must commit to a policy that precludes the production of any new fissile material. And third, states must be willing to destroy excess stocks of such materials whenever they can.[32]

The United States can make supporting these three goals a core objective of its national security strategy. This would include expanding the existing Nunn-Lugar cooperative threat reduction programs that already exist, with varying levels of success, with Russia; signing the Fissile Materials Cutoff Treaty and developing a plan for ensuring that no new states develop fissile materials—including Iran and North Korea; and eliminating surplus Cold War nuclear weaponry and encouraging Russia to do the same.

As for a biological attack, Allison suggests that a rigorous public health response capability, coupled with advance stockpiling of key medications and selective immunizations, could minimize the chances of a biological attack becoming an epidemic.[33]

Concluding Comments

Terrorism has evolved over time, reflecting the ideologies, organizational preferences, and technological sophistication of those who attempt to kill the innocent to achieve their political objectives. This evolution is not necessarily linear, but fourth-generation terrorists do seem unusually interested in generating mass casualty events. Future attacks could thus involve WMD, with levels of casualties and destruction heretofore never seen within the United States. But it is not a foregone conclusion that terrorists will want to use these weapons; there are good reasons to believe that a WMD incident could prove highly counterproductive from their perspective. As terrorists have already discovered, technical and operational challenges also have to be overcome if WMD is to be used to its fullest effect.

The evolution of U.S. counterproliferation and counterterror policy reflects the changing threat posed by WMD. The Clinton administration, largely responding to the discovery that Saddam Hussein's regime in Iraq possessed a significant chemical weapons capability and advanced biological and nuclear weapons programs, focused on the proliferation of WMD to state actors and its potential use on the battlefield. In the aftermath of the September 11 attacks on the World Trade Center and the Pentagon, the Bush administration redirected U.S. counterproliferation and nonproliferation programs to target clandestine traffic in WMD and to prevent these weapons from falling into the hands of terrorists. The threat of WMD terrorism has been identified and the Bush administration's response to this challenge to date appears pragmatic and reasonable. But in the aftermath of a future terrorist attack using WMD, their efforts will not look so reasonable, and people will justifiably ask the damning question, "Why didn't we do more to prevent this?"

A successful end to the global war on terror will require long-term international and national commitments. It will undoubtedly last a generation, during which time more attacks on the U.S. homeland may occur. Dealing with this potential threat therefore requires new ways of thinking, and new ways of coordinated interaction between national agencies and between states in the international system. As Wehling and Tamsett note in their chapter, prevention and response strategies also need to be better integrated to reduce the threat posed by nuclear and radiological weapons. Current policies are beginning to secure old stockpiles of WMD, but a long-term commitment will be needed to monitor clandestine terrorist networks to make sure that they cannot acquire or use chemical, biological, radiological, or nuclear weapons.

Endnotes

1. Ashton B. Carter, "How to Counter WMD," Foreign Affairs 83, no. 5 (September/ October 2004), 72–85.

2. National Commission on Terrorist Attacks upon the United States, The 9/11 Commission Report (New York: W.W. Norton & Co. 2004), 174–179.

3. Brian Jenkins, The Potential for Nuclear Terrorism, RAND Report P-5876 (Santa Monica, CA: RAND, 1977), 8.

4. Jessica Stern, "Terrorist Motivations and Unconventional Weapons," in Planning the Unthinkable, ed. Peter Lavoy, Scott D. Sagan, and James J. Wirtz (Ithaca, NY: Cornell University Press, 2000), 202–229.

5. Glen M. Segell, "Terrorism: London Public Transport—July 7, 2005," Strategic Insights 4, no. 8 (August 2005), www.ccc.nps.navy.mil/si/2005/Aug/segellAug05.asp.

6. Three plots were directed against targets inside the United States. One involved Jose Padilla's interest in launching an attack with a radiological device; the others involved the use of hijacked airliners to attack West and East Coast targets. See Peter Baker and Susan B. Glasser, "Bush Says 10 Plots by Al Qaeda Were Foiled," Washington Post, October 7, 2005, p. A1.

7. William Lind, Keith Nightengale, John Schmitt, Joseph Sutton, and Gary I. Wilson, "The Changing Face of War: Into the Fourth Generation," Marine Corps Gazette (October 1989): 22–26.

8. David Fromkin, "The Strategy of Terrorism," Foreign Affairs 53, no. 4 (July 1975): 683–698.

9. Phillip E. Devine and Robert J. Rafalko, "International Terrorism," On Terror, Annals of the American Academy of Political and Social Science 463 (September 1982): 49.

10. David C. Rapoport, "The Fourth Wave: September 11 in the History of Terrorism," Current History (December 2001): 419–424; and David Rapoport, "Terrorism," in Encyclopedia of Violence, Peace, and Conflict, vol. 3, ed. Lester R. Kurtz and Jennifer E. Turpin (London: Academic Press, 1999), 497–510.

11. Richard Shultz, "The Limits of Terrorism in Insurgency Warfare: The Case of the Viet Cong," Polity 11, no. 1 (Autumn 1978): 67–91.

12. Douglas Pike, PAVN: People's Army of Vietnam (Novato, CA: Presidio Press, 1986).

13. Brian Jenkins, Countering al Qaeda: An Appreciation of the Situation and Suggestions for Strategy (Santa Monica, CA: RAND, 2002), 6.

14. Audrey Kurth Cronin, "Terrorist Motivations for Chemical and Biological Weapons Use: Placing the Threat in Context," Defense & Security Analysis 20, no. 4 (December, 2004): 317.

15. Ahmed Rashid, "The Taliban: Exporting Extremism," Foreign Affairs 78, no. 6 (November/December, 1999): 22–35.

16. Lewis A. Dunn, Can al Qaeda be Deterred from Using Nuclear Weapons? Center for the Study of Weapons of Mass Destruction, Occasional Paper #3 (Washington, D.C.: National Defense University, July 2005).

17. Cronin, "Terrorist Motivations," 317.

18. Ibid., 315–316.

19. Dunn, Can al Qaeda be Deterred, 4–5.

20. Christopher Clary, "A. Q. Khan and the Limits of the Non-proliferation Regime," Disarmament Forum, no. 4 (2004): 33–42; D. Albright and C. Hinderstein, "Unraveling the A. Q. Khan and Future Proliferation Networks," The Washington Quarterly 28, no. 2 (2005): 111–128.

21. Ken Alibek with Stephen Handelman, Biohazard (New York: Delta, 1999).

22. Dunn, Can al Qaeda be Deterred, 4–5.

23. "Counterterrorism Before 9/11," 9/11 Commission Staff Statement No. 8, reprinted in James F. Hoge, Jr. and Gideon Rose, Understanding the War on Terror (New York: Council on Foreign Relations, 2005), 166.

24. Ibid.

25. The general organizing concept for this structure is expanded in Matthew Bunn, Anthony Wier, and John P. Holdren, Controlling Nuclear Warheads and Materials: A Report Card and Action Plan (Cambridge, MA: Project on Managing the Atom, Harvard University, March 2003).

26. James J. Wirtz and James Russell, "Preventive War and Preemption: Reassessing the U.S. Policy Toward Iraq and the War on Terrorism," Non Proliferation Review 10, no. 1 (Spring 2003): 113–123.

27. See Jeffrey A. Larsen and James M. Smith, Historical Dictionary of Arms Control and Disarmament (Lanham, MD: Scarecrow Press, 2005).

28. Robert G. Joseph, "The Bush Administration Approach to Combating the Proliferation of Weapons of Mass Destruction," Remarks to the Carnegie International Nonproliferation Conference, November 7, 2005, U.S. Department of State, at www.state.gov/t/us/rm/56584.htm.

29. Ibid.

30. Ibid.

31. Kerry quoted in Carter, "How to Counter WMD," p. 58.

32. Carter, "How to Counter WMD."

33. Ibid.

Chapter 7

Nuclear and Radioactive Threats to Homeland Security

Prevention and Response

Fred L. Wehling and Jeremy Tamsett

The authors focus on the nuclear and radiological threat posed by terrorist groups. After a review of the ways and means by which these groups could acquire and use such devastating weaponry, they consider how, among other factors, intelligence, port security, and the role of the Department of Homeland Security and other agencies fit into a strategic plan for dealing with this real-and-present threat. Given this analysis, they offer ten priorities for a national homeland security strategy. Wehling and Tamsett underscore that leadership at the political level as well as the formation of long-term collaborative relationships between working-level officials across institutional boundaries will be especially crucial for integrating prevention with response.

The resemblance of the collapse of the World Trade Center to the mushroom cloud of a nuclear explosion buttressed the burgeoning perception[1] that WMD could become a weapon of choice for terrorists. This new concern contributed to the creation of the U.S. Department of Homeland Security (DHS). DHS, along with other federal agencies, has spent billions of dollars to prevent and respond to the use of nuclear weapons or radioactive materials by terrorists, and nuclear and radiological incidents figure prominently in the National Response Plan (NRP). Do these efforts represent an adequate response to the nature and magnitude of nuclear and radioactive threats? Is a comprehensive strategy in place, or are there gaps that must be addressed? Our answer to these questions is that, although preparations for responding to nuclear and radiological emergencies are well underway, current efforts at preventing these incidents have significant deficiencies. With regard to radiological attacks, which in general represent high-probability, low-consequence events, this situation may be tenable, though action is still required in some areas. However, further action to prevent low-probability, high-consequence nuclear events is urgently needed.

This chapter begins its analysis of the current state of strategies for countering nuclear and radioactive terrorism by briefly characterizing the nature and severity of nuclear and radiological threats. A review of strategy and capabilities for meeting these threats then highlights the strengths and weaknesses of current approaches to the problem. We then use this review to recommend a "top 10" list of priorities for preventing and defending against nuclear and radioactive terror attacks. The potentially catastrophic consequences of a nuclear attack lead us to put urgently needed steps for preventing nuclear terrorism at the top of the list, but upgrading of capabilities to assess and mitigate radiological hazards should also receive high priority. The objective throughout is not to criticize current policies, leadership, or organizations, but to suggest how formulating a comprehensive strategy and implementing a well-considered set of priorities can improve the U.S. national capacity for protection against the well-publicized but still misunderstood threats of nuclear and radiological attack.

Characterizing Nuclear and Radioactive Threats

Possible motivations for terrorist groups to attack with nuclear or radioactive weapons, and potential pathways for acquiring and using these weapons, have been extensively described in open literature.[2] Our objective here is to clearly delineate the similarities and differences between these threats in order to show that although approaches for responding to both may be very similar, effective strategies for prevention must be radically different.

Terrorist attacks with nuclear weapons are the epitome of a low-probability, high consequence threat. While there is widespread agreement that the probability of a terrorist organization successfully acquiring and using a nuclear weapon to attack

U.S. territory is very low, the devastating impact of such an attack is the very definition of mass destruction. Al-Qaeda heads the list of terrorist organizations with motivations to use nuclear weapons not only because of its history of mass-casualty attacks and stated intentions to carry out more such strikes, but also because of reported attempts to purchase nuclear weapons from the former Soviet states and the capture of a diagram of a crude nuclear explosive from al-Qaeda affiliates in Afghanistan.[3] The simplicity of the captured diagram betrayed a lack of technical capability at the time it was prepared, but also emphasizes that a fairly unsophisticated improvised nuclear device (IND) constructed with highly enriched uranium (HEU) could produce a kiloton-range nuclear explosive yield.[4]

The explosive power of an IND could approach that of the nuclear weapons dropped on Hiroshima and Nagasaki and would have similarly destructive effects, including fatalities measured in the tens or hundreds of thousands if detonated in a densely populated area, and widespread radioactive contamination. An actual nuclear warhead would have even greater power to cause mass destruction.[5] Nuclear terrorism would therefore appeal only to terrorists desirous of causing appalling loss of human life, unconcerned about indiscriminate civilian casualties, and untroubled by large-scale environmental damage.

Obtaining and detonating a military nuclear weapon, most of which are protected by security devices such as Permissive Action Links (PALs) and/or require specific safing, arming, fusing, and firing procedures (SAFF), would present formidable challenges to even the most capable, highly motivated, and generously funded terrorist groups. While very unlikely, this possibility cannot be completely ruled out because serious concerns exist about the security of some nuclear weapons in the arsenals of Russia (particularly tactical weapons), Pakistan, and other countries. The possibility for terrorists to build and explode an IND must be considered much greater. For a major terrorist organization, such as the larger members of the al-Qaeda network, the only significant barrier to the construction and use of an IND is the acquisition of enough fissile material such as highly enriched uranium or, possibly, plutonium. Unfortunately, in many places around the world, this barrier is not high enough. An estimated total of 600 tons of highly enriched uranium was either in use or in storage in Russia alone in 2004 (not counting the material inside nuclear weapons), only 26 percent of which has been protected by comprehensive security upgrades installed through U.S.-Russian cooperative programs.[6] The U.S. Government Accountability Office (GAO) reported in 2004 that 20 kg or more of HEU were used at 128 civilian research reactors in 40 countries,[7] many of which have "no more security than a night watchman and a chain-link fence."[8] About 50 kg of HEU (enriched to 90% ^{235}U or greater) would be sufficient for an IND.[9] If a terrorist organization could somehow obtain enough fissile material, the level of resources and effort required to assemble an IND and detonate it in a U.S. city would be much less than what was needed to carry out the attacks of September 11, 2001.[10] Preventing terrorists from gaining access to HEU and plutonium useable in nuclear explosives is thus the highest priority and most effective means for combating nuclear terrorism.

In sharp contrast to the instant massive destruction of a nuclear attack, terrorist attacks with radiological agents could occur on a small scale, and might have effects so subtle that they would not be detected for months or years after the incident. There are three basic modes for terrorist attack using radioactive material (substances emitting ionizing radiation, including alpha particles, beta particles, and gamma rays).[11] The simplest is the use of a radiation emission device (RED) to expose persons, or even a single individual, to ionizing radiation from a point source. An example would be the emplacement of a cobalt-60 pellet in a washroom in an office building. An individual entering the area for only a short time might be unlikely to receive a harmful dose of radiation, but people who frequent the area could, over time, receive harmful or even fatal doses.[12] In this mode of attack, casualties might not be noticed, or attributed to radiation exposure, until years after the incident, when they might appear as a mysterious cancer cluster. At this point, the terrorists could plausibly claim responsibility for the attack.

A second mode of radiological attack involves the use of a radiological dispersal device (RDD) or "dirty bomb." RDDs use explosives to disperse a radiological agent over a wide area. Depending on the amount and type of radiological agent used, an RDD could contaminate a large area with radioactive material, cause casualties through external exposure or inhalation or ingestion of radioactive material, and induce psychological casualties through fear and panic.[13] Radioactive contamination could also require evacuation and decontamination of the affected area, likely leading to both short- and long-term economic damage. While the biological effects of an RDD detonation could take days, weeks, or even years to appear, the psychological impact would be immediate. The third mode of radiological terrorism, an attack on a nuclear power plant or other facility to breach containment and release radioactive material, would have similar effects, with the additional impact of damage or closure of the facility and, potentially, the economic and psychological shock of a major blackout.[14]

The wide range of modes and effects of radiological terrorism make these forms of attack potentially useful to a wide variety of groups and organizations. Terrorists could calibrate the physical and biological effects of an attack to suit their tactical and political objectives by using more or less radioactive material or causing exposure over a wide or a carefully defined target. Although radioactive materials are widely used in medicine, industry, research, and many other applications, only a small fraction of the millions of radioactive sources in commercial use pose serious risks for use in radiological terrorism due to their portability, dispersability, and high levels of radioactivity. Nevertheless, these high-risk isotopes (including americium-241, californium-252, cesium-137, cobalt-60, iridium-192, plutonium-238, and strontium-90) can be found in hospitals, laboratories, and industrial facilities in any major city, or could be smuggled into the United States with little difficulty.[15] Moreover, an unknown number of "orphan sources" have dropped out of regulatory control, unaccounted for or disposed of improperly. The wide availability of radioactive materials and ease of using radiological agents in terrorist attacks makes prevention of radiological attack extremely difficult. However, the ability of first responders and public health workers to detect radiological agents, recognize and treat injuries from radiation exposure, and decontaminate affected areas when provided with adequate training, equipment, and support allow development of a menu of options for both short- and long-term responses to radiological attack.[16]

Both prevention and response play important roles in meeting the threat of nuclear and radiological terrorism. However, the relative scarcity of the special materials and expertise needed to perpetrate a nuclear attack makes prevention the key to combating nuclear terrorism. Conversely, the wide availability and ease of use of radiological agents points to response as the cornerstone of the fight against radiological terrorism. While one prominent scholar[17] has called nuclear terrorism "the ultimate preventable catastrophe," radiological terrorism appears neither catastrophic nor preventable. As we will see, current U.S. strategy for homeland security does not always reflect these priorities.

Current National Prevention and Response Strategies

It has become increasingly evident in the post–September 11 environment that reliance on deterrence alone to forestall threats to U.S. homeland security from non-state actors is problematic at best. The formulation and implementation of robust antiterrorism measures, which are nonmilitary ways of countering or dissuading terrorism, play a key role in helping to prevent and respond to nuclear and radiological terrorism. Examples of current antiterrorism measures include increased protection of global nuclear power facilities and efforts to secure radiological materials potentially available to terrorists. However, antiterrorism measures can also encompass lesser known methods, such as increasing investments in advanced radiation detection systems, public education campaigns about the dangers posed by radiation and, concurrently, effective public risk communication, as well as improved crisis and consequence management techniques.

An RDD or IND could be detonated in virtually any location, and among the likely targets are large population centers where the element of surprise would increase the lethality of such an attack. Coordination among local, state or regional, and national agencies responsible for disaster response is critical for treating casualties, containing and controlling the area of destruction, and limiting the spread of radioactive contamination. For this reason, any homeland security strategy should be *national,* and not just federal, in nature.[18] This means that the federal government must empower states and local authorities to establish a sense of ownership as stakeholders in the formulation and implementation of policy as it relates to prevention, preparedness for, and response to a terrorist incident involving radioactive weapons.

Intelligence

The intelligence component of a national strategy to counter the threats posed by nuclear and radiological terrorism requires international cooperation. The timely exchange of important information, along with the occasional pooling of sensitive resources, can be used to thwart or disrupt potential terrorist activity. Many formal and informal agreements are in place between various members of the U.S. intelligence community (IC) and the security services of foreign governments. For example, the intelligence services of several European countries, including France, Britain, and Germany, work closely with the U.S. IC to ensure that relevant data is disseminated and back channels of communication are open and functioning properly.

On the domestic front, the Intelligence Reform and Terrorism Prevention Act of 2004 created not only the Office of the Director of National Intelligence (DNI), but also the National Counterterrorism Center (NCTC).[19] The NCTC draws upon the analytical capabilities of the preexisting, multi-agency Terrorist Threat Integration Center (TTIC), and seeks to expand its ability to assimilate and disseminate information to decision makers in a timely manner.

Other agencies are also enhancing their intelligence-gathering capabilities. For example, the Federal Bureau of Investigation (FBI) bolstered its counterterrorism efforts through the creation of an intelligence analysis unit in 2005. DHS created the Domestic Nuclear Detection Office (DNDO) in 2005, with an operating budget for 2006 more than double the amount spent on nuclear and radiation detection and prevention in 2005.[20] The DNDO had an operating budget of $500 million dollars in FY2007, a $163.6 million increase in funding over FY2006.[21] The purpose of the DNDO is to coordinate and build intelligence-sharing linkages between local, state, and federal agencies to better coordinate efforts in preventing and responding to nuclear or radiological emergencies. DHS has also created an Office of Intelligence and Analysis headed by an assistant secretary of homeland security and a chief intelligence officer who report directly to the secretary. This office is intended to be a clearing-house for intelligence collected by other government agencies related to homeland security. Once the office has analyzed the intelligence, it is tasked with disseminating that intelligence to local and state jurisdictions for further action. It remains to be seen, however, how sensitive information will be shared effectively with individuals at the state level who lack security clearances.[22]

Port Security

Detection of nuclear materials *before* they are placed on ships at their point of origin is crucial to the implementation of a strategy to prevent nuclear terrorism. A better tactic is to secure nuclear materials abroad and prevent shipments from leaving their respective home ports with deadly cargo than it is to deal with them once they have reached U.S. shores. Programs like the Megaports Initiative, overseen by the Department of Energy (DOE), and the Container Security Initiative (CSI), administered by DHS, are both designed to improve the screening and inspection of cargo for nuclear and radioactive materials at foreign ports before entering the United States. These programs have resulted in improved information sharing between U.S. and foreign customs operations.

There are three obstacles that must be overcome if international cooperation is to be improved and the goal of installing radiation detection devices at the world's largest twenty ports by 2010 is to become a reality.[23] For example, while it currently takes only around five seconds to screen trucks carrying containers unloaded from ships at the Port of Los Angeles, if radioactive materials are detected, more time is needed for a more thorough inspection to identify the source and determine the legitimacy of its presence and intended use.[24] Consequently, port authorities around the world are hesitant to sign agreements with DOE to place detectors at their ports because of concerns about a potential slowdown in commerce. Nevertheless, if containers are not scanned for dangerous cargo at their point of origin, it may be too late once the containers arrive in the United States. The problem is that containers are not individually scanned as they are unloaded off the ships; rather, the containers may sit at their destination in a U.S. port for hours or days before they are loaded onto the trucks and driven through the radiation portals. This simply ensures that a nuclear weapon or dirty bomb would not be able to leave the port, posing a serious problem if the intended target is the port itself.

The second challenge present in the detection of radiation is the ability of the personnel at the scene to know what types of materials at what levels pose a hazard and, hence, warrant further investigation and possibly a threat. Finally, if the United States installs radiation detection monitors at all official border crossings and at all foreign and domestic commercial ports, it is possible that all this will do is deter terrorists from bringing radioactive materials through commercial ports or official border crossings, but will not prevent them from crossing into the United States through unmonitored access routes or from using smaller watercraft to arrive on U.S. shores at noncommercial ports.

DHS Role in Preparedness and Response

The secretary of homeland security has budgetary authority over homeland security appropriations. Under the rubric of "threat, vulnerability, and consequence," DHS allocates fiduciary resources to local and state governments based on conclusions drawn in threat and risk assessments. Essentially, by linking threats with consequences, DHS prioritizes where money and training should be used to enhance the effectiveness of implementing national preparedness priorities. These priorities are outlined in the National Strategy for Homeland Security, and have been further iterated in the December 2004 National Response Plan (NRP).[25]

The National Response Plan (NRP) was created in December 2004 by Homeland Security Presidential Directive 8 (HSDP-8). It called for a single document to provide guidance for an all-hazards approach to disaster preparedness, response, and prevention.[26] The NRP incorporates and supersedes five preexisting plans; the FRP, National Contingency Plan (NCP), Interagency Domestic Terrorism Concept of Operations Plan (CONPLAN), and the Federal Radiological Emergency Response Plan (FRERP).[27] The NRP places an emphasis on planning, preparedness, and response at the local and state levels through the application of the National Incident Management System (NIMS), created by Homeland Security Presidential Directive 5 in February 2003.[28] The director of operations coordination is tasked with consolidating the efforts of the interagency process to conduct joint operations as well as coordinate and manage activities related to incident management.

The Office of Grants and Training (G&T) is the nexus of preparedness at DHS and is responsible for providing funding, training, and guidance to state and local authorities in the effort to help them prepare for, and respond to, terrorist incidents, including WMD disasters in accordance with the NRP.[29] G&T, formerly the Office for Domestic Preparedness (ODP), is headed by an assistant secretary who reports to the DHS undersecretary for preparedness, Directorate for Preparedness.[30] Under the auspices of HSPD-8, the Office of Grants & Training has awarded some $8.6 billion since 9/11 under its mandate to help local and state governments respond to incidents "involving chemical, biological, radiological, nuclear and explosive (CBRNE) incidents."[31]

Response to Nuclear and Radiological Incidents

Under the NRP, DHS is responsible for federal government coordination in the event of a radiological or nuclear incident.[32] DHS responds primarily through Regional Assistance Committees (RAC) comprised of regional DHS/FEMA personnel and attended by representatives from state emergency offices. In addition, DHS has established a Federal Radiological Policy Coordinating Committee (FRPCC), providing a conduit for the development and coordination of policies and procedures related to planning, preparedness, and response to radiological attacks with state and local governments.[33]

Depending on the source of the nuclear material used in the incident, other federal agencies may have lead operational and jurisdictional responsibilities, but DHS would remain in all cases the principal federal coordinator. For example, if an RDD or IND incident involved materials or facilities owned or operated by the Nuclear Regulatory Commission (NRC) or the Department of Defense (DoD), the controlling agency would assume responsibility for responding to the incident.

In all other cases, the Department of Energy assumes primary responsibility with many sub-tier federal agencies operating under its authority.[34]

During the response phase, three teams assembled from federal and local resources are deployed to the scene of the incident. The Interagency Modeling and Atmospheric Assessment Center (IMAAC) is responsible for "production, coordination, and dissemination of consequence predictions for an airborne hazardous material release." An Advisory Team for Environment, Food, and Health ("Advisory Team") provides advice on radiation protective measures. The Advisory Team is comprised primarily of personnel from the Center for Disease Control and Prevention (CDC), the Environmental Protection Agency (EPA), and the Food and Drug Administration (FDA). Lastly, a Federal Radiological Assessment and Monitoring Center (FRAMC) is set up near the scene to coordinate the efforts of IMAAC and the Advisory Team.[35]

At the appropriate time, determined on a case-by-case basis with state and local governments as well as DHS, the EPA will take over from DHS, or from whatever agency has lead authority depending on the circumstances as discussed previously to address clean-up issues. The Department of Health and Human Services (DHHS) is responsible for victim decontamination and long-term population monitoring after an event. This means that DHHS has responsibility to oversee the prescribing of medications needed in counter radiation, and administration of overall care of victims, including emergency personnel.[36]

Federal Guidance on Radiation

On January 3, 2006, the Department of Homeland Security released the "Application of Protective Action Guides for Radiological Dispersal Devices (RDD) and Improvised Nuclear Device (IND) Incidents."[37] This document, prepared by DHS, DHHS, DOE, DOD, NRC, EPA, Department of Commerce, and the Department of Labor, provides for a unified federal mechanism "to support decisions about actions that may need to be taken to protect the public when responding to or recovering from an RDD or IND incident."[38] Specifically, it applies the EPA's 1992 Protective Action Guide (PAG), written only to address nuclear accidents, and terrorist events involving radioactive materials.

The 2006 Guidance delineates three phases of response to an RDD or IND incident; the first phase directs emergency workers to "retrieve and care for victims, stabilize the scene, and public health protective actions (including sheltering-in-place or evacuation)." The second phase focuses on recovery and a "return to some state of normal activities," while the third phase is concerned with full recovery and cleanup.[39]

Prior to 2006, the 2003 Federal Guidance on Radiation contained the latest publicly available information on upper and lower boundaries of what were considered relatively safe and dangerous levels of radiation exposure following a nuclear or radiological incident.[40] The 2003 Guidance, produced jointly by DHS, DHHS, and the Department of Veterans Affairs, was written primarily as a guide for first responders and health care professionals to know how to respond to victims in the aftermath of an RDD explosion.[41]

There are several differences between the 2006 and 2003 Guidance documents. For example, the 2003 Guide stated that there were no upper boundaries of safe radiation levels for occupational emergency workers that limit their response to life-threatening emergencies. The Guidance went on to say, however, that for all non-life-threatening circumstances, first responders could enter an area if dose rates were around 10 rem/hr or less and should leave the area, unless attempting to save lives, if that dose rate exceeded 100 rem/hr.[42] The 2006 Guidance, on the other hand, because of the "broad range of potential impacts" from an RDD or IND, establishes no definitive "safe" boundaries for exposure. Emergency workers are advised, however, to limit their exposure to 5 rem/hr "or greater under exceptional circumstances." Radiation parameters for public exposure, in part designed to help authorities decide whether to order those affected to evacuate or shelter in place, are exactly the same figure, between 1 and 5 rem/hr.

Drawbacks to the Current Guidance

Operational Guidelines that implement the 2006 PAG and establish boundaries for acceptable levels of radiation contamination/exposure for a range of seven groups of property types are still under development. The Operational Guidelines are being developed by the Consequence Management Subgroup (CMS) of the RDD/IND Preparedness Working Group and will be published for public review on a roll-out basis on the Department of Energy's Web site.[43]

Survey of Public Resources for Nuclear and Radiological Terrorism Threats

The most widely known information source geared towards preparedness is Ready. gov, a DHS-sponsored Web site. The primary purpose of this site is to fulfill DHS's mandate to "educate the public, on a continuing basis, about how to be prepared in case of a national emergency."[44] While Ready.gov does have two sections dedicated to radiological threats, "Nuclear Blasts," and "Radiation Threats," no discussion exists about what radiation is or how it can affect the human body. The information provided states in general that one should "try to limit exposure."[45] FEMA has produced a slightly more detailed, all-hazards preparedness guide titled, "Are you Ready?" This guide, like Ready.gov, has two sections that cover nuclear blasts and RDDs, but provides no information about types of radiation (alpha, beta, and gamma), how each one interacts with the body, and what levels are considered safe or dangerous.[46]

In addition to clear recommendations from the government on what to do in case of a nuclear or radiological attack, people need to be told *why* they need to take certain actions and what the likely outcomes or consequences will be if they do not follow these guidelines. For example, it would be helpful for the public to know that first responders will treat conventional medical traumas before radiation victims are attended to. The reason is that it may take up to an hour for those exposed to near-fatal doses of radiation to express symptoms of ARS, such as vomiting, and those exposed to lower doses of radiation may not show symptoms for hours, days, or even weeks later, if ever.[47] If victims of an RDD or IND attack are not aware of this fact, it is likely that hundreds or thousands, or possibly tens of thousands in the case of a nuclear blast, will rush to area hospitals seeking treatment for radiation exposure when in all but the most severe cases, as long as people have been properly decontaminated and are safely removed from the vicinity of the incident, there is no justification for immediate radiation treatment.[48] Most individuals exposed to low doses of radiation, if they suffer any health effects at all, will recover naturally over time.[49]

Misperceptions about the danger that radiation poses stem from conflicting views on the risks of radiation exposure. Lack of consensus among top government officials and agencies breeds lack of trust, and may lead to frustration, anger, fear, and panic. Because clear and accurate communication of the risks of radiation exposure will be crucial in the aftermath of an RDD or nuclear attack, this information must be agreed upon well before an attack and made widely available to the public. By supplying the public with suggestions to minimize their exposure to radiation[50] without including even basic facts about radiation, the government is inadvertently confirming the public's often exaggerated fears of radiation. The fear of radiation, exacerbated by lack of knowledge about how radiation works, is the main reason why people are likely to panic in the event of a radiological or nuclear catastrophe, increasing the costs and consequences of response, especially in terms of clean-up and medical treatment of victims.

Assessment: A Strong Effort, but Gaps Remain

The above review of current national programs for preventing and responding to nuclear and radiological terrorism has shown that DHS and other agencies are undertaking a massive effort intended to protect the U.S. public from nuclear and radiological threats. Many aspects of this effort are well-suited to the character of the threat, but further action is needed in some key areas, and redirection of energy is called for in others. For example, DHS has made a substantial effort to develop and implement a public education campaign about terrorism, but has fallen short of providing specific guidance or information about the effects of radiation. Domestic intelligence agencies have made significant inroads in creating new offices and formulating new directives, but only time will tell if these efforts will prove valuable in improving the nation's ability to prevent nuclear terrorism and respond effectively to a radiological attack.

Finally, although programs to reduce the amount of nuclear and radioactive material potentially accessible to terrorists are understood as important elements of terrorism prevention at the political level, the national strategy and response plan per se does not give them sufficient attention. An effective strategy for preventing nuclear and radiological terrorism must include all of these components and prioritize them according to strategic objectives rather than extraneous political considerations.

Priorities for a National Homeland Security Strategy

With this in mind, the final section of this article offers a "top ten" list of priorities, ranked from highest to lowest, for improving the national strategy for countering nuclear and radiological terrorism. Most of these recommendations, particularly those addressing the threat of nuclear terrorism, focus on prevention, but the list also includes areas for improving response to nuclear and radiological incidents. The list is not exhaustive, as many other components of national strategy could benefit from reexamination or revision, but is intended to point out where new initiatives, different approaches, and higher levels of effort are most urgently needed.[51]

1. *Expand and accelerate the Global Threat Reduction Initiative.* The announcement of the Global Initiative to Combat Nuclear Terrorism at the 2006 G8 summit is further evidence of the high priority placed on preventing terrorism with nuclear materials.[52] Nevertheless, the scope of international efforts toward this goal requires further expansion.[53] The objective of the Global Threat Reduction Initiative (GTRI), announced by former U.S. Secretary of Energy Spencer Abraham in May 2004, is to identify, secure, remove, and facilitate the disposition of vulnerable nuclear and radiological materials and equipment on a worldwide basis.[54] Through the GTRI, the United States plans to work more intensively with Russia, the International Atomic Energy Agency (IAEA), and other global partners to return all Soviet-origin fissile material to safer storage in Russia and to return U.S.-origin research reactor spent fuel to the United States within 10 years.[55] GTRI partners also intend to convert all research reactors using HEU to operate on low-enriched uranium (LEU) fuel, focusing first on the most vulnerable facilities, and to identify and secure nuclear and radioactive materials not covered by other cooperative programs. DOE created an Office of Global Threat Reduction within the National Nuclear Security Administration (NNSA) in June 2004 to implement GTRI, and signed agreements with a number of countries and organizations on specific efforts for removal and repatriation of nuclear material. In May 2004, Russia and the United States signed an agreement to provide

technical and financial assistance to remove fresh and spent fuel from reactors in more than a dozen countries to safe storage in Russia. In August of the same year, Germany and the United States repatriated U.S.-origin nuclear fuel from three German reactors under the U.S. Foreign Reactor Spent Nuclear Fuel Acceptance Program. In future years, GTRI envisions plans involving over 90 countries to recover and dispose of unsecured nuclear and radioactive materials, facilitate disposition of civilian HEU, and convert civilian reactors from HEU to low-enriched uranium (LEU) fuel.[56]

Ambitious as its goals are, it is not surprising that implementation of many elements of GTRI has encountered difficulties and delays. For example, most Russian reactors using HEU still lack plans to convert to LEU. Moreover, the GTRI, as currently planned, will not secure all HEU that could be used to make nuclear weapons or INDs. Over twelve tons of U.S.-obligated HEU fuel shipped overseas is not covered under GTRI. The plan also does not cover HEU in facilities outside of research reactors, such as reactors used to produce medical radioisotopes, or fuel supplied by countries other than the United States or Russia. The expansion of GTRI to include all civilian HEU, together with accelerated implementation of all elements of the initiative, should be the number one priority in U.S. strategy for preventing nuclear terrorism.

2. *Increase intelligence on proliferation networks.* The emergence of networks for clandestine trade in nuclear technology, the most notorious one organized by Pakistani metallurgist and "father of the Pakistani Bomb" Abdul Qadeer Khan, has created a global black market for nuclear know-how.[57] The Proliferation Security Initiative (PSI) and other U.S.-led efforts to interdict smuggling of WMD materials can hinder the efforts of these twenty-first century merchants of death,[58] but reorientation of U.S. and allied intelligence capabilities to track nuclear and radioactive materials, and the individuals and firms that traffic in them, will be required to strengthen the vital second line of defense against nuclear terrorism.

3. *Train the public health workforce to respond to radiation hazards.* The public health workforce is a critical element in the national infrastructure for responding to radiological incidents. While firefighters or paramedics are the likely first responders to an RDD attack, discovery of an RED incident may initially arise in the course of an investigation into an unusual outbreak of symptoms associated with radiation exposure by public health workers. At the same time, public health officials will play a crucial role in communicating the risks associated with a radiation incident to the public rapidly, accurately, and credibly, thus reducing the number and severity of psychological casualties from radiological terrorism. The DHHS, CDC, and many state and county public health agencies have recognized this need and have launched initiatives to train the public health workforce in identifying radiation hazards, diagnosing effects of radiation on health, forensic epidemiology, and

other skills involved in response to terrorism,[59] but new ideas and additional resources for training an often-overtaxed public health workforce should be given high priority.

4. *Strengthen port security.* Screening maritime cargo entering the United States for WMD materials is a formidable challenge; over seven million cargo containers enter the United States each year. As of April 2006, Megaports Initiative programs were operational at six ports worldwide, including Greece, the Netherlands, the Bahamas, Singapore, Sri Lanka, and Spain, initiated at eight others, and agreements to begin work were under negotiation with an additional 20 countries.[60] However, the DOE has not yet developed a comprehensive strategic plan for the Initiative, and, as with many cooperative programs for nuclear security, political, economic, and operational considerations are limiting the scope and slowing the pace of work. Developing a strategic plan for the Megaports Initiative should be given high priority, and once the plan is in place, Megaports and CSI should receive additional resources to accelerate the pace of security upgrades. Closer coordination with the Coast Guard and the Department of Transportation, as well as port security authorities overseas, will likely be required to achieve the Initiatives' objectives.

In addition to bolstering domestic coordination and international cooperation, more needs to be done to reduce the amount of time needed to effectively scan cargo for nuclear materials to ensure the smooth flow of commerce at foreign ports. Improving the quality of training for personnel tasked with monitoring the type of radiation detection equipment implemented by Megaports Initiative and CSI is likely to contribute to a reduction in the number of reported false-positives and will increase the efficacy of the process. Finally, if nuclear materials happen to escape detection at their port of origin, then detection at sea becomes an important intermediate step that would carry the added benefit of allowing the United States to distinguish low-levels of radiation from background "noise" that can take a long period of time to detect. Container-based detectors may have the potential to detect dangerous materials before they enter U.S. ports, allowing authorities to stop ships before they are close enough to U.S. shores to pose a significant hazard.

5. *Increase the design basis threat for nuclear power plant security.* Security is a major concern in the design of any nuclear facility and, in general, operators and regulators of nuclear power plants have been diligent in planning and implementing protective measures. The Nuclear Regulatory Commission (NRC) and other agencies have reviewed and updated security plans since September 11, 2001 and, in particular, the NRC revised the design basis threat (DBT) used to develop security plans for nuclear plants.[61] Nevertheless, concern exists that the DBT, understandably hidden from public consumption, still does not correspond to the level of effort made by al-Qaeda in the September 11 attacks.[62]

Greater reliance on nuclear power, as proposed in the George W. Bush administration's energy plan,[63] is likely to present more targets for this form of nuclear terrorism and to increase the economic impact, both direct and indirect, from a successful attack on a nuclear facility. A greater role for nuclear energy could also increase the motivations of radical antinuclear groups to attempt strikes on nuclear power reactors. For all these reasons, it is vital that security plans for existing and future nuclear plants, as well as fuel fabrication, reprocessing, and waste disposal facilities, reflect the higher level of terrorist threat that must be assumed for the foreseeable future.

6. *Toughen regulations for disposal of radioactive sources and tighten enforcement.* The U.S. government also acted to improve control over radioactive sources after September 11. In particular, the DOE requested and received additional funding for its Offsite Source Recovery (OSR) Project, and EPA launched the Orphan Source Initiative, the first U.S. domestic program to bring orphan sources back under regulatory control. By February 2003, the OSR had recovered over 5,000 greater-than-class-C radioactive sources, and planned to recover over 14,000 such sources by the end of FY2010, assuming adequate storage facilities could be provided.[64] At the state level, the Conference of Radiation Control Program Directors (CRCPD), comprising members of state radiation control agencies, initiated a National Orphan Radioactive Material Disposition Program, partially funded by the NRC, in October 2001. Despite these efforts, it is estimated that a radioactive source is reported as orphaned every day. To put the issue in perspective, the potential threat posed by high-risk radiological sources probably exceeds that of low-level contamination by toxic chemicals, but does not receive nearly the same level of EPA effort or media attention. Although government regulators and industrial users have made admirable efforts to recover orphaned sources, stricter oversight and increased penalties for loss or improper disposal of radioactive sources are still needed, and Congress should provide full funding for OSR.[65]

7. *Ensure that standards for education include accurate information on radiation hazards.* A number of studies place "inoculation" of the public against unreasonable fear of radiation high on their list of priorities for combating nuclear terrorism. Public education and risk communication are widely considered important components of a response strategy after a nuclear or radiological incident and should be made a priority.[66] The public will be counting on the authorities to tell them whether they need to evacuate, or whether it is safe to go outside and leave a shelter. But the aftermath of an RDD attack is probably the worst time to attempt public education about radiation hazards. Fear and panic are not conducive to learning, and a number of government agencies and NGOs presenting conflicting information will hardly create a supportive environment for education. To avoid this situation, accurate information about radiation and its effects should be incorporated into science

and health curricula in public and private schools. In addition to conveying information about what is known and what is disputed about nuclear energy and radiation, curricula should incorporate learning objectives that demystify radiation and require students to use trustworthy sources and multiple perspectives to investigate issues surrounding radiation exposure, nuclear power, and related topics.[67]

According to the Center for Disease Control, people who live within ten miles of a nuclear power plant are provided with educational information on radiation, instructions for evacuation and sheltering, and about emergency warning systems in place.[68] Similar evacuation routes and procedures as well as recommendations for sheltering in place need to be disseminated to people living in high-density areas that are considered probable targets for a nuclear or radiological attack.

8. *Bring the Amended Physical Protection Convention into Force.* The Convention on Physical Protection of Nuclear Material, signed by 45 states and the European Atomic Energy Community (EURATOM), requires parties to meet standards of protection for peaceful nuclear material being shipped internationally. The original Convention did not set any standards for nuclear material used or stored within countries or for material used for military purposes.[69] In July 2005, amendments to the Convention were agreed to after a long and difficult process of negotiation. These amendments require all parties to protect civilian nuclear facilities and material, and provide for cooperation between states on recovering stolen material and mitigating consequences of radiological sabotage.[70] Because physical protection of fissile material is the first line of defense against nuclear terrorism, the United States, together with the IAEA, should place a high priority on bringing the amended Convention into force.[71] The G8 countries should also offer developing countries additional assistance in developing and implementing physical protection systems both through expansion of the IAEA's International Physical Protection Advisory Services and through new international and bilateral initiatives.

9. *Standardize and reform regulations for remediation after radiological attack.* As a 2004 study points out, DHS has yet to finalize guidance for protecting the public from radiation hazards in the event of an RDD attack or other radiological terrorist incidents. Deciding on the appropriate standards to apply is not a trivial task, as one study found at least 26 different standards or guidelines setting numerical values for acceptable radiation dosage.[72] As a result, federal, state, and local authorities have no clear basis on which to determine acceptable levels of radiation exposure in the aftermath of a radiological attack. The interim version of the DHS guidance, with standards based on EPA PAG guidelines,[73] has been criticized for weakening the standards for radiation exposure.[74] Some authorities argue instead for the stricter EPA Superfund standard. This limits allowable radiation after cleanup to levels corresponding to a 1 in 10,000 increased lifetime risk of developing can-

cer, or about 15 mrem per year. In contrast, the NRC enforces an all-source standard of 25 mrem per year above background radiation and considers a 1 in 1,000 increased lifetime cancer risk to be acceptable for the public. We should keep in mind that the average American receives about 360 mrem of background radiation annually. The difference may not appear very great, but the difficulty of decontamination increases substantially as the maximum allowable dosage decreases. In addition to raising the costs of decontamination after a major RDD incident by billions of dollars, the difference between a 25 mrem cleanup standard and a 15 mrem standard could make the difference between reoccupation and demolition of homes, workplaces, or public buildings.

It is vital to set standards for radiation cleanup before a major radiological terrorist incident occurs. If DHS waits until after such an incident, or takes the approach that standards should be negotiated with state and local governments on a case-by-case basis, the noise of the legal and political battle that will ensue will be louder than the explosion of the RDD. DHS should not be criticized too harshly for proceeding deliberately in issuing national guidance, because the confusion of current standards, the inability to reach a scientific consensus on the effects, if any, of low doses of radiation, and the interests of multiple stakeholders greatly complicates the process. Nevertheless, further research seems unlikely to produce greater clarity. The time has come to fight the political battles, finalize the standards reflected in DHS interim guidance for post-attack radiation exposure, and embed these standards in legislation before the first dirty bomb goes off.

10. *Develop advanced technologies for radioactive decontamination.* The discussion of radiation protection standards emphasizes that decontamination, as the final stage of response to a nuclear or radioactive attack, will be critical for mitigating the economic, environmental, and psychological impact of these forms of terrorism. Fire department HAZMAT teams and other first responders have upgraded training and equipment for decontamination after chemical and biological attacks, and some of the same equipment and procedures can be used for decontamination of personnel and areas affected by radioactive fallout. However, some forms of radiological attack can leave persistent contamination that simply hosing down with water or a bleach solution will not remedy. For example, cesium-137 chloride bonds to concrete, making it extremely difficult to remove from urban areas.[75] Because remediation plays such an important role in mitigating the long-term impact of a radiological incident, DHS-sponsored research at national laboratories and in the private sector should give higher priority to development of new equipment and procedures for radioactive decontamination.[76]

In addition, the government should be doing all that it can to promote radiation countermeasures, also known as radioprotectorants. An increased effort in this regard would serve several purposes. First, it would instill confidence in the public that the government was acting responsibly and pro-actively. Second, if people were aware that radioprotectorants were available to them prior to and after an attack, it might alleviate the pressures of panic and decrease the number of those in close proximity of the disaster area to self-evacuate. Third, countermeasures could dissuade terrorists from attacking if they knew that antidotes to the radiation released in a nuclear or radiological attack would be widely available.

Conclusion: Integrating Prevention and Response

Implementing the top ten priorities outlined above would not fill all the gaps in U.S. strategy to combat nuclear and radiological terrorism, but it would seal the most urgent breaches and repair the most obvious holes. Over the longer term, protecting the U.S. public from nuclear and radiological attack will require a broader perspective on the problem that no single agency is well suited to provide. In many areas, the agency that must play the leading role in preventing these forms of terrorism has little, if any, responsibility for responding in the event of an attack, and vice versa. Policies for protecting vulnerable nuclear material are formulated in Foggy Bottom, the Pentagon, and the Forrestal Building, but training the public health workforce to detect radiological events is coordinated in Atlanta. This is an understandable and unavoidable consequence of different competencies and jurisdictional boundaries, but it highlights the need for interagency cooperation. Just as the Departments of State, Defense, Energy, and the Treasury and the plethora of intelligence agencies have had to work together in order to advance the traditional national security interests of the United States, all of these departments plus Homeland Security, Health and Human Services, Justice, and the EPA must coordinate their roles in the national homeland security strategy. Leadership at the political level will obviously be critical for this, but the formation of long-term collaborative relationships between working-level officials across institutional boundaries will be especially crucial for integrating prevention with response. It is unrealistic to expect that all these governmental entities will see eye-to-eye on a majority of important issues, but those on the front lines of prevention and those charged with emergency response and their managers must be prepared to make trade-offs when submitting budget requests.

The fact that implementing many priorities for homeland security requires international cooperation emphasizes that in preventing nuclear and radiological terrorism, the "national security borders" of the United States extend far beyond its territorial boundaries. This is evidenced most dramatically in the need to protect nuclear weapons in Russia and Pakistan and secure fissile material in over 130 countries. Shoring up the first line of defense against nuclear terrorism will thus involve attentive leadership and financial investment, but if these activities are conducted according to a well-thought-out strategic plan under reasonable oversight, these investments will pay big security dividends. At the same time, "inreach" to domestic NGOs can help build public confidence in both the preventive and responsive components of national strategy.

Ultimately, although the distinction between prevention and response is analytically useful and comfortably fits institutional boundaries, it is somewhat artificial. The involvement of first responders in formulating strategy will help improve prevention, and input from agencies responsible for prevention will help strengthen response. Strategic emphasis should be placed and resources concentrated on the most effective point to block the pathway from terrorists' intentions to use nuclear or radioactive materials, to the use of those materials to cause human, economic, and environmental casualties. In fighting radiological terrorism, radioactive materials are widely available but limited in effect, so detection and decontamination will be most important. With nuclear terrorism, because fissile material is very rare but potentially devastating in sufficient quantity, an ounce of prevention will be worth kilotons of cure.

Endnotes

1. Peter R. Beckman et al., Nuclear Weapons, Nuclear States and Terrorism, 4th ed. (Cornwall-on-Hudson, NY: Sloan, 2007), 3.
2. Noteworthy analyses of nuclear and radiological terrorism include Charles D. Ferguson and William C. Potter with Amy Sands, Leonard S. Spector and Fred L. Wehling, The Four Faces of Nuclear Terrorism (New York: Routledge, 2005); Graham Allison, Nuclear Terrorism: The Ultimate Preventable Catastrophe (New York: Times Books, 2004); and Committee on Science and Technology for Countering Terrorism, National Research Council, "Nuclear and Radiological Threats," in Making the Nation Safer: The Role of Science and Technology in Countering Terrorism (Washington, D.C.: National Academy Press, 2002), Chapter 2.
3. This evidence is compiled in Center for Nonproliferation Studies WMD Terrorism Research Program, "Chart: Al Qa'ida's WMD Activities," Center for Nonproliferation Studies Web site, May 13, 2005, http://cns.miis.edu/pubs/other/sjm_cht.htm, accessed June 20, 2005. Osama bin Laden (in an ABC News interview published September 26, 2001) notoriously called the acquisition of weapons of mass destruction a "religious duty" for jihadists.
4. See for example Ferguson et al. Four Faces of Nuclear Terrorism, 131–142; Frank Barnaby, "Issues Surrounding Crude Nuclear Explosives," in Crude Nuclear Weapons: Proliferation and the Terrorist Threat. IPPNW Global Health Watch Report no. 1 (1996); and J. Carson Mark et al., "Can Terrorists Build Nuclear Weapons?" in Preventing Nuclear Terrorism, ed. Paul Leventhal and Yonah Alexander (Lanham, MD: Rowan & Littlefield, 1987).
5. Matthew Bunn and Anthony Wier discuss the possibilities for terrorists to acquire and use nuclear weapons from Russia and other countries in Securing the Bomb 2005: The New Global Imperatives (Cambridge, MA: Project on Managing the Atom,

Harvard University, and the Nuclear Threat Initiative, May 2005), http://www.nti.
org/e_research/report_cnwmupdate2005.pdf, accessed June 20, 2005; and "The
Seven Myths of Nuclear Terrorism," Current History (April 2005): 153–161. For other
perspectives, see Christopher F. Chyba, Harold Feiverson, and Frank von Hippel,
"Preventing Nuclear Proliferation and Nuclear Terrorism: Essential Steps to Reduce
the Availability of Nuclear-Explosive Materials," Center for International Security
and Cooperation report (March 2005), http://iisdb.stanford.edu/pubs/20855/Prvnt_
Nuc_Prlf_and_Nuc_Trror_2005-0407.pdf, accessed June 22, 2005; and Ferguson
et al. Four Faces of Nuclear Terrorism, 46–105.

6. U.S. Department of Energy, FY 2006 Defense Nuclear Nonproliferation Budget
Request, p. 485, cited in Bunn and Wier Securing the Bomb 2005, 27.

7. U.S. Government Accountability Office, Nuclear Nonproliferation: DOE Needs to
Take Action to Further Reduce the Use of Weapons-Usable Uranium in Civilian
Research Reactors, GAO-04-807 (Washington, D.C.: GAO, 2004), http://www.
gao.gov/new.items/d04807.pdf, accessed June 20, 2005.

8. Matthew Bunn and Anthony Wier, Securing the Bomb: An Agenda For Action
(Washington, D.C.: Nuclear Threat Initiative and the Project on Managing the Atom,
Harvard University, May 2004), http://www.nti.org/e_research/analysis_cnwmup-
date_052404.pdf, accessed June 20, 2005.

9. Ferguson et al. Four Faces of Nuclear Terrorism, 139.

10. Bunn and Wier ("Seven Myths of Nuclear Terrorism,") cite a finding from the Office
of Technology Assessment (OTA) in 1977 that a small group of individuals, without
any classified information, specialized equipment, or testing, could probably assemble a crude nuclear weapon at a cost of less than $1 million (p. 156). The same source
notes that smuggling an IND or the materials to make one into the United States
would not pose any major challenges.

11. Ferguson et al., Four Faces of Nuclear Terrorism, describe these modes of radiological
attack in detail.

12. There is still considerable disagreement on the effects of ionizing radiation, particularly at low doses, on human health. All studies agree that an acute radiation dose of
5,000 mrem or higher can cause observable biological effects and that higher doses
significantly increase the risk of injury or death. There is little evidence of risk to
health or safety from doses of 1,000 mrem or lower, but according to the Linear
No-Threshold (LNT) model of radiation effects, any dose of ionizing radiation could
pose some long-term risk of cancer or other illness. (The average American receives
about 360 mrem of ionizing radiation each year from natural and man-made sources.)
Good references for the effects of radiation on health are National Safety Council,
"Understanding Radiation: The Risks: Health Effects," December 10, 2002, http://
www.nsc.org/issues/rad/risks.htm, accessed June 21, 2005; and Kenneth L. Moss-
man et al., "Radiation Risk in Perspective," Health Physics Society Position Statement (revised August 2004).

13. Potential effects of radiological terrorism are discussed in Federation of American Scientists, "Dirty Bombs: Response to a Threat," FAS Public Interest Report 55 (March/April 2002); and Charles D. Ferguson, Tahseen Kazi, and Judith Perrera, "Commercial Radioactive Sources: Surveying the Security Risks," Center for Nonproliferation Studies Occasional Paper No. 11 (Monterey, CA: Monterey Institute of International Studies, January 2003), http://cns.miis.edu/pubs/opapers/op11/op11.pdf, accessed June 21, 2005; and James M. Acton, M. Brooke Rogers, and Peter D. Zimmerman, "Beyond the Dirty Bomb: Re-thinking Radiological Terror," Survival, 49, no. 3 (Fall 2007), 151–168.

14. For more on attacks on nuclear facilities, see Ferguson et al. Four Faces of Nuclear Terrorism, 190–259.

15. Ferguson et al., "Commercial Radioactive Sources."

16. For more on response to and remediation after radiological incidents, see U.S. Environmental Protection Agency (EPA), Radiological Emergency Planning and Preparedness, Title 44, Part 351.22, Code of Federal Regulations (revised October 1, 2002), "Protective Action Guidelines and Operational Guidelines for Radiological Dispersal Device (RDD); John MacKinney, "Guidance for Federal Protective Actions and Recovery After Radiological and Nuclear Incidents," NBC Report (Spring/Summer 2004); and Elizabeth Eraker, "Cleanup After a Radiological Attack: U.S. Prepares Guidance," Nonproliferation Review 11/3 (Fall/Winter 2004): 167–185.

17. Allison, Nuclear Terrorism.

18. This view is articulated by James Carafano, Paul Rosenzweig, and Alane Cochems, "An Agenda for Increasing State and Local Government Efforts to Combat Terrorism," Heritage Foundation, Backgrounder no. 1826, available at http://www.heritage.org/Research/HomelandDefense/bg1826.cfm, accessed November 23, 2005.

19. "President Signs Intelligence Reform and Terrorist Prevention Act," White House, December 17, 2004, available at http://www.whitehouse.gov/news/releases/2004/12/20041217-1.html, accessed August 23, 2005.

20. See "DHS Establishes Domestic Nuclear Detection Office," Metropolitan Medical Response System (MMRS) Press Release, April 20, 2005, available at https://www.mmrs.fema.gov/press/2005/pr2005-04-20.aspx, accessed October 8, 2006. See also: "Domestic Nuclear Detection Office," DHS Fact Sheet, available at http://www.dhs.gov/dhspublic/display?content=4474, accessed October 8, 2006.

21. "Conferees Approve FY2007 Homeland Security Appropriations Bill," U.S. Senate Committee on Appropriations, September 25, 2006, available at http://appropriations.senate.gov/hearmarkups/HomelandConferencePR07.mht, accessed October 8, 2006. See also "President Signs FY 2007 Homeland Security Appropriations," DHS Press Release, October 4, 2006, available at http://www.dhs.gov/dhspublic/display?content=5957, accessed October 8, 2006.

22. James Carafano et al., "Agenda for Increasing State and Local Government Efforts."

23. Jim Kouri, "Feds Focus on Preventing Nuclear Smuggling," American Chronicle, June 15, 2005, available at: http://www.americanchronicle.com/articles/viewArticle.asp?articleID=666, accessed August 10, 2005.

24. Alex Veiga, "Radiation Detectors to Scan all Incoming Cargo at LA Port Complex," San Francisco Chronicle, June 3, 2005, available at http://sfgate.com/cgibin/article. cgi?file=/n/a/2005/06/03/state/n000139D49.DTL, accessed August 10, 2005.

25. The National Strategy for Homeland Security is available at http://www.whitehouse. gov/homeland/book/nat_strat_hls.pdf, and the National Response Plan is available at: http://www.dhs.gov/interweb/assetlibrary/NRP_FullText.pdf.

26. White House Press Release, "December 17, 2003 Homeland Security Presidential Directive/Hspd-8," available at http://www.whitehouse.gov/news/releases/2003/12/20031217-6.html, accessed November 22, 2005.

27. National Response Plan Brochure, available at http://www.dhs.gov/interweb/assetlibrary/NRP_Brochure.pdf, accessed November 22, 2005.

28. National Memorial Institute for the Prevention of Terrorism, "Homeland Security Presidential Directive/HPSD-5," available at http://www.mipt.org/pdd-hspd5.asp, accessed November 23, 2005.

29. Office of Grants & Training (formerly the Office of Domestic Preparedness) Web site, available at http://www.ojp.usdoj.gov/odp/, accessed October 8, 2006.

30. DHS Organizational Chart, available at http://www.dhs.gov/interweb/assetlibrary/DHSOrgChart.htm, accessed November 22, 2005.

31. Office of Grants and Training Web site: "Program Highlights (FY2005)", available at http://www.ojp.usdoj.gov/odp/about/highlights.htm, and "G&T Mission" available at http://www.ojp.usdoj.gov/odp/about/mission.htm, accessed October 8, 2006.

32. Department of Homeland Security, National Response Plan, Incident Annexes, Nuclear/Radiological Annex, NUC-2, available at http://www.dhs.gov/interweb/assetlibrary/NRP_FullText.pdf, accessed on July 9, 2005. In any circumstance where nuclear or radiological materials are involved in a terrorist attack, known as an Incident of National Significance, it is referred to the Department of Homeland Security and is treated as a federal matter. Although local and state authorities will be called upon to cooperate with regional command centers, they will not have jurisdictional authority on scene.

33. National Response Plan, NUC-6.

34. There are many federal agencies that maintain offices or departments with specially trained personnel that are available to respond to a radiological emergency. For example, the EPA maintains a Radiological Emergency Response Team, see http://www.epa.gov/radiation/rert/respond.htm; the Oak Ridge National Laboratory maintains the Radiation Emergency Assistance Center/Training Site (REAC/TS), see http://www.orau.gov/reacts/intro.htm; response support available from the Defense Threat Reduction Agency (DTRA), see http://www.dtra.mil/toolbox/directorates/cs/index. cfm. In addition, the Department of Energy operates a number of Radiological Assistance Program (RAP) initiatives including Nuclear Incident Response Teams (NIRT), Search Response Teams (SRT), and Nuclear Emergency Search Teams (NEST). On top of these organizations, the Department of Defense maintains numerous response teams under the rubric of the Joint Special Operations Command. See Siobhan Gorman and Sydney J. Freedberg Jr., "Efforts to Combat Nuclear Terrorism Hindered by

Porous Borders," GovExec.com, June 17, 2005, available at http://www.govexec.com/dailyfed/0605/061705nj1.htm, accessed July 11, 2005, for more detailed information on how these various teams would operate together in response to a radiological terrorist attack.

35. National Response Plan, NUC-2, 11, 18.

36. Ibid., NUC-8.

37. "Fact Sheet: Proposed Protective Action Guides for Radiological Dispersion and Improvised Nuclear Devices," DHS Press Release, January 3, 2006, available at http://www.dhs.gov/dhspublic/display?content=5327, accessed October 8, 2006.

38. "Preparedness Directorate; Protective Action Guides for Radiological Dispersal Device (RDD) and Improvised Nuclear Device (IND) Incidents; Notice," Federal Register (Vol. 71, No. 1), January 3, 2006, available at http://frwebgate4.access.gpo.gov/cgi-bin/waisgate.cgi?WAISdocID=36195716208+0+0+0&WAISaction=retrieve, accessed October 8, 2006.

39. Ibid.

40. The previous Protection Action Guide (PAG) developed by the EPA in 1992 provided information about how to respond appropriately to nuclear incidents (accidents) unrelated to terrorism. Unlike the current PAG, the 1992 Guidance did not address issues related to long-term cleanup, Ibid.

41. Department of Homeland Security Working Group on Radiological Dispersal Device (RDD) Preparedness, Medical Preparedness and Response Sub-Group, May 1, 2003 Version, available at http://www1.va.gov/emshg/docs/Radiologic_Medical_Countermeasures_051403.pdf, accessed July 11, 2005.

42. Ibid., p. 9. Roentgen Equivalent Man (REM) is a measurement of human exposure to radiation (see note 11). In the context of a national disaster involving radiological weapons, people exposed to less than 100 rem will experience no signs of illness, but there will be a temporary decrease in white blood cells and platelets. Acute radiation syndrome (ARS) is likely to occur when a person is exposed to 100 rem or more, and those levels are not likely to be present in an RDD, according to the National Academies of Science and the Department of Homeland Security. Signs and symptoms of ARS include nausea, vomiting, and diarrhea. See also "Radiological Attack: Dirty Bombs and other Devices," Fact Sheet from the National Academies and the Department of Homeland Security, available at http://www.nae.edu/NAE/pubund-com.nsf/weblinks/CGOZ-646NVG/$file/radiological%20attack.pdf, accessed July 11, 2005.

43. DOE "representatives serve as Lead Coordinators for guiding the development of each Guidelines group" as quoted from "Operational Guidelines and Their Application within a Framework for Consequence Management of a Radiological Dispersal Device Incident," U.S. Department of Energy Web site, available at http://ogcms.energy.gov/overview.html, accessed October 8, 2006.

44. "About the Department of Homeland Security," Ready.gov, available at http://www.ready.gov/about.html, accessed on July 12, 2005.

45. Ready.gov, Radiation Threat, available at http://www.ready.gov/radiation.html, accessed on July 12, 2005.

46. FEMA, Are you Ready?, August 2004 print version, also available at http://www.ready.gov/radiation.html, accessed on July 12, 2005.

47. Ibid. (print version), p. 14.

48. According to the Federal Guidance on Radiation, there are no instances of radiation victims who require immediate medical treatment; only those with physical injuries or conventional trauma. Federal Guidance, p. 9.

49. Stanford University, Center for International Security and Arms Control, "Understanding Nuclear Terrorism," What to Do in an Attack: Response Guidance, available at http://cisac.stanford.edu/nuclearterrorism/index.html, accessed July 9, 2005.

50. The standard recommendations are: Time, Shielding, and Distance whereby a person needs to limit the amount of time spent near a radiation source, ensure that adequate shielding is between a person and the source, and increase the distance away from the center of the radioactive source.

51. Ferguson et al., Four Faces of Nuclear Terrorism; Bunn and Wier, Securing the Bomb 2005, Chyba et al., "Preventing Nuclear Proliferation," and Elizabeth Eraker, "Cleanup After a Radiological Attack: U.S. Prepares Guidance," Nonproliferation Review, 11, no. 3 (Fall/Winter 2004): 167–185. also offer recommendations for national strategy to counter nuclear and radioactive terrorism.

52. "Global Initiative to Combat Nuclear Terrorism: Joint Fact Sheet," Official Web site of the G8 Presidency of the Russian Federation in 2006, http://en.g8russia.ru/docs/7.html, accessed October 12, 2006.

53. Matthew Bunn and Anthony Weir discuss specific recommendations toward this objective in Securing the Bomb 2006 (Cambridge, MA: Project on Managing the Atom, Harvard University, and the Nuclear Threat Initiative, July 2006), NTI Web site, http://www.nti.org/e_research/stb06webfull.pdf, accessed October 12, 2006.

54. "Department of Energy Launches New Global Threat Reduction Initiative," U.S. Department of Energy Web site, May 26, 2004, http://www.doe.gov/engine/content.do?PUBLIC_ID=15956&BT_CODE=PR_PRESSRELEASES&TT_CODE=PRESSRELEASE, accessed June 21, 2005.

55. Rose Gottemoeller, Testimony before the U.S. House of Representatives, Committee on Homeland Security, Subcommittee on Prevention of Nuclear and Biological Attack, "Pathways to the Bomb: Security of Fissile Materials Abroad," June 28, 2005.

56. For more on GTRI, see Charles D. Ferguson, "Reducing the Threat of Nuclear Terrorism: A Review of the Department of Energy's Global Threat Reduction Initiative," testimony before the House Energy and Commerce Committee, Subcommittee on Oversight and Investigations, May 24, 2005, Council on Foreign Relations Web site, http://www.cfr.org/pub8130/charles_d_ferguson_ii/reducing_the_threat_of_nuclear_terrorism_a_review_of_the_department_of_energys_global_threat_reduction_initiative.php, accessed June 21, 2005.

57. Foremost among analyses of the A. Q. Khan network are Chaim Braun and Christopher F. Chyba, "Proliferation Rings: New Challenges to the Nuclear Nonproliferation Regime," International Security 29, no. 2 (Fall 2004): 5—49; and Gaurav Kampani, "Proliferation Unbound: Nuclear Tales From Pakistan," CNS Web site, http://www.cns.miis.edu/pubs/week/040223.htm, accessed June 21, 2005.

58. Thomas D. Lehrman analyzes PSI in "The Future of the Proliferation Security Initiative," Nonproliferation Review 11, no. 2 (Summer 2004): 1–45.

59. The role of public health in countering terrorism is summarized in U.S. Department of Health and Human Services, "Interim Public Health and Healthcare Supplement to the National Preparedness Goal," http://www.hhs.gov/ophep/index.html, accessed June 21, 2005. The skills that public health staff and management will require to respond to terrorist incidents are identified in Columbia University School of Nursing Center for Health Policy, "Bioterrorism and Emergency Readiness: Competencies for All Public Health Workers" (November 2002). The CDC sponsors efforts to improve terrorism preparedness training through a network of Centers for Public Health Preparedness; see http://www.asph.org/acphp/index.cfm, accessed June 21, 2005.

60. U.S. Government Accountability Office, "Preventing Nuclear Smuggling: DOE Has Made Limited Progress in Installing Radiation Detection Equipment at Highest Priority Foreign Seaports," GAO-05-375 (March 2005), GAO Web site, http://www.gao.gov/new.items/d05375.pdf, accessed June 22, 2005. See also: "Singapore and U.S. Cooperate to detect Nuclear-laden Shipments," XINHUA Online, http://news.xinhuanet.com/english/2005-03/10/content_2679883.htm, accessed August 10, 2005 and NNSA Fact Sheet (2006), NNSA Web site, http://www.nnsa.doe.gov/docs/factsheets/2006/NA-06-FS01.pdf, accessed April 26, 2006.

61. These updated measures are summarized in Nuclear Regulatory Commission, "Backgrounder on Nuclear Security Enhancements Since September 11, 2001" (February 2005), NRC Web site, http://www.nrc.gov/reading-rm/doc-collections/fact-sheets/security-enhancements.html, accessed June 22, 2005.

62. Ferguson et al., Four Faces of Nuclear Terrorism, 210–225.

63. The administration's energy plans are outlined in National Energy Policy: Report of the National Energy Policy Development Group (Washington, D.C.: GPO, May 2001), 5/15–5/17, DOE Web site, http://www.energy.gov/engine/doe/files/dynamic/195200312817_chapter5.pdf, accessed June 22, 2005. The major legislation to implement the policy is U.S. Congress, House of Representatives, Energy Policy Act of 2005, 109th Congress, and 1st session, H.R. 6, passed by the House on April 19, 2005 and by the Senate on June 28, 2005.

64. GAO, "Nuclear Nonproliferation: DOE Action Needed to Ensure Continued Recovery of Unwanted Sealed Radioactive Sources," GAO-03-438 (April 2003), GAO Web site, http://www.gao.gov/new.items/d03483.pdf, accessed June 22, 2005.

65. See also Ferguson et al., Four Faces of Nuclear Terrorism, 289–293, 332–333.

66. Among the studies emphasizing public education and risk communication are Committee on Science and Technology for Countering Terrorism, "Making the Nation Safer: The Role of Science and Technology in Countering Terrorism" (Washington, D.C.: National Academy Press, 2002); Allison, Nuclear Terrorism; and Ferguson et al., "Commercial Radioactive Sources." See also: National Council on Radiation Protection and Measurements, "Advising the Public about Radiation Emergencies," NCRP Commentary No. 10, November 30, 1994, available at http://www.ncrponline.org/Commentaries/NCRP%20Comm%20No.%2010.pdf.

67. An excellent resource for incorporating radiation into secondary school curricula is National Safety Council Environmental Health Center, "Understanding Radiation in Our World," http://www.nsc.org/ehc/rad/radbroch.HTM, accessed June 22, 2005. For a curriculum model that integrates study of radiation and radiological terrorism with development of critical thinking skills, see Critical Issues Forum, "2004-2005 Student Benchmarks and Activities: Radioactive Materials and Radiation Weapons," Critical Issues Forum Web site, http://homepage.mac.com/cifproject/bmks05.html, accessed June 22, 2005.

68. Centers for Disease Control and Prevention, Emergency Preparedness and Response Web site, "Facts about Evacuation during a Radiological Emergency," Fact Sheet, available at http://www.bt.cdc.gov/radiation/evacuation.asp, accessed July 8, 2005.

69. "The Convention on the Physical Protection of Nuclear Material," IAEA INFCIRC/274/Rev. 1 (May 1980), IAEA Web site, http://www.iaea.org/Publications/Documents/Infcircs/Others/inf274r1.shtml, accessed June 22, 2005.

70. International Atomic Energy Agency, "International Conventions and Agreements: Convention on the Physical Protection of Nuclear Material," IAEA Web site, http://www.iaea.org/Publications/Documents/Conventions/cppnm.html, accessed November 28, 2005.

71. Fritz Steinhausler, Chaim Braun, and George Bunn survey options for strengthening physical protection in "An Integrated Approach to Adapt Physical Protection to the New Terrorism Threats," Center for International Security and Cooperation (CISAC) conference/workshop report (September 2002), CISAC Web site, http://siis.stanford.edu/publications/20347, accessed June 22, 2005.

72. GAO, "Nuclear Health and Safety: Consensus on Acceptable Radiation Risk to the Public Is Lacking," GAO/RCED-94-190 (September 1994). For more on radiation standards, see Deborah Elcock, Gladys A. Klemic, and A. L. Taboas, "Establishing Radiation Levels in Response to a Radiological Dispersal Event (or 'Dirty Bomb')," Environmental Science and Technology 38 (2004): 2510.

73. See John McKinney, "Guidance for Federal Protective Actions and Recovery after Radiological and Nuclear Incidents," NBC Report (Spring/Summer 2004). Elizabeth Eraker, "Cleanup After a Radiological Attack" offers an excellent discussion of standards for radiation cleanup.

74. See for example "Planned Cleanup for Dirty Bombs Called Lax," Associated Press, December 2, 2004; and Nuclear Information and Resource Service, "Groups Criticize Homeland Security Plans to Relax Radiation Cleanup Standards for a 'Dirty Bomb' or Terrorist Nuclear Explosive," http://www.nirs.org/press/12-02-2004/1, accessed June 22, 2005.

75. For more on challenges to decontamination and new directions for decontamination technology, see Tammy P. Taylor et al., Radionuclide Decontamination Science and Technology Workshop: Workshop Summary and Findings, Los Alamos National Laboratory report LA_UR-03-8215 (September 16–17, 2003).

76. Ferguson et al., Four Faces of Nuclear Terrorism, 330–331.

SECTION 3

Strategy and the Safeguarding of Society and Its Infrastructure From Terrorism and Other Threats

---

Chapter 8

Comparative Risk Analysis

Biological Terrorism, Pandemics, and Other "Forgotten" Catastrophic Disaster Threats

Terrence M. O'Sullivan

The author thinks outside the box, taking a broad view of homeland security challenges, including, but not confined to, coping with terrorist threats. Although terrorism, including biological terrorism is a threat to the security of the homeland, so are natural disasters—earthquakes, hurricanes, tsunamis, floods, and disease epidemics. O'Sullivan notes how lacking any broad-based system for risk assessment or critical infrastructure prioritization, homeland security policy not unexpectedly defaulted to politically driven allocations, with less populous states receiving funds disproportionately large in comparison to either their demographics or the importance of their levels of disaster

> risk. Given his holistic view that includes both natural and human-induced threats, the author raises serious questions about the institutional capacities and organizational cultures within federal, state and local security agencies and infrastructures.

Both before and immediately after 9/11, "homeland security" almost exclusively reflected rising concerns about terrorism. But American public and governmental expectations of homeland security eventually broadened, impelled in part by a series of events that included some of the worst naturally occurring domestic and international disasters in generations. In 2004, the Great Sumatra Earthquake and accompanying tsunami, and the devastating Pakistan/Kashmir earthquake the following year, killed hundreds of thousands in Asia. These events coincided with a rising global awareness of the formidable global pandemic potential of the avian (H5N1) influenza virus, as outbreaks among birds and humans occurred across Asia, Eastern Europe, the Middle East, Africa, and the European Union.

Of the many sobering nonterrorist events that occurred around that particular time, though, among the most tangible and traumatic for Americans was a back-to-back set of domestic disasters that centered on Hurricane Katrina and the subsequent flooding of New Orleans, and the psychologically and institutionally damaging Hurricane Rita. Both were widely televised natural disasters compounded by pre- and post-event human errors. Because of those mistakes, Hurricane Katrina was the most costly natural disaster in modern U.S. history, with consequences on a scale rivaled only by the 9/11 terrorist attacks. And Hurricane Rita, which occurred only weeks later, was best characterized not by its relatively mild destruction, but by the fiasco of its chaotic mass evacuation, as fearful residents obeyed pleas to abandon the Galveston and Houston areas in Texas.

These events disturbed many Americans profoundly by vividly exposing U.S. failures in preparedness and response leadership and capability in the face of locally overwhelming natural calamities, and by logical extension highlighted similar shortcomings relevant to future terrorism preparation and response. Moreover, these revelations collectively helped muddy the homeland security waters by catalyzing a nascent, though ambivalent, conceptual, operational, and political reexamination of the U.S. government's security priorities. At the heart of these changes in thinking was the realization that, as much as possible, policymaking required comparing all threats across the security spectrum, and rationing limited resources for the most important and cost-effective risk areas.

This chapter integrates a set of issues that are intimately connected to effective "homeland security" strategy and policy. Natural disasters such as hurricanes, earthquakes, tsunamis, floods, and disease epidemics, as well as deliberate biological terrorism, are all threats that highlight the critical need for national, and global, policies based on *comparative risk analysis*. All of these cases have been, for various reasons, neglected or even "forgotten" dimensions of homeland security.[1] But they help illustrate collectively the critical need for comparatively weighing the relative threats, vulnerabilities and consequences associated with a broader spectrum of possible catastrophic disasters, whether natural or man-made, that might befall civilian populations.

The first section provides a backdrop by briefly noting some of the conceptual, operational, and political debates that have surrounded "homeland security," and the reasons that now motivate governmental emphasis on comparative risk analysis. Next, we address some of the elemental forces of nature that must be considered serious threats to domestic security in addition to terrorism. In the third section, we examine a unique category of disaster risk, *catastrophic infectious disease outbreaks (CIDOs)*, spanning both naturally occurring epidemic threats, such as severe acute respiratory syndrome (SARS) or the H5N1 "bird flu" pathogens, as well as bioterrorism (BT). Although BT is clearly under the domain of homeland security, it was not always treated as such.[2] Finally, to analyze all significant catastrophic threats to a country holistically, rather than merely in isolation, is a challenging enterprise. U.S. efforts to reassess more systematically the potential risk of *terrorism* were begun even before Hurricane Katrina altered the national priorities equation, but U.S. domestic security strategies must be rationally formulated in a context of limited resources, an adaptive adversary—be it terrorists *or* nature—and the interdependent domestic and global costs and benefits.

A Note About Comparative Risk Assessment

Risk has been a historically disputed term, but its essence is the desire to gauge the likelihood of something being a hazard, and to project the possible outcomes should they occur, so that the costs and benefits of mitigating, risk-reducing measures can be assessed. The Department of Homeland Security (DHS) adopted a definition that breaks risk down into three integrated components: threats, vulnerabilities, and consequences. This is not the only framework, but it is a useful standard for national, state, and local risk analysis of potential disasters. Broadly speaking, the threat includes the motivation, targets, and tactics of the terrorist, whose potential weapons would consist of a gun or a viral biological agent. The vulnerabilities would entail anything that might make the target or potential victims more or less susceptible to attack or harm, such as a bulletproof vest or a smallpox vaccination. Finally, the consequences could range from no injuries to many, no epidemic to a large one. Attempting to anticipate all three of these risk variables is important for coming back around full circle to assessing, comparatively and rationally, a variety of *different* potential threats and overall risks. This DHS risk framework will be used loosely below. For most catastrophic risk, prevention is usually the most cost-effective strategy; but for most natural disasters, and some human-caused threats such as biological terrorism, prevention can be very difficult or impossible, thus making adequate preparation and response capability the most important policy strategy.

Debates about Homeland Security Strategy in Theory and Practice

The concept of homeland security originally emerged most robustly in the 1990s as global terrorism concerns grew.[3] Federal government officials began using the terms "homeland defense" and "homeland security" to refer to various concepts of securing U.S. territorial borders. In February 2001, in its Phase III report, the Hart-Rudman Commission[4] recommended significant changes in U.S. government "homeland security" policies and activities. Among its recommendations was the establishment of a new agency, the National Homeland Security Agency, intended to integrate the Federal Emergency Management Agency (FEMA), the Customs Service, the U.S. Border Patrol, and the Coast Guard. Although policy officials continue to distinguish between "homeland defense" and "homeland security,"[5] the former belonging bureaucratically to the Defense Department and the latter to the Department of Homeland Security, in the public mind the two have become conflated.

Creation of the Department of Homeland Security, originally the Office of Homeland Security, OHS, was a direct political and strategic policy response to the 9/11 and October 2001 anthrax letter attacks, and was the largest reorganization of the federal government since the National Security Act of 1947. The national consensus seemed clear: securing the homeland specifically meant countering terrorism. Thus, the Homeland Security Act of 2002 chartered the DHS to first and foremost "prevent terrorist attacks within the United States; reduce the vulnerability of the United States to terrorism; and minimize the damage, and assist in the recovery, from terrorist attacks that do occur within the United States."[6] Although DHS as formed contained structural elements necessary for a broader mission beyond just terrorism, for years afterwards, federal resources previously aimed at naturally occurring disaster response were often redirected toward domestic terrorism priorities, the wars in Afghanistan and Iraq, and related military and law enforcement issues. In particular, FEMA, one of the 22 component agencies that the government haphazardly placed under the umbrella of DHS after 9/11, suffered from this neglect of naturally occurring disaster response.

The Muddled Homeland Security Mandate: FEMA the "Stepchild"

FEMA was a civilian, nonsecurity/nonlaw-enforcement entity chartered for natural disaster management and recovery, principally dealing with the effects of hurricanes. Though the original OHS mandate contained no specific mention of nonterrorist threats, by absorbing FEMA, DHS included at least an *implied* mandate for concern about naturally occurring, nonterrorist risks.[7] Notably, most of the other various federal agencies and organizations that were subsumed within DHS originally encompassed neither explicit civil defense nor military functions, per se, nor even primarily law-enforcement missions, with the exceptions of the Coast Guard, the Border Patrol/Immigration, Customs Service and Immigration and Naturalization Service (now together Immigration and Customs Enforcement), and the Secret Service.

The creation of DHS showed that conflicts between theory and practice, particularly in bureaucratic structure and execution, could have enormous security implications for prevention, preparation, response, and recovery from both potential terrorist and naturally occurring disasters. In February 2006, Congressional hearings held four months after Katrina and Rita, former FEMA director Michael Brown confirmed that the agency had experienced reduced status and neglect when it was put under the DHS umbrella.[8] In the days before and immediately after Katrina, despite numerous explicit reports and warnings, both DHS and the White House were slow to make the hurricane and subsequent flooding a major national priority. More broadly, Brown asserted that neither had truly cared about nonterrorist threats, and had demoted natural disasters to being a "stepchild" of national security. He testified, "It is my belief [that if] we've confirmed that a terrorist has [sic] blown up the 17th Street Canal levee, then everybody would have jumped all over that and been trying to do everything they could."[9] Indeed, even administration supporters reluctantly concluded that Katrina fell through the cracks in part because the agency typically in charge had been swallowed up by a security enforcement/counterterrorism organization.

The Elusive Comparative Risk Analysis Approach

Even within the terrorism aspects of homeland security, comparative risk prioritization proved difficult, given a frustrating lack of precedents, minimal field or research data, and the political realities of the day. In the immediate years after 9/11, U.S. government homeland security terrorism spending was rarely systematic or coherent. Complaints mounted about counterterrorism money misallocated on air-conditioned garbage trucks and other unnecessary schemes, about overlooked vulnerabilities in key areas such as port and border security or bioterrorism, or of complicated federal-state allocation formulas which valued petting zoos in rural areas on a par with New York City monuments.[10] Moreover, as late as fiscal year 2006, the Transportation Safety Administration, ostensibly responsible for *all* transportation security, was funded at a 10 to 1 ratio in favor of aviation.

Furthermore, lacking any broad-based system for risk assessment or critical infrastructure prioritization, homeland security policy also defaulted to politically driven population-based allocation, meaning that less populous states received funds disproportionately large in comparison to their demographics or the importance of their commercial activities. However, this began to change slowly, spurred by the realization that low-probability targets in less populous areas were receiving money at higher per-capita rates than high-probability cities such as New York, Los Angeles, and Washington, D.C.

Elemental Natural Disasters and *Forces Majeures*

The U.S. government's preparations before and response to Hurricanes Katrina and Rita shocked a world unaccustomed to seeing the United States fail to react relatively quickly and competently to a major domestic disaster. The following natural disaster threats begin to show why optimal domestic "homeland" security policy should comparatively weigh the potential risks from both nature and man.

Hurricanes

Hurricane Katrina was the biggest natural disaster in modern American history, projected to cost as much as $100 to 200 billion or more before its protracted aftermath was resolved. Yet it was the New Orleans canal levee floodwalls' failure and flooding, and not Katrina itself, that contributed most to the overall economic losses and that caused most of the 1,300 or so hurricane-related deaths. A National Science Foundation report concluded that had the levee floodwalls been properly designed, and had they held as they were supposed to, a large part of Katrina's consequences would have been avoided.[11] Similarly, subsequent investigations showed that despite the fact that local response was overwhelmed by the disaster, federal and state government response was slow, disorganized, and bureaucratically bogged down, adding considerably to the human suffering and chaos.[12]

Hurricane Rita occurred less than a month after Katrina. For a period of time after it had entered the Gulf of Mexico and was heading for the U.S. coast, Rita was among the most powerful (Category 5) hurricanes ever recorded. In the wake of Katrina, people feared an even greater calamity because of Rita's brief strong storm rating. Fears were further magnified by historic memories in southern Texas of the 1900 Galveston hurricane, the deadliest in U.S. history, with between 6,000 and 8,000 killed. Because of those fears, Rita triggered an enormous evacuation of Galveston, Houston, and neighboring areas in Texas. That evacuation went poorly, resulting in confusion, stranded motorists on jammed freeways, and accidental deaths. It further demonstrated a widespread lack of effective U.S. disaster planning and response.

Earthquakes

Seismologists often cannot pinpoint exact figures for energy release and damage, but any earthquake over a 5.5 on a logarithmic magnitude scale is generally considered significant. It is estimated that the largest earthquake ever recorded was a 9.5 magnitude off the coast of Chile, in 1960.[13] The deadliest earthquake ever recorded killed over 800,000 in Shansi Province, China, in 1556. And most recently, in December 2004, the 9.0 magnitude Great Sumatra Indonesia Earthquake, the fourth largest ever recorded, resulted in the infamous Indian Ocean tsunamis that killed up to 280,000 people from Thailand to Somalia. The following year, the 7.6 Pakistan/Kashmir earthquake killed over 80,000 and left over one million homeless.

Most Americans think of California and its San Andreas Fault when they consider U.S. catastrophic earthquake risk. To be sure, California has experienced damaging quakes, such as the 1987 5.9 Whittier Narrows, the 1994 7.1 magnitude Loma Prieta earthquake near San Francisco, and the 1994 6.7 Northridge earthquakes, the latter causing $40 billon in damage and 57 deaths.[14] And certainly various worst-case estimates put consequences to Los Angeles or San Francisco in the hundreds of millions of dollars—with potentially over 10,000 dead. Nevertheless, significant threats from major seismic events exist from *active* faults in other U.S. regions, such as Alaska, and the 700-mile-long Cascadia subduction zone, just off the Pacific Northwest coast. New York City sits on a network of faults thought to be capable of producing shaking equivalent to the 6.8 Kobe, Japan Earthquake.[15]

Tsunamis

Tsunamis are most frequently associated with earthquakes, but natural underwater landslides on the continental shelf, the collapse of dry landmasses such as volcanic islands, or ice shelves, into a body of water, or volcanic eruptions may all generate catastrophic events. A number of reports done after the calamitous December 2004 Indian Ocean tsunami warned of substantial U.S. tsunami risk, particularly in the Pacific Basin states of Washington, Oregon, Alaska, California, and Hawaii. In the twentieth century, most destructive American tsunamis originated in Alaska and Pacific Basin sites thousands of miles away. The 1960 Chilean 9.5 earthquake produced 80-foot tsunami surges and killed almost 2,000 within 30 minutes. But the same tsunamis also reached Hawaii, 6,500 miles and 15 hours later, with 35-foot waves that killed 61 people and caused $24 million in damage. Due in part to that event, Hawaii is now the best tsunami-prepared U.S. state.

Perhaps the greatest American tsunami threat potential is from the Cascadia subduction zone, which 300 years ago generated quakes with tsunamis as big as the 2004 Sumatra/Indian Ocean event. Indeed, every 500 years on average, it is believed to be capable of earthquakes substantial enough to generate tsunami surges from as much as 30 to 100 feet, hitting the coast within half an hour or less.[16] Moreover, tsunamis could be devastating to the economy of the United States, capable of crippling key trade facilities, such as those at the ports of Los Angeles and Long Beach. Even a smaller tsunami could cost up to $60 billion.[17]

Floods

The flood risk in New Orleans and the Mississippi Delta area was well established before Hurricane Katrina. Yet hurricanes continue to be a flooding threat until major, decades-long redesign and reconstruction of levees and floodwalls, as well as costly restoration of the deteriorating Delta itself, can be accomplished.

A less well known but similar threat from catastrophic levee breaches and flooding exists in California's critical San Joaquin-Sacramento River Delta. Among its many critical functions, the delta supplies up to half of the drinking water supply for more than 20 million Southern Californians. Unfortunately, projections estimate that worst-case levee/dike breaches could rival the Hurricane Katrina catastrophe, and devastate the California economy. One key report estimates a 60 percent chance of a catastrophic delta flood or levee-breaching earthquake by 2050. According to the state's top water official, failure of the decrepit levee/dike system would flood islands, damage highways and oil pipelines, submerge thousands of homes, and push Pacific Ocean saltwater eastward, potentially disrupting state water deliveries for more than a year.[18]

For Better *and* Worse: Globalization, Infectious Diseases, and the Biological Century

The scourge of pathogenic organisms is age-old. During the twentieth century alone, for example, up to 500 million people died of smallpox before that disease was eradicated from the natural environment. Diseases such as cholera, yellow fever, plague, typhoid fever, and polio have vexed humanity at different times throughout history.

The rise of the postwar liberal economic system has led to tremendous prosperity in many parts of the world, particularly among the Western industrialized countries. This material comfort has fostered dramatic advances in medical science, public health, standards of living, and life expectancy, through revolutions in immunization, antibiotics, and disease prevention methods. Such advances in health have led to most Western nations being *relatively* unworried about the effects of lethal infectious diseases.

The Bioterrorism-Bird Flu Nexus

The simplest reason for analyzing naturally occurring and bioterrorist-caused *catastrophic infectious disease outbreaks* (CIDOs) in tandem is that unlike other terrorist or nonterrorist threats, almost all prevention, preparation, protection, and consequence mitigating response strategies overlap, no matter what the causality. This reasoning is based on the following suppositions:

1. Naturally occurring disease pandemics have the potential to kill as many or even far more people than weapons of mass destruction (WMD) terrorism.
2. Bioterrorist WMDs have the potential to kill as many or even more people than nuclear terrorism.
3. Bioterrorism (BT) is very difficult to prevent, in part because bioweapons production, transportation, and dissemination is comparatively easy to conceal.
4. Unlike other potential weapons of mass destruction, homeland security strategies and resources needed to manage BT vulnerabilities and consequences are uniquely similar to those necessary for naturally occurring outbreaks.
5. Strategies to deal with microbial threat, regardless of causality, are uniquely different from most other terrorist countermeasures and should favor improving nontraditional *local and state* vs. federal "critical infrastructures" capabilities, such as public health, the overall health care system, emergency medical services, all of which would raise societal and global resiliency to both terrorism and naturally occurring catastrophes of all types.
6. Together, both outbreak sources illustrate the unusual strategic, jurisdictional, and conceptual problems inherent in such broadly cross-cutting subject areas.[19]

Globalization Externalities: Public Health Goods and "Bads"

For decades before anthrax, SARS, and avian influenza, warnings from the global public health expert community that globalization, population pressures, and neglect of public health infrastructure were rapidly increasing global microbial disease risks went largely unheeded.[20] Only after the turn of the millennium, with the interdependent world anxious over first SARS and then avian influenza, did policymakers and the public finally begin to respond to these naturally occurring threats.

Pathogenic microbial *threats*, the first component of *risk*, are the equivalent of the terrorist and his weapon(s). Pathogens are being aided by the unintended side effects, what economists refer to as externalities, of increasing globalization. Specifically, rapidly expanding trade, travel, urbanization, antibiotic and other antimicrobial drug misuse and overuse, and even organized crime growth have created significant transnational vulnerabilities to catastrophic infectious disease outbreaks, whatever their cause. Meanwhile, growing bioterrorism threats are a sinister externality of microbiological, pharmaceutical, and other scientific advances.[21] On the *vulnerability* and *consequences* side of the risk equation, both types of CIDO threats are also as high as they are because of continued neglect of public health, emergency medical systems, and the steady privatization of health care worldwide. From a disaster management standpoint, those "critical infrastructures" are just as important as electricity, fuel, food and water, and transportation systems, but they had not been viewed as such by most homeland security analysts until well into the first decade of the new century.

Although globalization has been a major catalyst for many of these related health and wealth advances, the world's economic system has simultaneously generated an ironic, growing burden. For its continued robust growth, the modern, integrated trading system has come to depend on the economic participation of more of the world's population than ever before. Overall global trade doubled during the 1990s.[22] Vulnerability to CIDOs arises because of the very changes that globalization has made in trade in goods and services, international tourism and travel, and the opening and integration of borders. This has created a veritable "trade" in pathogenic organisms and their vectors, improved the ease and speed with which microorganisms can spread, and conveniently herded humanity into interconnected cities, vastly improving the potential for infectious disease transmission.

Naturally Occurring Disease Outbreaks and Civilian Biodefense

Three fundamental characteristics or trends in the current economic regime collectively raise the likelihood that future catastrophic infectious outbreak problems, the indirect public health goods costs of globalization, will grow in magnitude. These include cross-border trade and travel, competitive privatization, and integration.

First, the tremendous volume and penetration of trade in goods and information services promote high levels of unintended "trade" in naturally occurring pathogens as well as deliberate, legal and illegal trade in the agents, equipment, technology, and expertise needed for bioterrorism. Second, private sector-oriented economic liberalization has privileged higher value-added private medical goods and services, and led to worldwide under-investment in and neglectful deterioration of important public health goods and infrastructure. The latter is necessary to mitigate the harsh disruption of human ecosystems that result in increasing infectious disease threats. Third, greater global economic integration has created a more favorable environment for catastrophic disease outbreaks to spread widely and quickly, by opening borders and promoting high volumes of rapid travel, economic migration, and urbanization. People are closer together and more quickly accessible to microbes. Ultimately, the risks from pathogenic outbreaks rise because, in a world that is more interdependent every year, the health of one person, nation, or region cannot easily be isolated from the health of all. Below, two of the most notable CIDO outbreaks since the turn of the century are described; each was aided and abetted by globalization.

SARS

In March 2003 the World Health Organization (WHO) issued the first of a series of rare global alerts about a novel viral outbreak that had alarmed the entire world with its suddenness, novelty, and mortality rates. Over 8,000 became ill, and over 800 perished, a 10 percent case mortality rate, in China, Hong Kong, Singapore, Vietnam, Canada, and more than a dozen other nations around the world. The pathogen, dubbed severe acute respiratory syndrome-corona virus (SARS-CoV), was a newly mutated strain, a cousin of a common cold microbe.[23]

China's SARS outbreak exemplified the need for increased international public health regulation. Early on, Chinese cover ups and belligerent assertions of sovereignty contributed to what might have become a global pandemic. The WHO was stymied during the crucial early stages of the outbreak by a lack of sanction ability, and forced to cajole and embarrass the Chinese regime into cooperating in the SARS investigation and control effort. Among the many other alarming characteristics of SARS was its ability to kill victims who had access to intensive emergency health care, leading public health experts at the time to wonder how much higher already impressive death rates would climb if SARS reached rural areas of China or other nations. For instance, the Canadian outbreak, centered in Toronto, compiled over a 10 percent mortality rate amidst some of the best medical care in the world.[24]

At its outset, some had even speculated that this could be the start of a deadly pandemic, akin to the notorious 1918 influenza. The broad WHO alert urged curtailed travel in affected areas, and led to significant economic losses to these tourism- and commerce-dependent regions, as well as heightened global public fears. Nevertheless, the WHO would later be applauded for its quick action. In the end, one model estimated *short*-term global losses from curtailed economic activity and trade, as well as within key economic sectors such as medical, travel, consumer confidence, and investment, at $80 billion. Actual medium- to long-term losses were clearly greater.[25]

Avian Influenza: The Inter-Pandemic Period, and Planning for the Inevitable

Influenza pandemics have occurred periodically throughout history, so much so that leading experts refer to times in between as "inter-pandemic period(s)." In 1997, the first indicator that the current inter-pandemic period might soon come to a close occurred in Hong Kong with the first H5N1 strain outbreak, which killed six people and led to the well-publicized slaughter of over a million virus-carrying chickens and fowl. As with the infamous 1918 influenza virus, this "avian" flu had apparently mutated from a benign form into one against which humans had little natural resistance. The Hong Kong outbreak had approximately a 33 percent mortality rate. As one observer stated: "While the outbreak highlighted the success of the [influenza] surveillance network, it also showed how dangerously mutable influenza viruses can be, and that, in their most deadly forms, they can be as deadly as any other disease known to man, more akin to Ebola than to the fevers and aches most people associate with flu."[26]

Highly pathogenic avian (H5N1) influenza fully emerged on the global radar around 2005.[27] While initially killing less than 100 people, the "bird" flu had more than a 50 percent case fatality/mortality rate, and an uncertain potential of mutating or reassorting to create a deadly global pandemic.[28] In October 2005, David Nabarro, World Health Organization (WHO) chief of avian influenza, declared that a human "bird flu" pandemic was inevitable, despite the fact that little or no human-to-human transmission had then occurred. Nabarro based his prediction on the observation that carried by migratory birds transmitting the virus to domestic bird flocks, the avian (H5N1) flu was spreading to every part of the world. With each animal and human exposure, there was a rising risk of viral mutation, or of H5N1 exchanging genetic material within the cauldron of a person co-infected with "normal" human flu. In November 2005, the WHO issued a report projecting the global gross domestic product (GDP) to decline by 2 percent during a modest flu pandemic. This is commensurate with quarterly losses sustained by Hong Kong and Toronto during the SARS epidemic.

Even in an average season, 40,000 to 50,000 Americans die, and 114,000 are hospitalized, due to influenza annually. These figures are projected to increase steadily, in all Western nations, with expanding susceptible elderly populations. Periodically, however, Type-A influenza viruses undergo significant genetic change, or *antigenic shift*, allowing "sudden, pervasive infection in all age groups."[29] Estimates on possible death and disruption from the next global influenza pandemic vary widely. The CDC estimates in the worst case a human-to-human transmissible H5N1 could cause 90,000 to 207,000 American deaths alone, almost a million hospitalizations, and potentially sicken a third of the U.S. population in a matter of months. The estimated economic impact might range from $70 to $170 billion dollars, not accounting for "disruptions to commerce and society."[30] A 2006 World Bank report asserted the economic losses in a worst case could exceed $550 billion for the high-income nations alone, $1 trillion to $3 trillion overall. The Asian Development Bank projected economic damage of $280 billion in the East Asia region, assuming 20 percent of the region's population falls ill. Other worst-case estimates put U.S. deaths between 200,000 and 1.9 million, with 92 million illnesses, and 100 to 300 million deaths worldwide, possibly within a ten-week period. Even a moderately severe pandemic, more akin to the 1968 flu outbreak, if adjusted for population, could cost $180 billion, not even including business disruptions.[31]

With proper collective international action, globalization's negative role in amplifying these rising pathogenic threats can be reduced, and its positive contributions to global health continued and enhanced. However, in an era of global integration the threat from catastrophic infectious diseases will never be eliminated.

Bioweapons and Bioterrorism: The Dark Side of the Biotechnology Revolution

Only recently have most security analysts or even medical experts fully fathomed the idea that biological weapons have a rapidly, inexorably growing potential for casualties on a scale not imagined since the Cold War. Frequently referred to as "public health in reverse," biological terrorism is a significant current and future threat to both Western and non-Western societies. Because of scientific advances, amidst proliferation of various possible terrorist weapons of mass destruction,[32] bioweapons may ultimately hold the greatest risk of all for creating terror, disruption, disease, and death. But unlike nuclear or even chemical weapons threats, it is far more difficult to police these technologies and materials. The increasingly available equipment and processing techniques for modern medical research and pharmaceutical production overlap considerably with technology and equipment needed to produce and disseminate biological agents for ill-purpose.

As a broad potential WMD category, BT risk assessment is uniquely challenging: it is more a future threat than one with a discernable historic pattern, and possesses difficult, complex first-response and consequence management dynamics, especially in worst-case scenarios. Indeed, it is not easy to comparatively rank BT risk by the pathogen or germ, given the importance of technological variables in genetic engineering, processing, delivery and dispersal, and environmental (including weather) conditions at the time of an attack. To some extent, these variables transcend the mere existence or availability of a historically deadly naturally occurring bug. Is smallpox more dangerous than anthrax or tularemia? The answer must always be "it depends," and on more than simple agent availability and traditional naturally occurring disease mortality rates.

Biological weapons, and other weapons of mass destruction as well as catastrophic terrorism in general are, as Ashton Carter noted: "destined to be a centerpiece of the field of international security"—the newest "A-list" security challenges for the twenty-first century.[33] Of these ascendant terrorist threats, biological terrorism has been the least understood within the security policy community. Among the reasons bioterrorism is misunderstood, and Western civilian biodefense preparation has been poor, is the unique nature of pathogenic agents and the disease outbreaks they can cause. Unlike virtually all other possible acts of terrorism, bioterrorism events are *public health disasters*, first and foremost. They are criminal acts as well. Indeed, effective bioterrorism policy should have ultimately less in common with traditional security measures, or even nuclear and chemical terrorism response, than it does with traditional public health, epidemiology, and emergency disaster preparedness and response. Bioterrorism preparation and countermeasures resemble other counter-WMD methods, and all terrorism, for that matter, primarily in the realm of intelligence gathering and covert operations aimed at prevention and interdiction. But the latter are far more difficult for bioterrorism than for other weapons of mass destruction and, thus, bioterrorism countermeasures are far more likely to be cost effective at the levels of vulnerability and consequence management. Bioterrorism is a uniquely dangerous form of terror-causing havoc, due to its ability to inflict intense combinations of death, disease, and disruption.

How Dangerous Is Bioterrorism? The BT Technology Growth Curve

Prior to 9/11 and to the 2001 anthrax attacks, few American security or terrorism analysts fully understood or appreciated the growing potential of biological threats. But for vulnerable civilian populations, whatever the current risk may be, the threat from bioweapons is growing. Considerable debate exists concerning the current *probability and potential* of mass casualty bioterrorism, ranging from those who claim bioterrorism is the greatest threat to humanity, exceeding even nuclear terrorism,[34] and others claiming that the probabilities are very small and over-hyped. Still others are concerned that bioterrorism has shifted attention away from other terrorism risks and serious public health priorities. The controversy over homeland security policy in the wake of the 2005 Hurricane Katrina debacle, in which critics charged DHS and the White House with excessive concentration on terrorism over naturally occurring threats mirrors, to some extent, the aforementioned debate about bioterrorism's purported importance.

One example that amply demonstrates some, though not all, of the potential for biological agents is *Bacillus anthracis*, the bacteria responsible for causing anthrax. Anthrax is believed to be a significant biological terrorism threat, particularly because it has already shown it has capabilities in two major historical incidents. The first was an inadvertent 1979 release of aerosolized anthrax spores at a military bioweapons facility in the Russian city of Sverdlovsk, an incident denied by the Soviets until after the Cold War's end, that resulted in up to 100 cases of civilian anthrax infection, and roughly 68 confirmed deaths. In October and November of 2001, the "anthrax letter" attacks targeted U.S. media and Congressional offices in Florida, Washington, D.C., and New York, among others. Around eleven cases of inhalation anthrax were confirmed, among whom five died. Decontamination and treatment alone cost tens of millions. The World Health Organization estimated in 1970 that in the event of an aircraft release of only 50 kg (around 30 lb) of dry, weaponized anthrax over a major urban area of 5 million people, 250,000 would be exposed and 100,000 might be expected to die. A well-known 1993 U.S. Congressional Office of Technology Assessment (OTA) report projected anywhere from 130,000 to 3 million deaths in Washington, D.C. in the event of a 100-kg aerosolized anthrax release from a private plane flying at night, upwind and under proper wind conditions. It noted that such casualty numbers rivaled those of a hypothesized hydrogen bomb.

If properly produced—by growing, freeze-drying (lyophilization), milling to optimal 1- to 5-micron particles, and treating with an antistatic coating—anthrax is a potent bioweapon. Colorless, odorless, and properly weaponized, such anthrax spores would float freely on the wind, almost as a gas, and if inhaled by unsuspecting victims, lodge deep in the lung's alveoli.[35] The first sign of infection, unless an attack was detected by bioagent detectors, would be patients entering emergency rooms with flu-like symptoms, starting around 36 to 48 hours after the attack. But the prognosis for symptomatic (those already ill) anthrax victims is very poor, even with antibiotic drug treatment and intensive medical support in modern hospitals. The U.S. Strategic National Stockpile (SNS) of key medicines and supplies is capable of flying prophylactic and treatment doses to any major city within twelve hours, but distribution to millions of residents in less than two days is extremely unlikely, and there is controversy about whether enough doses would be available on short notice for such a crash prophylaxis campaign.

Today, most knowledgeable analysts recognize that whatever the current level of threat from bioterrorism, the BT technology growth curve is steeper than any other known WMD threat. That is, regardless of how significant the current risk, future BT risk will eventually surpass other weapons with mass casualty potential (see Figure 8.1), largely because technological advances are making it easier to process or weaponize an agent, but also to genetically engineer more deadly varieties, or even new combinations of pathogens. There has been much ongoing discussion about weapons of mass destruction since the attacks on 9/11. Nuclear, biological, and chemical weapons are those *generally* considered to be WMD, in contrast to conventional arms. WMD are unique among terrorist weapons in that they are by definition terrifying and indiscriminate in whom they target.[36]

In comparison, nuclear weapons technology and techniques are fairly well established, and while the proliferation and availability of fissile material, the largest factor in nuclear terrorism, has the potential to change over time, it is unlikely to do so radically, given global efforts to keep it in check. The potential threat from chemical weapons is, for the moment, similarly on a flatter curve: major efforts are being made to destroy or secure Cold War-era military-grade chemical weapons. Even if such weapons were stolen, smuggled, and used, they would never be of much use for generating major mass casualties without massive quantities or highly technical dissemination methods. Finally, both nuclear and chemical weapons technology and materials are far easier to monitor through treaty provisions, export controls, and surveillance. Nuclear enrichment facilities are beyond the capability of any entity other than a nation-state. Furthermore, the technology, materials, and equipment for both nuclear and chemical weapons of any significance are all fairly specialized. In contrast, three major differences make biological weaponry stand out from other WMD:

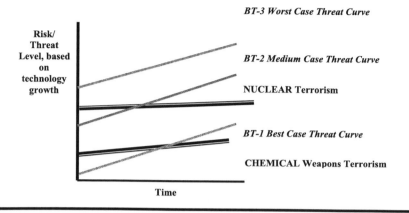

Figure 8.1 Comparing levels of bioterrorism (BT) risk/threat to nuclear and chemical terrorism, over time, given hypothetical technology trajectories.

1. The production and processing techniques potentially used for bioweapons are very similar and in many instances virtually identical to those used in the pharmaceutical, medical research, gene therapy, and biotechnology industries.
2. Much of the equipment used in the aforementioned global industries for producing beneficial biological products, drug and gene therapies, etc. can be used to mass produce and process biological agents for easier dissemination. Many of these technologies are widely available on the open market for pharmaceutical drug production.
3. Bioweapons are generally more easily concealed than other WMD.

Variables in Using BT Weapons

Whether successfully weaponized for maximal dispersal or spread by the cough or touch of an infectious victim, biological weapons provide considerable versatility for terrorists and unpredictability for potential targets. Biological weapons present a far more complex future terrorism risk than most. Broadly speaking, there are several variables that determine the likely success or failure of a biological attack: the specific biological agent, the environment in which it is disseminated, and the delivery and dissemination methods used. Any of these variables might render an attack ineffective; conversely, they might magnify its impact.

Although the *sine qua non* of any biological weapons attack is the disease-causing agent or pathogen, not all pathogen species or strains, nor the bioagents they are turned into, are equal. Among the CDC's highest-priority pathogens[37] deemed most likely to be used or most dangerous are *bacterial* agents, and the diseases they cause: *B. anthracis* (anthrax), *Yersinia pestis* (plague), *Francisella tularensis* (tularemia), and *C. botulinum* toxin (botulism). Threatening *viruses* include *variola* (smallpox) and numerous viral hemorrhagic fever-causing viruses (including Ebola, Marburg, Machupo, Junin, etc).

There are numerous inherent determinates of how effective the biological weapon agent might be, or the dynamics of the outbreak that might subsequently be caused. One is whether the pathogen and any strains or variations would be an effective disease-creating agent; most pathogenic microbes have multiple strains or variations. Next is the state and quality of how the agent has been processed, including whether it has been "weaponized" for easy dispersal in the air to the greatest number of people. As a rule, it is difficult to produce highly weaponized dry bioagent but easy to disperse such material, and easier to produce wet agent but difficult to aerosolize it for widespread dissemination. Environmental conditions are also critical to the success of a bioweapon attack: Aside from anthrax, sunlight can degrade the material, rain might literally dampen the impact, and high winds or those blowing in the wrong direction can prevent infection of those targeted. Alternatively, the interior of an enclosed building presents an ideal dissemination environment: cool, dry, with light, widely circulating air flow. Delivery and dissemination methods are particularly important for wet biological agents, necessitating very precise equipment for massive aerosolization (though perhaps only a perfume atomizer for small scale). Contrary to popular fears, a crop-dusting aircraft would have to be modified to present a threat from wet agent. Lastly is the susceptibility of the targeted population: If some or all have natural or induced immunity to the pathogenic bioagent, or are protected by preventive antibiotics, the attack may be less effective or even fail outright, the psychological impact notwithstanding.[38]

Agricultural Bioterrorism

Biological terrorism may be defined generally as the deliberate use of pathogenic (disease-causing) organisms or their byproducts to cause, or threaten to cause, a disease outbreak that sickens, kills, intimidates or otherwise sows fear or anxiety among people. Nevertheless, bioterrorism agents might be only indirectly targeted toward humans, and thus might be used to harm animals, crops, or even inanimate objects (see Table 8.1). Although terrorist infection of food crops or animals would not necessarily imply human casualties, such an attack could wreak considerable economic and psychological damage, disrupting food supply chains, causing massive, broadly disruptive quarantine areas. Just as a global avian flu pandemic could disrupt key supply chains, with rapid demand-driven price rises, so too could agricultural bioterrorism. Many crop spores, such as the wheat fungus *Puccinia*, already a destructive commercial crop pathogen, can spread with the wind for over 100 miles. If a bioterrorist was to mass produce such funguses, and process them into easily aerosolizable form, they could be used to destroy millions of acres of crops in a furtive attack. Many other crop disease organisms might be produced and deployed in such ways.

Table 8.1 Types of Bioterrorism

Target of Bioterror	Examples of Agents	Transmission Mechanisms	Possible Consequences
Humans	Anthrax, smallpox, plague, botulinum toxin, tularemia, E. coli, salmonella (various strains)	Aerosol delivery, food/water/ surface contamination, injection, human "suicide" attack	Human death, illness, fear, disruption, economic losses
Indirect to humans, via vector, zoonosis	West Nile virus, yellow fever, hantavirus, "mad cow" disease, VEE, EEE	Livestock, domestic fowl, wild animals, mosquitoes, birds, rats	Human death, illness, fear, disruption, economic losses
Agricultural crops	Corn, soybean, wheat rust, numerous other funguses, bacteria, viruses	Crop dusting, other aerosol, contaminate fertilizer, seed, wind-blown from infected crops, etc.	Mostly economic loss, fear, anxiety, disruption, possibly even hunger/famine
Animals	Bird flu (various), foot and mouth, anthrax, Rinderpest, brucellosis	Feed/water, animal to animal zoonosis, aerosol, soil contamination	Economic losses, anxiety, disruption
Inanimate materials, vehicle parts, etc.* *future threat	Technology under development (see microbial oil spill dispersal research, e.g.)	Contamination, timed release mechanism, aerosol transmission	Economic losses, disruption, and/or death/injury from sabotage (e.g., crash of aircraft, train/subway brake failure, etc.)

The Comparative Dimensions of Homeland Security Risk Analysis

The 2005 Gulf hurricanes, as well as the emergence of avian (H5N1) influenza, forced a reexamination among both the American public and policymakers of the operational definition and strategies behind homeland security. The question is not whether but how catastrophic natural disaster threats such as hurricanes, tsunamis, floods, earthquakes, and infectious diseases should be weighed against the risks of terrorism in the prevailing political, social, and fiscal environment. Homeland security must now account for a "new" critical infrastructure, including areas such as public health, emergency medical services, and the greater health care system in the United States. In these areas, security overlaps with social welfare, but so it must be when civilian public goods are at issue.

The Brave New World of Katrina and Osama—But With Tradeoffs

Terrorism-related preparation, response, and consequence management will remain an indispensable part of securing the overall well-being of the United States, but many of the risks posed by nonterrorist threats are great and growing. Some of these may exceed terrorism in probability and potential consequences to Americans, as well as the increasingly vulnerable, interdependent global economic system. However one defines "homeland security," the fact remains that in an era of growing risks to the nation and world from both man-made and natural threats, an integrated policy response is necessary, and comparative risk analysis is a central tool for assessing the variety of security challenges faced by the nation and the world.

But where does that leave us, now that extreme weather, earthquakes, and other natural catastrophes might, at least on paper, constitute "homeland security?" Should we assume that DHS has embraced this broader, though arguably ill-defined, crisis-driven mandate from Congress, the White House, and the American people? And if so, are DHS, DHHS and other government entities up to the tasks presented by these newly broadened priorities, and can they integrate them into the current bureaucratic and governmental security apparatus without major structural, conceptual, and "cultural" changes?

Considerable barriers remain to such change. The 2005 Gulf hurricanes, with their chaotic, troubling implications for disaster preparation and response, and the emergence of pandemic influenza, fundamentally changed most Americans' views of U.S. security priorities. Yet that does not mean these altered perspectives translated into significant changes in mission at DHS or other security-related federal agencies. Such institutions continued, as before those events, to illustrate the comparative weakness of nontraditional security constituencies compared to traditional ones, yet the American public believed that change would happen, and more would be done to address the disparity between terrorism and naturally occurring disaster countermeasures policy.

In U.S. homeland security strategy and policy, the natural disaster response function was and still is secondary, and the U.S. Department of Homeland Security until recently still considered itself primarily a security and law-enforcement agency.[39] Katrina was not unique, however, and potentially far greater globalization-related threats will challenge the homeland security paradigm even more. The most significant catastrophic nonterrorist threat of all will likely be from microbial diseases, including the risk of pandemic influenza. But bureaucratically, there are impediments in the current response system for dealing with catastrophic infectious disease outbreaks.[40] Historically, at the political level, terrorism, law enforcement, and traditional security interests have trumped natural threats. This is due to long-standing relative bureaucratic/political powerlessness of "low politics" civilian social welfare-oriented institutions associated with public health, emergency medicine, and emergency disaster response. The optimal national homeland security strategy for addressing both naturally occurring and man-made (terrorist) catastrophic risk may be to separate FEMA from DHS, and elevate the former to cabinet status in order to let both entities do what they do best, and in order to locate governmental capability and policy planning for naturally occurring disasters in a place of importance and power within the government bureaucracy.

Endnotes

1. For an analogous rethink, see Michael Howard, "The forgotten dimensions of strategy," Foreign Affairs (Summer 1979).
2. I acknowledge the importance of accidental catastrophes, such as industrial chemical, nuclear, or fuel storage mishaps, but these might also rise to become homeland security "incidents of national significance," just as any of those mentioned here, causes notwithstanding.
3. Particularly in the mid-1990s, with the Aum Shinrikyo Tokyo subway sarin attack, the Oklahoma City bombing, and the first World Trade Center bombing, among others.
4. Officially the U.S. Commission on National Security/21st Century, established in 1998 to assess global threats to domestic security and develop a national security strategy, headed by former senators Gary Hart and Warren Rudman.
5. See for instance, "An interview with Assistant Secretary of Defense for Homeland Defense, Paul McHale," in which the distinction is described as the following: "[H]omeland defense [is] the protection of U.S. sovereignty, territory, domestic population, and critical defense infrastructure against external threats and aggression or other threats as directed by the President, and that direction is pursuant to his authority as Commander in Chief. We define homeland security as a concerted national effort to prevent terrorist attacks within the United States, reduce America's vulnerability to terrorism, and minimize the damage and recover from attacks that do occur." Joint Force Quarterly (Issue 40, first quarter 2006). Available at www.ndupress.ndu.edu.
6. H.R. 5005-8 the Homeland Security Act of 2002. See the DHS Web site for links to its history and charter at http://www.dhs.gov/dhspublic/display?theme=59&content=411.
7. See for instance Planning Scenarios: Executive Summaries. The White House Homeland Security Council (July 2004), in which scenarios included the naturally occurring disasters, major earthquake, hurricane, and pandemic influenza.
8. Eric Lipton, "White House Knew of Levee's Failure on Night of Storm," New York Times, February 10, 2006.
9. Eric Lipton, "Ex-FEMA Leader Faults Response by White House," New York Times, February 11, 2006.

10. "Progress in Developing the National Asset Database," Department of Homeland Security, Office of the Inspector General, OIG-06-40 (June 2006); MSNBC News Services, "Inspector: Homeland Security Database Flawed," July 12, 2006, http://www.msnbc.msn.com/id/13822662/.

11. See for instance Bob Marshall, "17th Street Canal Levee Was Doomed," New Orleans Times Picayune, November 30, 2005. NOLA.com.

12. For a contemporaneous assessment of what went wrong, see for instance James Carney, Karen Tumulty, Amanda Ripley, and Mark Thompson, "Four Places Where the System Broke Down," Time, September 11, 2005.

13. Standard Richter and moment magnitude scales are logarithmic measures of gross energy output, but many now prefer the Modified Mercali Scale, which gauges the physical effects at any given point on the surface, and thus the amount of likely damage.

14. California Geological Survey, http://www.consrv.ca.gov/CGS/geologic_hazards/earthquakes/index.htm.

15. U.S. Geological Survey, "The Mississippi Valley—Whole Lotta Shakin' Goin' On," www.USGS.gov.

16. Sandi Doughton, "Tsunami Preparedness on Rise," Seattle Times, December 26, 2005. seattletimes.nwsource.com.

17. Sharon Bernstein, "Reports Warn of Tsunami Danger," Los Angeles Times, December 13, 2005; and Alicia Chang, "Report: California Unprepared for Tsunami," Associated Press, December 12, 2005.

18. Mike Lee, "Weak Levees Threaten the State's Economy and S.D. Water Supply," San Diego Union-Tribune, January 5, 2006.

19. In one key example, under the 2005 National Response Plan (NRP) and National Incident Management System (NIMS), the Department of Health and Human Services (DHHS), which includes the Centers for Disease Control and Prevention (CDC) and National Institutes of Health (NIH), is designated the lead agency for bioterrorism and pandemic flu disasters—despite the fact that DHS (Homeland Security) spends considerable time and resources on these very issues as well.

20. Joshua Lederberg, Robert E. Shope, and Stanley C. Oaks, Jr., Emerging Infections: Microbial Threats to Health in the United States (Washington, D.C.: Institute of Medicine, National Academy Press, 1992), 2; Sue Binder, A. M. Levitt, J. J. Sacks, and J. M. Hughes, "Emerging Infectious Diseases: Public Health Issues for the 21st Century," Science 284, no. 5418 (21 May 1999): 1311–1313.

21. Ali S. Khan and David A. Ashford, "Ready or Not—Preparedness for Bioterrorism," New England Journal of Medicine 345, no. 4 (July 26, 2001): 288.

22. World Trade Organization, various statistics, accessed at http://www.wto.org.

23. For an outstanding analysis, see especially Stacey Knobler, Adel Mahmoud, Stanley Lemon, Alison Mack, Laura Sivitz, and Katherine Oberholtzer, eds., Learning from SARS: Preparing for the Next Disease Outbreak (Washington, D.C.: National Academies Press, 2004).

24. See for instance Evelyn Iritani, "Illness May Slow Trade with China: California Firms Weigh Their Options as Concerns Grow About the Spread of the Respiratory Virus," Los Angeles Times, April 2, 2003; and Keith Bradsher, "Virus Spread Havoc on Businesses," New York Times, April 3, 2003.

25. Knobler et al., Learning from SARS, 9–11.

26. Erik Larson, "The Flu Hunters," Time, February 23, 1998, 55–64.

27. Although initial human deaths occurred in Hong Kong as early as 1997, much to the concern of global public health authorities, and led to wide-scale cautionary poultry slaughters even then.

28. A very good technical and historical summary of the H5N1 avian flu dilemma is Stacey Knobler, Alison Mack, Adel Mahmoud, and Stanley Lemon, eds., The Threat of Pandemic Flu: Are We Ready? (Washington, D.C.: National Academies Press, 2005).

29. Raymond A. Strikas, Gregory S. Wallace, and Martin G. Myers, "Preparing for Pandemic Influenza," Infectious Medicine 18, no. 12 (2001): 544–545.

30. Martin Meltzer, Nancy J. Cox, and K. Fakuda, "The Economic Impact of Pandemic Influenza in the United States: Priorities for Intervention," Emerging Infectious Diseases 5, no. 5 (September-October 1999): 659–671.

31. Patrick Dixon, "World Has Lost Control of Bird Flu," www.globalchange.com/bird-flu.htm.

32. CBNRE (chemical, biological, nuclear, radiological or high-explosive) weapons, assumed to include terrorist methods capable of causing mass casualties, large-scale economic losses and disruption, or all these.

33. Ashton B. Carter, "The Architecture of Government in the Face of Terrorism," International Security 26, no. 3 (Winter 2001/02): 5.

34. For a pre-9/11 view, see Graham S. Pearson, "Why Biological Weapons Present The Greatest Danger," The Seventh International Symposium on Protection against Chemical and Biological Warfare Agents, Stockholm, 15–19 June, 2001.

35. See for instance Ken Alibek, Thomas R. Dashiell, Adrian Dwyer, Scott Layne M.D., William C. Patrick III, Donald R. Ponikvar, Jane's Chem-Bio Handbook, 3rd ed. (Jane's Information Group, 2005).

36. Jessica Stern, The Ultimate Terrorists, 11–12.

37. See the CDC's Bioterrorism Agents Web page at http://www.bt.cdc.gov/agent/agentlist-category.asp. High-priority agents include pathogens that are rarely seen in the United States, and organisms that are believed to pose a risk to national security because they (1) can be easily disseminated or transmitted from person to person; (2) result in high mortality rates and have the potential for major public health impact; (3) might cause public panic and social disruption; and (4) require special action for public health preparedness.

38. Take as an example Bacillus anthracis, the agent responsible for anthrax. In one instance, the Japanese cult Aum Shinrikyo produced relatively large quantities of anthrax bacilli spores, and appeared to have successfully dispersed it in Japanese residential suburbs in "experiments" that failed primarily because they had inadvertently acquired a strain that was harmless to humans (a weak one used only to produce animal anthrax vaccine). In contrast, in the unsolved 2001 U.S. anthrax attacks, particularly in the case of the so-called Leahy letter, the agent was both potentially lethal and highly weaponized—at the right size to cause optimal lethality and treated to float freely and easily. Thus, with ideal indoor environmental conditions and an elegantly simple delivery and dispersal device (an opened letter), a few grams were used to infect dozens and contaminate a large area.

39. This was asserted in late 2005, even after Hurricane Katrina, by a high-level DHS official.
40. See Elin A. Gursky, "Drafted to Fight Terror: U.S. Public Health on the Front Lines of Biological Defense." ANSER (August 2004).

Chapter 9

Homeland Security Strategy and Policy Choices
A Local Government Perspective

Greg Moser

Federalism—the division of powers and authority among federal, state, county, municipal, and other local levels—poses a significant challenge to the making and implementation of strategy for homeland security as on so many other issues. Getting government departments and agencies to work together well is by no means an easy task. Having held state and county positions in emergency preparedness, the author has first-hand experience locally with planning for both natural disasters and man-made events. He is only too well aware of the difficulties among different government organizations and cultures at all levels in the making and implementation of strategy for securing the homeland.

Long-established ways and means or approaches to disaster preparedness—focusing on hazards, vulnerabilities, and risks—have not been easy to transfer to the domain of counterterrorism. For his part, the author favors an all-consequences focus regardless of cause as more cost-effective than dissipating limited human and material resources on preparations for particular hazards. Such an all-consequences approach is necessarily inclusive of all hazards, but relative emphasis is placed on potential outcomes—being prepared for all contingencies that can do harm or damage to communities or society as a whole.

Federal priorities typically are different from what most states and localities prefer to pursue. In this regard, the author takes the application of strategy to the tactical level of coordinating and directing the work of first responders who are so essential a part of the strategic effort to secure the homeland. Forging a comprehensive and dynamic strategy for homeland security depends on reconciling or accommodating alternative federal, as well as state and local government and private sector perspectives in a nationwide approach to the problems at hand.

The terrorist attacks of September 11, 2001 and catastrophic hurricanes and other weather events since provide several lessons that have yet to be integrated fully into a comprehensive strategy to make the nation safe from a growing range of hazards and disaster consequences. In the rush to adapt to the dangers of international terrorism, dramatic organizational and policy process changes were enacted often based more on the political need to take action than on a careful and critical analysis of what actions were needed to enhance homeland security.

One result has been the erosion of the federal government's ability to respond to natural disasters, as demonstrated most prominently by the hurricanes of 2005. These events have reminded us that natural disasters are also an important part of national security. As shown in Figure 9.1, the spectrum of hazards is growing, but we are failing to meet these strategic challenges. Prior to 9/11 the threat of terrorism was not fully appreciated by the American public, the country's leaders, or the emergency-response community. In the years since 9/11 we have fallen short in the effort to integrate strategic planning to prevent, limit the damage from, and manage consequences of terrorism with parallel efforts to deal with the dangers of natural

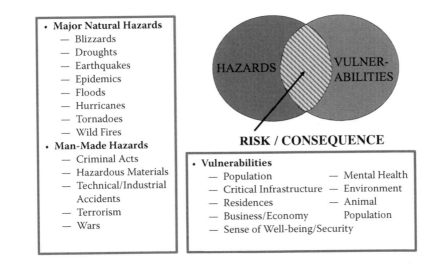

- **Major Natural Hazards**
  — Blizzards
  — Droughts
  — Earthquakes
  — Epidemics
  — Floods
  — Hurricanes
  — Tornadoes
  — Wild Fires
- **Man-Made Hazards**
  — Criminal Acts
  — Hazardous Materials
  — Technical/Industrial Accidents
  — Terrorism
  — Wars

HAZARDS

VULNER-ABILITIES

RISK / CONSEQUENCE

- **Vulnerabilities**
  — Population
  — Critical Infrastructure
  — Residences
  — Business/Economy
  — Sense of Well-being/Security
  — Mental Health
  — Environment
  — Animal Population

Figure 9.1   Hazards, vulnerabilities, and risks.

disasters and other, more traditional hazards that challenge officials particularly at state and local levels.

Constructing a framework that supports an integrated nationwide response is essential,[1] whether the threat is from the growing number of potential catastrophic events or the emergence of dangerous diseases as in an influenza pandemic. Since *prevention* and *mitigation* or limitation of damages may not always succeed, effective response and recovery depend on building preparedness in every community nationwide.

Hazards are defined broadly here as anything that potentially endangers the community or society as a whole. Hazards fall into two broad categories: natural and man-made. Historically, natural hazards have been the primary threat to local communities. Dealing with these environmental hazards and lesser man-made hazards, such as fires and violent crimes, continues to present the highest probability threats at the local level.

As society has developed, man-made hazards have become increasingly potent. These man-made hazards fall into two primary categories. First, technical-industrial hazards are a by-product of an increasingly technological world. The second category of man-made hazards includes criminal activity, terrorism, and war. Even though the scale of a natural disaster may be much larger, the death and destruction due to a natural disaster impacts society differently than does death and destruction caused by a terrorist attack. Although the 2004 tsunamis killed an estimated 240,000 and led to the initiation of an international effort to establish an Indian Ocean warning system,[2] the attacks of 9/11 initiated a global asymmetric war that will cost trillions of dollars, may last for decades, and could escalate into a much broader global conflict. These are clearly very different issues but conceptualization, strategic thinking, and policy-oriented discussions do not always make the necessary distinctions between either the dangers of natural disaster and terrorism or the means by which we respond to these challenges or threats.

Vulnerabilities refer to what is potentially endangered by hazards, including people in communities or society as a whole, critical infrastructure and key resources (CI/KR), the environment, and both public and non-governmental institutions. Although this category seems at first glance to be straightforward enough, CI/KR have proven in fact to be difficult to identify or specify easily. Each of the seventeen CI/KR sectors identified in national strategy documents[3] presents unique challenges that demand significant, highly specialized expertise that is often lacking in government and can be found only in the private sector. Vulnerabilities and the potential consequences associated with them have become fraught with both confusion and contention.

Finally, *risk* is defined as the relation between hazards and vulnerabilities. Reducing risk has long been the objective of homeland security efforts. The way in which we accomplish this objective, however, has been the source of much confusion, competition, in-fighting, and conflict. This has had the effect of undermining what worked before 9/11, while not fully addressing post-9/11 concerns about terrorism. Although both 9/11 and Hurricane Katrina provided examples of how risk may have increased, the federal emphasis since 9/11 has been to address terrorism[4] while leaving basic or core public safety preparedness in the traditional hands of local and state governments that often have little fiscal flexibility in an environment dominated by the practical priorities of day-to-day operations.

The bottom line on hazards, risks, and vulnerabilities is that all three are gradually increasing over time. This becomes particularly problematic when there is disproportionate focus on a single category of hazards, as was the case prior to both 9/11 and the hurricanes that came later. For their part, the thousands of local governments nationwide that are primarily responsible for funding, building, and sustaining the first-responder community rely on federal coordination to provide effective nationwide mobilization in response to large-scale disasters or catastrophic events. If the next generation of homeland-security efforts is to succeed, they must be guided by a comprehensive homeland security strategy that addresses each of these concerns

Consequences and Consequence Planning

Consequences have become a measure by which we set priorities in homeland security. In practical terms, we seek to prevent or mitigate all hazards. When these efforts fail, as they often do, we are faced with addressing consequences. In practical terms, the following list of generic consequences provides a baseline set of objectives for response and recovery efforts. Dealing with these consequences falls first and foremost upon local first responders, governments, and communities. All disasters present some combination of most if not all of these consequences:

- Dead, injured, displaced people
- Dead, injured, displaced animals
- Increased health and safety risks
- Loss of human and intellectual capital
- Endangered, damaged and destroyed property
- Loss of essential services
- Damaged or loss of critical infrastructure and key resources
- Economic losses
- Psychological trauma (to both the public and the responders)
- Environmental damage
- Cascading events or disasters
- Litigation
- Loss of confidence in public and private institutions

Although this short list of generic consequences can provide a focus for all-hazards response and recovery, it is also important to understand that not only does each hazard present a unique combination of consequences, but also that terrorism presents a set of unique consequences that must also be recognized and addressed.

In terms of domestic preparedness, significant media and congressional criticism of the traditional formulas used for federal preparedness grant distributions have driven the policy shift to consequence- or risk-based preparedness. This empirical approach has limitations that may not fully take into account those consequences that cannot be measured in simple terms of the numbers of dead, the value of property losses, or the loss of critical infrastructure and services. Although this approach has its merits, it continues to reflect a mind-set that does not fully account for the psychological aspects of terrorist attacks and the consequences terrorism has on domestic and national security policies.

Under this policy of prioritizing CI/KR and homeland security efforts based on analysis of potential consequences, only major attack scenarios are seen as a national priority. This disproportionate focus has now been extended to measuring local response-and-recovery preparedness for terrorist attacks using weapons of mass destruction, neglecting preparedness for much smaller and less exotic attacks, as well as the general preparedness needed for traditional hazards. In this regard, a single suicide bomber or attacks on the scale of the bombings in Madrid and London would drive policy consequences far beyond the loss of life or actual damage to critical infrastructure.

The consequences of terrorist attacks have more in common with warfare than they do with any other disaster. As with warfare, the strategic decisions translate into tactical realities and consequences at the local level. The tactical consequences outlined above do not define the limits of the consequences of terrorism. Once the bleeding stops and the fires are put out by local first responders, the longer-term systemic consequences of terrorism insert themselves into all levels of local, state, and national efforts.

The following is a short list of strategic terrorism-specific consequences that often have impacts disproportionate to the actual physical damage produced by these attacks:

■ A demand or expectation for apprehension, prosecution, and punishment
■ A demand or expectation of accountability from those entrusted with the security of fellow citizens, property, and way of life
■ An on-going sense of dread regarding possible future attacks
■ Increased policy and fiscal emphasis on intelligence, military, law-enforcement and first-responder operations related to terrorism and weapons of mass destruction
■ Decreased policy emphasis on social, political, economic, and informational engagement of on-going or underlying issues exploited by domestic and international terrorist organizations
■ Challenges to traditional norms of civil liberties, due process and rule of law, constitutional conventions, and fiscally responsible government
■ Demand for structural and mission changes within intelligence, military, law-enforcement and first-responder agencies
■ De-emphasis on traditional intelligence, military, law-enforcement and first-response missions
■ Loss of organizational or operational capabilities during reorganization efforts
■ Unfulfilled promises of justice and infallible prevention of future attacks
■ Policy frustration
■ Increased social stress that often manifests itself in hate crimes and other forms of racially motivated violence.

Terrorism thus has the unique capacity of having a strategic impact on all levels of response, government, and society.

Of note, both pre-9/11 planning guidance and current federal guidelines on response-and-recovery planning continue to be largely focused on hazard-based planning, *not* consequence-based planning. This is an important distinction that can detract from the objective of disaster and catastrophe response-and-recovery planning. By emphasizing hazards over consequences, we can spend an inordinate amount of time on the details of specific hazards and not enough time and effort on the core elements of consequences management needed for a solid, basic response-and-recovery effort. Response-and-recovery planning is not about dealing with specific hazards; that opportunity has passed once the event has occurred. The goal of response-and-recovery planning is dealing with consequences. A solid all-hazards or all-consequences basic plan, then, is the foundation of all effective response-and-recovery planning efforts.

Indeed, the National Strategy for Homeland Security defines homeland security as "a concerted national effort to prevent terrorist attacks within the United States, reduce America's vulnerability to terrorism, and minimize the damage and recovery from attacks that do occur." Despite subsequent acknowledgment of the need for an all-hazards approach, this definition still dominates the national strategy and the mind-set of national agencies to the detriment of a truly all-hazards or all-consequences national strategy. The current "consequence and risk"-based planning (see Figure 9.2) advocated by a DHS driven by its terrorism-prevention mission and culture, has resulted in an all too narrow concept of the hazards and risks facing communities. Within the counter- or antiterrorism-dominated culture of DHS, risk and consequences have also become an argument to reduce the role of the federal government in funding state and local homeland security efforts by seeking to set priorities based on expected terrorist targeting of critical infrastructure and key resources. On the surface, this is an intuitive and logical argument; however, in practice it is too narrow and also fails to recognize that terrorist target selection is tied to motivations, resources, capabilities, and the strategic consequences or goals of both violent domestic and international extremist organizations.

Regarding the effort to use risk- or consequence-based planning, both the 9/11 (and subsequent) commissions and the media have been highly critical of the distribution of homeland security grant funds. The traditional formula-based model for federal grant distribution guaranteed each state a minimum amount of grant funds;[5] the remaining funds were distributed in proportion to population size and a competitive process of risk analysis. Even so, the result has been a frequently cited distribution of funds in which low-population states have received a disproportion-

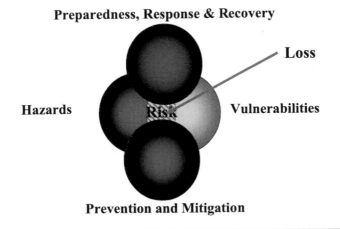

Figure 9.2   Risk/Consequence Reduction

ate per capita allocation while cities and states with large populations have received a lower per capita share. Nevertheless, the vast majority of homeland security grants funds in fact go to the large population centers most commonly cited as the likely targets of terrorist attacks.[6] It does not address the demographic realities of first-responder communities or the need to build national response capacity and reserves to support a nationwide mobilization in response to catastrophic natural events as well as terrorist attacks.[7]

Unlike any other hazard, terrorism is a deliberate, criminal-attack process. The ways, means and ends of the perpetrators largely define and limit this process. It is also important to remember terrorism is often a "farm to market" process in which the attack preparations may take place in various locations that have no relation to the location of the target.

The attacks on 9/11 were planned and prepared in various communities all over the United States and the rest of the world. There was little New York City or Arlington, Virginia could have done to prevent an attack using a commercial aircraft. Although improved CI/KR protection would have potentially defeated or mitigated the bombing of the Murrah Building in Oklahoma City, it is doubtful Timothy McVeigh, the principal perpetrator, would have sought an alternate target. Again, we must remember terrorism is a phenomenon conducted through a global network resulting in a wide range of tactical and strategic consequences involving all levels of response, government and societal. Indeed, terrorism prevention and preparedness require a cooperative national effort, not a competitive scramble focused on a limited set of assumed targets. Prevention depends on a coordinated national and global effort to detect and target every element of the attack process, regardless of the size or location of the community in which the elements of this process are being developed.

Prevention, Mitigation, and Preparedness

The language of domestic protective efforts has evolved significantly as perceptions of the threat have shifted over the years. In the years leading up to the attacks of 9/11, the Federal Emergency Management Agency (FEMA) had taken the lead in creating the framework of preparedness, mitigation, response, and recovery that forms much of the basis of the present-day Department of Homeland Security. If FEMA can be faulted for any single failure, it was its institutional tendency to think of terrorism as "hazmat [or hazardous materials] with an attitude."[8] Although this cliché captures some aspects of the dangers presented by weapons of mass destruction, it minimizes many of the consequences that are unique to terrorism.

The mission and strategies of FEMA had evolved significantly since its creation in 1979.[9] By 2001, it had evolved into an increasingly integrated national effort to lessen the impacts of natural disasters through mitigation and preparedness for the consequences of all hazards. The goal of prevention, mitigation, preparedness, response, and recovery is to reduce risk and minimize losses. One of the greatest accomplishments and assets of FEMA was the network of state and local relationships it built through its regional offices and their involvement in mitigation, preparedness, response, and recovery efforts. This network of partnerships is invaluable when it is in place and irreplaceably when it fails, as it did in the wake of Hurricanes Katrina and Rita. The declining effectiveness of FEMA since 9/11 is in no small part due to the failure to distinguish and preserve its all-hazards mitigation, preparedness, response-and-recovery mission from the very different primary mission of DHS to prevent terrorist attacks.

The methodologies of terrorism prevention are vastly different from the mitigation of natural hazards. Mitigation of natural hazards is primarily the responsibility of emergency management, planning, zoning, engineering, and property owners. The prevention of terrorism is primarily the responsibility of intelligence, law enforcement, border and port security, immigration and customs, and other security-related functions. Based on this primary mission, many of the various federal agencies with roles related to port and border security, immigration and customs were combined to form the bulk of the Department of Homeland Security.[10]

Having already noted FEMA's pre-9/11 failure to address prevention of terrorism, the post-9/11 efforts of the Department of Homeland Security must also be faulted for failing to address anything other than the tactical aspects of terrorism prevention. Mitigating natural hazards requires very specific strategies and long-term local, state, federal, and private-sector commitments. The strategies of preventing a terrorist attack require a very different set of agencies, resources, and strategies. The lessons of 2001 and hurricane disasters since make clear that to sacrifice one set of capabilities for another is perhaps penny wise, but certainly a pound-foolish approach. We cannot afford to neglect a comprehensive strategy of preventing terrorist attacks, mitigating natural hazards, and creating a nationwide response network capable of rapidly implementing effective all-consequences management efforts in response to any scale disaster, including such broad-area catastrophes as Hurricanes Katrina and Rita.

Capacity to perform this task will be dependent on the following factors:

- A clear and focused mission statement that also specifies authorities to act
- Leadership and accountability to maintain focus on the mission
- Consistent and adequate funding for staffing, equipment, planning, training, preparedness, and operations
- Staffing in the right numbers and skill sets to accomplish the mission
- Equipment that is appropriate to the duties of the staff and the focus of the mission
- Procedures to ensure the effective integration of mission, staffing, and equipment
- Training and planning that tie all these requirements into a functional capability to act

- Facilities and infrastructure (i.e., buildings, information technology, communications, transportation, etc.)
- Exercises and evaluation in support of continued development and program validation

Since 9/11, the United States has had what are reasonably assumed to be numerous successes in preventing terrorist attacks. This is not true for the mitigation of natural hazards. Had the levees around New Orleans been sufficiently improved to prevent the flooding that occurred, the human, economic, and political consequences of the hurricane would have been greatly reduced. Neither the probability of terrorist attacks prior to 9/11 nor the catastrophe that befell the Gulf Coast was unexpected. Indeed, the ambiguity prior to an event and the resistance to action it can create is at least as powerful as the clarity and the demand for action that emerges immediately after the event. Preparedness for mitigation by taking preparatory measures in advance has eroded dramatically in the post-9/11 world. It is yet to be seen if Hurricanes Katrina and Rita were sufficient to reinvigorate mitigation or damage limitation as a national priority.

Preparedness for response and recovery thus would seem to be a rather straightforward enterprise, but even this element of strategy has been the topic of a great deal of contention regarding the focus and responsibilities for such efforts. Following the 9/11 attacks the federal government initiated a dramatic expansion in funding to these local agencies—the overall aim of these efforts being to build a response-and-recovery capacity for terrorist attacks, particularly those using weapons of mass destruction. This focus has also ignited a heated national debate about how funds for first-responder preparedness are distributed in response to basic strategic-planning questions: "For what are we preparing, who is responsible, what is the desired end-state, and how do we measure progress?"

An often-overlooked aspect of homeland security preparedness has been the dramatic shift in federal involvement in first-responder funding since 9/11. Historically, the bulk of funding for fire, police, and emergency medical services (EMS) was provided by the approximately 87,000 local governments[11] and funded by local taxes. Preparedness of fire, police, EMS, public health and environment, public works, and volunteer service organizations was primarily the fiscal and legal responsibility of the thousands of state, municipal, and special district authorities that make up local government. This largely self-regulated system produced a highly fragmented national first-response community that was oriented toward local risk factors and funded according to local priorities. In the years immediately before 9/11, there was a growing recognition of the limitations this lack of standards in local response capacity had created. Although first responders continue to respond effectively to most routine emergencies and many traditional disaster events, effective response to large-scale disasters is dependent on the ability to mobilize nationwide mutual aid.

In principle this is a practical solution to meeting an historically rare need. In terms of preparedness for response to worst-case scenarios, this national network may not have sufficient staffing, equipment, procedures, or training. According to the National Fire Protection Association, in 2004 of some 1,100,750 fire fighters in the United States, 305,150 were career personnel and 795,600 were volunteers. Seventy-five percent of career fire fighters are in communities of 25,000 or more. Ninety-five percent of volunteers are in departments that protect populations of less than 25,000. More than fifty percent are in rural departments that protect populations of 2,500 or less.[12]

Law enforcement—another core first-responder function—is primarily staffed by paid personnel. There are currently approximately 800,000 sworn officers serving in over 35,000 agencies.[13] This staffing structure is designed primarily for routine operations and limited disaster events. Local law enforcement does have a limited surge capability, but sustaining this capacity during prolonged disaster events is problematic. Although the national fire and law enforcement staffing structures are adequate for most traditional contingencies, there is strategic need to maximize the overall capacity of these important albeit limited human resources.

Beyond law enforcement, emergency medical services, emergency management, and various other services will almost certainly face similar constraints. The overall capacity of the hoped-for national network of first-responder mutual aid will be defined by human and material resources. The final safety net for the network of national response also depends, of course, on the National Guard, the Department of Defense and other federal agencies, both church-affiliated and secular service and volunteer organizations, private-sector firms, and individual citizens.

Financing and Staffing State and Local Homeland Security Efforts

Current staffing reflects predominantly local perceptions of risk, need, and funding priorities. A consequence of these traditional local government priorities is that almost seventy-five percent of fire fighters are volunteers and most of these are in small or rural departments. The bulk of fire-fighting personnel resources is in communities that are unlikely to be targeted by international terrorism and the consequences to CI/KR or the population would be minimal (although substantial amounts of CI/KR are in low-population areas). An additional challenge is the difficulty volunteer organizations can experience in absorbing significant additional equipment, training, and technical skills. This absorption of resources often requires substantial investment in precious personnel hours. In the case of volunteers, this translates to additional time away from work or family.

Staffing clearly is the single greatest limiting factor in homeland-security planning. This factor dictates both the numbers available to support prevention, mitigation, response-and-recovery operations and the amount of training, equipment, and resources that can be absorbed to improve overall preparedness. Volunteers are and will continue to be a critical element of response capacity. But, until we assess the limitations imposed by this current staffing structure, we will have neither a clear picture of the national response capacity nor a defined benchmark to measure the amount of investment needed to maximize the effectiveness of these human resources.

The original federal HLS grants in 2003 of over $3.5 billion marked a tenfold increase in federal funding for first-responder equipment, planning, training, and exercises at the state and local levels. This level of federal investment in state and local first-responder preparedness gradually declined by about a half to some $1.7 billion in the FY2006 grant programs. The federal justification for the initial increase was twofold: (1) public demand for demonstrable investments to make the nation better prepared for terrorist attacks, particularly attacks by weapons of mass destruction, and (2) recognition that terrorism is a national security threat and therefore a funding responsibility of the federal government. The increase in federal funding for local first responders was politically expedient and it has significantly benefited these agencies across the nation. In the absence of a defined and sustainable "desired end-state," however, it also has created the perception at the state and local levels of a federal fiscal responsibility that did not previously exist and may not be sustainable in the long term. Reduced federal funding for these programs is due to fiscal constraints in the federal budget and continued frustration with state and local management of funds provided. Increasingly these programs have become fiscal and political liabilities due to the lack or absence of (1) a well-defined, desired end-state; (2) attainable and sustainable standards; (3) clear, accepted measures of success; and (4) practical means by which any standards can be enforced. Clearly, the pendulum of federal funding has begun to swing back to a traditional, limited role in state and local first response funding.

The need for clear goals has been recognized in Homeland Security, Presidential Directive – 8 (HSPD-8). As a result of this directive, the National Preparedness Guideline, Universal Task List and Target Capabilities List have been established. These first-generation documents reflect an awareness of the need for clear national goals and standards and a commitment to providing them.

The tradition of locally funded fire, law enforcement, and emergency management personnel is the result of more than two centuries of federalism and local government responsibility and control over these functions. Basic capacity of these agencies is almost entirely a function of local funding capabilities and priorities. They continue to provide heroic response to local emergencies and disaster events, but their ability to be integrated into a national response structure is limited by the lack of common equipment, communications, and procedures. Although Homeland Security Presidential Directives (HSPD) 5 and 8 mandate compliance with unprecedented national standards in order to remain eligible for federal grant dollars, these directives do not address the single greatest limiting factor of response-

and-recovery preparedness: staffing and basic funding and sustainment. These remain the responsibility of local government.

Increasingly the answer to the question of "who is responsible for funding first responders?" seems to be that it is a shared responsibility but one borne primarily by local government, which is responsible for staffing, benefits, and basic capabilities. For its part, the federal government funds additional equipment, training, planning, and exercises needed to prepare these local resources for integration into national response-and-recovery efforts with emphasis on dealing with a wide range of exotic terrorist attacks using weapons of mass destruction. Unfortunately, this federal focus on hazards rather than consequences effectively detracts from the overall goal of national preparedness and national response.

The final result of federal policy statements and funding initiatives is an inconsistent message with mixed results. HSPD-5 and HSPD-8[14] require regional approaches, mutual aid, and standardization. The "consequence-based" decisions and priorities of DHS and Congress send the message that most communities will be increasingly noncompetitive for the shrinking homeland security grant programs. Although the principles for standardized National Incident Management Systems[15] as described in the presidential directives are a valuable step toward an unprecedented level of national coordination of first responders, they are quickly becoming yet another in a long line of unfunded mandates that will limit dramatically the potential of these efforts.

Underlying these trends is a growing pressure to reduce the federal burden in what has traditionally been a local government responsibility. At the core of this issue is not only who pays, but also how we define the desired end-state. Indeed, establishing this benchmark has been one of the most elusive goals of homeland security efforts. One possible approach to resolving this benchmark problem is to base future spending levels on the costs of day-to-day locally funded staffing quite apart from costs associated with the consequences of an anticipated event.

The use of personnel costs as the basic preparedness benchmark offers a de facto baseline upon which equipment, planning, and training goals can be defined. Rather than basing preparedness goals on an ever-expanding list of desired capabilities, by tying preparedness goals to staffing we begin to base funding decisions on hard fiscal realities at the local level where first-responder staffing is based on locally assessed risk (and the degree of risk the community is willing to accept), local tax priorities, and capabilities. These factors are relatively stable, although it could be argued that they do not necessarily result in appropriate or correct local funding decisions.

Using the baseline of local first-responder staffing, we can define attainable end-states for equipment, planning, training, and exercises. An additional benefit of this shift in policy focus would be to move away from a competitive grant process to a system that encourages building capacity throughout the nationwide responder community. Communities with large response forces would receive funding proportionate to their staffing while smaller communities would also benefit. By building capacity throughout the responder community, we make all communities safer and build a strategic national reserve that also can be mobilized during both regional and national disasters.

Organizing and Coordinating Federal, State, and Local Efforts

The competition between communities most likely to be targeted by terrorists and the broader need for national, all-hazards preparedness is further complicated by the competition of the various first-responder organizations, as well as dispute over the relative priority of various homeland security missions. Although the first-responder communities are all committed to the common goal of protecting the public, they have very different missions, means, and cultures for doing so. The resulting competition among these organizations is similar to the rivalry among the military services.

As a federal bureaucracy, however, the Department of Defense has the statutory and fiscal authority required to meld the various services and their cultures into a force capable of supporting operational commanders around the world. By contrast, no such structure or authority exists for the Department of Homeland Security, much less for the first-responder communities. The task of building national preparedness among these diverse units is further complicated by the fact that unlike the military, first responders do not have a cycle of preparedness and deployment. The first-responder community is almost constantly engaged within its own "battle space." These distinctions are noteworthy because of the significant amount of cross flow between the military and first-response communities and the tendency to attempt to apply military organizational concepts to disaster preparedness response and recovery.

Although there are many concepts that can be effectively adapted from the military, the Incident Command System in Figure 9.3 being a case in point, we must be mindful of the organizational realities of the civilian first-response community. In addition to the challenges of unique mission cultures and the need to preserve mission integrity, another consequence of federalism is the organizational challenges of working with diverse peer-based networks in which *coordination* and control is more the practice than the *command* and control style one finds in military settings. Clear lines of authority are critical, of course, in tactical situations involving public safety. It is equally important to understand the need for peer-based networks, depicted in Figure 9.4, and unified command structures capable of coordinating efforts at the operational and strategic levels where there may not be a clear chain of command or single overriding authority.

The independence of diverse agencies and jurisdictions is a reality that must be accommodated in preparedness prevention, mitigation response-and-recovery

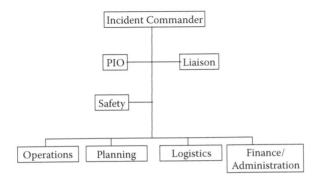

Figure 9.3   Basic Incident Command Structure

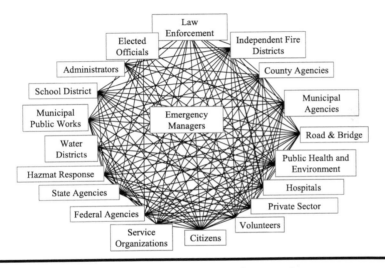

Figure 9.4   Response and Recovery Peer-Based Network

efforts. Although the concepts of unified command and multiagency coordination have been well developed by the wildfire community over more than three decades, they have not been integrated effectively into multidisciplinary, multijurisdictional operations nationwide. The result is a significant conceptual and organizational gap in ability to coordinate large-scale response to disaster events impacting broad geographical areas. This is a reality that is often overlooked by decision makers at all levels of government. The concepts and solutions needed to address this problem exist, but institutionalizing them into disaster-event response remains a daunting challenge.

Another area of competition within homeland security is that between terrorism prevention and all-hazards preparedness. The 9/11 attacks were highlighted by a failure at the national level to prevent terrorist attacks. Response to these attacks, however, was an overall success. Warnings of the dangers of major hurricanes were well known prior to their occurrence—warnings and available courses of action known at all levels of government and society. Whether due to a lack of political will or a casual acceptance of the risks involved, options to mitigate this danger were not acted upon beforehand.

Be that as it may, the experience of Hurricane Katrina offers very different lessons in the failure to respond and recover effectively. As catastrophic as the attacks on 9/11 were, the area impacted was significantly smaller than the 90,000 square miles devastated by hurricanes in 2005. Although terrorist attacks and hurricanes are two very different hazards, they produced many of the same consequences, except for noticeable differences in policy and political fallout. 9/11 drove a surge in public support for the Bush administration, a dramatic restructuring of government, and a significant debate over the balance between civil liberties and security. By contrast, Katrina significantly damaged public confidence in the Bush administration, but has yet to produce significant policy changes. In this regard, the Department of Homeland Security remains dominated by its primary mission of terrorism prevention and the cultures and disciplines primarily associated with that objective. Striking an appropriate balance between these antiterrorist and natural disaster missions will remain a difficult and ongoing challenge to the leadership of the Department of Homeland Security in relations with state and local authorities.

Concluding Comments

As is clear from the preceding discussion, one of the greatest challenges to dealing with consequences when disasters and catastrophic events occur continues to be the organizational gap that exists between local, state, and federal agencies. Although the national wildfire community has worked aggressively to address this issue over the past thirty years, many of the practices they have developed within the Incident Command System have not been effectively adopted by those outside the wildfire community. Local public safety is still a very complex jurisdictional issue for many communities. Although the National Incident Management System and Incident Command System provide guidelines for addressing this organizational gap, the demands of day-to-day operations will continue to hinder the ability to institutionalize these concepts nationwide. Historically, hurricanes, earthquakes, floods, and wildfires have been the only disasters that required the integration of hundreds of response agencies under a unified command structure. The wildfire community and FEMA have had the greatest experience and success with this concept. Implementation becomes more difficult in heavily populated areas where jurisdictional and organizational roles and responsibilities are more closely tied to local governments and the geographic area and constituencies upon which they are based. This legacy of federalism is a major stumbling block to the implementation of multiagency, multijurisdictional, and multidisciplinary response and recovery increasingly required in the wake of large disasters and catastrophic events. It also assumes that all future events will be geographically limited, thus allowing assistance from unaffected communities. In the case of the pandemic flu, this may not be the case.

A final stumbling block to creating an integrated homeland security structure is organizational culture. Mission drives the culture of an organization. Different missions attract different types of people. In the wake of 9/11 the overriding mission of the Department of Homeland Security has been the prevention of terrorist attacks. This is a critical mission that falls primarily to the disciplines of intelligence, law enforcement, the military, and immigration and customs officials. When DHS was created it sought to integrate the vastly different missions of terrorism prevention and all-hazards preparedness and consequence management.

The divergence of missions was further exacerbated by the disproportionate demographics of an organization in which the preparedness, response, and recovery element (FEMA) made up only 2,500 people—about one percent of the 220,000 members of the organization. This issue is not unique to DHS, of course. The Department of Defense has struggled with a similar challenge to its efforts to create an interoperable military force capable of joint military operations.

The military has found ways to overcome these problems for the most part, but it has required sustained multigenerational leadership and commitment by the Joint Chiefs of Staff, Congress and the military services to unifying doctrine on the use of force. By contrast, the bulk of operational field forces in homeland security are the thousands of independent response agencies in local communities across the nation. Although federal funding and direction increased dramatically after 9/11, the bulk of funding, policy, and leadership remain the responsibility of local governments and state authorities.

Overcoming these issues and balancing the integration of these diverse missions and cultures are essential for the future success of these efforts to secure the homeland. We cannot afford to sacrifice one mission for the other. We must create a truly integrated culture of homeland security that minimizes the possibilities of repeating the failures that led to 9/11 and both preceded and followed Hurricane Katrina.

After all, terrorism is just one of the many risk factors with which we must contend as we seek to make communities safer and better prepared. From the early days of militia and fire brigades to civil defense, FEMA and now DHS, domestic security and preparedness has had to adapt to changes in both the risk environment and societal expectations. 9/11 drove us to make dramatic changes in all levels of preparedness, mitigation, prevention, response, and recovery. These policy decisions have not always had the desired result and we will be living with the consequences for many years to come. Many of the lessons and legacies of the past were lost or forgotten. 9/11 and now Katrina continue to drive the evolution of concepts of domestic preparedness. It is increasingly clear that the next generation must build on these legacies without being confined by them. We must seek to prevent terrorist attacks, mitigate natural disasters, and be prepared to deal with the consequences of any disaster. Any and all communities must be able both to respond and to render mutual aid nationwide. The next generation of domestic preparedness must be based on a commitment to build a network that fully integrates the many agencies needed to make the homeland secure from all disasters.

Endnotes

1. The White House, Homeland Security Presidential Directive/HSPD-5 (Washington, D.C.: The White House, 2003).
2. Intergovernmental Oceanographic Commission of UNESCO, From Commitments to Action: Advancements in Developing an Indian Ocean Tsunami Warning and Mitigation System (Paris, France: United Nations Educational, Scientific and Cultural Organization [UNESCO], 2005).
3. Department of Homeland Security. National Department National Infrastructure Protection Plan: Washington D.C. Department of Homeland Security, 2006.
4. The National Strategy for Homeland Security defines homeland security as "a concerted national effort to prevent terrorist attacks within the United States, reduce America's vulnerability to terrorism, and minimize the damage and recover from attacks that do occur." Despite subsequent acknowledgment of the need for an all-hazards approach, this definition continues to dominate the strategic discourse (and the mindset of national agencies) to the detriment of formulating a truly all-hazards/consequences national strategy.
5. Shawn Reese, FY2006 Homeland Security Grant Distribution Methods: Issues for the 109th Congress (Washington, D.C.: Congressional Research Service-Library of Congress, 2006).
6. Department of Homeland Security, "FY 2006 State and Local Homeland Security Grant Awards." http://www.dhs.gov/xlibrary/assets/grants_st-local_fy06.pdf (retrieved October 29, 2006).
7. According to the National Fire Academy, there are approximately 25,000 volunteer fire departments nationwide. They estimate there were 1,064,150 firefighters in the United States in 2000. Of these 286,800 were career (full-time) and 777,350 were volunteer (NFA Facts & Figures*). The majority of career firefighters are in communities that protect 25,000 or more people. More than half of all volunteer firefighters are with small, rural departments protecting fewer than 2,500 people. (*From M. J. Karter, Jr., U.S. Fire Department Profile Through 2000 [National Fire Protection Association, December 2001]; Rita Fahy and Paul R. LeBlanc, "2001 U.S. Firefighter Fatalities," NFPA Journal [July/August 2002]; and Michael J. Karter, Jr. and Stephen G. Badger, "U.S. Firefighter Injuries," NFPA Journal [November/December 2001].)
8. This quote is commonly attributed to Louis O. Giuffrida, who was the first director of FEMA appointed by President Reagan in 1981. Although it is a catchy cliché, it reflects a dismissive attitude towards the unique aspects of terrorism that make it a national security threat.

9. Department of Homeland Security, "FEMA History." http://www.fema.gov/about/history.shtm (retrieved October 29, 2006).

10. United States Congress. "H.R. 5005—Homeland Security Act of 2002." http://www.dhs.gov/xlibrary/assets/hr_5005_enr.pdf (retrieved October 29, 2006).

11. Bureau of Census, "Types of Government Entities." http://www.census.gov/govs/www/class_ch3.html#S3.1 (retrieved October 29, 2006).

12. U.S. Fire Administration Web site, www.usfa.fema.gov.

13. Bureau of Justice Statistics Web site, www.ojp.usdoj.gov/bjs/sandlle.htm.

14. The White House. "Homeland Security Presidential Directive/HSPD-8." http://www.whitehouse.gov/news/releases/2003/12/20031217-6.html (retrieved October 29, 2006).

15. Department of Homeland Security. "National Incident Management System." (Washington, D.C.: Department of Homeland Security, 2004).

Chapter 10

Democracy, Civil Society, and the Damage-Limitation Component of Strategy

Alexander C. Diener and Timothy W. Crawford

Going beyond prevention measures, the authors focus on the ways and means to limit damage to political institutions, critical infrastructure, and other targets of value in American society. Finding ways to sustain governmental functioning is essential. With respect to critical infrastructure, particular attention needs to be given to aircraft, nuclear power plants, and chemical processing plants that can in effect be "weaponized" by terrorists—using them to attack (aircraft) or attacking them (nuclear or chemical plants) to wreak further damage on society. Establishing as much redundancy and substitutability as feasible in effect puts back-up assets in place should critical infrastructure be attacked. Intergovernmental and private-sector cooperation is essential as we prepare strategically to limit damage and respond to all hazards. Finally, civil-defense education can empower the population to help themselves and thus limit damage if or when attacks occur.

The threat of mass-casualty attacks by terrorists is unique in American history and has encouraged a concerted effort to address these dangers. U.S. policymakers urgently need to create a homeland security strategy that focuses on *limiting the damage* of terrorism, rather than merely seeking to *prevent* catastrophic terrorism. In doing so, we raise some fundamentally important issues concerning the role of democratic institutions, the political process, and civil society in the United States. The parochial nature of Congress in setting spending priorities for homeland security does not always lead to damage-limitation measures desirable from a national standpoint. Measures to limit damage may impose dangerous distortions in the balances of power and responsibility among local, state, and federal authorities, and, at the federal level, between the executive and legislative branches, and within the legislative branch itself. Similarly, before and after attacks occur, damage limitation and emergency-response measures may produce perverse shifts in relations between government and the diverse groups in civil society.

When constructing a homeland security strategy, it is readily apparent that any approach that ignores the domestic political context is doomed to fail. Indeed, remarkably little focus has been given in homeland security strategizing to the political modalities of U.S. democracy and the impact on civic culture. The purpose of this chapter is to begin to explore a few important links between the larger contours of democratic government and state-civil society relations, and problems forming and implementing damage-limitation policies in homeland security strategy.

We begin with a discussion of the need to sustain a central role for the popular voice in government responses through active congressional involvement in the aftermath of a catastrophic attack on the capital. The United States was founded on principles of separation of power and checks and balances. Accordingly, the preservation of federalism in practice and the constructive tension among the executive, judicial, and legislative branches is an essential damage-limitation mission that must be central to any U.S. strategy on homeland security.[1] Next, we explore the role of Congress in shaping homeland security strategy priorities and funding, especially in relation to the creation of effective damage-limitation capabilities. Finally, we discuss how damage-limitation capacities can be improved by doing more to integrate civil society with homeland security planning and preparations. In particular, we recommend greater commitment to civil-defense education and other programs aiming to capitalize on U.S. civic strengths that will have applicability in an "all-hazards" context.

Making Democracy Survivable

A major terrorist attack may impose enormous costs not just by the immediate destruction of lives and property, but also by disabling normal governing institutions and political processes, thus compromising the links between the governed and the government. These core links of the democratic process are threatened primarily when the public perception of the balance between safety and danger lurches toward the latter.[2] The costs may be difficult to quantify, but any disruption of balanced democratic government is harmful. By such a multiplier effect, the less tangible political costs of a catastrophic attack on organs of government can be huge. Thus, adopting stronger measures to ensure the continuity of democratic government after an attack must rank as a top priority in formulating homeland security strategy. Unfortunately, perhaps because the stakes are less tangible and tend not to generate strong political demands, major progress is still lacking.

It is imperative to maintain the constructive tension among the three federal branches and the distribution of their overlapping responsibilities in the wake of a catastrophic attack or indeed a sequence of them.[3] Well-established procedures for quickly reconstituting authority in the executive and judicial branches already exist. So there is less need to alter significantly the existing formulas for these branches.[4] By contrast, in the wake of a broadly debilitating attack, mechanisms for preserving the continuity of Congress, which tends already to be a reactive institution during emergencies, are "the biggest hole in our Constitutional system."[5] Although the Senate is better positioned to fill its ranks quickly through the process of gubernatorial appointment, it can be paralyzed by mass incapacitation of its members. The situation is especially dangerous for the House of Representatives, lacking any mechanism for quickly regenerating itself to sustain its representative function.[6] Failing to address these vulnerabilities means that an adversary can target the House in particular, and essentially cast the U.S. government into a pattern of emergency war-time rule heavily dominated by the executive branch and its political appointees.[7]

Since the House is so broadly representative a national institution, it would provide an especially tempting target for terrorists. In addition, maintaining existing *proportions* of power among the branches is the best guarantee of civil liberties, for the gravest incursions on civil liberties will not arise from excessive zeal in the executive branch alone, but from the paralysis of counteracting congressional influence in the face of such zeal.[8] This vulnerability can only truly be rectified by House legislative action, but so far the efforts at reform have been minimal at best. As congressional observer Norman Ornstein, a leading expert on continuity of government legislation, said the House's 2004 effort boiled down to a poorly drafted, poorly constructed bill simply to expedite special elections in the event of the death of a large number of Members, with no constitutional plan to deal with the possibility of widespread incapacitation," also adding, "a blatantly unconstitutional and partisan rule to allow the Speaker to redefine the meaning of 'quorum.'"[9]

The Senate blocked passage of the House bill, and the matter remains at a standstill. It is unlikely to be resolved without another attack to galvanize the necessary consensus and political will. In the interim the House has neither a legitimate system in place to expedite elections after mass vacancies have been created nor a plan for continuing to do business in the event many members are incapacitated and before such vacancies can be filled.

Ultimately, such fixes can only be produced and implemented through the existing political process. The problem of continuity of government poses a fundamental challenge for creating a damage-limitation strategy for democracy: the most important aspects defy abstract solutions. The unique permutations of popular government in the United States help to define the strategic problem as well as possible solutions. Consider, for example, the vulnerability to terrorist action created by presidential election cycles and the dramatic thinning of policy ranks when government changes hands. The depth and breadth of these transitions are testament to the effectiveness of democratic institutions, but nevertheless they routinely create an environment in which the executive branch's focus is often sidetracked, expertise on pressing issues drops, and the ability to react to developing challenges is blunted. However dangerous these vulnerabilities may be, they cannot be "fixed" within the existing political system for the essence of that system is the reliable promise of periodic government turnover.

Homeland Security Spending and Damage Limitation

As we have seen, protecting the institutions of government is an essential task in homeland security. Because of their openness, democratic societies have a daunting task defending against a determined foe bent on creating havoc in the country. How the United States is able to limit damage in the event of an attack is a function of how prepared it is for such an outcome. Mitigating damage means choices have to be made as to what most urgently needs protection. How and where the United States spends its precious capital is a critical determinant of whether its homeland security strategy as a whole will succeed or fail.

Two of the basic impediments to the formulation of strategy are analytical as well as political: how to judge and prioritize the most vulnerable of the many exposed flanks and how to measure progress in our efforts to better defend them?[10] The Department of Homeland Security (DHS) was created to overcome these problems by providing "the unifying core for the vast national network of organizations and institutions involved in efforts to secure" the country.[11] More concretely, DHS is to be the coordinator of efforts to prevent terrorist attacks within the United States, and to minimize damage and maximize recovery from attacks that do occur. If one includes the spending of other agencies involved in such efforts, expenditures on homeland security represents one of the largest and most rapid allocations of federal funding in the history of the United States.[12] Strong criticisms have been leveled, however, at the methods and processes used to formulate and implement homeland security strategy.

In DHS's initial efforts, the threat was treated as something more like a serial killer that had to be stopped than a virus requiring a re-evaluation of systemic vulnerabilities and resiliencies.[13] Yet given the wide range of targets for such terrorism, resources must also be mobilized and allocated in ways that try to minimize the impact of such attacks when they occur,[14] that is, in ways that are consistent with the logic of "hazards management" and a risk-assessment-based strategy.[15] To that end, Homeland Security Presidential Directive 8 gives DHS the lead role in rationalizing the funding of homeland security priorities and establishing a set of minimum essential response capabilities for every U.S. community. A DHS-led risk assessment to support this objective is currently underway, and will ultimately produce a comprehensive threat-vulnerability matrix and federal terrorism preparedness standards likely to be completed in 2008.[16]

Meanwhile, resources for damage limitation and other dimensions of homeland security will be allocated in ways that diverge markedly from nationwide risk-based priorities and instead reflect more parochial interests and disparate agendas.[17] Former Representative Christopher Cox illustrated the predicament by noting: "It is at the intersection of threat and vulnerability that our money should be directed [but] right now we are using seat-of-the-pants analysis" to determine the distribution of resources.[18] But so long as strategic confusion and "seat of the pants" analysis predominate, parochial politics will drive resource allocations even more than they normally do.[19] Hence, as former Senator Don Nickles noted: "Under the banner of homeland security," Congress has created programs that have more or less been used as "revenue sharing" by cities and states.[20] In other words, the analytical and political problems are partly related, for the absence of a strategic framework at the national level invites expenditures that "appear to be for a purpose other than security against an act of terrorism."[21]

A risk-assessment approach to homeland security spending must entail a commitment to thinking rigorously about how to determine the important priorities, because even sound general strategic concepts will not "spit-out" solutions to such matters. Such is the case for the underspecified concept of critical infrastructure (CI), essential to damage-limitation strategy. Because it lacks specificity, it has tended to reinforce rather than resolve the basic strategic problem, that is, what counts as "critical" is whatever someone deems to be worthy of extra protection. Indicative of this pattern is the fact that in the White House's Homeland Security Strategy the roster of critical infrastructure sectors was determined *before* the analytical framework for making such a determination had been developed. Thus, scarce resources appropriated to limit damage by protecting CI have been misdirected. For example, the relatively low level of funding for U.S. ports security included a disproportionate allocation of funds to small, inland ports and "projects that appeared to be more economic- than security-related."[22]

Unfortunately, the term critical infrastructure has been attached to sectors that are not truly crucial. Indeed, the term critical infrastructure is increasingly associated with all federal and state spending priorities. In recent years some 40 percent or more of homeland security funding was spent in agencies other than the Department of Homeland Security. Four agencies—the departments of Defense, Health and Human Services, Justice, and Energy—share approximately 81 percent of this non-DHS-controlled homeland security money.[23]

The haphazard pattern is even more pronounced in states' petitions for homeland security monies. Following the creation of the DHS in March 2003, each state government was asked to assess risk within its respective territory by identifying critical assets and people or groups that posed a threat. This process of "bottom-up" assessments will be in effect until the DHS's national threat-vulnerability matrix is completed in 2008. Unfortunately, the stop-gap measure has invited "critical asset" inflation as state officials have tended to list even the remotest risks rather than being viewed as negligent. In addition, a number of garden variety "pork-barrel" projects exist.[24] Examples from one homeland security budget include $200,000 to project Alert, a school-based drug prevention program for middle grade youth; $3,000,000 to Child Labor Enforcement; $7,100,000 for forensic support and grants to the National Center for Missing and Exploited Children; $100,000 to the Child Pornography Tipline; and $2.5 billion for "highway security," consisting of the building and improvement of roads. Although these projects may be worthwhile in their own right, one may call into question whether they are appropriate targets for homeland security funding.

Given finite resources for supporting efforts to limit damage by terrorist attacks, more discriminating choices are necessary, even if they are made by inherently political "muddling through" processes.[25] Elected officials and local administrators must be given a logical and defensible basis for saying to their constituents "we are not getting additional grants or as much as other areas and this is why." One attempt to provide such a foundation is the Urban Area Security Initiative Grant Program, which sets forth criteria for determining risk, including: (1) population density (half the weight), presence of critical infrastructure (one-third the weight), and the presence of a credible threat (about one-sixth the weight).[26] Similarly, HR3266, the "Faster Smarter Funding for First Responders Act of 2004," outlined a plan to authorize the secretary of the DHS to change the criteria used in the distribution of funding to DHS's major programs in order to base grants on potential damages, not population.[27]

The process of critical infrastructure assessment must be better insulated from pressures to use it for log-rolling measures and local pork projects. This is difficult to do because the formulation and implementation of homeland security strategy is exposed to a highly "pluralistic" political process that pushes up subnational concerns and priorities. Of course, the political process cannot be bypassed altogether. But, it is incumbent on policymakers to be aware of the stakes involved in the process. What is urgently required is a sharpening of the concept of critical infrastructure. We offer two ways: (1) the asset's capacity for weaponization, and (2) the asset's substitutability or redundancy.

Weaponization of civilian assets. For the purpose of focusing damage-limitation efforts, in specifying critical infrastructure we should identify elements of national infrastructure that can be used quickly to inflict catastrophic damage if weaponized (e.g., aircraft, nuclear power plants, chemical processing facilities). Distinguishing between assets that are *more or less* weaponizable is essential since virtually anything can be made into a weapon if one tries hard enough. Clean water supplies, for example, might be considered part of critical infrastructure, but water is difficult to weaponize by contamination, and thus not conducive to inflicting sudden catastrophic destruction. By contrast, dams are obvious elements of critical infrastructure, for if they can be made to fail, the resulting floods can cause enormous damage.

Redundancy and substitutability. The utility of the critical infrastructure concept can be further honed by considering redundancy and substitutability. Redundancy is associated with segments of national infrastructure that have many similar assets serving the same purpose, all of which can function at present or greater capacity even while others are impaired or cease functioning.[28] Substitutability is associated with segments of national infrastructure that serve needs that can be met by assets available in other segments. For example, postal, courier, and light-shipping systems are obvious targets but not critical because the overall shipping network—including both government and private actors—using roads, waterways, and air, is resilient by virtue of its diversification. By contrast, the port of New Orleans is essentially unsubstitutable, for it is the only possible facility for transferring goods coming down the Mississippi River to open-sea shipping.[29] Moreover, strong profit-based incentives to invest in security exist in some sectors, such as courier shipping, thus generating redundancy by proliferating competing firms. So the quality of redundancy gives some leverage in determining which assets most needed federal dollars. There is less need to channel resources to defending elements of critical infrastructure where the private incentives to create redundancies are high.

Employing criteria of substitutability and redundancy will not be easy. It will require study to ensure adequate coverage of population and territory. Further, coordination across political and organizational jurisdictions, a particularly vexing challenge to solve, is urgently needed. Finally, a concerted effort to educate the parties responsible for damage limitation and first response is necessary. It is to this latter consideration that we turn in the next section.

The Private Sector, Civil Society, and All-Hazards Response

Delving into the subject of critical infrastructure makes it clear that homeland security strategy requires intensive cooperation between the government and private sector. When it comes to damage limitation in particular, careful attention must be paid to these collaborative relations as they operate both before and after a large-scale terrorist strike.[30] Military assistance to civilian authorities in emergency situations is critical, considering the National Guard, under state or federal control, is often involved in emergency response. Although there are constitutional guidelines governing civil-military relations and customs regarding liaisons with local authorities, no well-established mechanisms exist for relations with nongovernmental groups. The most plausible starting point for building these bridges is to adapt military civil-affairs liaison roles, which have been well developed to support humanitarian relief operations abroad, to facilitate working with private-sector firms and civil society groups at home.

At the local level, certain private-sector firms may have a special responsibility because they make a given locale a bigger target and enhance the potential for secondary effects of attack (e.g., secondary explosions and chemical or biological contamination). Clearly, they will have a central role in recovery after an attack. Indeed, some industries have already become involved in this sort of planning. For example, Texas Instruments, Lockheed Martin, and oil and gas companies have their own emergency teams for responding to industrial disasters before, and in conjunction with, public emergency personnel.[31] Since the 1984 Union Carbide disaster in Bhopal, India, the Superfund Amendment and Reauthorization Act (SARA Title III) has required industries with reportable quantities of lethal chemicals to file Tier II reports which notify fire departments, Local Emergency Planning Committees, and the state agency in charge of emergency protection of the types, locations, and amount of hazardous material being moved or housed. Railroad companies are required by law to complete a shipping manifest that identifies the type and amount of hazardous materials being transported. Along with many trucking companies, railroad companies may also have specialized response teams to clean up hazardous materials. The Aviation Family Disaster Assistance Act of 1996 requires airlines to plan and prepare for responsibilities following an air disaster. These include information dissemination, body identification, and psychological counseling. Lastly, a long-standing mandate exists within the shipping industry to render assistance to seacraft in distress.[32] These are important sinews for broader collaboration of government and private sector actors interested in limiting the damage of disasters resulting from terrorist attacks or otherwise.[33]

Beyond private industry, a vast network of civic groups, such as Kiwanis, Rotary, Veterans of Foreign Wars (VFWs), and the Salvation Army, offer a largely untapped resource for promoting damage limitation in homeland security strategy. These groups can be thought of as ligaments in a decentralized national emergency-response capability. As McEntire notes, however, if they are to be utilized in this way, norms of collaboration between layers of civil society and government need also to be created so that the interaction does not weaken the private impulse.[34] After all, what gives civil society groups vitality is their autonomy from governmental control. The trick is to channel this dynamism without stifling the internal drive and creativity of popular voluntarism.

One way to effect this sort of engagement is to encourage social groups to be the locus for civilian volunteer and civil-defense education programs. We will say more about this in the next section, but here we want to emphasize one of the main goals: to enable local authorities to call upon these civil society assets during the emergency response to "all hazards," both man-made and natural.[35] As Mitchell observes, although the risks presented by terrorism are unique, the responses are not.[36] And "one clear conclusion from the record," notes Dennis Mileti et al., "is that our understanding of how to effectively communicate hazards to people transcends hazard type: people remain people regardless of the hazard type being investigated."[37] Thus, the "all-hazards" approach to damage limitation is a most compelling one.

A variety of organizations already serve as loose-fitting bridges between the public and private sectors, including the National Disaster Education Coalition, Project Impact, Disaster Recovery Business Alliance, Showcase Communities, and the Office of Private Sector Liaison. The latter should be expanded to include liaison with civil society actors as well.[38] From the perspective of broadening the reach of damage limitation in homeland security strategy, civil society mobilization is obviously attractive because it may lighten the load on public authorities during complex and demanding emergencies. For example, providing shelter, sustenance, and emergency hygiene for displaced persons is an obvious role for some civil society groups (e.g., the Red Cross, the Coast Guard auxiliary, civil-air patrol, ski-patrol). But, equally important, involving these players directly may achieve a larger objective, namely the amelioration of a popular sense of helplessness before a crisis, and the spread of panic afterwards. It is in relation to this latter goal that we turn to the subject of revitalizing civil-defense education.

Reviving Civil-Defense Education

As noted at the outset, the costs of terrorism are many layered, and go well beyond the physical. Terrorism not only results in deaths and damage but undermines the psychology of confidence and trust that is necessary for the functioning of a healthy society.[39] Perhaps more so in the United States than elsewhere, there is a deep reluctance to compromise the ethos of abundant security, by making robust protective measures routine features of daily life. Societies such as Israel and Russia have largely come to terms with the continual presence of terrorist threats. It is only since the 9/11 attacks that Americans have started to be aware of their own vulnerabilities. Naturally their first impulse has been to demand more security from their government, but Americans also have a tradition of self-reliance that does not seek or expect all the answers from the political authorities. We believe this deep-seated strain must be emphasized in the larger conception of homeland security strategy, especially in relation to the problem of damage limitation. Indeed, in the long run, citizens will want and should have a larger role to play in homeland security.

Recent studies present a compelling case for establishing a large-scale public education program that seeks not only to inform people about hazards but to change their behavior.[40] Widespread education can "prime" the public for a response to terrorism and other hazards by productively channeling volunteerism, suppressing the spread of panic, and assisting official first-response efforts. But the general proposition raises a key question: How should the federal government strike the balance between trying to catalyze civic involvement at the national level and passing that responsibility to state and local authorities who operate closest to the ground in communities? As Hurricane Katrina demonstrates, limiting the damage of a hazardous event obviously requires timely and significant federal commitment, and consequently, the coordination of multiple layers of authorities. However, the burden of controlling panic and organizing the initial response must always fall most heavily on local actors.

Typically, the real first responders are just citizens seeking to aid those in need.[41] In a pattern of "convergence," five different types of people tend to congregate at the scene of a catastrophe: the returnees, the anxious, the helpers, the curious, and the exploiters.[42] This is where the emphasis on all-hazards public education really gains traction. With effective federally supported public education, all but the exploiters may be helped to become positive forces in disaster response. In some cases, this may mean staying away from the disaster scene or at least out of the way, since researchers have noted that "spontaneous volunteers" can create additional problems for official first responders.[43] Thus, the federal government's most effective contributions may be to encourage and assist local authorities through civic education programs, as well as to marshal and integrate citizen volunteers who are not just willing but able to really contribute to the recovery process.

For damage limitation in the broadest sense to work, the natural forces of resilience within communities need to be cultivated. But people must know that such forces can make a difference in an actual crisis. If they do not, then the costs of terrorism will rise exponentially. Those who contend that robust civil-defense education will do more to aggravate fears than allay them underestimate the willingness and desire of the public to learn to act responsibly in conditions of crisis. Information that is credible and useful builds confidence, not fear. So it is essential to avoid superficial rules of thumb that aspire to little more than an easing of minds. Instead, people must be given the tools to act on their own behalf and in concert with others during emergencies in collectively beneficial ways.[44]

Imbuing citizens with the knowledge of how to respond properly in the event of an attack can be an empowering and relatively cheap measure with large positive ripple effects. Few could doubt the enormous value obtained from public education concerning personal safety during earthquakes, cardiopulmonary resuscitation, the Heimlich maneuver, and mouth-to-mouth resuscitation.[45] A central complaint of those seeking to volunteer after the events of 9/11 was that they felt they did not have the "right skills" to assist.[46] Perhaps even more than in the aftermath of natural disasters, terrorism evokes a desire to act with an "altruistic orientation."[47] Many people seek to channel their distress into efforts to help others. It is imperative to facilitate *this* psychological impulse as it represents one of the basic ways that the most fundamental damage of terrorism, the escalation of fear and helplessness, can be mitigated.

In sum, by combining programs to mobilize civil society organizations suggested above with this broader effort at civil-defense education, one can potentially improve the ability of Americans to act not only as "Good Samaritans" but "Smart Samaritans" in many emergency situations, thus directly yielding benefits to states and local first responders who must bear the brunt of crises.

Concluding Comments

Homeland security strategizing includes making trade-offs. Although the best way to limit the damage of terrorist attacks is to stop them from occurring in the first place, prevention is never perfect, and because it is not, much needs to be done to mitigate the impact of terrorist attacks that do occur. The fundamental problem of homeland security strategy is how best to spread resources between the twin goals of prevention and damage limitation, given the enormous constraints that arise from the government's need to pursue many *other* goals at home and abroad. But while, for some purposes, the cost-benefit analysis may best be confined to concrete and quantifiable values, our strategic thinking about the political workings of representative government, a thick and vibrant civil society, and a citizen ethos of self-help not only create vulnerabilities and impose limits on what can be done for defense, but also bring about opportunities for damage limitation.

Physical dangers are matched by potential self-imposed threats to values of proportionality in government. Some vulnerabilities, such as the danger to Congress of widespread incapacitation, or the misallocation of dollars for protection of critical infrastructure, are exacerbated by the realities of representative politics. Homeland security strategy cannot transcend these obstacles: they are part of the constraints in which strategy must operate. But the bigger picture also leads to a broader menu of options for limiting the damage of terrorist threats. While resources and responsibilities may be apportioned to federal, state, and local actors for damage limitation, the results can be enhanced by folding into the strategic calculus a role for private-sector and civil society groups at both the national and local levels. Indeed, even the role of private citizens should not be overlooked for an educated and prepared public is the best defense against the spread of fear. In the final analysis, efforts to empower the public are as much a part of damage limitation as measures to blunt the physical effects of terrorist attacks.

Endnotes

1. David Heyman and James J. Carafono, *DHS 2.0 Rethinking the Department of Homeland Security* (Washington, D.C.: The Heritage Foundation, 2004), 23.

2. James K. Mitchell, "Urban Vulnerability to Terrorism as Hazard," in *The Geographical Dimensions of Terrorism*, ed. Susan L. Cutter, Douglas B. Richardson, and Thomas J. Wilbanks (New York: Routledge, 2003), 21.

3. For a detailed and penetrating legal study of this problem, see Bruce Ackerman, "The Emergency Constitution," *Yale Law Journal* 113, no. 5 (2005): 1029–1091.

4. For a review of the basic protocols for executive and judicial continuity, see Continuity of Government Commission, *Preserving our Institutions: The Continuity of Congress* (Washington, D.C.: American Enterprise Institute, 2003), 4–5.

5. *Preserving our Institutions*, 5.

6. Ronald Keith Gaddie, "Restoring the U.S. House of Representatives: A Skeptical Look at Current Proposals," *Policy Analysis* (Cato Institute), no. 510, February 17, 2004.

7. Ibid.

8. Ackerman, "The Emergency Constitution."

9. Norman J. Ornstein, "How Many Warnings Does Congress Need before Protecting Itself?" *Roll Call*, May 31, 2005.

10. John H. Marburger, "Foreword," in Cutter et al., *Geographical Dimensions*, xvii.

11. http://www.dhs.gov/dhspublic/interapp/editorial/editorial_0413.xml.

12. See Budget of the United States, Fiscal Year 2005, Table S-6; and Office of Management and Budget, "Securing the Homeland, Strengthening The Nation," http://www.whitehouse.gov/homeland/homeland_security_book.pdf. According to de Rugy, the TSA budget now exceeds that of the FBI, and spending on homeland security is up 180 percent from 2001–2003 (Veronique de Rugy, *What Does Homeland Security Spending Buy?*, American Enterprise Institute for Public Policy Research Working Paper, no. 107, October 29 [Washington, D.C.: AEI, 2004], 24, 2).

13. Cutter et al., *Geographical Dimensions*, 3.

14. Though some posit that nuclear, biological, and chemical attacks may be more difficult to enact than often thought (see, e.g., Dafia Linzer, "Could They Pull it Off? Atomic Weapons Capabilities May Elude al Qaeda Terrorists, Experts Say," *Washington Post*, December 29, 2004, 6-9) the possibilities of attack are no less spatially disparate or challenging to mitigate.

15. See Cutter et al., *Geographical Dimensions*, 7.

16. Heyman and Carafono, *DHS 2.0*, 24.

17. For examples, see Alice Lipowicz, "North Pole Receives Homeland Security Funds," *Congressional Quarterly*, October 22, 2002; and Mimi Hall, "Homeland Security Money Doesn't Match Terror Threat," *USA Today*, October 29, 2003, 1.

18. Quoted in Eric Lipton, "Big Cities Will Get More in Antiterrorism Grants," *New York Times*, December 22, 2004, 20.

19. For criticisms of homeland security funding that pinpoint the lack of a "risk assessment" basis for expenditure as a fundamental flaw, see National Research Council, *Terrorism: Reducing Vulnerabilities and Improving Responses U.S.–Russian Workshop* (Washington, D.C.: National Academies Press, 2004); Council on Foreign Relations, *Still Unprepared, Still in Danger*, Task Force Report, no. 41 (New York: Council on Foreign Relations, 2002); de Rugy, "What Does Homeland Security Spending Buy?"; Eric Lipton, "Big Cities"; Eric Lipton, "Audit Faults U.S. for Its Spending on Port

Defense," *New York Times*, February 20, 2005, 1. Eric Lipton, "U.S. Report Lists Possibilities for Terrorist Attacks and Likely Toll," *New York Times*, March 16, 2005; and Heyman and Carafano, *DHS 2.0*.

20. *Congressional Quarterly*, February 25, 2004. For more on the reasons for maldistribution of homeland security resources, also see Benjamin Friedman, "Think Again: Homeland Security," *Foreign Policy* (July/August 2005), 22; John Mueller, "Simplicity and Spook: Terrorism and Dynamics of Threat Exaggeration," *International Studies Perspectives*, no. 2 (2005): 208–235.

21. Lipton, "Big Cities." Also see de Rugy, *What Does Homeland Security Spending Buy?*", 8–24.

22. Lipton, "Audit Faults U.S.," 1.

23. de Rugy, *What Does Homeland Security Spending Buy?*", 10.

24. Kate O. O'Beirne, "Introducing Pork Barrel Homeland Security," *National Review*, September 8, 2003.

25. See Bruce Schneirer, *Beyond Fear: Thinking Sensibly About Security in an Uncertain World* (New York: Copernicus Books, 2003), 3.

26. http://www.dhs.gov/dhspublic/display?content=755, http://hsc.house.gov/release.cfm?id=167, http://hsc.house.gov/release.cfm?id=181; and House Select Committee on Homeland Security, "An Analysis of First Responder Grant Funding" (2004), 6.

27. See http://homelandsecurity.house.gov/release.cfm?id_216; and Alice Lipowicz, "First Responder Groups Endorse Risk Based Grants Formula," Congressional Quarterly, October 22, 2004.

28. For further discussion of redundancy see de Rugy, *What Does Homeland Security Spending Buy?*", 20; David A. McEntire, Robie J. Robinson, and Richard T. Weber, "Business Responses to the World Trade Center Disaster: A Study of Corporate Roles, Functions, and Interaction with the Public Sector" in *Beyond September 11th: An Account of Post Disaster Research Program on Environment and Behavior,* Natural Hazards Research and Applications Information Center, Public Risk Institute, and the Institute for Civil Infrastructure Systems, , Special Publication no. 39 (University of Colorado Boulder: Institute of Behavior Science Natural Hazards Research and Application Research Center, 2003), 435–437; and Andre Le Duc, Robert Parker, and Kathy Lynn, "Natural Hazards Mitigation in Oregon: A Case Study," in *Beyond September 11th*, 581.

29. George Friedman, "The Ghost City," *New York Review of Books*, October 6, 2005, 4–6.

30. Heyman and Carafano, *DHS 2.0*, 16; Paul W. O'Brien, "Risk Communication and Public Warning Responses to the September 11th Attack on the World Trade Center," in *Beyond September 11th*, 355–372; David McEntire, *Towards a Theory of Coordination: Umbrella Organizations and Disaster Relief in the 1997 Peruvian El Nino*, Quick Response Paper no. 105 (Boulder, Colorado: Institute of Behavior Science Natural Hazards Research and Application Research Center of University of Colorado, 1998); Richard T. Weber, David A. McEntire, and Robie J. Robinson, *Public/Private Collaboration in Disaster: Implications From the World Trade Center Terrorist Attacks*, Quick Response Paper no. 155 (Boulder, Colorado: Institute of Behavior Science Natural Hazards Research and Application Research Center of University of Colorado Boulder, 2003); McEntire et al., "Business Responses to the World Trade Center Disaster";

Le Duc et al., "Natural Hazards Mitigation in Oregon"; Claire B. Rubin, *Emergency Management in the 21st Century: Coping with Bill Gates, Osama bin-Laden and Hurricane Mitch*, Natural Hazards Research Working paper no. 104 (Boulder, Colorado: Institute of Behavior Science Natural Hazards Research and Application Research Center of University of Colorado Boulder, 2003).

31. McEntire et al., "Business Responses to the World Trade Center Disaster," 435.

32. For a detailed discussion of private sector activities in disaster relief, see McEntire et al., "Business Responses to the World Trade Center Disaster," 433–453.

33. For further examples of the private sector's potential role in the damage limitation and emergency-response efforts, see McEntire et al., "Business Responses to the World Trade Center Disaster." On activities taken up by faith-based organizations and other components of civil society, see Jeanette Sutton, "Complex Organizational Adaptation to the World Trade Center Disaster: An Analysis of Faith Based Organizations," in *Beyond September 11th*; William H. Form and Sigmund Nosow, *Community in Disaster* (New York: Harper, 1958); Thomas Drabek and William H. Key, *Conquering Disaster: Family Recovery and Long Term Consequences* (New York: Irvington Publishers, 1984); E. L. Quaranteli, "Emergent Behavior at the Emergency Time Periods of Disasters," Final Project Report (Columbus, OH: Disaster Research Center, Ohio State University, 1983); E. L. Quaranteli, "Emergent Citizen Groups in Disaster Preparedness and Recovery Activities," Final Project Report (Columbus, OH: Disaster Research Center, Ohio State University, 1985); and Martin H. Smith, "American Religious Organizations in Disaster: A Study of Congregational Response to Disaster," *Mass Emergencies*, no 3 (1978): 133–142.

34. McEntire, "Toward a Theory of Coordination." McEntire also discusses achieving the proper balance between public and private cost sharing that creates incentives to provide security both vertically (adjacent spatial jurisdictions) and horizontally (local, state, federal, and private sector) within society. Also see Gerald E. Galloway, "Emergency Preparedness and Response: Lessons Learned from 9/11," in Cutter et al., *Geographical Dimensions*, 32.

35. See Sutton, "Complex Organizational Adaptation," 424; Barbara P. Buttenfield, "Terrorism, Information Technology and Vulnerability," *Annals of the Association of American Geographers*, no 4 (2004), 993–994; and Cutter et al., *Geographical Dimensions*.

36. See Mitchell, "Urban Vulnerability to Terrorism as Hazard," 18–19, 22.

37. Dennis Mileti, Sarah Nathe, Paula Gori, Marjorie Greene, and Elizabeth Lemersal, *Public Hazards Communication and Education: The State of the Art* (Boulder, Colorado: Institute of Behavior Science Natural Hazards Research and Application Research Center of University of Colorado Boulder, 2003), 3.

38. See McEntire et al., "Business Responses to the World Trade Center Disaster," 431; Mileti et. al., "Public Hazards Communication," 11; and Heyman and Carafono, *DHS 2.0*, 14.

39. Mitchell, "Urban Vulnerability to Terrorism as Hazard," 25.

40. Mileti et al., "Public Hazards Communication."

41. Seana Lowe and Alice Fothergill, "A Need to Help: Emergent Volunteer Behavior after September 11th," in *Beyond September 11th,* 309; Dennis Mileti, *Disasters by Design* (Washington, D.C.: Joseph Henry Press, 1999); Kathleen J. Tierney, Michael K. Lindell, and Robert W. Perry, *Facing the Unexpected: Disaster Preparedness and Response in the United States* (Washington, D.C.: Joseph Henry Press, 2001).

42. Lowe and Fothergill, "A Need to Help," 294; and Charles E. Fritz and J. H. Mathewson, *Convergence Behavior in Disasters: A Problem in Social Control,* Committee on Disaster Studies Research Group (Washington, D.C.: National Research Council, National Academy of Sciences, 1957).

43. Lowe and Fothergill, "A Need to Help," 294; A. H. Barton, *Communities in Disaster: A Sociological Analysis of Collective Stress Situations* (Garden City, NY: Doubleday, 1969); Tierney et al., *Facing the Unexpected.*

44. Joshua Sinai, "How Israel Approaches Homeland Security," *Journal of Counter Terrorism and Homeland Security International,* no. 1 (2003): 1–6.

45. Mileti et al., "Public Hazards Communication," 4, lists "Quit Smoking," "Fasten Seatbelts," and "Don't Litter" as other examples of highly successful efforts to change public behavior.

46. Lowe and Fothergill, "A Need to Help," 296, 302.

47. Mileti, *Disasters by Design,* 145.

Chapter 11

Transportation as a Component of Homeland Security Strategy

Joseph S. Szyliowicz

The intermodal transportation system—road, rail, air, and sea—and terminals or nodes are an enormously complex network that is extraordinarily difficult to defend. The stakes are indeed high for the economy and society. Given this challenge, homeland security strategy necessarily turns to risk-management methodologies. Also essential is a layered approach to strategy, with back-up elements activated when security breaches occur. Beyond technological innovations, some of which can be circumvented by equally innovative terrorists, is the need for homeland-security education customized to the needs of private-sector and government employees in all transportation modes. The author underscores the importance of strategic thinking about transportation intermodally with attention also directed to the entire network of terminals or nodes that serve as linking pins for the system as a whole.

In the aftermath of the tragic events of 9/11, transportation security has emerged as a major focus in the effort to defend the United States against terrorist attacks. This episode demonstrated a breakdown in many areas of security, necessitating a period of profound change and adjustment to the new realities of the situation. As a result, the federal government, the states, and the private sector have created new structures, reorganized existing ones, and adopted new policies to safeguard the nation's critical infrastructure—its food, water, and energy supplies, its defense industries, banking and financial sectors, and such facilities as nuclear power plants, chemical plants, and dams.[1] In February 2003, the National Strategy for the Physical Protection of Critical Infrastructures and Key Assets was published.[2] However, concern with protecting such key assets dates back to the Clinton era when the Oklahoma bombing and the failed attempt to destroy the twin towers in New York led to the establishment of the President's Commission on Critical Infrastructure and the publication of its report in 1997.[3] In both reports, transportation was identified as one of the key infrastructures. The 1997 report noted: "The physical distribution infrastructure is critical to the national security, economic well-being, global competitiveness and quality of life in the U.S. … [It] provides this nation a distinct competitive advantage in the global economy."[4]

In this chapter, I examine the vulnerabilities of the U.S. transportation system. It forms a major element in our assessment of critical infrastructure. I start by addressing the importance of transportation to the country and economy as a whole. The bulk of the analysis is geared toward an understanding of the concept of modes of transportation. Simply put, I argue U.S. policymakers and analysts need to move toward conceiving the transportation system in *inter*modal, rather than strictly *intra*modal terms. Terrorists have grown increasingly sophisticated and possess a rich knowledge of the inner workings of advanced industrialized societies. They understand that where citizens and goods come together presents a rich target to kill vast numbers of people and produce havoc in the global economy, as well as to focus needed attention on their respective cause. So I examine the vulnerabilities in the air, water, rail, and road nodes or connection points where various modes come together. The final section outlines different dimensions of transportation security that must be considered, such as science and communications technologies, areas that must be incorporated into any long-term strategy of homeland security.

Transportation is an attractive target because of its role in the national and global economic systems. This sector accounts for over 10 percent of the U.S. GDP and about 20 percent of a household's expenditures, and employs over fourteen million people.[5] Such numbers belie, however, the true significance of transportation as it is linked to every sector of the economy. As the 2003 report noted: "Interdependencies exist between transportation and nearly every other sector of the economy. Consequently a threat to the transportation sector may impact other industries that rely on it."[6] In fact the world is characterized by supply chains that foster international trade and these are vulnerable to disruption. For example, if the freight system in the United States or another major economy were successfully attacked, exporting industries and importers alike would incur tremendous losses, as trade would be brought to a virtual standstill. In short, transportation facilities present tempting targets to any terrorist group seeking to wreak economic havoc in the United States, a goal specifically articulated by al-Qaeda.

Modes of Transportation

Terrorists are also attracted to transportation targets so as to be able to inflict mass casualties, as illustrated by the bombings of London's underground and Madrid's train stations. Moreover, they are fully aware that such facilities often have great symbolic importance, as exhibited by attacks on the World Trade Center in 1993 and 2001. Overall, transportation accounted for roughly 20 percent of all targets and 15 percent of all fatalities between 1968 and 2005.[7]

The London and Madrid attacks also demonstrated yet again that the transportation sector is a security risk because all of its vehicles—not just aircraft—can be turned into deadly weapons. Truck and car bombs have been notoriously effective, much as hijacked planes became deadly missiles on 9/11. So, transportation is a channel for terrorists to travel to their targets and as a way to ship their weapons. Thus, it is appropriate to consider *all* terrorism as involving transportation security in one way or another.

Unfortunately, transportation systems have certain characteristics that make them especially difficult to safeguard. They encompass several decidedly different modes, notably air, water, rail, and road. Each mode contains its own unique characteristics and vulnerabilities. To put it another way, aviation and airport issues are very different from those confronting ocean traffic and seaports and rail or road passenger and cargo transportation systems.

Until 9/11 aviation was the only mode that received much attention concerning security. This mode continues to be the primary beneficiary of public spending on security, even though other modes have also been successfully attacked by terrorists. Indeed, any coherent effort to enhance transportation security requires an analysis of the ways each mode can be safeguarded from attack.

Furthermore, transportation systems have been undergoing dramatic change in recent decades that further complicate efforts to enhance security. Today they have become more reliant on telecommunications, to such a degree that every transportation mode is highly dependent upon a functioning cyber network. For example, the air traffic control system is critical to safe airline operations. Any disruptions of telecommunications networks will have profound consequences for global, regional, and national transportation systems, yet they are not yet secure.

Moreover, technological progress in transportation and telecommunications continues to aid globalization by reducing obstacles to international commerce and facilitating transnational interactions of all kinds. Thus, the problem of safeguarding transportation systems is further complicated because it is a global as well as a national issue. But world politics is largely characterized by the interactions of independent international states with varying degrees of power and influence. So, national and international security concerns require a strong measure of cooperation, often a challenging task when attempting to create a new regime.

An array of national, international, and transnational actors has dealt rather effectively with transportation security. The Asia Pacific Economic Cooperation (APEC), for example, has adopted various measures to enhance the transportation security of member states. These include the establishment of the Secure Trade in the APEC Region (STAR) initiative, by which member economies are to take action to screen people and cargo better, as well as to protect ships, planes, airports, and seaports. To achieve these goals, a Counter Terrorism Task Force has been established along with a Transportation Security Experts Group, with task groups for such areas as cyber, maritime, and aviation security.[8] Although helpful, the full impact of these activities and those undertaken by the International Maritime Organization (IMO) and the International Civil Aviation Organization (ICAO) remains to be seen.

Technological developments have also led to the increasing integration of the individual modes into a complex system that utilizes the strengths of each. The critical points in this intermodal system are the terminals or nodes that link different modes together. These are very attractive targets because of their economic and social significance. Traditional security challenges are multiplied by numerous new problems of coordination and integration, such as clearly defining the roles of the many different types of personnel working in these terminals and ensuring that they understand their proper roles in the security program and can manage them effectively. For example, the new emphasis on direct rail connections to airports means that security practices for the railway and aviation modes need to be harmonized. Of course, ensuring that all rail passengers are subject to rigorous aviation screening standards is no simple matter. [9] Thus, intermodalism greatly complicates security calculations, particularly when we continue to think of security purely within one mode at a time.

Modal thinking is reinforced by the tendency of virtually all governmental agencies to function in a reactive mode by responding to particular threats, rather than taking a more holistic view of the situation. For example, the airline hijackings and problem of bombs aboard airplanes that emerged in the late 1950s and 1960s resulted in government-mandated, stepped-up security measures by the airlines and at airports. By contrast, little focus was given at the time to security measures in road, rail, or sea-going modes, a lack of preparedness that remains largely unchanged today.

Another complicating factor is that attacks against transportation systems can take many forms. The weapons available to terrorists have proliferated and each poses unique problems for transportation planners and managers. Explosives, originally in the form of suitcase bombs in planes, remain the most common. They range from common commercial products to powerful plastic explosives (PBX, RDX, and HMX) that are difficult for x-ray machines to detect and are available on the black market in Europe.[10] Bombings accounted for 60 percent of all attacks, 80 percent of all injuries, and 52 percent of all fatalities between 1968 and 2005.[11] Moreover, they appear to be an integral part of al-Qaeda's strategy: in 2002 to 2003, it launched twelve car bombs, one boat bomb, and two truck bombs, killing 439 persons in 15 attacks conducted in ten countries.[12] Indeed, al-Qaeda and its affiliated groups continue to use these tactics.

Cyber attacks are also common, and can take many forms. A specific database of a transportation owner or operator can be attacked in order to gain information. An attacker can seek out a weakly defended pathway for access to a network. The purpose can be to shut down service or to introduce harmful instructions. Attacks can be launched against highway traffic, train control centers, and air traffic control systems, as well as port, power, and telecommunications systems. Although the Department of Homeland Security (DHS) is the lead agency for cyber security of critical infrastructure, it has been slow to develop threat and vulnerability assessments or recovery plans.[13] Recognizing the need for urgent action, DHS secretary Michael Chertoff has established a new office under an assistant secretary for cyber security and telecommunications to attend to this issue.[14]

Transit of nuclear and radiological materials also poses threats. If terrorists can acquire 50 kg of highly enriched uranium (HEU), in principle they can assemble a bomb; however, building such a bomb remains a difficult task even with these materials and the technical know how. More likely is a radiological attack using a "dirty bomb," or other radiological dispersal device (RDD) that disseminates radioactive materials in intermodal facilities or is scattered in powdered form from a plane. Such materials are readily available since they are widely used in many civilian activities such as x-rays. RDDs are also relatively easy to build.

Chemical and biological weapons have already been used. Terrorists can easily acquire numerous agents that cause such diseases as plague, botulism, and smallpox. A few grams of microbes can prove as deadly as attacks with anthrax have proven. Such an attack took place in Tokyo on March 20, 1995 when five members of a religious cult carrying bags of the deadly nerve agent sarin entered the subway during the morning rush hour, punctured the bags with umbrellas and fled. Fifteen different subway stations were affected as people left the train and subsequently collapsed. At first, the cause was unknown so people continued to be infected as operators tried to clean up the puddles and the trains continued to operate, spreading the contamination. It took three hours for the cause to be identified. Fortunately the terrorists were not efficient; if they had been, the number of casualties would have been much higher. Even so, the toll was 12 dead and some 1,600 seriously injured.[15]

Intermodal Passenger Systems

The Tokyo attack as well as the ones in London and in Madrid illustrate all too clearly that intermodal passenger systems and their terminals are attractive terrorist targets. Achieving security of these intermodal passenger systems is ultimately a fully unachievable goal given their extent, openness, accessibility, and complexity. Compounding this problem is that greater security measures in the realm of aviation have contributed to terrorists focusing more of their efforts on railways, particularly since they are so difficult to secure and terrorists can escape more easily. The number of passengers who use light rail, subways, buses, inter-city rail, and commuter rail and flow through the system is so high that it is difficult to apply preventive screening measures. Every day, over ten million trips are taken on metro and commuter rail systems in the United States.[16] An obvious conflict exists between securing such a system and the inconvenience such measures cause passengers.

Managing an attack is no simple matter. The Tokyo case highlighted the challenges that responders confront. These include:

1. Structural issues—the Tokyo government was in charge, but had poor communications with the military, which had the necessary equipment but was under the control of the prime minister.
2. Poor and conflicting information reached the prime minister's office.
3. Diagnosis and reaction times were slow.
4. Staff and managers were unprepared for this kind of attack.
5. A lack of communication with the public led to panic, which was a major reason so many became ill.
6. Emergency response preparation (medicines, hospitals, communications) were inadequate.[17]

These lessons learned are applicable at a general level to all attacks on passenger systems and have been widely disseminated, but not necessarily acted upon.

In the United States, various steps have been taken at both the national and local levels to improve transit security. At the national level, the Federal Transit Association has taken the following steps:

1. Carried out a number of threat and vulnerability assessments of major transit systems
2. Deployed technical assistance teams to help transit agencies develop and implement security programs
3. Accelerated the deployment of technologies, especially a chemical detection system
4. Promoted training and regional collaboration
5. Developed a public awareness program
6. Disseminated guidelines and action items to guide local agencies[18]

These urge transit agencies both to (1) establish a specific integrated security program that includes emergency-management plans that incorporate and update such measures on the basis of threat information and (2) incorporate design criteria, for new facilities and systems an organized incident-management system with defined security responsibilities for all employees, including managers who are accountable for security within their separate domains. Security awareness is stressed for all employees, with ongoing training programs; new employees are to be checked and undergo security orientations. Public awareness is also emphasized and appropriate materials are to be distributed widely.[19]

The efficacy of such measures remains to be seen but public transit officials are worried about the limited resources that have been made available to harden passenger systems and to improve security. During the first few years following 9/11, for example, the federal government allocated a mere $250 million to mass transit, compared to over $15 billion for aviation security.[20]

Railroads and highways are also part of the infrastructure of the surface passenger transportation systems that require attention. Although difficult to protect, trains run along specific routes and can be controlled. If taken over by terrorists, for example, the train can be diverted from its original route. Though passenger and baggage screening of rail passengers is difficult to implement owing to the high costs, delays, and number of personnel required, the Transportation Security Administration (TSA) initiated a pilot project involving a modified procedure designed to assess the impact on passenger flows of checking for explosives.[21] The sheer size of highway systems with their miles of roads and thousands of bridges makes prevention virtually impossible for the system as a whole and extraordinarily difficult even for particular segments thought to be threatened. On the other hand, although bridges or tunnels can be destroyed relatively easily, the impact tends to be limited to the specific corridors struck.

Planning for the security of surface intermodal passenger systems requires a decision approach based on clearly defined goals and risk assessment methodologies that link actions to potential threats. It should include criteria to identify key assets and choke points, such as bridges and tunnels, intermodal nodes, highway interchanges, and border crossings that, if successfully attacked, could lead to major public health and safety problems or have serious economic consequences. Such planning should include the development of comprehensive risk, threat, and vulnerability assessments; guidelines and criteria for identifying choke points; standards for threat reduction at these points; plans to harden industry infrastructure; the use of biometrics and other relevant technology; response plans to handle incidents, including direction and control; and creation of national transportation security education and awareness programs for planners, managers, and operators.

Any attempt to increase the security of passenger or cargo systems must therefore begin with a plan that is based on threat perception analysis and incorporates all elements of the system from design and construction through operations and response. Thus, facilities should be designed and constructed with such security considerations as lights, visibility, and nonhazardous materials in mind. All relevant technologies should be deployed, such as closed-circuit video surveillance, alarms, detection, and screening technologies. Communications technologies are especially critical for responders, operators, and managers, who must be able to share information and decisions among themselves through multimode communication systems and procedures. Contingency planning by the key stakeholders, such as the transportation authority, ministries, health organizations, and first responders must be part of the plan, which should include measures to deal with various types of attacks, including weapons of mass destruction (WMD). The plan should also provide for a clear decision-making process for system shut down and evacuation, effective communications between stations and surface, operators and managers, and between various organizations, improved security awareness at all levels of the relevant organization, and guidelines for response and training programs, including emergency drills and seminars. It should also deal with such issues as detection, alarm, and communications systems, as well as the availability of appropriate equipment such as vaccines. The goal should be to mitigate or limit casualties, damage, and disruption because, given the vulnerability of both passenger and cargo systems, deterrence and prevention are unlikely to work 100 percent of the time. Of course, every effort should be made to maintain a high level of awareness through constant training of staff and personnel and the involvement of the public through signs and announcements,. Still, even a well-prepared system is not immune to attack, as the bombings of London's underground clearly demonstrated.

A Government Accountability Office (GAO) report found that well-known risk-management principles had not been implemented. In its words:

> Implementation of risk management principles and improved coordination could help enhance rail security. Using risk management principles can help guide federal programs and responses to better prepare against terrorism and other threats and to better direct finite national resources to areas of highest priority. In addition, improved coordination among federal entities could help enhance security efforts across all modes, including passenger and freight rail systems. We reported in June 2003 that the roles and responsibilities of the Transportation Security Administration (TSA) and the Department of Transportation (DOT) in transportation security, including rail security, have yet to be clearly delineated, which creates the potential for duplicating or conflicting efforts as both entities work to enhance security.[22]

Congress has taken the initiative to improve this situation with calls for the development and implementation of a security plan as well as prioritizing and authorizing vastly increased expenditures for rail security.[23] Of course, this is merely an attempt to diminish the gap between the lavish spending on the aviation passenger system compared to the relatively paltry amount dedicated to rail security.

In regard to the aviation system since 9/11 the United States has attempted to increase security through various measures, the most expensive and visible being the replacement of private-company screeners who tended to be poorly paid, badly trained, and inefficient compared to a larger, better-funded force of federal workers. The degree to which their activities enhance security remains debatable for, although the federal screeners have seized a huge number of potential weapons, testers have been able to take weapons past screeners in at least 15 airports. Further evidence that the screening process was in need of improvement came from a GAO report that criticized the TSA's training efforts. These needed to be updated, required additional staff as well as better intranet and Internet connections, and internal controls including monitoring and evaluation mechanisms. Moreover, screening remained focused on passengers and baggage did not receive the attention that is required.[24]

Whether better training would significantly reduce the hassle factor that presently bedevils travelers is unclear, but sentiment appears to be growing that change is required, specifically that a passenger who has smuggled a pair of scissors on board does not represent a major threat. Measures such as the "registered traveler" that would facilitate the process may be desirable, although many object to the infringement on privacy involved in transferring the necessary personal information to security authorities.

Be that as it may, former DHS secretary Tom Ridge, during whose tenure most of the existing practices and protocols were established, admitted: "I think we probably overreacted. ... We need to move from looking for weapons to paying attention to people who are or could be terrorists."[25] A study by the RAND Corporation that evaluated the potential threats did not even list hijacking. Explosives were at the top of the list on a threat spectrum or scale ranging from 0 to 100:[26]

Insider plants bomb 100
Bomb in uninspected cargo 100
Large truck bomb 71
Luggage bomb 45
Curbside car bomb 33
Attack on terminal passenger areas 26
Attack on airplane runway areas 26
Shoulder fired missile 13
Attack on control tower or utility plant 12
Sniper attack 8
Mortar attack 3

Although missiles ranked relatively low, primarily because few attempts have succeeded in downing a plane, the potential threat that they pose led Congress to instruct the DHS to test a missile defense system that could cost as much as $10 billion.[27] This is another area where cooperation is essential, yet the airlines have always been reluctant for these cost reasons to make major investments in security.

To deal with other threats, various measures have included background checks of airport workers and staff, restricted access to various airport areas, and the appointment of some 158 federal security directors who are responsible for all 429 major airports. Notwithstanding huge investments, significant deficiencies remain. A team of police experts, for example, concluded that:

> [airport] security in the United States is best characterized as in its developmental stage. ... First and foremost there is a glaring worldwide deficiency in the intelligence gathering capabilities of both governments and airport facilities. ... The integration between TSA and law enforcement needs significant improvement. ... Law enforcement needs a significant attitude change regarding its role in security and that it needs to be trained to a higher level of activity to be able to respond to an attack.[28]

Nor can one overlook the role of general aviation. It is quite simple to rent or steal a small, privately owned plane or even a large corporate jet. Safeguarding thousands of airports and large numbers of planes is a very costly proposition and, though some modest steps have been taken, access to these airports and their planes remains relatively open. The Aircraft Owners and Pilots Association (AOPA), a powerful lobby, argues that their planes are not a major threat, that they have taken effective voluntary actions, and that small airports are secure and planes not easily stolen;[29] however, many other experts believe that the threat is real. In May 2005 a small single-engine plane accidentally intruded into forbidden air space over Washington, D.C., causing all three branches of the government to evacuate. Indeed, the GAO has urged the TSA to develop a risk-management approach to identify threats and vulnerabilities, and then apply risk communication principles.[30]

Freight Systems

In addition to its role in passenger transportation, aviation provides an important freight system function. Air cargo represents a potential threat not only to the freight carriers, but also to passenger planes that also carry large amounts of cargo. Freight passes through many transfer points in its journey from the shipper to a plane so that opportunities for tampering are quite extensive. Furthermore, cargo planes are just as powerful weapons as loaded passenger planes, but access to the cargo ramps is not monitored closely. Nor is all cargo checked. Some experts claim that the "trusted shipper" program ensures safety, but the high level of air cargo theft, drug smuggling, and other illegal activities indicates the degree to which the system is vulnerable. A terrorist attack aimed at blowing up several cargo planes simultaneously would have very damaging consequences for any economy and for global trade generally.

The security risks involving cargo have been recognized for some time and various measures have been implemented in the past decade by the Federal Aviation Administration (FAA) and the air cargo companies; however, air freight continues to be accorded a lower priority than passengers. Measures such as work on explosive detection or cargo profiling are ongoing, but no effective, comprehensive cargo-security plan has been developed thus far by the FAA or the TSA.

Such an approach is also relevant for other elements of the freight system. Railroads carry tons of bulk commodities and thousands of containers. In addition, trucks and containers often carry hazardous materials. An appropriate decision system to handle and track such shipments is vital. Contingency plans should be developed that deal with such important questions as:

1. When do you shut down the corridor or system?
2. How quickly can traffic resume?
3. Are alternative routes available?
4. What, if anything, should be exempt from the shutdown?
5. How will the containers be marked so that first responders are alerted to the specific nature of the cargo, without using a system that can easily be decoded by terrorists?

The most critical elements in the freight system are the intermodal nodes—the ports through which millions of containers flow each year. Like all other terminals, ports are attractive, vulnerable targets. Ports are accessible by both land and water, have large numbers of workers and visitors, are close to crowded metropolitan centers, cover large land areas that often contain petrochemical and other dangerous storage facilities, and are intermodal nodes that link shipping to rail and road nodes, thus providing ready access to other locations. In addition to such difficulties as size, complexity, and diversity of port operations, other problems include the difficulties of achieving coordination by all the actors involved, developing a set of standards for the nation so that the level of security is the same for all ports and within ports as different facilities owned by different operators may have different security levels, funding provisions, as well as obstacles to sharing of intelligence and information between the port authority and other governmental agencies.

These vulnerabilities have been exploited by criminal elements for decades. Smuggling of drugs and other illicit goods is an active international industry. They are often hidden in containers that are part of regular cargoes. The number of containers that are handled in international commerce is immense, thus creating great security challenges. The imports number about nine million containers per year, any one of which could be used to introduce a nuclear device or dirty bomb into the United States. Checking each of these containers, or even a statistically significant percentage, is an impossible task because it would bring commerce to a standstill. Another issue is that ports also handle a considerable amount of hazardous cargo.

As early as 2002, Congress passed the Maritime Transportation Security Act (MTSA) that called for various initiatives to safeguard U.S. ships and ports. These included threat and security assessments of ports and vessels, national and area security plans, a National Maritime Security Advisory Committee and regional committees, vessel and facility security and response plans. Closely related is the Container Security Initiative (CSI). CSI, a U.S. Customs program, was launched in January 2002, and places U.S. Customs inspectors at major foreign ports from which most U.S.-bound containers originate so that high-risk containers can be prescreened. As many as 37 ports are participating in the program.[31]

Despite the importance and relevance of achieving such international cooperation, however, the effectiveness of this effort remains in doubt. Moving the inspection overseas inevitably raises questions about the integrity, reliability, and honesty of the local officials who are responsible for checking suspected containers. Indeed, a GAO study found that 35 percent of the "potentially dangerous" containers were not screened in foreign ports due to diplomatic consideration and inadequate staffing. Furthermore, the equipment at various ports varies and, in the absence of minimal standards, even a checked container may still pose a danger. In addition, no strategic plan with performance measures that would permit an evaluation of its effectiveness has yet been fully implemented, even though the GAO called for such action in a 2003 report and, a year later, pointed out that the program did not adequately incorporate risk management principles.[32]

Similarly, a "trusted shipper" program, whereby manufacturers, shippers, and carriers who meet certain security standards are eligible for fast-track cargo processing by U.S. Customs, also contains vulnerabilities. Recognizing that the cooperation of the private sector is essential to any attempt at achieving supply chain and border security, the trusted-shipper initiative is designed to promote such cooperation. Firms that commit themselves to analyze their security practices and policies and to upgrade them throughout their supply chain to a specific standard benefit because their goods pass through borders faster as they will be subjected to fewer inspections. The GAO found, however, that the process that customs agents used to check that the security standards were in fact appropriate was severely flawed, that Customs "grants benefits before members undergo the validation process.... To date it has validated 11%. ... Further, the validation process is not rigorous." Nor has Customs determined how to manage validations in order to minimize risks, established any performance measures, or maintained adequate records.[33]

A number of ports have also received grants either to assess their vulnerabilities or to implement additional security measures, but this program too has not led to enhanced security. It has been bedeviled by conflicting goals and administrative procedures regarding priorities, funding criteria, and the like. As a result, the acting inspector general of the DHS concluded that "the majority of projects have not been completed and the program has not yet achieved its intended results in the form of actual improvements to port security."[34]

Finally, the concern with freight also led to the establishment of Operation Safe Commerce (OSC), a public-private partnership designed to bring together the largest ports and various federal agencies in an effort to develop new cargo management systems that would safeguard international commerce from terrorist threats. Various pilot projects have been implemented to test existing security practices and technologies, the goal being to develop a secure and monitored system for freight shipments from their point of origin to their final destination. The effectiveness and impact of these activities is also problematic.

The overall conclusion to be drawn is that, although each of these projects has yielded some positive results, lack of clear guidance and unclear roles for port owners and operators has delayed adequate implementation of appropriate solutions. The Coast Guard, the lead agency under the MTSA, is responsible for developing new regulations and conducting port and harbor security assessments. Though it has implemented a number of important measures in this and other areas, much remains to be done, and it is not obvious that it possesses the manpower or the expertise to carry out its new functions. Three areas are of particular concern. First, to increase security, the Coast Guard has been developing an Automatic Identification System (AIS) to track vessels, but lacks adequate resources. Second, the port security assessments are not based on a "defined management strategy, specific cost estimates, and a clear implementation schedule" so this vital activity is not as effective as is necessary. Third, the Coast Guard's efforts to ensure that security measures are implemented appropriately are not adequate in such areas as staffing, training and managing inspectors, and carrying out inspections.[35]

Not surprisingly, port authorities and consultants argue that the funding problem continues to handicap efforts to achieve port security. The Maritime Security Act intended to improve port security but provided no funding mechanism and since its passage Congress has not yet allocated the funds the Coast Guard estimates will be required to safeguard the ports by 2012. Less than 10 percent of the ports' requests were funded, the Bush administration maintaining that the private sector should assume most of these costs.[36] Certainly, the program has suffered from serious management issues, including the fact that the limited available resources were not targeted sharply. Some 360 cities were initially eligible for port security grants. DHS Secretary Chertoff focused on the most critical, declaring that only 66 cities could apply under this program.

That ports remain vulnerable is generally accepted by all experts. Specific measures that can be taken include maintaining secure loading docks monitored by cameras; outfitting containers with electronic seals; installing sensors within containers to ensure that they are not opened illegally during transit; conducting background checks of truck drivers and others who access or work in the port, providing them with biometric identification cards; using electronic transponders and geopositional satellites (GPS) to track the movement of trucks and rail cars to and within the port; requiring advance notice of all movements to the port from the supply chain, that is, from product origin to delivery, as well as security and awareness training of all personnel. Lastly, detection of weapons of mass destruction deserves a high priority, with at least all major ports having radiation coverage.

Yet, the most important problem is to ensure the security of the entire supply chain, but all the efforts cited above are essentially focused on preventing a terrorist attack aimed at the ports. This is a real and significant danger, especially since al-Qaeda has mounted some successful maritime operations and is believed to own over 20 vessels that it can utilize for smuggling nuclear and other weapons and as means of attack.[37] A RAND study noted a lack of focus on the viability of the supply chain, the "fault tolerance or resilience of the system." Accordingly, the authors suggest that there is a need to assess existing and proposed policies, apply a systems approach, evaluate the contribution of technological developments, and gain a better understanding of how security considerations affect trade flows and corridors. Above all, the government should take the lead in promoting measures to enhance resiliency and focus research and development activities on the development of low-cost, high-volume scanning devices.[38]

The Dimensions of Transportation Security

Certain basic lessons emerge from this consideration of transportation security that need to be emphasized. Transportation systems are complex interconnected systems. The more complex the system, the greater the vulnerability. One element contributing to this complexity is the large number of actors. Many key actors are in the private sector. Their cooperation is essential if appropriate levels of security are to be achieved but, historically, the airlines and other private sector firms have not been interested in funding the necessary security measures, apart perhaps from theft prevention. If this pattern is to change, incentives motivating the private sector to adopt different policies will have to be devised. The goal should be to create a situation in which the private sector achieves economies of scale while security is enhanced.

Collaboration across modes and organizations is necessary. The many and diverse organizations that are involved must cooperate in joint efforts to break down existing barriers and obstacles that prevent the integration of security measures. This has to take place at many levels and include such measures as information sharing, training, and planning. These should be based on an evaluation of existing strengths and weaknesses in all relevant areas, including technology, identifying gaps and ways to fill them. Transportation-dependent organizations, such as shippers and tourism industries, should also be involved in the process. At the national level, issues of national policy and funding require attention. At the local level, issues of responses and mitigation need to be addressed.

The traditional approach to securing intermodal and other facilities is with a "guards, guns, and gates" strategy. Such a strategy is essentially a perimeter defense that, if breached, can lead to the destruction of the entire facility. This happened on 9/11 when the terrorists were able to smuggle their weapons onto the planes. What is required is a "layered" approach that is systematic and comprehensive because breaching a particular security feature means that other elements will provide backup.

When considering transportation security, it is necessary to consider all aspects of the system, specifically planning, design, implementation, and operation. The goal should be to incorporate security into each of these aspects to the greatest extent possible. At the core of such an approach is a decision process based on clearly defined goals. For example, what are the goals in the aviation sector? Is it to decrease the overall risk to passengers? If so, then more stringent measures should be enacted. Is it to enhance the well-being of the airlines? If so, should they not be expected to bear a share of the high costs? Is it to protect the national economy? If so, air cargo requires more attention. Is it to prevent the release of chemical or biological agents? If so, private planes merit greater focus. Is it to increase consumer confidence? If so, the least invasive procedures are probably desirable. Because some of these goals may well be contradictory, beyond difficulties in attempting to achieve them all, conflicting policies likely will be the outcome. The alternatives need to be thought through, priorities set, and allocations of cost determined in exchanges between government and the private sector.

Once goals and objectives are specified, risk assessment methodologies that relate actions to potential threats and costs can be utilized. These should be based on a realistic appraisal of the potential threat and include such basic factors as the terrorists' training, skill levels, resources, attack methods and weapons, including chemical, biological, radiological, and nuclear, as well as more traditional ones.

This approach requires that consideration be given to an analysis of the range of possible actions, their costs and benefits, and impacts upon security at each of the three principal stages:

1. Analysis and planning—develop a national transportation security assessment that identifies the weakest links in the transportation system and its infrastructure, and prioritizes the value of these links to terrorists.
2. Preparedness—develop a protection strategy.
3. Response—develop a response strategy at all levels.

These activities must be supplemented by the development of a training and preparedness program at all levels. Well-prepared first responders can mitigate impacts of terrorist acts so it is necessary to:

1. Establish national standards with appropriate regional variations.
2. Establish programs and funding for training key personnel.
3. Work with professional associations and others to develop training programs.

Such programs should include system and modal security awareness for employees who should be trained to understand their roles and responsibilities, alerting them to recognize suspicious persons, activities, and devices, and to communicate information to appropriate personnel. Management and supervisors should be trained to understand their roles and responsibilities and how to carry them out. Communicating with the public is also important. In particular, a specific plan should be developed to communicate threat alerts to the public through channels such as the media and cell phone networks.

Science and technology will inevitably comprise important elements in such a strategy. There is no doubt that technology can reduce vulnerabilities in many important ways. The United States is carrying out a large research and development effort to identify new methods of safeguarding telecommunications systems, of detecting biological, chemical, and nuclear agents, of checking baggage for explosives, and of tracking and protecting containers. Ideally the new technologies will increase efficiency at the same time that they enhance security. Such technologies are obviously more likely to be accepted rapidly by the private sector.

Communications technologies are critical. Attacks have occurred against several modes so intermodal communication and interorganizational communication is essential. Fast and coordinated information exchange must be the goal. This requires more than common radio frequencies for first responders, such as secure and standardized procedures. Other relevant technological areas include the use of biometrics to improve security at key points of access, the identification and deployment of container- and cargo-screening capabilities, identification and deployment of explosive detection technologies, and design processes that build security into basic system designs as much as possible.

To be effective, new technologies have to be integrated into existing systems through the following steps:

1. Identify the modes, nodes, infrastructure, and stakeholders that are vulnerable
2. Analyze the relationships among these elements
3. Pay special attention to intermodal and transfer facilities
4. Consider all the modes and their interactions when developing security policies and practices in terms of:
   a. Existing capabilities and strengths that can be built upon
   b. Funding priorities at all levels
   c. Cross-modal interactions
5. Incorporate security requirements when setting new standards
6. Define best practices and assess their relevance for other areas
7. Look for effective but simple and affordable technologies

Technology cannot deliver a "silver bullet" to safeguard transportation, despite its appeal and efforts to accelerate the development of new technologies, such as "sniffers" to detect bombs at a distance, computer programs to identify suspicious activities, and machines to screen large numbers of people quickly and accurately. All such technologies may hold promise but they only too frequently may be circumvented by equally innovative terrorists.

Technology ultimately depends on people. It is human beings who operate the technologies, who must interpret the results that technological tools provide. Since every aspect of transportation—its planning, design, operation, and maintenance—requires organizational and technological change, professionals with appropriate skills and perspectives will be required. Only recently have educational and security issues received any attention so that few transportation professionals in either the public or the private sector possess an appropriate understanding of the issues or the relevant skills required to function effectively in the new environment. An appropriate level of security will be achieved when all levels of all transportation-related organizations assume ownership of security; however, this will take time and be dependent on improving the technical and conceptual skills of all members of the aviation sector, from truck drivers delivering cargo to clerical staff opening the mail and entering data to corporate-level executives and government officials planning and implementing policy. Developing a coherent strategy to tackle such educational and training needs is an issue of great urgency.

Concluding Comments

It is no longer adequate to consider security in terms of individual modes. Intermodal linkages, or nodes, must be included and this growing connectivity has dramatically increased the vulnerability of transportation. It is obviously essential to think of security not in intramodal but in intermodal terms, a difficult challenge because commercial firms and government agencies are usually organized on the basis of modes.

Transportation professionals must, therefore, be sensitive to the security issues that this new transportation system creates. They must be prepared to develop plans and policies that are designed to prevent attacks, reduce the vulnerabilities of intermodal facilities, and prepare for response and recovery should a disaster occur. Intermodal professionals have a responsibility to pay attention to each of these dimensions in order to ensure that personal mobility and the movement of freight and goods continue as smoothly as possible, as failure to do so would seriously hinder national development and pose significant obstacles to future growth.

With a finite number of dollars and competing budgetary priorities, of course we simply cannot protect all of our assets all the time despite our best intentions. Thus, we will need to assess our vulnerabilities as well as the nature and extent of the threat. In the final analysis, a balanced risk assessment must be a critical ingredient if we are to construct and implement an effective homeland security strategy. In this endeavor the public and private sectors will each have to play a major role. Working together at all levels in a cooperative fashion must be a hallmark of any successful strategy to address this major and growing homeland security problem.

Endnotes

1. This chapter draws upon a module on transportation security that was prepared under the auspices of the Asia-Pacific Economic Cooperation (APEC), as part of a week-long course on intermodal transportation that was field tested in Indonesia, December 2005, as well as on a presentation to the Istanbul Conference on Democracy and Global Security, June 2005. It also draws upon my articles, "Aviation Security: Promise or Reality," Studies in Conflict and Terrorism 27, no. 1 (2004); and "International Transportation Security," Review of Policy Research 21, no. 3 (May 2004).

2. "The National Strategy for the Physical Protection of Critical Infrastructures and Key Assets." Available at http://www.dhs.gov/interweb/assetlibrary/Physical_Strategy.pdf.

3. "Critical Foundations." Available at http://www.tsa.gov/interweb/assetlibrary/Infrastructure.pdf.

4. Ibid., p. A11.

5. U.S. Department of Transportation, Pocket Guide to Transportation (Washington, D.C.: U.S. Department of Transportation, 32, 33, 35.

6. "The National Strategy," 54.

7. Calculated from the MIPT Terrorism Knowledge Base, available at www.tbk.org.

8. http://www.apec.org/apec/apec_groups/som_special_task_groups/counter_terrorism/secure_trade_in_the.html.

9. A. Boyd and J. Caton, "Securing Intermodal Connections" (2001). Available at http://gulliver.trb.org/publications/security/intermodal_facilities.pdf.

10. H. Timmons, "A Black Market for Bomb Materials Is Said to Flourish in Europe," New York Times, July 17, 2005, A9.

11. Calculated from the MIPT Terrorism Knowledge Base available at www.tbk.org.

12. Robert Pape, "Al Qaeda's Smart Bombs," New York Times, July 9, 2005, A29.

13. Government Accountability Office, "Department of Homeland Security Faces Challenges in Fulfilling Cybersecurity Responsibilities," May 2005, GAO-05-434.

14. Larry Greenemeier, "Changes in the Works," Information Week, July 18, 2005.

15. T. Okumura et al., "Lessons Learned from the Tokyo Subway Sarin Attack," available at http://pdm.medicine.wisc.edu/Okumura.htm.

16. Data is available from the American Public Transit Association's (APTA) Web site at http://www.apta.com/research/stats/.

17. Okumura et al., "Lessons Learned."

18. http://transit-safety.volpe.dot.gov/Security/Default.asp.

19. http://transit-safety.volpe.dot.gov/Security/SecurityInitiatives/Top20/default.asp.

20. See comments by Bill Millar, president, APTA, at http://www.apta.com/media/releases/050620senate_cuts.cfm.

21. M. L. Wald, "Train Station as Test Site for Screening of Passengers," New York Times, April 16, 2004, http://www.nytimes.com/query.fullpage.html.res9C01E2DBF935A25757COA9629C8B63.

22. http://www.gao.gov/htext.d04598.html.

23. http://www.csoonline.com/read/080105/wonk_wonk.html.

24. Government Accountability Office, "Aviation Security: Screener Training and Performance Measurement Strengthened, but More Work Remains," May 2005 C.F. GAO-05-457, 18 May 2005. Available at: http://www.gao.gov/new.items/do5457.pdf.

25. Joe Sharkey, "Don't Let That Ticket Out of the Screener's Sight," New York Times, August 20, 2005, C7.

26. Eric Lipton, "U.S. Set to Test Missile Defenses Aboard Airlines," New York Times, May 29, 2005, A1, 16.

27. Ibid.

28. Maine Community Policing Institute, "Executive Report," January 6, 2003, 4, 5.

29. http://www.aopa.org/whatsnew/newsitems/2002/020621_homeland_security.html.

30. Government Accountability Office, "General Aviation Security: Increased Federal Oversight Is Needed but Continued Partnership with the Private Sector Is Critical to Long-Term Success" November 2004, GAO-05-144.

31. http://www.customs.gov/xp/cgov/border_security/international_activities/csi/.

32. Government Accountability Office, "Container Security: A Flexible Staffing Model and Minimum Equipment Requirements Would Improve Overseas Targeting and Inspection Efforts," April 2005, GAO-05-557.

33. Government Accountability Office, "Homeland Security: Key Cargo Security Programs Can be Improved," statement by R. M. Stana, director, Homeland Security and Justice Issues, May 26, 2005.

34. OIG, DHS, "Review of the Port Security Grant Program," January 2005.

35. Government Accountability Office, "Coast Guard. Observations on Agency Priorities in Fiscal Year 2006 Budget Request," March 17, 2005.

36. Zeltech, LLC, "Port Security Faces a Funding Abyss," available at: http://www/zeltech.com?News/News_Sept_11_04_Portsecurityfacesfundingabyss.asp; see also the American Association of Port Authorities at www.aapa-ports.org.

37. J. Sinai, "Future Trends in Worldwide Maritime Terrorism," The Quarterly Journal, March 2004.

38. H. Willis and D. Ortiz, "Evaluating the Security of the Global Containerized Supply Chain," The RAND Corporation, Santa Monica, CA, 2004.

Chapter 12

Redefining U.S. Energy Security in the Twenty-First Century

Kevin King

The author examines energy infrastructure in relation to national and homeland security. Much like transportation, energy and other parts of national infrastructure are vulnerable to one form or another of terrorist attack. Beyond the extraordinarily difficult and expensive task of defending the energy infrastructure, which is also closely tied to and dependent on the transportation sector, King also addresses other vulnerabilities that pose significant challenges to national security. Continuing availability and access to a sufficient supply of fuels are central to economic security. At the same time, reliance on fossil fuels contributes to global warming, which is itself a national security challenge.

In these early years of the twenty-first century, the national focus on war and instability in the Middle East and climbing domestic energy prices is drawing attention to the nexus between energy and national security once again. During the 1970s and early 1980s, energy policy and national security were tightly linked, but the primacy of this relationship tended to wane in salience with the resolution of international petroleum supply crises and with petroleum prices that have facilitated Organisation for Economic Co-operation and Development (OECD) member countries' economic development on the whole. By the late 1990s, however, attention was redirected toward this relationship when oil industry insiders presaged world peak oil production and an impending oil shortage by 2010.[1] Following these warnings were the 9/11 attacks in 2001, raising serious questions about U.S. critical vulnerabilities and possible terrorist targets, including the U.S. energy system. Further heightening concerns today are a multitude of problems that appear to have no easy solutions and affect world energy markets: surging oil demand in developing countries; political instability in Nigeria; soured U.S. relations with Venezuela; the U.S. military intervention in Iraq, the ongoing insurgency, and Iraq's oil sector operating at suboptimal levels; the durability of al-Qaeda's leadership and the diffusion of affiliated terror groups; Saudi Arabia's internal militant Islamic jihadist problem; the stalled Israeli-Palestinian peace process and associated conflicts; as well as Iran's nuclear program, pledges to destroy Israel, and threats to use the oil weapon if provoked.

Even more daunting is a long-term set of challenges that confront the United States over the next thirty to forty years. The U.S. must attain its energy security in the face of decreasing domestic energy supply and increasing energy consumption, growing dependence on foreign sources of fossil fuels, the exponentially rising costs of maintaining intervention policies in the Persian Gulf to ensure the free flow of oil, and precipitous and irreversible decline in world oil production predicted before 2040.[2] The urgency of this situation is underscored by the inescapable fact that the U.S. economy, the world's largest at over $13 trillion,[3] rests fundamentally on "an energy foundation,"[4] and this foundation is built primarily out of hydrocarbon fuels.

Indeed, at the core of this energy base is the strategic commodity petroleum and its related products, all of which are demanded in greater quantities annually. This makes the expected twilight of the petroleum age a massive dilemma for the United States, at least as large as its present dependence on foreign oil imports. Not only is the United States growing more dependent on imported oil daily, this trend is not expected to reverse until and unless a technological breakthrough leads to an energy revolution, public policy provides the leadership and framework necessary for meeting tomorrow's energy needs through a variety of alternative energy solutions, or world peak oil collapses the present system altogether. Furthermore, as exploitable world petroleum resources shrink in the coming years concomitant with more global competition for these resources, it is hard to see how the United States will be less vulnerable to energy shocks absent a comprehensive energy security strategy to create a more resilient and diversified energy system.

Complicating this picture is the prospect of finding viable alternatives to fossil fuels that can be economically exploited within the coming decades to meet higher energy demands, a situation that will require tremendous innovation and farsighted public policy. Energy solutions that come too late, or further contribute to severe environmental imbalances, or are insufficient to meet energy requirements would almost certainly have cascading economic, political, social, and ecological effects. Stability of the present hydrocarbon energy system is not simply desirable, it is presently vital to the functioning of U.S. society and integral to the prosperity of its economy. Yet how the United States eventually transitions to an alternative and more sustainable energy system will determine its success and security tomorrow.

In this chapter, I seek to explore this critical link between energy and national security, ubiquitously known as energy security. The goal is threefold. First, I develop a framework for understanding the nature of how energy security is broadly conceived. The energy position of the United States is explained in relation to its main energy sectors. Second, the critical infrastructure and key assets pertaining to energy production, transmission and transport, storage, and end use are outlined for major components of the energy system. Finally, this chapter discusses U.S. national energy strategy in light of current dilemmas and concludes with the issue of energy system transition.

Conceptualizing Energy Security

Since conceptions concern the elements that make energy systems secure, it is useful to begin by clarifying what these terms mean. An energy system pertains to the integrated network of primary energy sources, fuel refinement and power generation processes, and infrastructure that distribute energy for residential, commercial, industrial, military, and transportation end-use sectors.[5] An energy system is like other systems, in that it has inputs, or supply chains of primary energy sources that are the raw materials, such as crude oil; throughputs, or chemical, electrical, nuclear, thermal, and other conversion processes; and outputs, or refined fuels, electricity, heat, pollution, and waste—in short, all of the intended and unintended effects from energy conversion and consumption; and throughout the system there is the complex web of infrastructure and human resources that manage the inputs, throughputs, and outputs within the context of corporate and government policies and legal constraints to transform and deliver energy to end users.

The task of defining energy security beyond the traditional scope of oil security is not easy, complicated by factors such as a relative conceptual nascency and lack of scholarly consensus. It has only been in the last decade that broader scholarly attention to the subject has emerged in real force, in contrast with the vast bulk of literature the oil crises generated in the 1970s and 1980s. As yet there is no universally accepted paradigm, but rather a variety of approaches that emphasize different issues and policies that are explored in this section.

Besides conceptual nascency and competing approaches, another factor complicating defining energy security is its tainted legacy from its use by policymakers. Often public officials who speak of energy security never make an attempt to define it, but use it as the rationale for executive or legislative action. U.S. politicians of all political stripes have been particularly adept at using energy security as the pretext for enacting legislation that is purportedly promoting the greater good and protecting America.[6] This may be useful in rallying support for the passage of an energy bill, but it is hard to see how America's energy system is more secure when such legislation tends to benefit special interests with powerful lobbies, and resource allocation is largely directed away from America's renewable energy programs.[7] As a result, some view energy security as "a woolly and much-abused notion,"[8] deployed to justify resource nationalism, industry protectionism, and a virtual constellation of bad policy decisions.[9] Thus, it becomes necessary to distinguish between the political uses of energy security versus its meaning in a rigorous academic context. It is this scholarly milieu that is the focus of this section.

In its simplest articulation, energy security is a population's "secure access to adequate supplies of primary energy at affordable cost."[10] For example, Bielecki reiterates these central themes, defining energy security as "uninterrupted supply that fully meets the needs of the global economy," while noting that "reasonable prices" is a problematic generalization depending on the dimensions of time and individual perception.[11] Nevertheless, Bielecki decides that reasonable prices are "cost-based and determined by the market based on supply/demand balances." Barton et al. similarly stress energy supply reliability and affordability, stating that energy security is the "condition in which a nation and all, or most, of its citizens and businesses have access to sufficient energy resources at reasonable prices for the foreseeable future free from serious risk of major disruption of service."[12] As far as definitions go, these first appear to be parsimonious. But upon reflection, they raise more questions than answers. For instance, why is importance attached to energy supply reliability but not energy system resiliency and resistance to critical failure? Are market preferences the central important aspects of secure energy systems, even beyond critical infrastructure protection and designing less vulnerable networks? One can also ask why energy security is confined to all or most of a nation's citizens and businesses, and why energy security is apparently achieved when risk of major service disruption is presumed to be absent. One would assume in the age of modern terrorism that such risk would be omnipresent, especially given the prevalence of centralized generation networks and their well-known vulnerabilities. Moreover, should demand-side management be at least as important as supply-side management? Likewise, environmental issues impacting domestic populations and the global commons are not mentioned in these definitions. Are we to infer, therefore, that they are of little importance in how we should approach the concept of energy security? Many simple definitions fall short for the reason that they ignore elements integral to the optimal functioning and robust protection of energy systems, as well as the recognition that new threats require adaptive change.

Though the simple definitions circumvent the issue of threats posed to energy systems by terrorists, the post-September 11 world requires that conceptual thinking take such threats into account. Terrorism is no longer something that occurs in places distant temporally and psychologically, but a real and serious threat at home and abroad to critical infrastructure and global supply chains. Similarly, easy definitions also ignore central policy themes. Government policies impact the security of energy systems by setting priorities and standards, regulating industries, providing parameters for negotiations and agreements, and allocating resources. In the twenty-first century, modern industrial countries must meet their rising energy needs while competing for scarce resources with rapidly developing states, and addressing international pressures for sustainable development, pollution abatement, and cooperation on climate change. Thus, definitions that ignore critical realities, or are centered on one issue or almost entirely concerned with aspects of one fuel alone fail to help us understand energy security in its totality. For these reasons, conceptual understandings of energy security that articulate the core challenges, threats, and goals to securing energy systems are preferred to pithy definitions.

Before turning to more recent work, we need to examine a seminal Cold War study of the U.S. energy system, a path-breaking work originally conceived for the Defense Civil Preparedness Agency and later completed under the aegis of the Federal Emergency Management Agency.[13] This report remains a definitive analysis of critical vulnerabilities, potential and real threats, and solutions that remain salient today. In fact, the authors recognized over twenty years ago that "energy is more than oil, and energy security is far more than ability to keep the oil coming," also adding that America's energy system is "brittle—easily shattered by accident or malice."[14] The study aptly assessed vulnerabilities that still plague the U.S. energy system, notably its highly centralized and rigid networks, hazardous materials/fuels intensity, the lack of large-scale fuel substitutability, as well as complex system components designed for reliability but nevertheless prone to unpredictable interactions that can result in system-wide failures having potentially catastrophic consequences. In light of these vulnerabilities and human threats, the study concluded that national energy insecurity requires designing resilience into the energy system.

After the Cold War, new research began to assess whether the United States was still vulnerable to the old threats, as well as assess emerging and future threats. Of particular note is a white paper the Pacific Northwest Laboratory prepared for the U.S. Department of Energy in the early 1990s that addressed future energy security concerns. The authors concluded that the "meaning of energy security for the United States in the post-Cold War era will be different than previously conceived due to changes in politics, economics, technology and the environment on a global scale."[15] Important contributions from this white paper are its findings that energy crises are not usually precipitated by a single problem or event, but are the product of a confluence of complex interactions. Future energy crises may arise from any combination of the following: (1) unanticipated and rapid political changes that intersect in time to result in supply disruptions, such as those caused by regime change, civil unrest, numerous but separate regional conflicts, and/or terrorism, and perhaps even nuclear terrorism against high-value targets such as oil infrastructure; (2) restrictive environmental regulation decreasing energy production due to rising concerns about human-caused environmental harm and "the need to include ecological considerations in plans for economic growth and industrial development"; (3) transportation problems arising from accidents or shipping congestion at vital choke points, such as the Suez Canal or any of the main tanker routes funneling heavy traffic through narrow straits; and (4) destabilizing effects from rapid economic growth in the developing world, or devaluation of the dollar making energy imports unaffordable or perhaps even the loss of the dollar as the benchmark currency for foreign energy commodities.[16] These are all either manifestly real or highly possible scenarios and each of the identified areas has public policy implications.

Another post-Cold War security context is provided in a 1996 Trilateral Commission report by Martin et al.[17] Maintaining security of oil supply and stable oil prices is necessarily part of their analysis given the present oil dependency of the Trilateral countries, but they also take a broader view that looks beyond oil and incorporates the environment. Their "three faces" of energy security are:[18]

1. Limiting vulnerability to [energy supply] disruption given rising dependence on imported oil from an unstable Middle East
2. Over time, the provision of adequate supply for rising demand at reasonable prices—in effect, the reasonably smooth functioning over time of the international energy system
3. The energy-related environmental challenge. The international energy system needs to operate within the constraints of "sustainable development"—constraints which, however uncertain and long-term, have gained considerable salience in the energy policy debates in [Trilateral] countries.

In relation to limiting vulnerability, the authors warn against lowering inventories in strategic petroleum stockpiles, the problem of absent stockpiles in rapidly developing states, and the necessity that the United States "continue to protect the Gulf region from possible aggressors."[19] At the same time, they urged Trilateral countries to find alternatives to Persian Gulf oil where possible, and to slow oil demand growth by adopting policies that stress increased energy efficiency and alternative energy technologies.[20]

Thus, Martin et al. acknowledged the strategic importance of maintaining oil security while dependence on petroleum is growing, but they also pivotally introduced output environmental effects and sustainable development as part of a new energy security equation.[21] In relation to the environment, they considered the three most significant negative externalities linked to conventional fossil fuel consumption to be the threat of global climate change, such as global warming, the regional environmental challenge of acid rain, and urban air pollution. Of these, potential cumulative human contributions to global warming is the only real albeit controversial element, the scientific mainstream holding that natural variability alone is insufficient to explain observed climatic phenomena.[22] Moreover, cogent and forceful reasons exist for policymakers to address both the economic price tag of government action in attempts to mitigate climate change, as well as the costs to be paid as a result of inaction.[23] Since the anthropogenic contributions to global warming have become clearer and pressures are mounting on governments to provide energy policy solutions to help alleviate correlated environmental effects,[24] emerging energy-security concepts now incorporate the expanded view of the Trilateral Commission report.

A 1998 energy security working paper by the Nautilus Institute for Security and Sustainable Development was another forward-looking conceptual reorientation on the subject of energy security. The authors recognized the long-term challenge posed by international terrorism and diverged from the traditional approach to energy security, identified in the report as "the conventional view" centered upon the "problem of securing oil resources."[25] The report outlined a more comprehensive energy security construct that incorporated the challenges national energy policies confronted in the late 1990s and beyond:

1. Integrating international environmental problems linked to energy consumption (e.g., acid rain and global warming) into a new energy security concept.
2. Assessing long-term risks associated with advanced technologies that tend to be miscalculated (e.g., nuclear power plant accidents and the failure of synthetic fuel, fast breeder reactor, and solar thermal research and development programs).
3. Utilizing the demand-side management (DSM) of energy consumption, difficult because it involves uncertainties related to consumer behavior and reacting to demand surges as well as negative demand growth.
4. Investigating the sociocultural factors that impact policymaking, such as local opposition in the siting of important energy facilities, legal disputes and economic compensation to aggrieved parties, and the issue of promoting public confidence in energy policy decisions.
5. Adapting to the post-Cold War changes in international relations and rise of potential regional military confrontations that exist in an environment of greater uncertainty, also characterized by the threat of nuclear terrorism and proliferation.

This rationale for an expanded view of energy security seems well justified years later, as these challenges persist.

Yergin's evolving conceptions of energy security warrant mention here given his influence in policy formation circles. In the late 1980s, Yergin specified that the key role of energy security "is to assure adequate, reliable supplies of energy at reasonable prices and in ways that do not jeopardize major national values and objectives."[26] This definition omits much for the sake of brevity, and is problematic when one considers the disagreement that obtains in relation to defining national values and objectives. Yergin has since expanded his view of energy security to include ten key principles constituting energy security:[27]

1. Diversification of fuel supply
2. Recognition that only one oil market exists and it is international in scope
3. A security margin (strategic reserves, spare capacity, etc.)
4. Resisting temptations to interfere in markets (using price controls, allocation schemes, etc.)
5. Building cooperative relations with energy exporting countries
6. Maintaining cooperative relations with energy importing countries
7. Designing and implementing a proactive security framework involving producers and consumers that responds to threats and attacks on supply chains
8. Better information flows from government and the private sector to the public during tight market conditions and supply disruptions in order to alleviate panic-driven responses
9. A healthy, technologically driven energy industry for continued exploration and production in environmentally sound ways that operates under reasonable and predictable rules
10. Commitment to research, development, and innovation across energy systems (hydrocarbon to alternative) and involving government, university, and private cooperation to achieve diversification, respond to environmental considerations, and try to meet growing world energy needs

Though Yergin advocates cooperation between government and the private sector, he does not advocate a greater role for government in shaping public policy to change market steering currents. He prefers the view that markets are largely self-adjusting, stressing the lessons from the 1970s and earlier, when government policies damaged the market's ability to allocate resources efficiently and exacerbated conditions for already stressed supply chains. Yergin has called for a widened energy security construct that is more global in outlook and requiring international cooperative efforts to stabilize and protect energy markets.[28]

It is important to note an increasingly persuasive challenge to the conventional wisdom maintaining that the unfettered free market will find expedient and monetarily feasible technological solutions to the energy challenges that lie ahead. There are those who point out that the time horizon for these solutions is shrinking rapidly, depending on differing world peak oil predictions, with mean estimates suggesting it will occur by 2040. With possibly only three decades in advance of the need to transition to a more diversified array of energy sources, if not an entirely new energy system, technological advancements must occur within a compressed time frame.

Yet technological solutions often require extensive periods of research and development before technology transfer occurs on a large scale. Recognizing this, Kenderdine and Moniz make the important observation: "Energy security is not easily achieved. As a 'public good,' it is a government responsibility."[29] In their vision of energy security, market preferences do not inevitably lead to greater security. Government has the imperative to facilitate technology development that is not taking place and cannot take place within the time horizon that is necessary without large public expenditures.

Kenderdine and Moniz note that the last thirty years of public energy research and development investment has a mixed track record of successes and failures, but most of it has accrued to public benefit by enhancing national security, furthering knowledge, advancing technology development, and achieving significant cost savings.[30] The coming decades require that the U.S. government reevaluate its approach to the energy sector and set "strategic energy objectives, revise those objectives where appropriate, and more closely align its energy R&D programs with its energy security objectives."[31]

In sum, energy security conceptions are broadening to capture previously ignored complexities, and vary considerably in their assessment of the essential issues and public policy roles. Although the different approaches reviewed in this chapter by no means represent a new consensus, they nevertheless are an effort toward developing a more comprehensive energy security paradigm that is necessary for redirecting national energy policies to work for better management of critical problems. Most simple definitions of energy security frame it within the context of maintaining reliable supplies of primary energy at affordable costs, but these definitions do little to delineate priorities in securing energy systems given a range of vulnerabilities, new threats, and remediation necessities. This is especially important as pertains to petroleum-dominated systems having global supply chains jeopardized by increasing competition for resources in tight markets, exacerbated by serious political instabilities in major producing countries and regions, and the specter of global terrorism. Indeed, the urgency to protect critical aspects of the global energy system has never been greater.

The U.S. Energy System: Vital Energy Sectors and Critical Infrastructure Protection

The United States ranks as the world's largest energy consumer, producer, net importer, and single largest contributor of anthropogenic greenhouse gas emissions,[32] yet it only possesses approximately 4.6 percent of the world's population. The country's energy system is built upon three major energy sectors: petroleum, natural gas, and electricity. All of these sectors are dominated by fossil fuels that collectively meet 86 percent of current energy demand, almost totally eclipsing alternatives.[33] Thus, while renewable and alternative energy sources hold great promise for the future, this chapter necessarily confines its analysis to the sectors that are critical at this moment in time and that will be dominant for years to come.

Petroleum

Petroleum is the most important U.S. fuel and constitutes a strategic energy sector. Petroleum has become essential to modern industrialized societies because it is easily converted into a multitude of fuels and chemicals and is already in a liquid state, unlike coal or natural gas, and exceeds them in applications far beyond heating and power generation. Even high world nominal crude prices have done little to dampen oil demand. Indeed, the United States is more dependent on oil, devouring roughly 25 percent of the world's petroleum production.[34] Petroleum accounts for 41 percent of America's overall fuel consumption, the highest of any fuel, and comprises a staggering 98 percent of the nation's transportation fuel needs.[35] While about 90 percent of petroleum is converted into gasoline and other fuels, the rest is used as a feedstock in the manufacture of plastics, chemicals, pharmaceuticals, foods, and other consumer products too numerous to mention here.[36] It is hard to think of many contemporary goods that are not derived from or do not utilize petroleum or its related products, in whole or in part, at some point in their development, transport, storage, or end use. One could say that petroleum is not merely a commodity or fuel source, but the basis for a way of life.

Its utility notwithstanding, the bottom line is that the United States is overwhelmingly dependent on petroleum, but it is unable to produce all of the oil it needs. Of the approximately 21 million barrels (bbl) of oil a day the United States consumes, over 12 million are imported. As demand goes up and domestic production continues to decline, the percentage of imported oil can only increase. The problem is fundamentally one of high domestic demand coupled with falling domestic supply. The United States has the eleventh largest recoverable oil deposits in the world, approaching 21.4 billion bbl of conventional proved reserves.[37] Production from these reserves is inadequate to meet daily demand. Even with new discoveries and reserves additions to older fields, the overall situation is one of net depletion. The maturity of U.S. oil fields is quite problematic, given that oil consumption is rising, on average, 1 to 2 percent annually, while domestic crude production has been falling at about the same rate. In fact, U.S. Energy Information Administration (EIA) models indicate that petroleum demand will rise by approximately 1.4 percent annually through 2025, when Americans will consume almost 28 million bbl a day and 19 million of those will be imported. This means imports account for approximately 60 percent of consumption now, and through 2025 this could trend toward 68 percent or higher unless high crude prices are sustained over time and lower import projections.[38]

Since the petroleum market is international in scope, U.S. demand should be contextualized within the rubric of overall world demand, both present and future projections. According to the International Energy Agency (IEA), world oil demand in 2004 stood at 82.46 million bbl per day (30.1 billion bbl annually), an increase of 2.68 million bbl per day (978.2 million bbl annually) over the previous year.[39] In fact, world demand was surprisingly high in 2004, and about

750,000 bbl a day higher than analysts previously had predicted.[40] Although the world average demand growth was about 3.4 percent, the largest jump in demand occurred in China, with a significant increase of over 15.5 percent from the year before. Consuming 6.5 million bbl per day in 2004, China has surpassed Japan to become the world's second largest consumer of petroleum. This increase accounted for approximately 40 percent of world oil demand growth in 2004.[41] Although it is true that this strong demand growth was not sustained into 2005, IEA forecasts that China will increase its oil consumption by 5.3 percent in 2006.[42] Moreover, China's consumption is expected to double by 2025, but given its strong economic growth in recent years, this may be a conservative estimate. China, India, and other non-OECD countries are areas to watch for strong oil demand increases in the coming years, increases that will compete with rising OECD demand in a tight market supply situation. The EIA anticipates world oil demand to rise to 121 million bbl per day by 2025, an increase requiring almost 40 million bbl per day of extra supply to be largely provided by OPEC's 70 percent share of estimated remaining world oil reserves.[43] This has led some to question whether the industrialized countries are taking seriously the need to secure future import supplies while the rapidly industrializing economies, particularly China, are busy conducting oil diplomacy in the Middle East, Asia, Canada, and South America, tying up future imports and perhaps sidelining OECD countries.[44]

Although the U.S. economy is built fundamentally on a petroleum foundation today, this may prove unsustainable in the coming decades as mounting resource competition drives prices higher. Real questions arise as to how much capital can flow out of the United States to sustain future oil import demands before there are serious economic consequences. In 2005 alone, nearly $252 billion were spent on petroleum and related products imports. Price volatility and the balance of payments issue, coupled with increasing resource scarcity, paint an uncertain picture. Taken together with serious oil-related environmental and geopolitical problems, these issues illustrate why lessening oil dependency is in the long-term interest of the United States and the entire industrialized world.

Natural Gas

The second major energy sector is natural gas, the cleanest of the fossil fuels. Natural gas is strategically important because it currently provides 22 percent of total U.S. annual primary energy requirements and has over 175 million consumers in the residential, commercial, and industrial end-use sectors. Almost everyone in the United States benefits from natural gas in some way. This may be due to its use in heating and cooling buildings and homes, or the products created from its use as a chemical feedstock. Natural gas has also been in greater demand over the last decade for electric power generation, rising in recent years to approximately 17 to 18 percent of total annual megawatt hours generated.[45] Electricity capacity additions will overwhelmingly come from natural gas-fired plants until 2015, when more coal-fired plants start to come online.[46] A very small percentage of vehicles have been modified to use natural gas as a transportation fuel, amounting to less than 1 percent of overall consumption. Transportation fuels for existing vehicle fleets can be made from natural gas using gas-to-liquids technologies, and there are those who are calling for more investment in this area to offset petroleum dependence.

The United States has the sixth largest conventional natural gas reserves in the world, currently estimated to be 193 trillion cubic feet (tcf) and about 3 percent of world supply.[47] Unconventional natural gas resources should also be included in this analysis, since they will constitute the largest domestic source of natural gas supplies in the future and expand the resource base possibly as high as 215 tcf by 2020, assuming high resource access and improved production technology.[48] Nevertheless, reserve replacements are not always exceeding what is annually produced, and the current trend for the United States is its outpacing of production with consumption. Furthermore, even with new discoveries, the U.S. Department of Energy's Office of Fossil Energy assumes that new oil and natural gas discoveries will increasingly be smaller, assuming that the largest reserves have already been discovered due to extensive exploration in mature basins,[49] and new fields and wells will peak earlier in their histories because newly discovered reserves will be depleted more quickly based on increasing consumption rates.[50] In 2004, the United States consumed about 22 tcf but only produced 18.7 tcf, meaning the country is importing about 15 percent of its natural gas requirements, mostly from Canada. The EIA forecasts domestic natural gas demand to climb to 30.7 tcf per year by 2025, representing a 26 percent increase from 2005.[51] Such demand growth in light of insufficient domestic natural gas production trends will require more foreign imports. According to the EIA, liquefied natural gas (LNG) imports are expected to rise from well under 5 percent in recent years to account for 20 percent of U.S. natural gas supply by 2025.[52] The Middle East will play prominently in meeting future world LNG needs, possessing over 40 percent of estimated recoverable natural gas reserves.

On balance, natural gas offers the United States a mixed bag in relation to its energy security. Natural gas is the cleanest-burning fossil fuel. The United States has large supplies of natural gas, both conventional and unconventional, and thus possesses a more advantageous natural gas position than oil position. The main short- and mid-term natural gas issues will be restoring hurricane-damaged production capacity in the Gulf of Mexico, and accessing the nation's most remote deposits, as in the case of Alaska's North Slope[53] or Gulf of Mexico frontier regions. Long-term issues will be the problem of lessening vulnerability to import disruptions, a problem since much of the world's natural gas reserves are stranded or located in geopolitical hot spots.

Electricity

Electricity is the third major energy sector vital to national security. Electricity is unlike petroleum and natural gas, in that it is not a primary fuel but must be generated from primary energy sources. Like petroleum, electricity is a cornerstone of economic development and modern social organization and activity, allowing humans to control indoor climates, light millions of dwellings, and power a virtually endless list of devices and mechanical systems. The U.S. utility industry that provides electricity to all end-use sectors is vast. In 2004, more than 136 million U.S. consumers purchased over 3,548 million megawatt hours of electricity.[54]

The electricity sector is characterized by a high degree of interdependency, meaning that a power loss in one aspect of the system can result in a cascading series of failures elsewhere. Interdependency so defined is "the mutual functional reliance of essential services—on other networks, utilities, services, or auxiliary nonutility systems."[55] These interdependencies are physical, cyber, geographical, and institutional in nature. Cyber interdependencies are increasingly important, as banking and finance and e-commerce depend on network reliability and stability. Physical interdependencies mean that loss of fuel or power supply can cause cyber systems to crash, resulting in the loss of a whole range of dependent services. In such scenarios, it is possible that critical communications systems lose capacity or all functionality. Additionally, transportation services need electricity for power supply and traffic control systems, as in the case of subways, railroads, airports and air traffic, energy terminals and seaports, and motor vehicle traffic management. Power loss means public and private services of all kinds may be drastically reduced or totally ceased, including emergency response, health care, and government. Even if there are backup generators for these infrastructures, full services may not be restored to levels prior to the blackout and for the duration that may be needed—days, weeks, or even months. Loss of electricity is not just inconvenient, it can be life threatening. And it can also have costly economic repercussions. Take, for example, the worst power failure to ever afflict the United States and Canada, which occurred on August 14, 2003. This outage resulted in a loss of electricity to over 50 million people, lasted for days in the United States and weeks in Canada, and economic damage estimates suggest losses totaling $4 to $10 billion.[56] The reasons for this blackout were not even clear initially, requiring months of investigation to determine the exact causes and initiating sequences of events. This evolution of complex, interdependent infrastructures has led to system rigidity, meaning there are multitudes of opportunities for disruptions at the same time that there are lowering tolerances for disruptions. Centralized generation and control are vulnerable, in the sense that "failure in one part of the network can spread unpredictably almost instantaneously, including to the centralized control elements."[57] This has led to the call for highly sophisticated self-healing energy infrastructure networks, such that they can identify, isolate, and repair problems closer to their origins and thereby optimize system operations through more resiliency.

The U.S. electricity sector is a network of three major grids, known as the Eastern, Western, and Texas Interconnections[58] or Interconnected Systems, also tied in to the Province of Quebec Interconnection. These four main grids comprise an interdependent system for the purpose of maximally linking power generation with consumer demand over geographically distant locations. The U.S. grid network is massive, possessing a generating capacity exceeding 960 gigawatts and valued at over $1 trillion in assets.[59] Coal, natural gas, and nuclear power plants are the most important electricity sources in the United States today, with less than 13 percent of generation attributed to conventional hydroelectric, renewables, and petroleum. Since natural gas has already been discussed as a fuel and energy sector, the remaining focus will be centered on coal and nuclear power given their importance.

Coal

Coal is the world's most abundant fossil fuel. It is especially plentiful in the United States, which has 25 percent of world estimated recoverable reserves, the highest of any country and leading many to call the United States the "Saudi Arabia of coal."[60] Coal currently provides 23 percent of U.S. total primary energy requirements. At present rates of consumption, approximately one billion short tons per year, the EIA projects that the United States has over 250 years of coal supplies left, far exceeding any of its other fossil fuel reserves. Coal is widely distributed geographically and relatively cheap to produce, historically providing a cost-effective fuel source for large electricity-generating power plants. In fact, coal-fired power plants account for approximately 92 percent of U.S. coal consumption and generate about half of U.S. electricity, or 1,979 million megawatt hours in 2004. Investment in coal-fired power plants slackened in the last decade, primarily owing to high capital costs associated with new construction and the fact that natural gas-fired plants had become increasingly attractive due to the cleaner nature of their emissions. With the tightening of natural gas supplies in recent years and concomitant natural gas price volatility, however, an additional 72 coal-fired power plants are planned or under construction[61] and most will begin generating electricity in the United States after 2015.[62] Coal will inevitably be an integral component in meeting tomorrow's energy needs, and its share of electricity generation will rise through at least 2025.

Nuclear Power

U.S. nuclear electric power generation provided over 780 million megawatt hours of electricity in 2004 or about 20 percent of total electricity generation.[63] The EIA projects that no new nuclear plants will be built before 2025, when most "nuclear units will be beyond their original license expiration dates."[64] The Three Mile Island and Chernobyl incidents highlighted the dangers associated with fission reactors and marred public perceptions of this energy source. The nuclear waste generated may also be a trade-off with the lack of greenhouse gas emissions, especially given the controversy surrounding siting nuclear waste storage facilities in this country. In the new domestic security context defined by the threat of global terrorism, expanding nuclear energy's role in the domestic energy portfolio also raises serious national security questions, especially the threat of nuclear proliferation because fuel and waste must be transported into and out of facilities.[65]

Next-generation technologies, such as pebble bed modular reactors that are smaller and generate less waste, are touted as "designed for safety, proliferation resistance, and ease of operation."[66] Some propose a migration from the present petroleum economy to a blended nuclear-hydrogen economy in three or more decades, arguing that nuclear energy is the only energy source that would efficiently generate the needed amounts of hydrogen while protecting the environment.[67] Yet public opposition to constructing new nuclear plants remains quite significant in the United States, thus nuclear energy's role in electricity generation is expected to fall as more coal and natural gas-fired generation comes online in the next two decades.

Critical Infrastructure Protection

This chapter adopts the conventions used in The National Strategy for the Physical Protection of Critical Infrastructures and Key Assets for the sake of consistency and clarity. In particular, that report identified critical infrastructures as the "facilities, systems, and functions" comprised of "human assets and physical and cyber systems that work together in processes that are highly interdependent" and reliant on "key nodes" for their operation.[68] Nodes can be thought of as hubs,[69] or important junctions in energy pathways. Nodes are places where lines of connection, otherwise thought of as links,[70] intersect to convert, divert, gather, store, and transfer power or fuels or fuel products through the system. An example of an energy system node would be a pumping station along a pipeline route, where the pipeline would be the link. Determining whether an infrastructure is critical in nature hinges upon whether its destruction results in a disruption "to the continuity of critical services at the national level,"[71] thereby constituting a national security threat. In reality, there are uncertainties associated with determining the status of an infrastructure and thus the potential to exclude vital and vulnerable infrastructures.[72] Beyond critical infrastructure, key assets are "individual targets whose attack—in worst-case scenarios—could result in not only large-scale human casualties and property destruction, but also profound damage to our national prestige, morale, and confidence," such as pertains to nuclear power plants and dams.[73]

The United States has no shortage of energy infrastructure to contend for critical or key asset status. In fact, the system is so vast and so complex that it would be impossible to protect all of it at every point in space and time. To put the scale of the problem into context, here are some key U.S. statistics and observations:[74]

- More than 2,000,000 miles of pipelines transport oil, natural gas, condensate, refined products, hydrogen, and other hazardous materials.
- Major oil pipelines transport over two-thirds of the nation's shipped oil volumes through 161,000 miles of pipe. Refined products pipelines span over 95,000 miles. Additionally, there are 1,400,000 miles of natural gas pipelines that move almost all of the natural gas transported throughout the United States. Nearly half of the natural gas pipeline system traverses commercial and public infrastructure, such as airports, businesses, and highways.
- Roughly 700,000 oil and natural gas wells are classed as active. Drilling activity has been on the rise in recent years, with nearly 41,000 new wells drilled in 2005 alone.
- 2,000 petroleum storage terminals and 17 LNG facilities are operated nationwide. Another 38 LNG terminals are either proposed or approved.
- More than 17,000,000 bbl of oil are refined per day at 151 operable refineries. Forty-three percent of this total is processed by clusters of refineries located along the Gulf of Mexico between Alabama and Texas, with the majority concentrated in Louisiana and Texas.
- There are 580 natural gas plants that treat more than 60 billion cubic feet daily. More than 50 percent of the total is treated by plants located in just two states: Louisiana and Texas.
- Approximately 11,000 conventional coal, petroleum, natural gas, and dual-fired electric power plants are operated by more than 3,000 independent utilities. Electricity is routed over approximately 181,000 miles of high-voltage transmission lines. There are millions of miles of distribution lines to homes and businesses.
- Sixty-five percent of coal is shipped by railroad, at least for part of its journey. Varying regionally, some utilities have only one or two railroads that provide coal deliveries for their area.
- There are 104 nuclear reactors in operation, and 36 more research and test reactors are located primarily at educational institutions.

Though infrastructures on this scale make system-wide protection daunting, what is at issue is the preservation of key services to populations, thereby making the identification of critical nodes more important than protecting every link. Auerswald et al. persuasively argue that "the policy goal should be to build capabilities for the prevention of attacks that interrupt such services and for effective response and rapid recovery when such attacks do occur."[75] Besides, it is not entirely clear that all possible threats and vulnerabilities to energy infrastructures can be identified and quantified.[76] This shifts the focus to planning for worst-case scenarios and improving system security margins for the most critical nodes.

Protecting the energy system is complicated by bureaucratic confusion. The agencies and departments responsible for regulating the energy industry and coordinating critical infrastructure protection comprise a complex and entangling network. The list begins with the Department of Homeland Security (DHS), the Department of Commerce (DOC), the Department of Energy (DOE), the Department of the Interior (DOI), the Department of Transportation (DOT), the Environmental Protection Agency (EPA), the Federal Energy Regulatory Commission (FERC), the National Association of Regulatory Utility Commissioners (NARUC), the North American Electric Reliability Council (NERC), and the Nuclear Regulatory Commission (NRC), but a host of other federal and state agencies are also involved.

President George W. Bush's National Energy Policy Development Group released a comprehensive report[77] on U.S. energy policy in 2001, but it failed to address substantively this issue of bureaucratic overlap and confusion. Sandia National Laboratories subsequently studied the problem in depth and determined:[78]

> The energy infrastructure as a system has lost integrity. No individual organization has full responsibility for its maintenance and reliability. … With a market, rather than national, focus on energy, there is little interest in energy security. In the absence of actual dramatic attacks, it is difficult to persuade taxpayers that the public should pay for infrastructure security improvements.

Because most of the energy infrastructure in the United States is privately owned, its protection has in fact been left primarily to the private sector. Therein resides a central problem, in that "energy industries have secured their assets and operations against ordinary threats such as theft, low-level vandalism, and commercial espionage. To do so, relatively modest efforts were all that were required, and less-than-perfect prevention was acceptable."[79] The emergence of globally connected terror groups has changed the internal logic of this approach. Indeed, private industry's preoccupation with increasing efficiencies by minimizing costs and eliminating uneconomic redundancies narrows security margins, and in effect increases the vulnerabilities.

Critical Vulnerabilities and Homeland Security Implications

Some of the most significant vulnerabilities have been assessed authoritatively by the National Research Council's Committee on Science and Technology for Countering Terrorism, subsequently referred to here as the Committee.[80] This body's main assessments of the nation's most crucial energy sectors are summarized briefly below.

The petroleum sector's most vulnerable infrastructures are refineries and pipeline pumping stations. Their vulnerability to physical attack is well understood given that these are large and high-value fixed targets. The Committee noted that refinery densities along the Gulf Coast create vulnerability, especially since they serve as critical nodes in oil and refined products supply chains to the populous Northeast. Refineries and pipelines are also vulnerable to cyber attack, given that they rely heavily on Supervisory Control and Data Acquisition (SCADA) computer systems for monitoring and control, typically in relation to geographically dispersed infrastructures.[81] SCADA systems are especially vulnerable as they are moved from standalone mainframe systems to integration with a company's main systems, vulnerable to intranet and possibly Internet subterfuge.[82] Such integration can have its bureaucratic rationale, but nevertheless opens the door for cyber attacks.

The natural gas sector is more vulnerable than the petroleum sector because it lacks the same storage infrastructures and import capacities. Identified as potential targets vitally important to the U.S. energy system are key links, such as transmission pipelines, and key nodes, such as pipeline interconnections, compressor stations, city gate stations, LNG terminals, and SCADA control systems. The Committee particularly stressed that "a well-planned and coordinated terrorist attack could take out the nation's gas transmission systems and keep key pipelines out of service for an extended period of time," resulting in "enormous personal and economic damage."[83]

Finally, the electricity sector is vulnerable in relation to physical and cyber attacks, plus the additional threat posed by electromagnetic attack. The highly centralized nature of power generation in the United States, as opposed to distributed generation, means that large power plants, substations, and important transmission lines are obvious physical targets. Moreover, other critical nodes such as control centers present special protection challenges, because they are vulnerable to physical, cyber, and electromagnetic attack. SCADA is also employed in the electricity sector, and may well be the Achilles' heel of the energy system. A worst-case scenario would be simultaneous attacks on multiple nodes, perhaps bringing down an entire grid or multiple grids. An attack on one or more nuclear power plants is a variant on this theme. In fact, disabling multiple nuclear power plants could take significant amounts of electricity off the grid, not to mention result in great loss of life. In such a scenario, classifying nuclear power plants as key assets instead of critical infrastructure becomes meaningless.

The National Commission on Energy Policy (NCEP) also made important assessments regarding strengthening the U.S. energy system. Although the NCEP made a host of recommendations to government and private-sector decision makers, NCEP analysis of three key issue areas bears upon the current topic of critical infrastructure protection. First, the NCEP recommends greater efficiency in siting energy infrastructure, often hampered by public opposition and lengthy bureaucratic impediments. Chronic siting problems can lead to protracted delays across every aspect of the energy system, but the most significant siting problems pertain to "high voltage electricity transmission lines ... new LNG facilities, and high-level nuclear waste storage."[84] Second, the NCEP urges greater attention to protecting the most valuable infrastructure that is likely to be targeted by terrorists. NCEP policy recommendations include identifying cyber vulnerabilities in relation to control systems, examining surveillance options for monitoring energy infrastructure, threat simulation development and analysis to predict and prepare for various disruptions and possible attacks, and deployment of multisensor warning systems to move toward self-healing systems. Third, the NCEP report acknowledges the problem presented by lack of diversification in transportation fuels. Such reliance on one fuel source creates vulnerability, especially as regards tight refining capacity. Since there have been no new refineries built in the United States since the 1970s, there is a need to expand this capacity and also move toward diversifying transportation fuels and producing them domestically.

Summary Conclusions

From the standpoint of U.S. vital interests, energy security ranks among the most paramount. The tremendous instabilities in the Middle East and other oil producing regions, as well as the dangerous rise of globally connected terror groups that target energy infrastructure, represent new challenges. Given the U.S. fuel positions and current energy policies, protecting the most critical infrastructure nodes is an urgent problem. It will not be feasible to protect the entire energy system, especially when supply chains span the globe. Policy must also address stronger security margins, a real problem given the scale of U.S. infrastructure and vulnerabilities in the petroleum, natural gas, and electricity sectors.

The fossil fuels appear to be the fuels that will supply the majority of U.S. primary energy requirements through at least 2025. U.S. coal resources are the largest in the world, but natural gas and petroleum estimated proved reserves are not able to supply demand. The United States is thus in a situation where its reliance on foreign fuel imports will grow significantly over the next twenty years, and likely beyond until world oil midpoint depletion occurs. The problem is that world peak oil is estimated to occur by 2040, given EIA data and assumptions, though some analysts warn that this estimate is too optimistic. Even assuming the optimists are correct, U.S. policymakers may only have about three decades to have the research, development, phase-in, and wide deployment of the necessary next-generation alternative fuels in place. Some envision transition to a hydrogen economy, but generating enough hydrogen in an economic and environmentally sensitive way faces many hurdles and perhaps a fifty-year transition period.[85] Thus, renewable energy sources, such as biofuels, will almost certainly be an important part of the intermediate transition away from petroleum addiction, but more funding needs to be directed toward this end. Current U.S. energy policy is one of primarily encouraging the growth of the fossil fuels industry and allowing markets and the private sector to largely steer the nation's energy policy. Markets do not always flexibly reorient themselves to changing circumstances and necessities, and this may be compounded by the absence of clear market signals in relation to peak oil. Moreover, the private sector will be preoccupied with the tremendous challenge of exploiting remaining opportunities that coincide with the nation's established hydrocarbon-dominated energy system. Visionary public policy is needed that understands the new energy exigencies of this century, and creates and implements strategic energy policy to integrate more alternative and renewable resources into the nation's energy portfolio. Policymakers need to be thinking this way now, not thirty years down the road when it might be too late.

The United States is in a state of deepening energy insecurity. Stability in the vital regions that serve the international petroleum and natural gas markets will not be enough, even if this is possible to achieve. The U.S. energy system is almost certainly going to transition this century, whether imposed exogenously by events or purposively by leadership. Let us hope tomorrow's policymakers understand this and develop the strategy necessary to protect the long-term interests of the United States.

Endnotes

1. Chief among the oil resource analysts who are warning of world oil midpoint depletion by 2010 are Colin J. Campbell and Jean H. Laherrère. The world peak oil debate is hotly contested, and there is no consensus that world oil production will reach its peak by 2010. Campbell first fueled the fires of the current peak oil controversy when he published The Coming Oil Crisis (Essex: Multi-Science Publishing Company & Petroconsultants S.A., 1997). Campbell and Laherrère followed this with a short but widely read and provocative article titled "The End of Cheap Oil" in Scientific American 278, no. 3 (March 1998).

2. See the Arlington Institute's A Strategy: Moving America Away from Oil (Arlington, VA: The Arlington Institute, 2003), 29. Also see John H. Wood, Gary R. Long, and David F. Morehouse, Long-Term World Oil Supply Scenarios: The Future is Neither as Bleak nor Rosy as Some Assert (Washington, D.C.: DOE, 2003).

3. "National Economic Accounts," [online] Bureau of Economic Analysis, U.S. Department of Commerce, available from http://www.bea.gov/bea/dn/gdplev.xls, accessed May 10, 2006.

4. Daniel Yergin, "U.S. Energy Policy Goals," in Global Challenges for U.S. Energy Policy: Economic, Environmental and Security Risks held in Washington, D.C. 5 March 2004, by the Brookings Institution, the National Commission on Energy Policy, the American Enterprise Institute, and the AEI-Brookings Joint Center for Regulatory Studies (Washington, D.C.: The Brookings Institution, 2004).

5. For an overview of the U.S. energy system and an in-depth examination of its energy options for the future, see the previously cited report by The Arlington Institute, A Strategy: Moving America Away from Oil. For a substantive background on energy systems, see Godfrey Boyle, Bob Everett, and Janet Ramage, eds., Energy Systems and Sustainability: Power for a Sustainable Future (Oxford: Oxford University Press, 2003).

6. A case in point is the recent Chinese National Offshore Oil Corporation (CNOOC) bid to acquire the United States' eighth largest oil company, Unocal. Amid fears widely spouted in the U.S. Congress that such a merger needed to be prevented as a matter of vital U.S. energy security, there are many reasons to believe that this argument has been very thinly presented. The Economist makes the logical case that as a result of "denying China access to energy assets through legitimate means, America might expose itself to bigger threats. Some think that China might now seek energy security more aggressively; for instance, by competing more directly for access to the oil and gas from Russia and Central Asia that the West so prizes." For more see "Bogus Fears Send the Chinese Packing," [online] The Economist Global Agenda, 2005, available from http://www.economist.com/agenda/displayStory.cfm?story_id=4244565, accessed August 15, 2005.

7. The U.S. Energy Policy Act of 2005 is exemplary of what many consider to be bad energy legislation. Most of its funding provisions are directed at the nuclear power industry (an alternative but not renewable form of energy), and the oil and natural gas sector which has been riding high on the largest corporate profits in U.S. history.

8. "Oil in Troubled Waters: A Survey of Oil," The Economist 375, no. 8424 (April 30–May 6, 2005), 14.

9. See Vito Stagliano, "The Ghost of OPEC," in Energy and National Security in the 21st Century, ed. Patrick L. Clawson (Honolulu: University Press of the Pacific, 2002), 125–133.

10. Robert McFarlane, "A Declaration of Energy Independence," Wall Street Journal, 20 December 2004, A15.

11. J. Bielecki, "Energy Security: Is the Wolf at the Door?" Quarterly Review of Economics and Finance 42, no. 2 (2002): 237.

12. Barry Barton et al., Energy Security: Managing Risk in a Dynamic Legal and Regulatory Environment (Oxford: Oxford University Press, 2004), 5.

13. Amory B. Lovins and L. Hunter Lovins, Brittle Power: Energy Strategy for National Security (Andover, MA: Brick House Publishing Co., 1982).

14. Ibid., 1, 5.

15. M. T. Freund, J. A. Wise, C. A. Ulibarri, B. R. Shaw, H. E. Seely, and J. M. Roop, "Energy Security in the Post-Cold War Era: Identifying Future Courses for Crises," in Energy and National Security in the 21st Century, ed. Patrick L. Clawson (Honolulu: University Press of the Pacific, 2002), 154.

16. Ibid., 1–16.

17. William F. Martin, Ryukichi Imai, and Helga Steeg, Maintaining Energy Security in a Global Context: A Report to the Trilateral Commission (New York: The Trilateral Commission, 1996).

18. Ibid., 4.

19. Ibid., 16–17.

20. Ibid., 103.

21. The three faces of energy security are apparent in the 2001 National Energy Policy report submitted to President George W. Bush containing policy recommendations intended to promote "dependable, affordable and environmentally sound energy for the future."

22. An authoritative report on global warming has been published by the National Academy of Sciences. See the National Research Council, Committee on the Science of Climate Change, Climate Change Science: An Analysis of Some Key Questions (Washington, D.C.: The National Academies Press, 2001).

23. Robert W. Fri, "Taking the Lead on Climate Change," in New Approaches on Energy and the Environment, ed. Richard D. Morgenstern and Paul R. Portney (Washington, D.C.: Resources for the Future, 2004), 12–13.

24. While scientists believe that climate change has a component of natural variability, top scientific organizations are finding the observed climate data unexplained without including anthropogenic contributions.

25. Synthesis Report for the Pacific Asia Regional Energy Security (PARES) Project, Phase 1: A Framework for Energy Security Analysis and Application to a Case Study of Japan. [Online]. The Nautilus Institute for Security and Sustainable Development, 1998. Available from http://www.nautilus.org, accessed August 12, 2005.

26. Daniel Yergin, "Energy Security in the 1990s," Foreign Affairs 67, no. 1 (Fall 1988): 111.

27. Daniel Yergin, "Energy Security and Markets," in Energy and Security: Toward a New Foreign Policy Strategy, ed. Jan H. Kalicki and David L. Goldwyn (Washington, D.C.: Woodrow Wilson Center Press, 2005), 55–58.

28. Daniel Yergin, "Ensuring Energy Security," Foreign Affairs 85, no. 2 (March/April 2006): 76–78.

29. Melanie A. Kenderdine and Ernest J. Moniz, "Technology Development and Energy Security," in Energy and Security: Toward a New Foreign Policy Strategy, ed. Jan H. Kalicki and David L. Goldwyn (Washington, D.C.: Woodrow Wilson Center Press, 2005), 453.

30. See National Research Council, Commission on Engineering and Technical Systems, Energy Research at DOE: Was It Worth It? Energy Efficiency and Fossil Energy Research 1978 to 2000 (Washington, D.C.: The National Academies Press, 2001).

31. Kenderdine and Moniz, "Technology Development," 426.

32. U.S. Department of Energy, Energy Information Administration (DOE/EIA), "United States of America Country Analysis Brief," [online], available from http://www.eia.doe.gov/emeu/cabs/usa.html, accessed August 26, 2005.

33. Ibid., accessed June 8, 2006.

34. The reader should assume that the primary data source for this article's examination of U.S. energy positions is DOE/EIA, the organization responsible for collecting energy statistics and publishing energy forecasts for the U.S. government.

35. Petroleum consumption equals approximately 27.4 quadrillion BTUs out of 28 quadrillion BTUs of annual transportation energy consumption. See DOE/EIA, "Monthly Energy Review: Energy Consumption by Sector," [online], available from http://www.eia.doe.gov/emeu/mer/consump.html, accessed June 6, 2006.

36. DOE/EIA, "Petroleum Products Information Sheet," [online], available from http://www.eia.doe.gov/neic/infosheets/petroleumproducts.htm, accessed June 8, 2006.

37. "Worldwide Look at Reserves and Production," Oil & Gas Journal 103, no. 47 (December 19, 2005): 24–25.

38. DOE/EIA, Annual Energy Outlook 2005 (Washington D.C.: EIA, 2005), 5–7.

39. IEA, Monthly Oil Market Report (Paris: IEA, February 2005), 5.

40. BBC News, "World Oil Demand Estimate Raised," [online] BBC News UK Edition, 2005, available from http://news.bbc.co.uk/1/hi/ business/3554462.stm, accessed March 9, 2005.

41. DOE/EIA, "China Country Analysis Brief," [online], available from http://www.eia. doe.gov/emeu/cabs/china.html, accessed June 8, 2006.

42. IEA, Monthly Oil Market Report (Paris: IEA, May 2006), 4.

43. "Worldwide Look at Reserves and Production," 25.

44. For example, see Irwin M. Stelzer, "The Axis of Oil," Weekly Standard, February 7, 2005, 25–28.

45. DOE/EIA, "Electricity," [online], available from http://www.eia.doe.gov/fuelelectric. html, accessed September 10, 2005.

46. DOE/EIA, Annual Energy Outlook 2005, 87.

47. "Worldwide Look at Reserves and Production," 25.

48. DOE/EIA, Accelerated Depletion: Assessing Its Impacts on Domestic Oil and Natural Gas Prices and Production (Washington, D.C.: DOE, 2000), 23.

49. There are notable exceptions to this general expectation. There are world-class giant oil fields, those with reserves exceeding 500 million bbl, continuing to be discovered in the Gulf of Mexico and indicated in Arctic frontier regions. Even in the well-explored interior of the lower 48, such as the Central Utah Overthrust Belt, tens of millions of barrels of oil continue to be found. Some are now expecting this part of Utah to be a billion-barrel province with other undiscovered fields along this thrust belt system. See David Brown, "Covenant Field Keeping Promises: Utah Play Makes Lots of Headlines," AAPG Explorer 26, no. 4 (April 2005): 4, 8.

50. DOE/EIA, Accelerated Depletion, 11.

51. DOE/EIA, Annual Energy Outlook 2005, 9.

52. Ibid., 4. Also see Phyllis Martin, "EIA: LNG Will Supply More Than 20% of U.S. Gas by 2025," Oil & Gas Journal 103, no. 12 (March 28 2005): 60.

53. In the Alaska Natural Gas Pipeline Act of 2002, the U.S. Congress pledged to compensate private investors up to 80 percent of the principal of any loan associated with the proposed $20 billion pipeline cost in the event the project fails, EIA reports. Though such a guarantee was surely intended to stimulate private interest in this project, it is still on the drawing board at the time of this writing. Given the estimated more than 30 tcf North Slope natural gas reserves, this project will almost certainly proceed once all legal and political barriers are resolved.

54. DOE/EIA Office of Coal, Nuclear, Electric and Alternate Fuels, Electric Power Annual 2004 (Washington, D.C.: EIA, 2005).

55. The National Association of Regulatory Utility Commissioners, Technical Assistance Briefs: Utility and Network Interdependencies: What State Regulators Need to Know (Washington, D.C.: NARUC, 2005), 1.

56. U.S.-Canada Power System Outage Task Force, Final Report on the August 14, 2003 Blackout in the United States and Canada: Causes and Recommendations (2004), 1.

57. Massoud Amin, "Toward Self-Healing Energy Infrastructure Systems," IEEE Computer Applications in Power 14, no. 1 (January 2001): 25.

58. The Texas Interconnection is also known as the Electric Reliability Council of Texas (ERCOT) Interconnection.

59. U.S.-Canada Power System Outage Task Force, 1.

60. DOE/EIA, "International Energy Outlook 2004," [online], available from http://www.eia.doe.gov/oiaf/ieo/coal.html, accessed February 26, 2005.

61. Mark Clayton, "New Coal Plants Bury 'Kyoto'," Christian Science Monitor, December 23, 2004, 1.

62. DOE/EIA, Annual Energy Outlook 2005, 87.

63. DOE/EIA, Electric Power Annual 2004, 2.

64. U.S. Department of Energy, Energy Information Administration, Annual Energy Outlook 2005, 75, 89.

65. Coal presents a proliferation threat too. A 1,000 megawatt electric coal-fired power plant produces, on average, about 74 pounds of uranium-235 per year as a byproduct of combustion, posing a real proliferation hazard given the plentitude of coal and the ability to refine uranium-235 into plutonium given the proper technological means. See Richard Rhodes and Denis Beller, "The Need for Nuclear Power," Foreign Affairs 79, no. 1 (January/February 2000): 32–33.

66. Ibid., 42.

67. Leon Walters and Dave Wade, "Hydrogen Production from Nuclear Energy," AIP Conference Proceedings 671, no. 1 (2003): 116–117.

68. The National Strategy for the Physical Protection of Critical Infrastructures and Key Assets (Washington, D.C.: The White House, 2003), viii.

69. Ted G. Lewis, Critical Infrastructure Protection in Homeland Security: Defending a Networked Nation (Hoboken, NJ: John Wiley & Sons, 2006), 2.

70. Lovins and Lovins, Brittle Power, 192.

71. The National Strategy for the Physical Protection of Critical Infrastructures and Key Assets, viii.

72. John Moteff and Paul Parfomak, Critical Infrastructure and Key Assets: Definition and Identification (Washington, D.C.: The Library of Congress, Congressional Research Service, 2004), 14, RL32631.

73. Ibid.

74. Statistics from CRS, DOE (EIA & NETL), DOT (BTS & PHMSA), EEI, FERC, NRC, NSTAC/IATF, and the Oil & Gas Journal. Data are through 2004 in most cases as the 2005 data are either not yet released or preliminary at the time of writing.

75. Philip Auerswald, Lewis M. Branscomb, Todd M. La Porte, and Erwann Michel-Kerjan, "The Challenge of Protecting Critical Infrastructure," Issues in Science & Technology 22, no. 1 (Fall 2005): 78–79.

76. Thomas H. Karas, Energy and National Security (Albuquerque, NM: Sandia National Laboratories, 2003), 27, SAND2003-3287.

77. Reliable, Affordable, and Environmentally Sound Energy for America's Future: Report of the National Energy Policy Development Group (Washington, D.C.: The White House, 2001).

78. Karas, Energy and National Security, 27.

79. Alexander Farrell, Hisham Zerriffi, and Hadi Dowlatabadi, "Energy Infrastructure and Security," Annual Review of Environment and Resources 29 (2004): 427.
80. National Research Council, Committee on Science and Technology for Countering Terrorism, Making the Nation Safer: The Role of Science and Technology in Countering Terrorism (Washington, D.C.: The National Academies Press, 2002).
81. Lewis, Critical Infrastructure Protection, 223.
82. National Research Council, Committee on Science and Technology for Countering Terrorism, Making the Nation Safer, 201–203.
83. Ibid., 197–198.
84. The National Commission on Energy Policy, Ending the Energy Stalemate: A Bipartisan Strategy to Meet America's Energy Challenges (Washington, D.C.: NCEP, 2004), 87.
85. National Research Council and National Academy of Engineering, The Hydrogen Economy: Opportunities, Costs, Barriers, and R&D Needs (Washington, D.C.: The National Academies Press, 2004), 116–122. Also see Peter Hoffman, Tomorrow's Energy: Hydrogen, Fuel Cells, and the Prospects for a Cleaner Planet (Cambridge, MA: MIT Press, 2001).

Afterword

Terrorism and Securing the Homeland

Michael A. Opheim and Nicholas H. Bowen

> "Fighting terrorism is like being a goalkeeper. You can make a hundred brilliant saves but the only shot that people remember is the one that gets past you."
>
> **—Paul Wilkinson**

In Lewis Carroll's classic novel, *Alice's Adventures in Wonderland,* Alice becomes lost, only to happen upon a Cheshire Cat sitting on a tree branch. "Would you tell me, please, which way I ought to go from here?" inquires Alice. "That depends a good deal on where you want to get to," responds the Cat. "I don't much care where," replies Alice. "Then it doesn't matter much where you go," reasons the Cat. "So long as I get *somewhere*," Alice added. "Oh, you're sure to do that, if you only walk long enough," the Cat said grinning.

Much like Alice, the United States still stands at a fork in the road years after the tragic events of 9/11. An absence of strategic thinking continues to permeate the corridors of power in Washington, D.C. Despite the rhetorical flourish of most politicians and decision makers, this dearth of profound strategic thinking at the highest levels of government has prevented the United States from exploring all of its options in the post-9/11 national security environment. There cannot be any doubt that countries do not effectively chart a direction if they have not agreed on a final destination. Gone are the early heydays of the Cold War when President Harry Truman was able to fashion bipartisan support for what became the long-standing policy of containment. Rather, there exists today a situation in which the two major U.S. political parties are engaged in bitter partisan politics, unwilling or unable to engage in a bold, imaginative strategic debate necessary for any future understanding of homeland security.

The contributors to this volume have called for a new strategic vision for dealing with terrorism—homeland security situated within a multinational context. The response thus far to the events of 9/11 still falls short. Efforts thus far do not serve adequately U.S. national interests, particularly in light of continued opposition to the United States, both at home and abroad not only from adversaries, but also from allies and other friendly countries.

A more systematic examination of the threat, the capabilities of the United States and its friends and allies, as well as a more thorough understanding of those active hostile forces against the United States would have been preferable. Robert Dorff is absolutely right to suggest that strategy can be neither rigid nor dogmatic. This is especially true today where unpredictability is the norm. Strategizing is a dynamic process. So, with a host of challenges and amorphous threats, the present environment defies easy characterization, further necessitating the need for sound analytical thought.

The contributors to this volume have underscored in Part 1 the importance of developing a comprehensive and dynamic strategy for securing the homeland. Strategy for homeland security begins with the causes—grievances or interests— that motivate the formation of groups, movements, or insurgencies prone to use terror and other forms of political violence to serve their aims. Terrorism and weapons of mass destruction are the focus of Part 2; the safeguarding of society and its infrastructure is addressed in Part 3.

But it is not just a matter of *thinking* strategically; it is about *acting* strategically as well. Although no attempt has been made here to impose a particular strategy or strategic view of homeland security, the book is a clarion call for policies driven by a greater strategic understanding of what is at issue and what is to be done. Developing such strategy is (to say the least) overdue. Assuring national security requires attention to the homeland and looking abroad to the sources of terrorism, as well as taking steps domestically to prevent, limit damage, and manage consequences of terrorist and other threats to the country. In pursuing this purpose, strategy needs to be understood as an ongoing, flexible process aiming to match appropriate means to the ends we pursue.

With an inward focus, some regard homeland security as consisting largely of domestic or *internal* efforts and policy initiatives that deal with protecting the country's population and critical infrastructure—national, state, and local measures to prevent, limit damage, and manage consequences. Others have sought to secure the homeland primarily by taking an *externally* focused, macro-approach— pursuing aggressively a "global war on terror" (or, as we prefer to call it, a campaign against groups, movements, and insurgencies using terror and other forms of political violence to advance their aims). As Terrence O'Sullivan and Greg Moser make clear, however, focusing primarily on the dangers of international terrorism creates a policy imbalance that underemphasizes (and underfunds) domestic preparations for a wide spectrum of hazards that continues to grow. What is needed, of course, is strategy that contains both of these internal and external elements.

As with many issues relating to government, progress has been greater in certain areas of the homeland-security effort than in others. Most of the core competencies of homeland security are addressed by the contributors to this volume. Both Dorff and Viotti correctly observe that any proper assessment of homeland security must be made in a strategic context—a position with which all of our contributors would concur. Indeed, waging defense requires an overarching strategy along with practical, affordable tactics in pursuit of homeland-security objectives—a systematic understanding of ends, ways, and means. Ends are defined as the objectives or goals sought; means are categorized as the resources available to pursue the objectives; and ways are described as the concepts or methods for how one organizes and applies the resources.

Any examination of strategy is an admission that individuals have a discernible role to play. As our coeditor has observed elsewhere: "Strategy is a voluntarist formulation by which states (i.e., their government officials) try to maximize their positions, achieving at least an adequate degree of security or defense capability in a potentially hostile world."[1] To be sure, political leaders exercising their will are often constrained by events in both the domestic and the external arenas. Nevertheless, our contributors would adhere to the notion that "formulation of a strategy amounts to an assertion that statesmen can make a difference."[2] We might also extend this to decision makers at the state and local levels who have a myriad number of responsibilities in ensuring domestic preparedness against a growing array of hazards and disaster consequences. Simply put, leadership matters.

Leadership is particularly vital in developing clear, unambiguous objectives, a crucial element since ends matter. Indeed, ends matter most[3] and utilizing effective means to these ends helps to shape the strategic environment. Means must be practical and part of an overall organizational architecture designed to bring about the implementation of policy based on sound strategy. They involve diplomatic, economic, informational, and military courses of action.

An international focus must permeate all aspects of United States security strategy. Securing borders is important but insufficient. Providing security for day-to-day domestic processes and networks of communication and action is impossible without multinational and transnational cooperation, as explored by Veronica Kitchen and Gregory Moore. If the viability of terrorism can be undermined as a means toward political ends pursued by U.S. adversaries, the United States will be more secure. It is for this reason that what Paul Viotti calls a comprehensive and dynamic U.S. strategy for dealing with hostile groups, movements, or insurgencies in the post-9/11 world is so important to assuring American homeland security.

Hard decisions regarding ends, ways, and means have to be made, particularly since all countries are resource-constrained—none possessing an infinite quantity of needed resources.[4] Developing strategy is all the more difficult given the fragmentation of political authority and the bureaucratic proliferation of competing governmental actors that occur under federalism and a separation of powers. Some authors observe how catastrophic events in the United States since 9/11, such as Hurricane Katrina and other natural disasters, continue to show the wholesale organizational failures of multiple levels of U.S., state and local government, and private-sector institutions. With 9/11 and Hurricane Katrina now in the past, the United States unfortunately has yet to come to grips fully with the theoretical and practical challenges posed by these monumental events.

When considering the import of these episodes on U.S. foreign and national security policy, it is critical to remember that the United States does not operate in a vacuum. Not only do U.S. actions have external, sometimes adverse, effects on others, but also reactions from abroad can blow back with negative consequences for the United States. While domestic measures designed to safeguard people and critical infrastructure at home likely will not elicit much foreign opposition, counterterrorist actions taken abroad—the "away game" element of homeland security—impacts other populations within which target groups, movements, or insurgencies operate, often with adverse consequences. Indeed, effective implementation of a comprehensive strategy to secure the homeland is fraught with difficulties that require adept and flexible handling by policy makers sensitive to these complexities.

Daniel M. Gerstein notes that in this Information Age *how strategy will be received internationally* must be an important component for consideration. Thus, owing to the increasing influence of globalization, he includes the geo-strategic environment along with the more traditional ends, ways, and means. Gerstein emphasizes his point by observing:

> Ends, ways, and means all apply to the country developing the strategy. The ends are the desired outcomes from the perspective of the country developing the strategy. The means are the resources and the ways are the processes or techniques that will be employed; but both of these are also "owned" by the country developing the strategy. So, where do we consider how the strategy will be received internationally? Or whether, in the case of conflict, the desired ends are even feasible for the country.[5]

While we can expect U.S. policymakers to continue to act in accordance with what they believe to be the best interests of the country, our authors see them as better served in most cases by seeking partners for multilateral actions rather than by acting unilaterally. It is an indicator of strength, not weakness, to be in a position to assemble coalitions—an acknowledgment that it is usually better to work in concert with allies and other coalition partners.

Although our contributing authors agree that homeland security strategizing must focus on the deterrence (or dissuasion) and prevention of terrorist attacks, much needs to be done to mitigate the impact and manage the consequences of terrorist attacks that do occur. Indeed, our contributors see the role of private citizens as an essential part of preserving civil society—an educated public the best defense against the spread of fear. Efforts to empower the public are as much a part of damage limitation as measures to blunt the physical effects of terrorist attacks. It is indicative of the fact that little will change in a positive direction if elites and citizens alike remain too set in their outmoded ways of thinking.

In any war or military campaign, the operational and logistical elements of conducting war have traditionally received the greatest amount of attention. In the current struggle, however, we cannot allow ourselves to be locked into that mindset because the nature of the conflict is so fundamentally different. The campaign against those using terror and other forms of political violence goes beyond the scope of any single battlefield. So, the instruments used to wage this particular campaign will differ from those applicable to other conflicts. We cannot be caught fighting the last war. While Confederate General Nathan Bedford Forrest talked about getting there the "firstest with the mostest," it is perhaps this "forgotten" social dimension of warfare that perhaps emerges as one of the most important.[6] Undoubtedly, addressing grievances that give rise to terrorist actions must be a fundamental tenet of any successful security strategy.

As our coeditor stated in the Introduction, we make no pretense here about offering a grand strategy for homeland security in the twenty-first century. Our objective is more modest. Rather, we seek only to identify the variables or factors critical in formulating a comprehensive strategy for homeland security policy. So, what are these essential elements that can be distilled from the foregoing analysis?

1. *Strategic thinking must be dynamic.* Clausewitz talked about incidents accumulating in war that undercut in practice the effectiveness of efforts to achieve desired objectives. When implemented plans made in advance necessarily confront friction—unforeseen obstacles that can mar or even blunt their effectiveness. It is this concept of friction that separates war gaming in concept from the real-world heat of battle. When possible, exercises or practice implementations of plans can help us identify errors, leading to revisions of particular plans and even the strategy of which they are a part. Of course, friction can never be eliminated entirely, not to mention the uncertainties captured by the Clausewitzian "fog of war." There is no shame, then, in deviating from the battle plan if the battle plan itself exhibits deficiencies, as it almost certainly will. So, a certain amount of flexibility must be built into the implementation process. Decision makers must not eschew open discourse as a more thorough airing of views has the virtue of mitigating the worst excesses of potentially devastating strategic miscalculation.

2. *To be truly comprehensive, the "home" and "away games" of security policy should be merged more closely together.* Homeland security issues transcend boundaries like never before. Veronica Kitchen and Gregory Moore note the distinction between antiterrorism policy made by the Department of Homeland

Security (DHS), the FBI, and the Justice Department, and counterterrorism, largely under the purview of the State Department, Defense Department (DoD), and the CIA. DHS is also charged with the homeland *security* tasks of protecting the borders as well as the interior of the country, while DoD (especially its Northern Command) remains responsible for homeland *defense*. Increasingly, distinction among these realms seems at best artificial, if not dysfunctional. But, the difference is real to those officials who toil in their respective departments. This can be problematic if little discussion is taking place across these various agencies, especially if their greatest concern becomes in day-to-day practice the protection not so much of the homeland, but rather of their respective bureaucratic turfs. Moreover, homeland security in a multinational context must incorporate both the home and away games if it is to be truly effective over the long term. While changes have occurred in the aftermath of 9/11, it is still the case that the security architecture of the United States remains woefully inadequate organizationally for the challenges in the present and beyond.

3. *Education is a vital part of preserving civil society.* In fact, education could be considered the cornerstone of any effective homeland security strategy. Many contributors emphasized several different aspects of education. David Goldfischer makes the case that homeland security education can "build and improve integrated networks within and between allied states." With greater emphasis on education, the United States can perhaps change its culture to one that more fully embraces homeland security and defense. This is true particularly in the aftermath of hurricanes Katrina and Rita which served as clarion calls to action. Smith and Talbot make the case that education can play an important role in marginalizing the message of the terrorist. Fred Wehling and Jeremy Tamsett argue that to be forewarned is to be forearmed. By educating the public as to the danger of radiation hazards before an attack, we are more likely to prevent mass confusion and chaos than if no information had been disseminated. Science and health curricula can be established in both private and public schools. In this way, a sustained policy of education can mitigate the worst effects of an attack. For their part, Alexander Diener and Timothy Crawford cogently note the work of vibrant civic groups free from governmental control as being at the center of civil defense education programs. With civil defense comes a sense of civic responsibility. To the extent more citizens and organizations are involved with homeland security so much the better.

4. *We must not confuse strategizing about homeland security with a "War on Terror."* Such an approach misses the point that one cannot wage war against a tactic. Although perhaps an effective rhetorical device, such erroneous characterizations cause the focus of effort to be misplaced. Instead, what is required is a better understanding of the groups and insurgents responsible for engaging in such action. Larsen and Wirtz examine the goals and techniques of terrorist groups such as al-Qaeda along with a thorough analysis of

how terrorism has changed over time. Terrorists are not stupid. Rather, they are engaged in the rational use of the irrational. By understanding their goals and motivations, as well as working to the greatest extent possible to drain the swamp of grievances in which terrorists reside, great strides can potentially be made in a wide-ranging campaign against terrorism. At the same time, crafting a strategy that focuses on the hard core, seemingly irreconcilable terrorist leadership and organization is equally necessary.

5. *Globalization is a double-edged sword.* To the extent globalization is equated with Westernization (or even Americanization), the United States might be viewed negatively by those unable or unwilling to hop aboard the globalization train. Globalization is often looked upon as positive because it has brought about enormous tangible benefits to great numbers in the world in the economic as well as social domain. But, globalization is equally threatening to the life-style and customs of traditional societies. More than anything, figuring out how traditional values and modernity can coexist in the twenty-first century will be a primary challenge for the international community. Joseph Szyliowicz discusses how technological progress in transportation and telecommunications has increased the level and scale of globalization. Similarly, Kevin King observes how energy flows and related infrastructures have also become very global in scope. Put another way, what were once national issues are now worldwide in scope. Due to increasing integration of energy, transportation modes (air, rail, road, and sea), and telecommunications, these systems provide more tempting targets now compared to even just a few years ago. That someone with a backpack and some explosives can cause so much death and destruction to people and the infrastructure on which they depend makes clear how vulnerable we are. Lest we focus only on explosives, Terrence O'Sullivan also reminds us of the threat from catastrophic infectious disease outbreaks, including both the naturally occurring disease threats, such as SARS, as well as bioterrorism. In short, while many may be prone to extol the virtues of globalization, we need also to expose this adverse side of the globalization coin—that increasing interconnectedness increases vulnerability to terrorist or other forms of political violence both at home and abroad.

6. *Cooperation is the key.* An important tactic in homeland security is the leadership recognizing that all of us are in this together, which makes us all part of an effective response to the threats and challenges to civil society. Greg Moser emphasizes the relations between the federal, state, and local authorities in dealing with preventing, mitigating, preparing for, and responding to an attack on U. S. critical infrastructure. Typically, we think of cooperation between governments, but establishing and nurturing links beyond the intergovernmental are equally critical. Or, as Veronica Kitchen and Gregory Moore put it, cooperation must be both multinational and transnational, encompassing networks at all levels of government. Certainly more work can be accomplished to forge and sustain these external links important to

dealing with the gravity of the problem, especially in areas such as intelligence, law enforcement, and judicial action, and protecting energy, transportation, telecommunications, and other infrastructures and networks.

7. *Don't lose sight of civil liberties.* As Benjamin Franklin cogently noted, "They who would give up an essential liberty for temporary security, deserve neither liberty nor security." So, how do we balance civil liberties with the need for social protection? The 9/11 episode demonstrates the need for discussion. The Patriot Act was passed quickly following the 9/11 attacks. Subsequently amended, statutory expansion of what many see as intrusive law-enforcement measures remain in place—not to mention those pursued without legal certification. In short, the appropriate balance between security measures taken by state authorities and the protection of privacy rights and civil liberties remains an unresolved, highly controversial set of issues.

Be that as it may, developing an effective strategy to secure the homeland requires a multifaceted approach on the part of the United States. Without a doubt, the military dimension is important when the nation is faced with an irreconcilable enemy that eschews any form of negotiation, but it is equally important in this long-term campaign for the United States to consider other, nonmilitary measures that address the social dimension of the problem abroad and at home.

More often than not, unilateral measures on the part of the United States play into the hands of adversaries, particularly those using terror or other forms of political violence. Because other countries also have felt the wrath of terrorist actions or expect they may do so in the future, there is common ground on which to cultivate allies and coalition partners—a foundation on which to build solidarity against the threat as well as being an important source of support. We offer a quote commonly attributed to British Prime Minister Winston Churchill: "It is better to jaw jaw than to war war." A multilateral approach facilitates greater cooperation when needed not only in the combat arena, but also in diplomatic actions, intelligence sharing, law enforcement, military and police training, civic actions, and other collaborative pursuits.

The contributions of Carl von Clausewitz have been cited in numerous places throughout this work. But, perhaps it is to Sun Tzu that we may owe an even greater debt. In this age of asymmetric terrorist warfare, he reminded us that we need to know ourselves and our enemy, and that we will not succeed if we know neither. Ultimately, we need to avoid fighting the last war. Although the political tremors of the Cold War are largely over, the political earthquakes that have emerged in its wake are only beginning. Learning how to deal with challenges posed by nonstate actors using terror and other forms of political violence have thus far been a work in progress for the leading countries of the world. Alice may not have cared where she needed to go. The United States, however, cannot afford that luxury. It must examine the path itself and the direction it is taking if the journey in this twenty-first century is to be a positive one.

Endnotes

1. Paul R. Viotti, "International Relations and the Defense Policies of Nations: International Anarchy and the Common Problem of Security," in *The Defense Policies of Nations*, 3rd edition, ed. Douglas J. Murray and Paul R. Viotti (Baltimore, MD: Johns Hopkins University Press, 1994), 12.

2. Ibid.

3. See Robert H. Dorff's chapter in this volume.

4. For a view grounded in the belief that it is not the lack of a grand strategy that is the problem, but rather its ineffective implementation by national security strategists, see Clark A. Murdock, *Improving the Practice of National Security Strategy: A New Approach for the Post-Cold War World.* (Washington D.C.: Center for Strategic and Defense Studies, 2004). Of particular interest is the relationship between national security strategy versus business strategy. Many of the generic lessons learned in business also resonate well in national security strategizing. Although one may be skeptical of checklists, they do provide a modicum of guidance for the strategist. These lessons include: (1) successful strategies often emerge as the strategist learns what will work; (2) strategists must learn while doing in order to avoid being trapped in a bad or ineffective strategy; (3) establishing clarity about the ends being sought is critical for good strategy making; (4) converting words to action is often the greatest challenge for any strategist; (5) when contemplating action, the strategist should avoid the trap of indecisiveness and half measures and act decisively, even if the decision is to do nothing; (6) deciding what to do is important, but actually doing it is what really matters. p. 28.

5. Daniel M. Gerstein, *Securing America's Future: National Strategy in the Information Age* (Westport, CT: Praeger, 2005), 135. Gerstein goes on to identify five elements that will be vital in guiding the development of any new security strategy. They are: (1) *Foundations*—because values and ideals form an important part of the U.S. character, any future strategy cannot ignore ideology; (2) *Transparency*—information technologies such as Radio Free Europe will multiply and lead to more accountability of leaders and individuals. However, we must be mindful that it will also have the effect of limiting flexibility of action; (3) *Perspective*—Besides looking at issues from a calculation of national interests, an effective strategy would be to look at the world from the perspective of others; (4) *Legitimacy*—Are the actions perceived to be for the greater good or perceived as self-interest. However, exceptions can be made, such as the U.S. operation in Afghanistan in the aftermath of 9/11; (5) *Balance*—Strike a balance between the elements of power internally and competing interests around the globe. The key is to ensure the United States avoids a short-term view of events against a foe adopting a more long-term orientation. pp.136-141. This is not to say that each of these points will necessarily be adopted. More than anything, it is an acknowledgment that to play an effective role, the United States may have to rethink some aspects of past policies in a new era.

6. Michael Howard, *The Causes of War*, 2nd edition (Cambridge, MA: Harvard University Press, 1984), 107. This particular chapter from Howard, "The Forgotten Dimensions of Strategy" was drawn from the journal *Foreign Affairs*, Summer 1979.

The National Strategy for Homeland Security

This is an Executive Summary of this document first prepared in 2002. The full text is at WhiteHouse.gov.

This document is the first *National Strategy for Homeland Security*. The purpose of the Strategy is to mobilize and organize our Nation to secure the U.S. homeland from terrorist attacks. This is an exceedingly complex mission that requires coordinated and focused effort from our entire society—the federal government, state and local governments, the private sector, and the American people.[1]

People and organizations all across the United States have taken many steps to improve our security since the September 11 attacks, but a great deal of work remains. The *National Strategy for Homeland Security* will help to prepare our Nation for the work ahead in several ways. It provides direction to the federal government departments and agencies that have a role in homeland security. It suggests steps that state and local governments, private companies and organizations, and individual Americans can take to improve our security and offers incentives for them to do so. It recommends certain actions to the Congress. In this way, the Strategy provides a framework for the contributions that we all can make to secure our homeland.

The *National Strategy for Homeland Security* is the beginning of what will be a long struggle to protect our Nation from terrorism. It establishes a foundation upon which to organize our efforts and provides initial guidance to prioritize the work ahead. The Strategy will be adjusted and amended over time. We must be prepared to adapt as our enemies in the war on terrorism alter their means of attack.

Strategic Objectives

The strategic objectives of homeland security in order of priority are to:

Prevent terrorist attacks within the United States;
Reduce America's vulnerability to terrorism; and
Minimize the damage and recover from attacks that do occur.

Threat and Vulnerability

Unless we act to prevent it, a new wave of terrorism, potentially involving the world's most destructive weapons, looms in America's future. It is a challenge as formidable as any ever faced by our Nation. But we are not daunted. We possess the determination and the resources to defeat our enemies and secure our homeland against the threats they pose.

One fact dominates all homeland security threat assessments: terrorists are strategic actors. They choose their targets deliberately based on the weaknesses they observe in our defenses and our preparedness. We must defend ourselves against a wide range of means and methods of attack. Our enemies are working to obtain chemical, biological, radiological, and nuclear weapons for the purpose of wreaking unprecedented damage on America. Terrorists continue to employ conventional means of attack, while at the same time gaining expertise in less traditional means, such as cyber attacks. Our society presents an almost infinite array of potential targets that can be attacked through a variety of methods.

Our enemies seek to remain invisible, lurking in the shadows. We are actively engaged in uncovering them. Al-Qaeda remains America's most immediate and serious threat despite our success in disrupting its network in Afghanistan and elsewhere. Other international terrorist organizations, as well as domestic terrorist groups, possess the will and capability to attack the United States.

Organizing for a Secure Homeland

In response to the homeland security challenge facing us, the President has proposed, and the Congress is presently considering, the most extensive reorganization of the federal government in the past fifty years. The establishment of a new Department of Homeland Security would ensure greater accountability over critical homeland security missions and unity of purpose among the agencies responsible for them.[2]

American democracy is rooted in the precepts of federalism—a system of government in which our state governments share power with federal institutions. Our structure of overlapping federal, state, and local governance—our country has more than 87,000 different jurisdictions—provides unique opportunity and challenges for our homeland security efforts. The opportunity comes from the expertise and commitment of local agencies and organizations involved in homeland security. The challenge is to develop interconnected and complementary systems that are reinforcing rather than duplicative and that ensure essential requirements are met. A national strategy requires a national effort.

State and local governments have critical roles to play in homeland security. Indeed, the closest relationship the average citizen has with government is at the local level. State and local levels of government have primary responsibility for funding, preparing, and operating the emergency services that would respond in the event of a terrorist attack. Local units are the first to respond, and the last to leave the scene. All disasters are ultimately local events.

The private sector—the Nation's principal provider of goods and services and owner of 85 percent of our infrastructure—is a key homeland security partner. It has a wealth of information that is important to the task of protecting the United States from terrorism. Its creative genius will develop the information systems, vaccines, detection devices, and other technologies and innovations that will secure our homeland.

An informed and proactive citizenry is an invaluable asset for our country in times of war and peace. Volunteers enhance community coordination and action, whether at the national or local level. This coordination will prove critical as we work to build the communication and delivery systems indispensable to our national effort to detect, prevent, and, if need be, respond to terrorist attack.

Critical Mission Areas

The *National Strategy for Homeland Security* aligns and focuses homeland security functions into six critical mission areas: intelligence and warning, border and transportation security, domestic counterterrorism, protecting critical infrastructure, defending against catastrophic terrorism, and emergency preparedness and response. The first three mission areas focus primarily on preventing terrorist attacks; the next two on reducing our Nation's vulnerabilities; and the final one on minimizing the damage and recovering from attacks that do occur. The Strategy provides a framework to align the resources of the federal budget directly to the task of securing the homeland.

Intelligence and Warning. Terrorism depends on surprise. With it, a terrorist attack has the potential to do massive damage to an unwitting and unprepared target. Without it, the terrorists stand a good chance of being preempted by authorities, and even if they are not, the damage that results from their attacks is likely to be less severe. The United States will take every necessary action to avoid being surprised by another terrorist attack. We must have an intelligence and warning system that can detect terrorist activity before it manifests itself in an attack so that proper preemptive, preventive, and protective action can be taken.

The *National Strategy for Homeland Security* identifies five major initiatives in this area:

> Enhance the analytic capabilities of the FBI;
>
> Build new capabilities through the Information Analysis and Infrastructure Protection Division of the proposed Department of Homeland Security;
>
> Implement the Homeland Security Advisory System;
>
> Utilize dual-use analysis to prevent attacks; and
>
> Employ "red team" techniques.

Border and Transportation Security. America historically has relied heavily on two vast oceans and two friendly neighbors for border security, and on the private sector for most forms of domestic transportation security. The increasing mobility and destructive potential of modern terrorism has required the United States to rethink and renovate fundamentally its systems for border and transportation security. Indeed, we must now begin to conceive of border security and transportation security as fully integrated requirements because our domestic transportation systems are inextricably intertwined with the global transport infrastructure. Virtually every community in America is connected to the global transportation network by the seaports, airports, highways, pipelines, railroads, and waterways that move people and goods into, within, and out of the Nation. We must therefore promote the efficient and reliable flow of people, goods, and services across borders, while preventing terrorists from using transportation conveyances or systems to deliver implements of destruction.

The *National Strategy for Homeland Security* identifies six major initiatives in this area:

> Ensure accountability in border and transportation security;
>
> Create "smart borders";
>
> Increase the security of international shipping containers;
>
> Implement the Aviation and Transportation Security Act of 2001;
>
> Recapitalize the U.S. Coast Guard; and
>
> Reform immigration services.

The President proposed to Congress that the principal border and transportation security agencies—the Immigration and Naturalization Service, the U.S. Customs Service, the U.S. Coast Guard, the Animal and Plant Health Inspection Service, and the Transportation Security Agency—be transferred to the new Department of Homeland Security. This organizational reform will greatly assist in the implementation of all the above initiatives.

Domestic Counterterrorism. The attacks of September 11 and the catastrophic loss of life and property that resulted have redefined the mission of federal, state, and local law enforcement authorities. While law enforcement agencies will continue to investigate and prosecute criminal activity, they should now assign priority to preventing and interdicting terrorist activity within the United States. The Nation's state and local law enforcement officers will be critical in this effort. Our Nation will use all legal means—both traditional and nontraditional—to identify, halt, and, where appropriate, prosecute terrorists in the United States. We will pursue not only the individuals directly involved in terrorist activity but also their sources of support: the people and organizations that knowingly fund the terrorists and those that provide them with logistical assistance.

Effectively reorienting law enforcement organizations to focus on counterterrorism objectives requires decisive action in a number of areas. The *National Strategy for Homeland Security* identifies six major initiatives in this area:

Improve intergovernmental law enforcement coordination;
Facilitate apprehension of potential terrorists;
Continue ongoing investigations and prosecutions;
Complete FBI restructuring to emphasize prevention of terrorist attacks;
Target and attack terrorist financing; and
Track foreign terrorists and bring them to justice.

Protecting Critical Infrastructure and Key Assets. Our society and modern way of life are dependent on networks of infrastructure—both physical networks such as our energy and transportation systems and virtual networks such as the Internet. If terrorists attack one or more pieces of our critical infrastructure, they may disrupt entire systems and cause significant damage to the Nation. We must therefore improve protection of the individual pieces and interconnecting systems that make up our critical infrastructure. Protecting America's critical infrastructure and key assets will not only make us more secure from terrorist attack, but will also reduce our vulnerability to natural disasters, organized crime, and computer hackers.

America's critical infrastructure encompasses a large number of sectors. The U.S. government will seek to deny terrorists the opportunity to inflict lasting harm to our Nation by protecting the assets, systems, and functions vital to our national security, governance, public health and safety, economy, and national morale.

The *National Strategy for Homeland Security* identifies eight major initiatives in this area:

Unify America's infrastructure protection effort in the Department of Homeland Security;
Build and maintain a complete and accurate assessment of America's critical infrastructure and key assets;

Enable effective partnership with state and local governments and the private sector;

Develop a national infrastructure protection plan;

Secure cyberspace;

Harness the best analytic and modeling tools to develop effective protective solutions;

Guard America's critical infrastructure and key assets against "inside" threats; and

Partner with the international community to protect our transnational infrastructure.

Defending against Catastrophic Threats. The expertise, technology, and material needed to build the most deadly weapons known to mankind—including chemical, biological, radiological, and nuclear weapons—are spreading inexorably. If our enemies acquire these weapons, they are likely to try to use them. The consequences of such an attack could be far more devastating than those we suffered on September 11—a chemical, biological, radiological, or nuclear terrorist attack in the United States could cause large numbers of casualties, mass psychological disruption, contamination and significant economic damage, and could overwhelm local medical capabilities.

Currently, chemical, biological, radiological, and nuclear detection capabilities are modest and response capabilities are dispersed throughout the country at every level of government. While current arrangements have proven adequate for a variety of natural disasters and even the September 11 attacks, the threat of terrorist attacks using chemical, biological, radiological, and nuclear weapons requires new approaches, a focused strategy, and a new organization.

The *National Strategy for Homeland Security* identifies six major initiatives in this area:

Prevent terrorist use of nuclear weapons through better sensors and procedures;

Detect chemical and biological materials and attacks;

Improve chemical sensors and decontamination techniques;

Develop broad spectrum vaccines, antimicrobials, and antidotes;

Harness the scientific knowledge and tools to counter terrorism; and

Implement the Select Agent Program.

Emergency Preparedness and Response. We must prepare to minimize the damage and recover from any future terrorist attacks that may occur despite our best efforts at prevention. An effective response to a major terrorist incident—as well as a natural disaster—depends on being prepared. Therefore, we need a comprehensive national system to bring together and coordinate all necessary response assets quickly and effectively. We must plan, equip, train, and exercise many different response units to mobilize without warning for any emergency.

Many pieces of this national emergency response system are already in place. America's first line of defense in the aftermath of any terrorist attack is its first responder community—police officers, firefighters, emergency medical providers, public works personnel, and emergency management officials. Nearly three million state and local first responders regularly put their lives on the line to save the lives of others and make our country safer.

Yet multiple plans currently govern the federal government's support of first responders during an incident of national significance. These plans and the government's overarching policy for counterterrorism are based on an artificial and unnecessary distinction between "crisis management" and "consequence management." Under the President's proposal, the Department of Homeland Security will consolidate federal response plans and build a national system for incident management in cooperation with state and local government. Our federal, state, and local governments would ensure that all response personnel and organizations are properly equipped, trained, and exercised to respond to all terrorist threats and attacks in the United States. Our emergency preparedness and response efforts would also engage the private sector and the American people.

The *National Strategy for Homeland Security* identifies twelve major initiatives in this area:

Integrate separate federal response plans into a single all-discipline incident management plan;
Create a national incident management system;
Improve tactical counterterrorist capabilities;
Enable seamless communication among all responders;
Prepare health care providers for catastrophic terrorism;
Augment America's pharmaceutical and vaccine stockpiles;
Prepare for chemical, biological, radiological, and nuclear decontamination;
Plan for military support to civil authorities;
Build the Citizen Corps;
Implement the First Responder Initiative of the Fiscal Year 2003 Budget;
Build a national training and evaluation system; and
Enhance the victim support system.

The Foundations of Homeland Security

The *National Strategy for Homeland Security* also describes four foundations—unique American strengths that cut across all of the mission areas, across all levels of government, and across all sectors of our society. These foundations—law, science and technology, information sharing and systems, and international cooperation—provide a useful framework for evaluating our homeland security investments across the federal government.

Law. Throughout our Nation's history, we have used laws to promote and safeguard our security and our liberty. The law will both provide mechanisms for the government to act and will define the appropriate limits of action.

The *National Strategy for Homeland Security* outlines legislative actions that would help enable our country to fight the war on terrorism more effectively. New federal laws should not preempt state law unnecessarily or overly federalize the war on terrorism. We should guard scrupulously against incursions on our freedoms.

The Strategy identifies twelve major initiatives in this area:

Federal level
    Enable critical infrastructure information sharing;
    Streamline information sharing among intelligence and law enforcement agencies;
    Expand existing extradition authorities;
    Review authority for military assistance in domestic security;
    Revive the President's reorganization authority; and
    Provide substantial management flexibility for the Department of Homeland Security.
State level
    Coordinate suggested minimum standards for state driver's licenses;
    Enhance market capacity for terrorism insurance;
    Train for prevention of cyber attacks;
    Suppress money laundering;
    Ensure continuity of the judiciary; and
    Review quarantine authorities.

Science and Technology. The Nation's advantage in science and technology is a key to securing the homeland. New technologies for analysis, information sharing, detection of attacks, and countering chemical, biological, radiological, and nuclear weapons will help prevent and minimize the damage from future terrorist attacks. Just as science has helped us defeat past enemies overseas, so too will it help us defeat the efforts of terrorists to attack our homeland and disrupt our way of life.

The federal government is launching a systematic national effort to harness science and technology in support of homeland security. We will build a national research and development enterprise for homeland security sufficient to mitigate the risk posed by modern terrorism. The federal government will consolidate most federally funded homeland security research and development under the Department of Homeland Security to ensure strategic direction and avoid duplicative efforts. We will create and implement a long-term research and development plan that includes investment in revolutionary capabilities with high payoff potential. The federal government will also seek to harness the energy and ingenuity of the private sector to develop and produce the devices and systems needed for homeland security.

The *National Strategy for Homeland Security* identifies eleven major initiatives in this area:

Develop chemical, biological, radiological, and nuclear countermeasures;
Develop systems for detecting hostile intent;
Apply biometric technology to identification devices;
Improve the technical capabilities of first responders;
Coordinate research and development of the homeland security apparatus;
Establish a national laboratory for homeland security;
Solicit independent and private analysis for science and technology research;
Establish a mechanism for rapidly producing prototypes;
Conduct demonstrations and pilot deployments;
Set standards for homeland security technology; and
Establish a system for high-risk, high-payoff homeland security research.

Information Sharing and Systems. Information systems contribute to every aspect of homeland security. Although American information technology is the most advanced in the world, our country's information systems have not adequately supported the homeland security mission. Databases used for federal law enforcement, immigration, intelligence, public health surveillance, and emergency management have not been connected in ways that allow us to comprehend where information gaps or redundancies exist. In addition, there are deficiencies in the communications systems used by states and municipalities throughout the country; most state and local first responders do not use compatible communications equipment. To secure the homeland better, we must link the vast amounts of knowledge residing within each government agency while ensuring adequate privacy.

The *National Strategy for Homeland Security* identifies five major initiatives in this area:

Integrate information sharing across the federal government;
Integrate information sharing across state and local governments, private industry, and citizens;
Adopt common "meta-data" standards for electronic information relevant to homeland security;
Improve public safety emergency communications; and
Ensure reliable public health information.

International Cooperation. In a world where the terrorist threat pays no respect to traditional boundaries, our strategy for homeland security cannot stop at our borders. America must pursue a sustained, steadfast, and systematic international agenda to counter the global terrorist threat and improve our homeland security. Our international anti-terrorism campaign has made significant progress since September 11. The full scope of these activities will be further described in the forthcoming National Security Strategy of the United States and the National Strategy for Combating Terrorism. The *National Strategy for Homeland Security* identifies nine major initiatives in this area:

Create "smart borders";
Combat fraudulent travel documents;
Increase the security of international shipping containers;
Intensify international law enforcement cooperation;
Help foreign nations fight terrorism;
Expand protection of transnational critical infrastructure;
Amplify international cooperation on homeland security science and technology;
Improve cooperation in response to attacks; and
Review obligations to international treaties and law.

Costs of Homeland Security

The national effort to enhance homeland security will yield tremendous benefits and entail substantial financial and other costs. Benefits include reductions in the risk of attack and their potential consequences. Costs include not only the resources we commit to homeland security but also the delays to commerce and travel. The United States spends roughly $100 billion per year on homeland security. This figure includes federal, state, and local law enforcement and emergency services, but excludes most funding for the armed forces.

The responsibility of providing homeland security is shared between federal, state and local governments, and the private sector. In many cases, sufficient incentives exist in the private market to supply protection. Government should fund only those homeland security activities that are not supplied, or are inadequately supplied, in the market. Cost sharing between different levels of government should reflect the principles of federalism. Many homeland security activities, such as intelligence gathering and border security, are properly accomplished at the federal level. In other circumstances, such as with first responder capabilities, it is more appropriate for state and local governments to handle these responsibilities.

Conclusion: Priorities for the Future

The *National Strategy for Homeland Security* sets a broad and complex agenda for the United States. The Strategy has defined many different goals that need to be met, programs that need to be implemented, and responsibilities that need to be fulfilled. But creating a strategy is, in many respects, about setting priorities—about recognizing that some actions are more critical or more urgent than others.

The President's Fiscal Year 2003 Budget proposal, released in February 2002, identified four priority areas for additional resources and attention in the upcoming year:

Support first responders;
Defend against bioterrorism;
Secure America's borders; and
Use 21st-century technology to secure the homeland.

Work has already begun on the President's Fiscal Year 2004 Budget. Assuming the Congress passes legislation to implement the President's proposal to create the Department of Homeland Security, the Fiscal Year 2004 Budget will fully reflect the reformed organization of the executive branch for homeland security. That budget will have an integrated and simplified structure based on the six critical mission areas defined by the Strategy. Furthermore, at the time the *National Strategy for Homeland Security* was published, it was expected that the Fiscal Year 2004 Budget would attach priority to the following specific items for substantial support:

Enhance the analytic capabilities of the FBI;
Build new capabilities through the Information Analysis and Infrastructure
    Protection Division of the proposed Department of Homeland Security;
Create "smart borders";
Improve the security of international shipping containers;
Recapitalize the U.S. Coast Guard;
Prevent terrorist use of nuclear weapons through better sensors and procedures;
Develop broad spectrum vaccines, antimicrobials, and antidotes; and
Integrate information sharing across the federal government.

In the intervening months, the executive branch will prepare detailed implementation plans for these and many other initiatives contained within the *National Strategy for Homeland Security*. These plans will ensure that the taxpayers' money is spent only in a manner that achieves specific objectives with clear performance-based measures of effectiveness.

Endnotes

1. The *National Strategy for Homeland Security* defines "State" to mean "any state of the United States, the District of Columbia, Puerto Rico, the Virgin Islands, Guam, American Samoa, the Canal Zone, the Commonwealth of the Northern Mariana Islands, or the trust territory of the Pacific Islands." The Strategy defines "local government" as "any county, city, village, town, district, or other political subdivision of any state, any Native American tribe or authorized tribal organization, or Alaska native village or organization, and includes any rural community or unincorporated town or village or any other public entity for which an application for assistance is made by a state or political subdivision thereof."

2. The distribution of the *National Strategy for Homeland Security* coincides with Congress' consideration of the President's proposal to establish a Department of Homeland Security. The Strategy refers to a "Department of Homeland Security" only to provide the strategic vision for the proposed Department and not to assume any one part of the President's proposal will or will not be signed into law.

Bibliography

Books

Adams, James. *The Financing of Terror*. New York: Simon & Schuster, 1986.

Alibek, Ken, with Stephen Handelman. *Biohazard*. New York: Delta, 1999.

Allison, Graham. *Nuclear Terrorism: The Ultimate Preventable Catastrophe*. New York: Times Books, 2004.

Andreas, Peter, and Thomas Biersteker. *The Rebordering of North America: Integration and Exclusion in a New Security Context*. New York: Routledge, 2003.

Arlington Institute. *A Strategy: Moving America Away from Oil*. Arlington, VA: The Arlington Institute, 2003.

Auersweld, Philip, Lewis Branscomb, Todd M. La Porte, and Erwann Michel-Kerjan. *Seeds of Disaster, Roots of Response: How Private Actions Can Reduce Public Vulnerability*. New York: Cambridge University Press, 2006.

Barber, Benjamin. *Jihad vs. McWorld: How Globalism and Tribalism are Reshaping the World*. New York: Ballantine Books, 1996.

Baylis, John, and James J. Wirtz, eds., *Strategy in the Contemporary World*. London: Oxford University Press, 2002.

Benjamin, Daniel, and Steve Simon. *The Age of Sacred Terror*. New York: Random House, 2002.

———. *The Next Attack: The Failure of the War on Terror and a Strategy for Getting it Right*. New York: Henry Holt and Co., 2005.

Bergen, Peter L. *Holy War Inc.: Inside the Secret World of Osama bin Laden*. New York: The Free Press, 2001.

Bloom, Mia. *Dying to Kill: The Allure of Suicide Terrorism*. New York: Columbia Press, 2005.

Bodansky, Yossef. *Bin Laden: The Man Who Declared War on America*. Roseville, CA: Prima Publishing, 2001.

Booth, Ken, and Tim Dunne. *Worlds in Collision: Terror and the Future of Global Order*. New York: Palgrave-Macmillan, 2002.

Boulden, Jane, and Thomas G. Weiss, eds., *Terrorism and the UN: Before and After September 11*. Bloomington, IN: Indiana University Press, 2004.

Bovard, James. *Terrorism and Tyranny: Trampling Freedom, Justice and Peace to Rid The World of Evil.* New York: Palgrave Macmillan, 2003.

Boyle, Godfrey, Bob Everett, and Janet Ramage, eds., *Energy Systems and Sustainability: Power for a Sustainable Future.* Oxford: Oxford University Press, 2003.

Bunn, Matthew, and Anthony Wier. *Securing the Bomb 2005: The New Global Imperatives.* Cambridge, MA: Project on Managing the Atom, Harvard University, and the Nuclear Initiative, May 2005.

Bunn, Matthew, Anthony Wier, and John P. Holdren. *Controlling Nuclear Warheads and Materials: A Report Card and Action Plan.* Cambridge, MA: Project on Managing the Atom, Harvard University, March 2003.

Campbell, Colin J. *The Coming Oil Crisis.* Essex: Multi-Science Publishing Company and Petroconsultants S.A., 1997.

Campbell, Kurt, and Michelle Flournoy. *To Prevail.* Washington, D.C.: Center for Strategic and International Studies, 2001.

Carafano, James Jay, and Paul Rosenzweig. *Winning the Long War: Lessons from the Cold War for Defeating Terrorism and Preserving Freedom.* Washington, D.C.: The Heritage Foundation, 2005.

Charters, David A., and Graham F. Walker, eds. *After 911: Terrorism and Crime in a Globalised World.* Halifax, Nova Scotia: University of New Brunswick Centre for Conflict Studies and Dalhousie University Centre for Foreign Policy Studies, 2005.

Clausewitz, Carl von. *On War.* Translated by Michael Howard and Peter Paret from Clausewitz's 1831 original work. Princeton, NJ: Princeton University Press, 1984.

Clawson, Patrick L., ed., *Energy and National Security in the 21st Century.* Honolulu: University Press of the Pacific, 2002.

Cohen, David B., and John W. Wells. *American National Security and Civil Liberties in an Era of Terrorism.* New York: Palgrave Macmillan, 2004.

Cole, David, and James X. Dempsey. *Terrorism and the Constitution: Sacrificing Civil Liberties in the Name of National Security.* New York: The Free Press, 2002.

Collins, Joseph, and Michael Horowitz. *Homeland Security: A Strategic Approach.* Washington, D.C.: Center for Strategic and International Studies, 2000.

Combs, Cindy. *Terrorism in the Twenty-First Century.* Upper Saddle River, NJ: Prentice Hall, 2005.

Committee on Science and Technology for Countering Terrorism, National Research Council. *The Role of Science and Technology in Countering Terrorism.* Washington, D.C.: National Academy Press, 2002.

Continuity of Government Commission. *Preserving Our Institutions: The Continuity of Congress.* Washington, D.C.: American Enterprise Institute, 2003.

Cordesman, Anthony H. *Terrorism, Asymmetric Warfare, and Weapons of Mass Destruction.* Westport, CT: Greenwood Publishing Group, 2001.

Crenshaw, Martha, ed. *Terrorism in Context.* University Park, PA: Pennsylvania State University Press, 1995.

Cronin, Audrey Kurth, and James M. Ludes. *Attacking Terrorism: Elements of a Grand Strategy.* Washington, D.C.: Georgetown University Press, 2004.

Cutter, Susan L., Douglas B. Richardson, and Thomas J. Wilbanks, eds. *The Geographical Dimensions of Terrorism.* New York: Routledge, 2003.

Daalder, Ivo, et al., *Assessing the Department of Homeland Security*. Washington, D.C.: Brookings Institution Press, 2002.

Dittrich, Mijam. *Facing the Global Terrorist Threat: A European Response,* Working Paper no. 14. Brussels: European Policy Centre, January 2005.

Drabek, Thomas, and William H. Key. *Conquering Disaster: Family Recovery and Long-Term Consequences*. New York: Irvington, 1984.

Dunn, Lewis A. *Can Al Qaeda be Deterred from Using Nuclear Weapons?* Center for the Study of Weapons of Mass Destruction, Occasional Paper no. 3. Washington, D.C.: National Defense University, July 2005.

Ebinger, Charles K. *The Critical Link: Energy and National Security in the 1980's*. Cambridge: Ballinger Publishing Co., 1982.

Ehrenfeld, Rachel. *Funding Evil: How Terrorism Is Financed and How to Stop It*. Chicago: Bonus Books, 2003.

Ferguson, Charles D., and William C. Potter, with Amy Sands, Leonard S. Spector, and Fred L. Wehling. *The Four Faces of Nuclear Terrorism*. New York: Routledge 2005.

Findlay, Paul. *Silent No More: Confronting America's False Images of Islam*. Beltsville, MD: Amana Publications, 2001.

Firestone, Reuven. *Jihad: The Origin of Holy War in Islam*. New York: Oxford University Press, 1999.

Forrest, James. *The Making of a Terrorist: Recruitment, Training, and Root Causes*. Westport, CT: Praeger Security International, 2006.

Friedman, Thomas L. *The World Is Flat: A Brief History of the Twenty-First Century*. New York: Farrar, Straus and Giroux, 2005.

Flynn, Stephen. *America the Vulnerable*. New York: Harper Collins, 2004.

Gerstein, Daniel M. *Securing America's Future: National Strategy in the Information Age*. Westport, CT: Praeger, 2005.

Goldfischer, David. *The Best Defense: Policy Alternatives for U.S. Nuclear Security From the 1950s to the 1990s*. Ithaca, NY: Cornell University Press, 1993.

Goodwin, Craufurd D., ed., *Energy Policy in Perspective: Today's Problems: Yesterday's Solutions*. Washington, D.C.: The Brookings Institution, 1981.

Gottfried, Ted. *Homeland Security versus Constitutional Rights*. New York: Lerner Books, 2003.

Gunaratna, Rohan. *Inside al Qaeda: Global Network of Terror*. New York: Columbia University Press, 2002.

Hanle, Donald J. *Terrorism: The Newest Face of Warfare*. Washington D.C.: Pergamon-Brassey, 1989.

Heyman, David, and James J. Carafano. *DHS 2.0: Rethinking the Department of Homeland Security*. Washington, D.C.: The Heritage Foundation, 2004.

Hoffman, Bruce. *Inside Terrorism,* 2nd ed. New York: Columbia University Press, 2005.

Hoffman, Peter. *Tomorrow's Energy: Hydrogen, Fuel Cells, and the Prospects for a Cleaner Planet*. Cambridge, MA: MIT Press, 2001.

Hoge, James F. Jr., and Gideon Rose. *Understanding the War on Terror*. New York: Council on Foreign Relations, 2005.

Holst, Johan J., and William Schneider Jr., eds. *Why ABM? Policy Issues in the Missile Defense Controversy*. New York: Pergamon Press, 1969.

Horgan, John. *The Psychology of Terrorism*. London: Routledge, 2005.

Howard, Michael. *The Causes of War,* 2nd ed. Cambridge, MA: Harvard University Press, 1984.

Howard, Russell D., and Reid L. Sawyer, eds., *Terrorism and Counterterrorism: Understanding the New Security Environment—Readings and Interpretations.* Dubuque, IA: McGraw Hill, 2006.

Ikenberry, G. John. *After Victory.* Princeton, NJ: Princeton University Press, 2001.

International Energy Agency (IEA). *IEA The First Twenty Years, Volume Two: Major Policies and Actions.* Paris: IEA, 1994.

Juergensmeyer, Mark. *Terror in the Mind of God: The Global Rise of Religious Violence.* Berkeley, CA: University of California Press, 2000.

Kalicki, Jan H., and David L. Goldwyn, eds., *Energy and Security: Toward a New Foreign Policy Strategy.* Washington, D.C.: Woodrow Wilson Center Press, 2005.

Karas, Thomas H. *Energy and National Security.* Albuquerque, NM: Sandia National Laboratories, 2003.

Kepel, Gilles. *Jihad: The Trail of Political Islam.* Cambridge, MA: The Belknap Press of Harvard University, 2002.

———. *The War for Muslim Minds.* Cambridge, MA: Harvard University Press, 2004.

Keohane, Robert, and Joseph Nye. *Power and Interdependence,* 3rd Ed., London: Longman, 2000.

Knobler, Stacey, Alison Mack, Adel Mahmoud, and Stanley Lemon, eds. *The Threat of Pandemic Flu: Are We Ready?* Washington, D.C.: National Academies Press, 2005.

Knobler, Stacey, Adel Mahmoud, Stanley Lemon, Alison Mack, Laura Sivitz, and Katherine Oberholtzer, eds. *Learning from SARS: Preparing for the Next Disease Outbreak.* Washington, D.C.: National Academies Press, 2004.

Krasner, Stephen D. *International Regimes.* Ithaca, NY: Cornell University Press, 1983.

Kurtz, Lester R., and Jennifer Turpin, eds. *Encyclopedia of Violence, Peace and Conflict,* Vol. 3. London: Academic Press, 1999.

Labeviere, Richard. *Dollars for Terror: The United States and Islam.* New York: Algora, 2000.

Lansford, Tom. *All for One: Terrorism, NATO, and the United States.* Aldershot, UK: Ashgate, 2002.

Laqueur, Walter. *The Age of Terrorism.* Boston: Little, Brown, 1987.

———. *The New Terrorism: Fanaticism and the Arms of Mass Destruction.* New York: Oxford University Press, 1999.

———. *No End to War: Terrorism in the Twenty-First Century.* NY: Continuum, 2003.

Larsen, Jeffrey A., and James M. Smith. *Historical Dictionary of Arms Control and Disarmament.* Lanham, MD: Scarecrow Press, 2005.

Lavoy, Peter, Scott D. Sagan, and James J. Wirtz, eds. *Planning the Unthinkable.* Ithaca, NY: Cornell University Press, 2000.

Lederberg, Joshua, Robert B. Shope, and Stanley C. Oaks, Jr. *Emerging Infections: Microbial Threats to Health in the United States.* Washington, D.C.: Institute of Medicine, National Academies Press, 1992.

Leventhal, Paul, and Yonah Alexander, eds. *Preventing Nuclear Terrorism.* Lanham, MD: Rowan & Littlefield, 1987.

Lewis, Ted G. *Critical Infrastructure Protection in Homeland Security: Defending a Networked Nation.* Hoboken, NJ: John Wiley & Sons, 2006.

Limaye, Satu P., Robert G. Wirsing and Mohan Malik, eds. *Religious Radicalism and Security in South Asia*. Honolulu: Asia Pacific Center for Security Studies, 2004.

Lovins, Amory B., and L. Hunter Lovins. *Brittle Power: Energy Strategy for National Security*. Andover, MA: Brick House Publishing, 1982.

Nacos, Brigitte L. *Mass-Mediated Terrorism: The Central Role of the Media in Terrorism and Counterterrorism*. New York: Rowman & Littlefield, 2002.

Marburger, John H. "Foreword," in *The Geographical Dimensions of Terrorism*, edited by Susan L. Cutter, Douglas B. Richardson, and Thomas J. Wilbanks. New York: Routledge, 2003.

Martin, William F., Ryukichi Imai, and Helga Steeg. *Maintaining Energy Security in a Global Context: A Report to the Trilateral Commission*. New York: The Trilateral Commission, 1996.

Mileti, Dennis. *Disasters by Design*. Washington, D.C.: Joseph Henry Press, 1999.

Mitchell, James K. "Urban Vulnerability to Terrorism in Hazard," in *The Geographical Dimensions of Terrorism*, edited by Susan L. Cutter, Douglas B. Richardson, and Thomas J. Wilbanks. New York: Routledge, 2003.

Morgenstern, Richard D., and Paul R. Portney, eds. *New Approaches on Energy and the Environment*. Washington, D.C.: Resources for the Future, 2004.

Murdock, Clark A. *Improving the Practice of National Security Strategy: A New Approach for the Post-Cold War World*. Washington, D.C.: Center for Strategic and Defense Studies, 2004.

Murray, Douglas J., and Paul R. Viotti, eds. *The Defense Policies of Nations*, 3rd ed. Baltimore: Johns Hopkins University Press, 1994.

Napoleoni, Loretta. *Modern Jihad: Tracing the Dollars behind the Terror Networks*. London: Pluto, 2003.

National Academies. *Making the Nation Safer: The Role of Science and Technology in Countering Terrorism*. Lewis M. Branscomb and Richard Klausner, co-chairs. Washington, D.C.: National Academies Press, 2002.

National Commission on Terrorist Attacks Upon the United States. *The 911 Commission Report*. New York: W. W. Norton & Co., 2004. See also the Web site www.9-11commission.gov.

National Research Council, Commission on Engineering and Technical Systems. *Energy Research at DOE: Was It Worth It: Energy Efficiency and Fossil Energy Research 1978 to 2000*. Washington, D.C.: National Academies Press, 2001.

National Research Council, Committee on the Science of Climate Change. *Climate Change Science: An Analysis of Some Key Questions*. Washington D.C.: National Academies Press, 2001.

Nanda, Ved. *Law in the War on International Terrorism*. Ardsley, NY: Transnational Publisher, 2005.

Nesi, Giuseppe, ed., *International Cooperation in Counterterrorism: The United Nations and Regional Organizations in the Fight Against Terrorism*. Burlington, VT: Aldershot, 2006.

O'Hanlon, Michael, et al., *Protecting the American Homeland: A Preliminary Analysis*. Washington, D.C.: Brookings Institution, 2002.

O'Neill, Bard. *Insurgency and Terrorism: From Revolution to Apocalypse*. Washington, D.C.: Potomac Books, 2005.

Parra, Francisco. *Oil Politics: A Modern History of Petroleum*. London: I.B. Tauris, 2004.

Patai, Raphael. *The Arab Mind*. New York: Charles Scribner's Sons, 1983.

Pike, Douglas. *PAVN: People's Army of Vietnam*. Novato, CA: Presidio Press, 1986.

Pillar, Paul. *Terrorism and U.S. Foreign Policy*. Washington, D.C.: Brookings Institution Press, 2001 (updated 2003).

Quester, George. *Offense and Defense in the International System*. New York: Wiley, 1977.

Reich, Walter, ed., *Origins of Terrorism: Psychologies, Ideologies, Theologies, States of Mind*. Cambridge: Cambridge University Press, 1990.

Ricks, Thomas E. *Fiasco: The American Military Adventure in Iraq*. New York: Penguin Press, 2006.

Rose, Mark H. *Interstate: Express Highway Politics, 1939–1989*, rev. ed. Knoxville, TN: University of Tennessee Press, 1990.

Ruggie, John. *Multilateralism Matters: The Theory and Praxis of an Institutional Form*. New York: Columbia University Press, 1993.

Safir, Howard. *Security: Policing Your Homeland, Your State, Your City*. New York: St. Martin's Press, 2003.

Sageman, Marc. *Understanding Terror Networks*. Philadelphia, PA: University of Pennsylvania Press, 2004.

Sauter, Mark A., and James Jay Carafano. *Homeland Security*. New York: McGraw Hill, 2005.

Scheuer, Michael. *Imperial Hubris*. Washington, D.C.: Potomac Books, 2004.

Schneier, Bruce. *Beyond Fear: Thinking Sensibly About Security in an Uncertain World*. New York: Copernicus Books, 2003.

Schwartz, Stephen I., ed. *Atomic Audit: The Costs and Consequences of U.S. Nuclear Weapons since 1940*. Washington, D.C.: Brookings Institution Press, 1998.

Schweizer, Peter. *Victory*. New York: The Atlantic Monthly Press, 1994.

Sidel, Mark. *More Secure, Less Free? Antiterrorism Policy and Civil Liberties after September 11*. Ann Arbor, MI: University of Michigan Press, 2004.

Slaughter, Anne-Marie. *A New World Order*. Princeton, NJ: Princeton University Press, 2004.

Smith, James M., and William C. Thomas, eds. *The Terrorism Threat and U.S. Government Response: Operational and Organizational Factors*. USAF Academy, CO: Institute for National Security Studies, March 2001.

Stagliano, Vito A. *A Policy of Discontent: The Making of the National Energy Strategy*. Tulsa: Penn Well Corporation, 2001.

———. "The Ghost of OPEC," in *Energy and National Security in the 21st Century*, edited by Patrick L. Clawson. Honolulu: University Press of the Pacific, 2002.

Stern, Jessica. *Terror in the Name of God: Why Religious Militants Kill*. New York: Harper Collins, 2003.

Sweet, Kathleen M. *Terrorism and Safety Concerns*. Upper Saddle River, NJ: Pearson, 2004.

Thomas, Troy S. *Beneath the Surface: Intelligence Preparation of the Battlespace for Counterterrorism*. Washington, D.C.: Joint Military Intelligence College, November 2004.

Tierney, Kathleen J., Michael K. Lindell, and Robert W. Perry. *Facing the Unexpected: Disaster Preparedness and Response in the United States*. Washington, D.C.: Joseph Henry Press, 2001.

Vale, Lawrence. *The Limits of Civil Defence in the USA, Switzerland, Britain and the Soviet Union*. New York: St. Martin's Press, 1987.

Weber, Max. *The Theory of Social and Economic Organization*. New York: The Free Press, 1947.

White, Jonathan R. *Terrorism and Homeland Security*, 5th ed. Belmont, CA: Thomson Wadsworth, 2006.

Woodward, Bob. *Bush at War*. New York: Simon & Schuster, 2002.

———. *Plan of Attack*. New York: Simon & Schuster, 2004.

———. *State of Denial*. New York: Simon & Schuster, 2006.

Yergin, Daniel. *The Prize: The Epic Quest for Oil, Money and Power*. New York: Free Press, 1992.

Articles

Ackerman, Bruce. "The Emergency Constitution." *Yale Law Journal* 113, no. 5 (2005): 1029–1091.

Albright, David, and Corey Hinderstein. "Unraveling the A.Q. Khan and Future Proliferation Networks." *The Washington Quarterly* 28, no.2 (Spring 2005): 111–128.

Albright, Madeleine. "Bridges, Bombs, or Bluster." *Foreign Affairs* 82, no. 5 (September/October 2003): 2–19.

Alhajji, A. F. "The Oil Weapon: Past, Present, and Future." *Oil and Gas Journal* 103, no. 17 (May 2005): 22–33.

Auerswald, Philip, Lewis M. Branscomb, Todd M. La Porte, and Erwann Michel-Kerjan. "The Challenge of Protecting Critical Infrastructure." *Issues in Science & Technology* 22, no. 1 (Fall 2005): 77–83.

Bensahel, Nora. "International Cooperation against Terrorism." *Studies in Conflict and Terrorism* 29, no. 1 (January 2006): 35–49.

Betts, Richard. "The New Threat of Mass Destruction." *Foreign Affairs* 77, no. 1 (January–February 1998): 26–41.

———. "Fixing Intelligence." *Foreign Affairs* 81, no. (2002): 43–59.

Braun, Chaim, and Christopher F. Chyba. "Proliferation Rings: New Challenges to the Nuclear Nonproliferation Regime." *International Security* 29, no. 2 (Fall 1994): 5–49.

Campbell, Colin J., and Jean H. Laherrère. "The End of Cheap Oil." *Scientific American* 278, no. 3 (March 1998).

Carter, Ashton, John Deutch, and Philip Zelikow. "Catastrophic Terrorism: Tackling the New Terrorism." *Foreign Affairs* 77 no. 6 (November–December 1998): 80–94.

Carter, Ashton, and William Perry "The Architecture of Government in the Face of Terrorism." *International Security* 26, no. 3 (Winter 2001–2002): 5–23.

Chyba, Christopher F., Harold Feiverson, and Frank von Hippel. "Preventing Nuclear Proliferation and Nuclear Terrorism: Essential Steps to Reduce the Availability of Nuclear-Explosive Materials." *Center for International Security and Cooperation Report* (March 2005).

Clary, Christopher. "A.Q. Khan and the Limits of Non-proliferation Regime." *Disarmament Forum*, no. 4 (2004): 33–42.

Cronin, Audrey Kurth. "Behind the Curve: Globalization and International Terrorism." *International Security* 27, no. 3 (Winter 2002/03): 30–58.

Cronin, Audrey Kurth. "Terrorist Motivations for Chemical and Biological Use: Placing the Threat in Context." *Defense & Security Analysis* 20, no. 4 (December 2004): 313–320.

Dory, Amanda J. "American Civil Security: The U.S. Public and Homeland Security." *The Washington Quarterly* 27, no. 1 (Winter 2003–2004): 37–52.

Dubois, Dorine. "The Attacks of 11 September: EU-US Co-operation against Terrorism in the Field of Justice and Home Affairs." *European Foreign Affairs Review* 7, no. 3 (2002): 317–335.

Elcock, Deborah, Glagys A. Klemic, and A. L. Taboas. "Establishing Remediation Levels in Response to a Radiological Dispersal Event or ('Dirty Bomb')." *Environmental Science and Technology* 38, no. 9 (2004): 2505–2512.

Eraker, Elizabeth. "Cleanup After a Radiological Attack: U.S. Prepares Guidance."*Nonproliferation Review* 11, no. 3 (Fall/Winter 2004): 167–185.

Ferguson, Charles D., Tahseen Kazi, and Judith Perrera. "Commercial Radioactive Sources: Surveying the Security Risks." *Center for Nonproliferation Studies Occasional Paper No. 11.* Monterey, CA: Monterey Institute of International Studies, January 2003. Accessible at http://cns.miis.edu/pubs/opapers/op11/op11.pdf.

Farrell, Alexander, Hisham Zerriffi, and Hadi Dowlatabadi. "Energy Infrastructure and Security." *Annual Review of Environment and Resources* 29 (2004).

Flynn, Stephen. "The Neglected Homefront." *Foreign Affairs* 83, no. 1 (September–October 2004): 20–33.

Fromkin, David. "The Strategy of Terrorism." *Foreign Affairs* 53, no. 4 (July 1975): 683–698.

Fri, Robert W. "Taking the Lead on Climate Change." In *New Approaches on Energy and the Environment*, edited by Richard D. Morganstern and Paul R. Portney. Washington, D.C.: The National Academies Press, 2001.

Goldfischer, David. "Rethinking the Unthinkable After the Cold War: Toward Long-Term Nuclear Policy Planning." *Security Studies* 7, no. 4 (Summer 1998): 128–157.

Hardy, Victoria, and Phil Ross. "International Emergency Planning for Facilities Management." *Journal of Facilities Management* 2, no. 1 (2003): 7–25.

Heyman, Philip. "Dealing with Terrorism: An Overview." *International Security* 26, no. 3 (Winter 2001–2002): 24–38.

Homer-Dixon, Thomas. "The Rise of Complex Terrorism." *Foreign Affairs* 81, no. 1 (January/February 2002): 52–62.

Howard, Michael. "The Forgotten Dimensions of Strategy." *Foreign Affairs* 57 no. 5 (Summer 1979): 975–986.

Johnson, Jeannie L. "Exploiting Weaknesses in the Far Enemy Ideology." *Strategic Insights* 4, no. 6 (June 2005). Accessible at www.ccc.nps.navy.mil.

Joskow, Paul L. "Energy Policies and Their Consequences after 25 Years." *Energy Journal* 24, no. 4 (2003): 17–49.

Khan, Ali S, and David A. Ashford. "Ready or Not—Preparedness for Bioterrorism." *New England Journal of Medicine* 345, no. 4 (July 26, 2001): 287–289.

Kibble, David G. "The Threat of Militant Islam: A Fundamental Reappraisal." *Studies In Conflict and Terrorism* 19, no. 4 (1996): 353–364.

Kitchen, Veronica. "Smarter Cooperation in Canada-US Relations?" *International Journal* 59, no. 3 (Summer 2004): 693–710.

Lehrman, Thomas D. "The Future of the Proliferation Security Initiative." *Nonproliferation Review* 11, no. 2 (Summer 2004): 145.

Luck, Edward C. "The U.S., Counterterrorism, and the Prospects for a Multilateral Alternative." In *Terrorism and the UN: Before and After September 11,* edited by Jane Boulden and Thomas G. Weiss. Bloomington, IN: Indiana University Press, 2004.

Luft, Gal, and Anne Korin. "Terrorism Goes to Sea." *Foreign Affairs* 83 (November/December 2004): 61–71.

Meltzer, Martin, Nancy J. Cox, and K. Fakuda, "The Economic Impact of Pandemic Influenza in the United States: Priorities for Intervention." *Emerging Infectious Diseases* 5, no. 5 (September–October 1999): 659–671.

Mathews, Jessica Tuchman. "Power Shift." *Foreign Affairs* 76, no. 1 (January/February 1997): 50–66.

Morse, Edward L. "A New Political Economy of Oil?" *Journal of International Affairs* 53, no. 1 (Fall 1999): 1–29.

Mueller, John. "Simplicity and Spook: Terrorism and Dynamics of Threat Exaggeration." *International Studies Perspectives* 6, no. 2 (May 2005): 208–234.

Muir, Angus. "Terrorism and Weapons of Mass Destruction." *Studies in Conflict and Terrorism* 22, no. 1 (1999): 79–91.

Nye, Joseph S. Jr., "The Decline of America's Soft Power." *Foreign Affairs* 83, no. 3 (May/June 2004): 16–20.

Ozernoy, Ilana. "Ears Wide Shut." *Atlantic Monthly* 298, no. 4 (November 2006): 30–32.

Posen, Barry. "The Struggle against Terrorism: Grand Strategy, Strategy, and Tactics." *International Security* 26, no. 3 (Winter 2001–2002): 39–55.

Rapoport, David. "Terrorism." In *Encyclopedia of Violence, Peace and Conflict,* Vol. 3, edited by Lester R. Kurtz and Jennifer E. Turpin, 497–510. London: Academic Press, 1999.

———. "The Fourth Wave: September 11 in the History of Terrorism." *Current History* (December 2001): 419–424.

Rashid, Ahmed. "The Taliban: Exporting Extremism." *Foreign Affairs* 78, no. 6 (November/December 1999): 22–35.

Rhodes, Richard, and Denis Beller. "The Need for Nuclear Power." *Foreign Affairs,* 79, no. 1 (January/February 2000): 30–44.

Rudner, Martin. "Hunters and Gatherers: The Intelligence Coalition against Islamic Terrorism." *International Journal of Intelligence and CounterIntelligence* 17, no 2 (2004): 193–230.

Scheuer, Michael. "Al-Qaeda's Next Generation: Less Visible and More Lethal." *Terrorism Focus*2, no. 2 (October 2005): 5–7.

Segell, Glen M. "Terrorism: London Public Transport—July 7, 2005." *Strategic Insights* 4, no. 8 (August 2005). Accessible at www.ccc.nps.navy.mil/si/2005/Aug/segellAug05.asp.

Shultz, Richard. "The Limits of Terrorism in Insurgency Warfare: The Case of the Viet Cong." *Polity* 11, no. 1 (Autumn 1978): 67–91.

Smith, James M. "A Strategic Response to Terrorism." In *After 911: Terrorism and Crime in a Globalised World,* edited by David A. Charters and Graham F. Walker. Halifax, Nova Scotia: University of New Brunswick Centre for Conflict Studies and Dalhousie University Centre for Foreign Policy Studies, 2005.

Smith, James M., and William C. Thomas. "The Real Threat from Oklahoma City: Tactical and Strategic Responses to Terrorism." *Journal of Conflict Studies* 18, no. 1 (Spring 1998): 119–138.

Stern, Jessica. "Terrorist Motivations and Unconventional Weapons." In *Planning the Unthinkable,* edited by Peter Lavoy, Scott D. Sagan, and James J. Wirtz. Ithaca: NY: Cornell University Press, 2000.

Szyliowicz, Joseph S. "Aviation Security: Promise or Reality." *Studies in Conflict and Terrorism* 27, no. 1 (January–February 2004): 47–63.

———. "International Transportation Security." *Review of Policy Research* 21, no. 3 (Fall 2004): 351–368.

Tucker, Johnathan B., and Robert P. Kadlec. "Infectious Disease and National Security." *Strategic Review* 29, no. 2 (Spring 2001): 12–20.

Ullman, Richard. "Redefining Security." *International Security* 8, no 1 (Summer 1983): 129–153.

Viotti, Paul R. "International Relations and the Defense Policies of Nations: International Anarchy and the Common Problem of Security." In *The Defense Policies of Nations,* 2nd ed., edited by Douglas J. Murray and Paul R. Viotti, 10–22. Baltimore: Johns Hopkins University Press, 1994.

Wirtz, James J., and James Russell. "Preventive War and Preemption: Reassessing the U.S. Policy Toward Iraq and the War on Terrorism." *Non Proliferation Review* 10, no. 1 (Spring 2003): 113–123.

Wilkinson, Paul. "The Media and Terrorism: A Reassessment." *Terrorism and Political Violence* 9, no. 2 (Summer 1997): 51–64.

Yergin, Daniel. "Energy Security in the 1990's." *Foreign Affairs* 67, no. 1 (Fall 1988): 110–132.

———. "Energy Security and Markets." In *Energy and Security: Toward a New Policy Strategy,* edited by Jan H. Kalicki and David L. Goldwyn. Washington, D.C.: Woodrow Wilson Center Press, 2005.

———. "Ensuring Energy Security." *Foreign Affairs* 85, no. 2 (March/April 2006): 69–82.

Documents

Bureau of Census. "Types of Government Entities." Accessed at: http://www.census.gov/govs/www/class_ch3.html#S3.1.

Burgos, Russell A., Timothy W. Crawford, Alexander C. Diener, Anne-Marie Gardner, William Josiger, Veronica M. Kitchen, Ritu S. Lauer, and Gregory J. Moore. *Homeland Security in a Multinational Context: A New Strategic Vision." Report of the Fred A. Sondermann Summer Seminar.* Denver and Vail, CO: University of Denver and Vail Cascade Resort, August 2004.

Carafano, James, Paul Rosenzweig, and Alan Cochems. "An Agenda for Increasing State and Local Government Efforts to Combat Terrorism." Heritage Foundation, Backgrounder no. 1826. Accessible at http://www.heritage.org/Research/Homeland-Defense/bg1826.cfm.

Center for Nonproliferation Studies WMD Terrorism Research Program. "Chart: Al Qa'ida's WMD Activities." Center for Nonproliferation Studies Web site, http://cns. miis.edu/pubs/other/sjm_cht.htm.

Cragin, Kim, and Sara A. Daly. *The Dynamic Terrorist Threat: An Assessment of Group Motivations and Capabilities in a Changing World*. Santa Monica, CA: RAND, 2004. Accessed at: http://www.rand.org/publications/MR/MR1782/MR1782.pdf.

Department of Energy. "Department of Energy Launches New Global Threat Reduction Initiative." Available at http://www.doe.gov/engine/content.do?PUBLIC_ID_CODE=PR_PRESSRELEASES&TT_CODE=PRESSRELEASE .

Department of Energy. *National Energy Policy: Report of the National Energy Policy Development Group*. Washington, D.C: Government Printing Office, May 2001. Available at http://www.energy.gov/engine/doe/files/dynamic/195200312817_chapter5.pdf.

Department of Health and Human Services. "Interim Public Health and Healthcare Supplement to the National Preparedness Goal." Available at http://www.hhs.gov/ophep/index.html.

Department of Health and Human Resources—Centers for Disease Control and Prevention. "Facts About Evacuation during a Radiological Emergency." Fact Sheet. Available at http://www.bt.cdc.gov/radiation/evacuation.asp.

Department of Homeland Security. National Response Plan, Incident Annexes, Nuclear/Radiological Annex, NUC-2. Available at http://www.dhs.gov/interweb/assetlibrary/NRP_FullText.pdf.

Department of Homeland Security. National Response Plan Brochure. Available at http://dhs.gov/interweb/assetlibrary/NRP_Brochure.pdf.

Department of Homeland Security. Press release. "Fact Sheet: Proposed Action Guides for Radiological Dispersion and Improved Nuclear Devices." Available at http://www.dhs.gov/dhspublic/display?content=5327.

Department of Homeland Security. Working Group on Radiological Dispersal Device (RDD) Preparedness. *Medical Preparedness and Sub-Group*, May 1, 2003. Version. Accessible at http://www.1.va.gov/emshg/docs/Radiologic_Medical_Countermeasures_051403.pdf.

Department of Homeland Security. *National Incident Management System*. Washington, D.C.: Department of Homeland Security, 2004.

Department of Homeland Security. National Infrastructure Protection Plan. Washington, D.C.: Department of Homeland Security, 2006.

Department of Homeland Security. "FY2006 State and Local Homeland Security Grant Awards." Accessed at http://www.dhs.gov/xlibrary/assets/grants_st-local_fy06.pdf.

Department of Homeland Security. "FEMA History." Available at http://www.fema.gov/about/history.shtm.

Flynn, Stephen, with Daniel B. Prieto. *"The Neglected Defense: Mobilizing the Private Sector to Support Homeland Security."* New York: Council on Foreign Relations Special Report, May 2006.

Government Accountability Office. "Nuclear Nonproliferation: DOE Action Needed to Ensure Continued Recovery of Unwanted Sealed Radioactive Sources." GAO-03-438 (April 2003). Available at http://www.gao.gov/new.items/d03483.pdf.

Government Accountability Office. "Preventing Nuclear Smuggling: DOE Has Made Limited Progress in Installing Radiation Detection Equipment at Highest Priority Foreign Seaports." GAO-05-375 (March 2005). Available at http://www.gao.gov/new.items/d05375.pdf.

Hart-Rudman Commission. *"Phase 3 Report of the U.S. Commission on National Security/ 21ˢᵗ Century, Roadmap for National Security: Imperative for Change.* Preface and pages 10–29 accessed at http://www.fas.org/irp/threat/nssg.pdf.

Intergovernmental Oceanographic Commission of UNESCO. *From Commitments to Action: Advancements in Developing an Indian Ocean Tsunami Warning and Mitigation System.* Paris, France: United Nations Educational, Scientific and Cultural Organization (UNESCO), 2005.

International Atomic Energy Agency. International Conventions and Agreements: Convention on the Physical Protection of Nuclear Material." Available at http://www.iaea.org/Publications/Documents/Conventions/cppnm.html.

Jenkins, Brian. *The Potential for Nuclear Terrorism.* RAND Report P-5876. Santa Monica, CA: RAND, 1977.

——. *Countering al Qaeda: An Appreciation of the Situation and Suggestions for a Strategy.* Santa Monica, CA: RAND, 2002. Accessible at http://www.rand.org/publications/MR/MR1620/index.html.

Kayyem, Juliette, and Arnold M. Howitt, eds., *Beyond the Beltway: Focusing on Hometown Security.* Cambridge, MA: Harvard University Press, 2002.

Moteff, John, and Paul Parfomak. *Critical Infrastructure and Key Assets: Definition and Identification.* Washington, D.C.: The Library of Congress, Congressional Research Service, 2004, 14, RL32631.

National Academies. *Start Making the Nation Safer: The Role of Science and Technology in Countering Terrorism.* Lewis M. Branscomb and Richard Klausner, co-chairs. Washington, D.C.: National Academies Press, 2002.

National Academies and the Department of Homeland Security. Fact Sheet. Radiological Attack: Dirty Bombs and Other Devices." Available at http://www.nae.edu/NAE/pubundcom.nsf/weblinks/CGOZ-646nvg/$file/radiological%20attack.pdf.

The National Commission on Energy Policy. *Ending the Energy Stalemate: A Bipartisan Strategy to Meet America's Energy Challenges.* Washington, D.C.: NCEP, 2004.

National Council on Radiation Protection and Measurements. "Advising the Public About Radiation Emergencies." *NCRP Commentary No. 10* (November 20, 1994). Available at http://www.ncrponline.org/Commentaries/NCRP%20Comm%20No.%2010.pdf.

National Research Council, Committee on Science and Technology for Countering Terrorism. *Making the Nation Safer: The Role of Science and Technology in Countering Terrorism.* Washington, D.C.: The National Academies Press, 2002.

National Research Council and National Academy of Engineering. *The Hydrogen Economy: Opportunities, Costs, Barriers, and R&D Needs.* Washington, D.C.: The National Academies Press, 2004.

National Safety Council. "Understanding Radiation: The Risks: Health Effects." December 12, 2002. Accessible at http://www.nsc.org/issues/rad/risks.htm.

National Safety Council Environmental Health Center. "Understanding Radiation in Our World." Available at http://www.nsc.org/ehc/rad/radbroch.HTM.

9/11 Commission. *"Final Report on 9/11 Commission Recommendations,"* December 5, 2005. Accessed at http://www.9-11pdp.org/press/2005-12-05_report.pdf.

Nuclear Information and Resource Service. "Groups Criticize Homeland Security Plans to Relax Radiation Cleanup Standards for a 'Dirty Bomb' or Terrorist Nuclear Explosive." Accessible at http://www.nirs.org/press/12-02-2004/1.

Nuclear Regulatory Commission. "Background on Nuclear Security Enhancements Since September 11, 2001." February 2005. Accessible at http://www.nrc.gov/reading-rm/doc-collections/fact-sheets/security-enhancements.html.

Office of Grants and Training. "Program Highlights (FY2005)." Available at http://www.ojp.usdoj.gov/odp/about/highlights.htm.

Office of Grants and Training. "G&T Mission." Accessible at http://www.ojp.usdoj.gov/odp/about/mission.htm.

Reese, Shawn. "FY2006 Homeland Security Grant Distribution Methods: Issues for the 109th Congress." Washington, D.C.: Congressional Research Service—Library of Congress, 2006.

Stanford University, Center for International Security and Arms Control. "Understanding Nuclear Terrorism." *What to Do in an Attack: Response Guidance.* Available at http://www.cisac.stanford.edu/nuclearterrorism/index.html.

U.S. Commission on National Security Strategy in the 21st Century. *New World Coming: American Security in the 21st Century.* Arlington, VA: U.S. Commission on National Security Strategy, 1999.

U.S. Congress. "H.R. 5005-Homeland Security Act of 2002." Accessible at www.dhs.gov/xlibrary/assets/hr_5005_enr.pdf.

U.S. Government Accountability Office. *Nuclear Nonproliferation: DOE Needs to Take Action to Further Reduce the Use of Weapons-Usable Uranium in Civilian Research Reactors.* GAO-04-807. Washington, D.C.: GAO, 2004. Accessible at http://www.ntiorg/e_reserach/analysis_cnwupdate_052404.pdf.

White House. *Reliable, Affordable, and Environmentally Sound Energy for America's Future: Report of the National Energy Policy Development Group.* Washington, D.C.: The White House, 2001.

White House. *The National Strategy for Homeland Security.* Washington, D.C.: Office of Homeland Security, the White House, 2002. Accessible at http://www.whitehouse.gov/homeland/book/.

White House. *National Strategy for Combating Terrorism.* Washington D.C.: The White House, February 2003.

White House. National Strategy for Homeland Security. Available at http://whitehouse.gov/homeland/book/nat_strat_hls.pdf.

White House. *The National Strategy for the Physical Protection of Critical Infrastructures and Key Assets.* Washington, D.C.: The White House, 2003.

White House. Press Release. "December 17, 2003 Homeland Security Presidential Directive/HSPD-8. Available at http://www.whitehouse.gov/news/releases/2003/12/20031217-6.html.

White House. "President Signs Intelligence Reform and Terrorist Prevention Act." December 17, 2004. Accessible at http://www.whitehouse.gov/news/releases/2004/12/20041217-1.html.

White House. "The Federal Response to Hurricane Katrina: Lessons Learned." February 23, 2006. Accessible at http://www.whitehouse.gov/reports/katrina-lessons-learned/letter.html.

Web sites

Bureau of Justice Statistics: http://www.ojp.usdoj.gov/bjs/sandlle.htm

Center for Arms Control and Non-Proliferation: Terrorism Prevention: http://www.armscontrolcenter.org/terrorism/handbook

Center for Defense Information: Terrorism Project: http://www.cdi.org/terrorism

Center for Democracy and Technology: http://www.cdt.org/policy/terrorism/html

Center for Nonproliferation Studies: Terrorism: http://cns.miis.edu/reserach/terror.htm

Centre for the Study of Terrorism and Political Violence: http://www.st-and.ac.uk/academic/intrel/research/cstpv

Customs-Trade Partnership Against Terrorism (C-TPAT): http://www.customs.gov/import/commercial_enforcement/ctpat.html

Council on Foreign Relations: http://www.cfr.org

Council on Foreign Relations—Questions Regarding Terrorism Answered: http://www.terrorismanswers.com

Defense Threat Reduction Agency: http://www.dtra.mil/toolbox/directorates/cs/index.cfm

Department of Energy: http://www.doe.gov

Department of Health and Human Services: http://www.hhs.gov

Department of Health and Human Services—Centers for Disease Control and Prevention: http://www.bt.cdc.gov

Bioterrorism Agents Web page: http://www.bt.cdc.gov/agent/agentlist-category.asp

Department of Homeland Security: http://www.dhs.gov

Department of Homeland Security Organizational Chart: http://www.dhs.gov/interweb/assetlibrary/DHSOrgChart.htm

Department of Homeland Security's Ready America Project: http://www.ready.gov

Environmental Protection Agency: http://www.epa.gov

Environmental Protection Agency's Radiological Emergency Response Team: http://www.epa.gov/radiation/rert/respond.htm

GlobalSecurity.org: http://www.globalsecurity.org

Government Accountability Office: http://www.gao.gov

Government Publications on Terrorism: http://www.lib.umd.edu/GOV/terrrorism.html

Homeland Security Project: http://www.homelandsec.org

International Association for Counterterrorism Professionals: http://www.iacsp.com

International Atomic Energy Agency: http://www.iaea.org

Jane's Terrorism and Insurgency Centre: http://jtic.janes.com

Marshall Center Information Resource on Terrorism: http://www.marshallcenter.org

Monterey Institute of International Studies Center for Nonproliferation Studies Critical Issues Forum: http://homepage.mac.com/cifproject/bmks05.html

National Council on Radiation Protection and Measurements: http://www.ncrponline

National Safety Council: http://www.nsc.org

National Security Council: http://www.whitehouse.gov/nsc

Nuclear Information and Resource Service: http://www.nirs.org

Nuclear Regulatory Commission: http://www.nrc.gov

Oak Ridge National Laboratory's Radiation Emergency Assistance Center/Training Site (REAC/TS): http://www.orau.gov/recats/intro.htm

Office of Grants and Training (formerly the Office of Domestic Preparedness): http://www.ojp.usdoj.gov/odp

RAND Corporation: www.rand.org

State Department: http://www.state.gov

Teaching Terror—Resource Guide for the Study of Terrorism: http://www.teachingterror.com

Terrorism Research Center: http://www.terrorism.com

United States Fire Administration: http://www.usfa.fema.gov

United States Institute of Peace—Terrorism/Counterterrorism Web links: http://www.usip.org/library/topics/terrorism/html

University of Michigan's Documents Center—America's War against Terrorism: http://www.lib.umich.edu/govdocs/usterror.html

White House—Homeland Security: http://www.whitehouse.gov/homeland

Glossary

ABM Treaty (Anti-Ballistic Missile Treaty): 1972 agreement between the United States and the Soviet Union precluding militarily significant defenses against missiles. Specifically, it prohibited deployment by the United States and the Soviet Union (later the Russian Federation) of ABM systems for territorial defense, limited ABM deployments for defense of a state's national capital or one ICBM-launcher complex; prohibited development, testing, or deployment of sea-based, air-based, space-based, or mobile land-based ABM systems; prohibited transfer of ABM systems or components to other states; and provided for national technical means of verification while prohibiting concealment measures. The treaty went out of force in June 2002, six months after the United States provided notice it would no longer adhere to the treaty.

Active defenses: Weapons systems that spring into action in order to shoot down an enemy's offensive forces (e.g., bombers or missiles) as they approach their targets.

Aerosol (aerosolized): A fine mist or spray that contains very small particles that can float easily in the air, and thus readily be inhaled into the lungs. Hair spray or air freshener, for example, is aerosolized when it leaves the nozzle.

Agent: Any biological organism or "**pathogen**" capable of causing **infectious disease** (e.g., bacteria spores, viruses, prions, or other germs) used for **bioterrorism**.

al-Arabiya: Satellite television news channel established in 2003 and based in the United Arab Emirates. Considered by some to be more moderate than its al-Jazeera counterpart.

al-Jazeera: Round the clock Arab television news network operating out of Qatar since 1996. Defended in Arab lands for bringing a new perspective on issues in the region while criticized by some in the West for being a mouthpiece for jihadists.

All-hazards approach: Approach designed to build capability in preparedness, mitigation, response, and recovery in tackling both natural and man-made disasters.

"All terrorism is local": The notion that in a crisis, one's perceptions are reality. Local factors significantly shape those perceptions of the most directly impacted targeted audience. It is a modification of former Speaker Thomas P. "Tip" O'Neil's famous dictum that "all politics is local."

Antibiotic: Any drug intended to retard or prevent the disease-causing ability of bacteria.

Antiproliferation: An attempt to prevent the spread of nuclear, biological, and chemical weapons. *See also* counterproliferation and nonproliferation.

Antiterrorism: Coordinated *defensive* measures to detect, prevent, and respond to terrorism. Part of an overall effort to minimize damage and maximize recovery. *See also* counterterrorism. The Department of Homeland Security has jurisdiction in these matters.

Anthrax: A natural bacterial toxin that has been enhanced by programs of weapons. A person can be infected through inhalation, exposure through the skin, or by eating contaminated food.

Antimicrobial: A general term for any drug or treatment intended to retard or prevent the disease-causing ability of microbial, disease-causing organisms, such as bacteria, viruses, funguses, etc.

Aum Shinrikyo (more recently referred to as Aleph): Japanese cult, or religious group, founded by Shoko Asahara. They gained fame by placing the chemical agent sarin on Tokyo subway cars in March 1995, killing eleven and injuring 6,000. Earlier that same year they attempted to aerosolize anthrax in Tokyo neighborhoods.

Australia Group: Informal group of countries established in 1985 to help reduce the spread of chemical and biological weapons by monitoring and controlling the spread of technologies required to produce them.

Avian influenza: Any influenza virus that infects birds (wild or domestic), but between 1997 and the present, most people use this term in reference to a particular strain of avian flu, H5N1, which crossed the **species barrier** to become a disease organism for humans also. Currently, H5N1 flu virus, which up to 2006 had over a 60 percent case fatality rate, is feared to hold the potential for **mutation**. If so, it could be sufficient to become **transmissible** from human to human, just like standard strains of human influenza, and possibly start a global **pandemic** that could kill millions.

Away game: Phrase used by the Pentagon to describe a situation of forward defense, and international efforts to deal with security, distinguished from the "home game" of domestic homeland security. It influences homeland security in that it prevents individuals and groups from adopting terrorism as a tactic in the first place.

Bacteria: A particular type of single-celled microorganism, ranging in size from 1 to 20 micrometers, usually visible under a light microscope. *Examples* of bacterial infectious diseases include cholera, anthrax, tuberculosis, and plague. Bacteria in the CDC's Category A of biological weapons include anthrax, pneumonic plague, and botulin toxin.

bbl: The conventional shorthand for barrels is bbl. It stands for blue barrels, after Standard Oil decided to standardize barrels to hold 42 U.S. gallons and painted them blue to signify this.

Bin Laden, Osama: Founder and current leader of al-Qaeda. A rich, exiled Saudi financier who built a reputation as a logistics and construction expert during the war against the Soviet Union in Afghanistan. His influence demonstrates the growing importance of non-state actors in international politics today.

Biosecurity: Biological security or defense measures taken to prevent, monitor, research, respond to, and otherwise increase the protection of civilian and military populations against biological threats, such as catastrophic infectious disease outbreaks, caused either by deliberate bioterrorism or naturally occurring infectious pathogens or toxins.

Biological weapon (BW): Any weapon that uses living microorganisms, such as bacteria or viruses, to deliberately sicken or kill humans, animals, or plants. Often distinguished from either chemical or toxin weapons, bioweapons are potential *weapons of mass destruction (WMD)*, and now considered to be primarily an instrument of terrorism.

Bioterrorism (BT): Terrorism using biological microorganisms or related agents. Biological diseases and the agents that might be used for terrorism include viruses, bacteria, Rickettsiae, fungi, and biological toxins.

Btu: British thermal unit. A measure of heat energy required to raise the temperature of one pound of water by one degree Fahrenheit.

Caliphate: Divinely inspired government. Islamic government representing political leadership and unity of the Muslim world with application of Islamic law. Establishing a caliphate by driving away the "faraway enemy" from Islamic lands and the downfall of corrupt "near enemy" governments is one of the central goals of jihadists in the global arena today.

Catastrophic infectious disease outbreak (CIDO): Any infectious disease outbreak, naturally occurring or deliberate biological terrorism, which is likely to create anxiety, panic, disruption, demoralization, and even political chaos where it occurs.

Civil defense: A direct pre-September 11, 2001 antecedent of the phrase "homeland security," it refers to attempts to prepare civilians for military attack and subsequent emergency operations of response, evacuation, and recovery.

Civil Defense Act of 1950: Act creating the Federal Civil Defense Administration, which was an attempt by President Truman to give a positive nod toward the embryonic concept of homeland security.

Civil security: The protection of critical infrastructure, and the networks and processes that support global trade, government, civil-society relations, and ensuring the secure movement of people.

Richard Clarke: Former terrorism "czar" in the George W. Bush administration.

Clash of Civilizations: The term was introduced by the scholar Samuel P. Huntington to describe conflict in the post-Cold War era. Rather than states attacking other states, fighting would take place along civilizational and cultural lines.

Clausewitz, Carl von: Prussian general and writer whose 1832 work, *On War*, is considered a classic treatise in strategy. He advocated the total destruction of an enemy's forces as one of the strategic targets of warfare. Clausewitz also saw war as an extension of political policy and not merely as an end in itself.

Co-infection: Infection by more than one disease organism at the same time, which may cause one or both diseases to be worse, or more easily transmitted, than they might without the presence of the other. Example: HIV/AIDS and tuberculosis in Africa are common, devastating co-infections.

Comparative risk analysis: Risk is the likelihood that bad things may happen. Risk is conceptualized by DHS as a combination of threat, vulnerability, and consequence probabilities.

Consequences: A leading measure by which priorities are set in homeland security since prevention and mitigation of all hazards is nearly an impossible task.

Container Security Initiative (CSI): The Custom and Border Protection's major initiative for securing goods by prescreening, using tamper-resistant containers, targeting containers that pose a risk, and using automated detection technology.

Continuity of democratic government: Ensuring the maintenance and viability of the institutions of democratic society even after a catastrophic event.

Conventional oil: Oil that is less than 20.0 degrees API gravity and is producible through wells using primary, secondary, improved, enhanced, or tertiary methods.

Counterproliferation: Active measures to reduce or eliminate existing weapons systems and nuclear, chemical, and biological agents as opposed to simply preventing the spread of such weapons, technology, and knowledge which is associated with nonproliferation. *See also* antiproliferation and nonproliferation.

Counterterrorism: Coordinated *offensive* efforts and measures to prevent attacks, minimize damage, and maximize recovery. It is largely the bailiwick of the State Department, the Defense Department and the CIA. See also *Antiterrorism*.

Counter-Terrorism Committee (CTC): Committee established by the United Nations as part of UN Security Council Resolution 1373 requiring UN member states to ensure that terrorist groups do not receive funds, haven, or support of any kind from member states.

Creutzfeldt-Jacob disease (CJD), and new variant Creutzfeldt-Jacob disease (vCJD): vCJD is a rapidly progressive, degenerative neurological condition in human beings. Dementia and destruction of healthy brain tissue most notably characterize it. Most commonly believed to be transmitted to humans via meat or other byproducts ingested from cattle infected with *bovine spongiform encephalopathy* **(BSE), or "mad cow disease,"** as it's colloquially known. It is currently incurable and believed to be 100 percent fatal.

Critical infrastructure/key resources (CI/KR): The assets, systems, and functions vital to our national security, governance, public health and safety, economy, and national morale.

Customs-Trade Partnership Against Terrorism (C-TPAT): Public-private partnership concerned with expediting the passage of precleared goods. The emphasis is on self-policing rather than customs inspection and is an important development in civil security cooperation.

Damage limitation: Strategy based on the realization that prevention of terrorist attacks can never be perfect. Concern is geared toward mitigation of attacks that do occur with emphasis on creating a more vibrant civil society and a citizen ethos of self-help.

Denial of capability: At an operational level, the emphasis is to deter any campaign or series of terrorist actions. This is achieved primarily through the disruption of organizational recruitment and sustainment, as well as their training, access to weapons and sanctuary, communications, finance, and whatever other resources needed to initiate terrorist operations.

Denial of objectives: At this highest strategic level, the goal is to deter terrorism itself by marginalizing the terrorist message from both its target population and its support base.

Denial of opportunity: The base, or tactical level, of deterrence which delinks the terrorist action cadre from its intended victim or victims. This is accomplished primarily through either denying the victim to the terrorist through protection and hardening, or by denying the terrorist access to the victim or weapon through entry and movement management.

Department of Homeland Security (DHS): U.S. cabinet-level department under the executive branch (president) designated to "detect, prepare for, prevent, protect against, respond to, and recover from terrorist attacks within the borders of the United States."

Deterrence: Threat of the use of force aimed at persuading another actor not to do what it intends or may like to do. It is a psychological effect on an opponent that results in a rational decision to desist because of the expected consequences of attacking or starting a war.

Disease: A condition in which the functioning of the body or a part of the body is interfered with or damaged. In a person with an infectious disease, the infectious agent that has entered the body causes it to function abnormally in some way or ways. The type of abnormal functioning that occurs is the disease. Usually the body will show some signs and symptoms of the problems it is having with functioning. Disease can be infectious (able to be transmitted from another person, animal, or insect, or gotten from a germ or pathogen in the environment, such as the soil or air) or *non*infectious (*not* able to be transmitted person to person, such as cancer or diabetes).

Emergency medical services (EMS): Generally refers to state or local level government agencies charged with overseeing and providing public health facilities and training to deal with critical care medical emergencies, including mass casualty events. Such services would involve coordinating ambulances and emergency rooms in hospitals, for instance.

Emerging infectious disease (EID): Pathogens that either have newly appeared in the population or are expanding their range or severity.

Empathetic analysis: Quality of putting oneself in the shoes of a rational adversary in an attempt to create an effective counter strategy.

Energy system: System pertaining to the integrated network of primary energy resources, fuel refinement, and power generation processes and infrastructure that distribute energy for residential, commercial, industrial, military, and transportation end-use sectors. It consists of: inputs, or supply chains of primary energy sources that are the raw materials, such as crude oil; throughputs, or chemical, electrical, nuclear, thermal, and other conversion processes; and outputs, or refined fuels, electricity, heat, pollution, and waste.

Epidemic: The condition in which an infectious disease spreads rapidly through a population in which that disease is not normally present or is present at a lower level.

Epidemiology: The study of epidemic disease, with a view to finding means of control and future prevention. This can include not only classic infectious diseases, but chronic disease (cancer, e.g.) or those caused by or contributed to by lifestyle (diabetes, heart disease) as well.

Faraway enemy: Label used by Islamic radicals to describe the United States and the state of Israel since they are geographically further away. *See also* near enemy.

Fatwa: Religious ruling.

FEMA (Federal Emergency Management Agency): A civilian natural disaster management and recovery agency originally chartered to respond to hurricanes, and later all natural disasters. Absorbed into the Department of Homeland Security in 2003, it was reduced to "a stepchild of national security," according to Michael Brown, its former director, and was criticized for not responding adequately to the 2005 Hurricane Katrina.

First wave of terrorism: First of four waves of terrorism expounded on by David Rapoport emerging in the late 1800s when rebel and revolutionary movements embraced sensational violence to attack local regimes. The *Nar-*

odnaya Volya (People's Will) is a clear example of this wave. Wave seen as ending with the assassination of the Austrian Archduke on the eve of World War I. *See also* second wave of terrorism, third wave of terrorism, and fourth wave of terrorism.

Flatteners: Term developed by Thomas L. Friedman to trace the process of contemporary globalization through developments such as the globalization of business and the exponential growth of information.

Fog of war: The idea that in combat one encounters enormous difficulties as circumstances change so quickly that one may not be aware of essential details about what is happening.

4 D's: Four fundamental goals laid out by President George W. Bush in 2003 in the U.S. National Strategy for Combating Terrorism. They are: (1) defending U.S. citizens and interests at home and abroad; (2) defeating and destroying terrorist organizations; (3) denying sanctuary and support to terrorist organizations; and (4) diminishing the underlying causes of terrorism.

Fourth wave of terrorism: Fourth of four waves of terrorism expounded on by David Rapoport. It emerged in the aftermath of the Soviet defeat in Afghanistan and the rise of Islamic fundamentalism in Iran. It demonstrated the growing power of religion as a way to motivate people to terrorism. *See also* first wave of terrorism, second wave of terrorism, and third wave of terrorism.

French Revolution: Event from 1789 to 1799 in which republicanism replaced absolute monarchy in France. It is considered by many to be the seminal event in the birth of modern war and modern terrorism as perpetrated by the state in the form of the Committee of Public Safety, symbolized by use of the guillotine.

Friction: Concept taken from Carl von Clausewitz in which real-world, often unexpected factors may hamper war plans from being implemented as fully planned.

Globalization: The continual increase in transnational and worldwide economic, social, and cultural interactions that transcend the boundaries of states, aided by advances in technology.

Global Threat Reduction Initiative: Effort launched in 2004 designed to secure, remove, and facilitate the disposition of vulnerable nuclear and radiological materials and equipment on a worldwide basis.

GTL: Gas to liquids. A process that combines the carbon and hydrogen elements in natural gas molecules to make synthetic liquid petroleum products, such as diesel fuel. GTL synthetic liquids can be shipped in traditional tankers.

"Guards, guns, and gates strategy": A perimeter defense strategy for airports.

Hart-Rudman Commission (formally The United States Commission on National Security/21st Century): Independent panel created by Congress and chaired by former Democratic Senator Gary Hart of Colorado and former Republican Senator Warren Rudman of New Hampshire. It consisted of three phases. Phase one went from July 1998 to August 1999. The second phase lasted from August 1999 to April 2000. Finally, phase three's duration was a period from April 2000 until February 2001, concluding just months before the September 11, 2001 attacks on the United States. It was charged to "conduct the most comprehensive review of American Security since the National Security Act of 1947 was signed into law over 50 years ago." More concretely, the objective of the report was to "design a national security strategy" suitable for the new international environment of the twenty-first century.

Hazards: Anything that potentially endangers our community. Hazards are either natural or man-made. Natural hazards include blizzards, drought, earthquakes, epidemics, floods, hurricanes, tornados, or wild fires. Man-made hazards include criminal acts, hazardous materials, technical/industrial accidents, terrorism, and war.

Herd immunity: The existence of a presumed threshold of individuals in a given population (the "herd") with immunity against a pathogen in sufficient (or insufficient) numbers to reduce or even prevent a broader outbreak. This does not require universal immunity among all the population, but a variable percentage, depending on many factors.

Home game: Domestic effort revolving around actions taken to harden victims against attack, to limit terrorist access to those victims, and to limit access to weapons of choice to carry out attacks. It equally involves efforts to mitigate the effects of attacks that do take place. Its efforts are largely concentrated in the Department of Homeland Security.

Homeland defense: Measures a state takes to protect what lies within its borders—its people along with the physical and institutional foundations of human sustenance and society. Though there is obvious overlap, homeland security before Hurricane Katrina was aimed exclusively at domestic and external terrorism attack threat and vulnerability reduction, and consequence mitigation.

Homeland security: Refers to the "home game" of defense within U.S. borders. The Department of Homeland Security, which emerged in the aftermath of the September 11 attack, represents a new generation of domestic security and public safety and sets as its goals preparedness, prevention, mitigation, response, and recovery from an attack. It is situated as distinct from the "away game" of operations more commonly associated with the Department of Defense.

Homeland Security Presidential Directive 5 (HSPD-5): Directive designed to prevent, prepare for, respond to, and recover from terrorist attacks, major disasters, and other emergencies. It established the secretary of homeland security as the main federal official responsible for domestic incident management. Its purpose is to enhance the management of domestic incidents by establishing a single, comprehensive national incident management system.

Homeland Security Presidential Directive 8 (HSPD-8: Directive serving as a follow up to Homeland Security Presidential Directive 5 for preparedness. It mandated compliance with national standards to remain eligible for federal grant dollars. It created the National Response Plan calling for a single document to provide guidance for an all-hazards approach to disaster preparedness, response, and prevention.

Hydrocarbon: An organic chemical compound of hydrogen and carbon in the gaseous, liquid, or solid phase. The molecular structure of hydrocarbon compounds varies from the simplest (methane, a constituent of natural gas) to the very heavy and very complex.

Incubation period: The period of time, from infection to noticeable disease, that it takes for an infectious microbe to multiply and spread sufficiently to cause disease symptoms in the infected organism (human, animal, etc.).

Infection: The entry and development of a pathogenic disease agent in the body of a person, animal, or other organism. In an apparent "manifest" infection, the infected person outwardly appears to be sick. In an *in*apparent infection, there is no outward sign that an infectious agent has entered that person at all. Infection should not be confused with **disease**.

Influenza: See **avian influenza.**

Integrated Border Enforcement Team (IBET): Operational level of cooperation between the United States and Canada composed of immigration, law-enforcement, and customs officials often operating from shared facilities, to target cross-border crimes.

International Atomic Energy Agency (IAEA) Nuclear Suppliers Group: Group formed in the mid-1970s seeking to control exports of nuclear materials, equipment, and technology, both dual use and specially designed and prepared.

Intermodalism: Connection between two or more modes. Same as nodes. An example is direct rail to airports.

International organizations: The multilateral institutions created by states in order to pursue common goals that usually cannot be achieved as easily by states acting unilaterally. The United Nations and its associated agencies serve as examples.

Intramodalism: Within one mode at a time. Currently, the dominant mode of thought regarding transportation and security.

Jihadists: Islamic radicals who have accepted the call of jihad (holy war) against those who stand in opposition to strict Muslim interpretation of faith.

Khan, A. Q.: Pakistani metallurgist and "father of the Pakistani bomb" whose efforts created a global black market for nuclear knowledge and expertise.

LNG: Liquefied natural gas. Natural gas (primarily methane) that has been liquefied by reducing its temperature to -260 degrees Fahrenheit at atmospheric pressure. LNG must be shipped in special LNG tankers.

MAD: Mutually (also mutual) assured destruction. The nuclear deterrence doctrine that avoids resort to war by reciprocal threat of punishment through an unacceptable level of (or mass) destruction, should either party commit aggression or take other hostile action against the other that would provoke such a response.

Mad cow disease: Informal term for either bovine spongiform encephalopathy (BSE) or sometimes for the human version, new variant Creutzfeldt-Jacob disease (vCJD), believed to be acquired by consuming beef products contaminated with BSE.

Madrassah: Islamic school.

Man made hazards: *See* hazards.

Maritime Transportation Security Act: Act enacted in 2002 which calls for various initiatives to safeguard U.S. ships and ports. This includes: threat and security assessments of ports and vessels, material and area security plans, a National Maritime Security Advisory Committee and regional committees, vessel and facility security and response plans.

Mass casualty: Any large number of casualties produced in a relatively short period of time which is usually the result of a single incident or armed attacks that exceeds the capabilities of local logistics support.

Massive retaliation: Doctrine articulated by U.S. secretary of state John Foster Dulles in January 1954 that stated the United States would protect itself, Western Europe, and other allies mainly through the threat of nuclear attacks.

Megaports Initiative: 2003 initiative established by the United States to deter, detect, and interdict illicit trafficking in special nuclear materials and other radioactive materials throughout the global maritime network.

Modes of transportation: Air, water, rail, and road ways of transportation, each of which has particular characteristics and vulnerabilities.

Mortality: Death; or, the death rate or ratio of number of deaths to a given population over time. Related to "case-fatality rate," which is the rate of deaths for identified people ill with a particular disease.

Multilateralism: Working issues jointly, usually emphasizing a thicker form of cooperation involving content and not just form.

Multinational: Relationships between central governments. It is often viewed as a thin form of cooperation.

Mutation or mutability: The ability of a microorganism, such as a human pathogenic disease germ, to change its genetic makeup, and thus potentially adapt to natural threats (e.g., the human immune system) and/or man-made threats (e.g. antibiotics, antiviral drugs, or vaccine-derived immunity).

Mutation may allow a new pathogen strain to succeed where a previous version failed to flourish in a particular external or internal environment.

Mutually assured destruction (MAD): The nuclear deterrence doctrine that avoids resort to war by reciprocal threat of punishment through an unacceptable level of destruction, should either party commit aggression or take other hostile action against the other that would provoke such a response.

NCEP: *See* National Commission on Energy Policy.

Naming and shaming: A form of criticism by the UN and the international community in which a state, having taken an action regarded negatively by the international community, may be named and held up in contempt. May result in severe enough pressure for the named state to alter course and change its behavior.

National Commission on Energy Policy: Bipartisan group of leading energy experts established in 2002 focusing on long-term issues: oil security, climate change, and energy infrastructure adequacy and siting.

National Incident Management System: System directed by Homeland Security Presidential Directive 5 (*see* HSPD-5). It is a drive to standardize the organization and vocabulary of response to emergencies among different federal, state, and local agencies.

National Response Plan (NRP): Plan created in December 2004 by Homeland Security Presidential Directive 8 which itself called for an all-hazards approach to disaster preparedness, response, and prevention. The NRP incorporated and superseded several preexisting plans: the Federal Response Plan, the National Contingency Plan, the Interagency Domestic Terrorism Concept of Operations Plan, and the Federal Radiological Emergency Response Plan. The National Response Plan places an emphasis on planning, preparedness, and response at the local and state levels through the application of the National Incident Management System, created by Homeland Security Presidential Directive 5 in February 2003.

Natural hazards: *See* Hazards.

Naturally occurring infectious diseases: Microbial pathogens that emerge or emanate from the natural environment to cause illness in any organism, versus those that originate from a laboratory, particularly those grown by humans for **bioterrorism**.

Near enemy: Term used by Islamic radicals to describe what they see as nearby corrupt Arab and other Muslim state governments that prevent the implementation of *sharia* and whose existence prevents the unification of the umma under a single caliphate. *See also* faraway enemy.

Nodes: Intermodal linkages. Hubs where two modes of transportation come together. An example is direct rail to airports. In the energy sector, it refers to important junctions in energy pathways. Specifically, in the realm of energy it means where lines of places of connection intersect to convert, divert, gather, store, and/or transfer power or fuels/fuel products through the system. An example of an energy system node would be a pumping station along a pipeline route where the pipeline would be the link.

Non-governmental organization (NGO): Transnational organizations with a standing independent of governments, often with a diversified membership, that work to fulfill specific political, social, or economic goals that may benefit or have some positive or negative impact on a wide range of persons. An example of this would be Doctors Without Borders.

Nonproliferation: Focus on attempting to prevent proliferation directly through multilateral treaties, export controls, and norms of cooperation.

Nuclear warfighting: Strategic nuclear doctrine based on denial in which the goal is to destroy or substantially weaken an enemy's war-making capability. Predicated on the notion that by talking credibly about fighting and prevailing in a nuclear war was also the belief that by doing so, such a chance would never come to fruition.

OAPEC: Organization of Arab Petroleum Exporting Countries. Member countries are Algeria, Bahrain, Egypt, Iraq, Kuwait, Libya, Qatar, Saudi Arabia, Syria, and the United Arab Emirates. Tunisia is a former member.

OECD: Organisation for Economic Co-operation and Development. Member countries are Australia, Austria, Belgium, Canada, the Czech Republic, Denmark, Finland, France, Germany, Greece, Hungary, Iceland, Ireland, Italy, Japan, Korea, Luxembourg, Mexico, Netherlands, New Zealand, Norway, Poland, Portugal, the Slovak Republic, Spain, Sweden, Switzerland, Turkey, the United Kingdom, and the United States of America.

Office of Grants and Training (G&T): Department of Homeland Security office that is responsible for providing funding, training, and guidance to state and local authorities in the effort to help them prepare for, and respond to, terrorist incidents including weapons of mass destruction in accordance with the National Response Plan.

OPEC: Organization of the Petroleum Exporting Countries. Member countries are Algeria, Indonesia, Iran, Iraq, Kuwait, Libya, Nigeria, Qatar, Saudi Arabia, the United Arab Emirates, and Venezuela.

Operation Safe Commerce: A public-private partnership designed to bring together the largest ports and various federal agencies in an effort to develop new cargo management systems that would safeguard international commerce from terrorist threats.

Oppenheimer, J. Robert: U.S. physicist who served as the scientific director of the Manhattan Project. Often known as the "Father of the Atomic Bomb." After World War II, he chaired a 1952 Report of the Panel of Consultants on Disarmament which recommended that the United States needed a continental defense. Seeing what the bomb could do, his later work involved lobbying for international control of atomic energy.

Pandemic: An epidemic so widely spread that vast numbers of people in different countries are affected. The Black Death, the fourteenth century plague that ravaged much of Europe and Eurasia; the 1918 "Spanish" Influenza; the 1994 cholera outbreak in Peru; as well as global HIV/AIDS are among the many pandemics in history.

Passive defenses: Measures such as radar detection designed to give warning or cope with the consequences of an attack.

Pathogen: Any microorganism (germs such as bacteria, viruses, etc.) or substance capable of producing a disease.

Patriot Act: The Uniting and Strengthening America by Providing Appropriate Tools Required to Intercept and Obstruct Terrorism Act of 2001, known as the USA PATRIOT Act or simply the Patriot Act, was signed into law by President George W. Bush on October 26, 2001. Although the bill enjoyed widespread congressional and presidential support it is a very controversial piece of federal legislation. Originally passed after the September 11, 2001 attacks, the act was written in response to the terrorist attacks against the United States, and dramatically expanded the authority of U.S. law enforcement for the stated purpose of fighting terrorism in the United States and abroad.

Pattern of convergence: Pattern of first responders tending to congregate at the scene of a catastrophe. Those converging on the scene tend to be of five types: the returnees, the anxious, the helpers, the curious, and the exploiters.

Petroleum: A broadly defined class of liquid hydrocarbon mixtures. Included are crude oil, lease condensates, unfinished oils, refined products obtained from the processing of crude oil, and natural gas plant liquids.

Petroleum products: Petroleum products are obtained from the processing of crude oil (including lease condensates), natural gas, and other hydrocarbon compounds. Petroleum products include unfinished oils, liquefied petroleum gases, pentanes plus, aviation gasoline, motor gasoline, naphtha-type jet fuel, kerosene-type jet fuel, kerosene, distillate fuel oil, residual fuel oil, petrochemical feedstocks, special naphthas, lubricants, waxes, petroleum coke, asphalt, road oil, still gas, and other products.

Plague: Either (1) a generic term for any widespread, deadly epidemic of any origin—derived originally from the specific *Yersinia* "black plague"; or (2) the plague bacterium, *Yersinia pestis*, believed to be responsible for Europe's Black Death and other periodic pandemics throughout history.

Presidential Decision Directive 39 (PDD 39): A directive that established the FBI as the lead federal agency for crisis management of a terrorist attack. It further established FEMA as the lead official for consequence management of a terrorist incident.

Presidential Decision Directive 62 (PDD 62): Codified change in perspective regarding terrorism in May 1998 establishing the creation of a small group within the National Security Council focusing on the terrorist threat.

Preventive war: Term for a type of war where public justification is proclaimed as a type of self-defense, an attack before the fact based on the assumption that conflict is likely imminent.

Proliferation Security Initiative (PSI): Initiative announced by President George W. Bush on May 31, 2003 whereby the United States would take a lead in an effort to interdict the transfer of weapons of mass destruction, their delivery systems, and related materials to or from states of proliferation concern.

Proved reserves: An estimate of remaining recoverable resources that is based on economic and technical parameters. The EIA version of this definition stresses that proved reserves are estimated quantities of energy sources that analysis of geologic and engineering data demonstrates with reasonable certainty are recoverable under existing economic and operating conditions. The location, quantity, and grade of the energy source are usually considered to be well established in such reserves.

Public health: The health of the human population as a whole; or the field of medicine that attempts to promote such health.

Radiological dispersal device: Conventional bomb wrapped in radioactive material. When it is detonated, radioactive material is spread by the blast. It is commonly referred to as a "dirty bomb."

Redundancy: Concept associated with segments of national infrastructure that have many similar assets serving the same purpose.

Regional Assistance Committees: Groups comprised of Department of Homeland Security and Federal Emergency Management Agency personnel, and according to the National Response Plan, is the primary vehicle for federal government coordination in the event of a radiological or nuclear incident.

Risk: The relationship between hazards and vulnerabilities.

Risk assessment (or analysis): See **Comparative risk analysis**.

Sarin: Toxic substance used as a nerve agent chemical weapon. Its use has been banned by the United Nations.

Second wave of terrorism: Second of four waves of terrorism expounded on by David Rapoport. It emerged in the aftermath of World War I, prompted by the forces of decolonization. Instead of targeting senior officials, nationalists typically attacked instruments of colonial control, such as police and military outposts. The Irgun attacking the British in Palestine is a clear example of this wave. The wave demonstrated that terrorism could be integrated into an overall effective political strategy. *See also* first wave of terrorism, third wave of terrorism, and fourth wave of terrorism.

Secure Trade in the Apec Region: See STAR Program.

Severe acute respiratory syndrome (SARS): SARS appeared early in 2003 in China, but soon spread and created a significant global outbreak. SARS prompted the WHO's first ever worldwide travel alert for a newly emerging viral disease, and was thought to be a mutated strain of the coronavirus, normally one of three viruses responsible for the common cold. Its animal hosts are uncertain.

Sharia: Law of Allah.

Short ton: A unit of weight equal to 2,000 pounds.

Soft power: Concept associated with political scientist Joseph Nye which stressed the capacity to persuade and influence others through elements such as popular culture, institutions, and values rather than merely the hard power of military force.

Smallpox: The disease caused by the pathogenic Variola major virus, a member of the *Orthopoxvirus* genus and Poxviridae family. After a concerted, immunization campaign around the world in the 1960s and 1970s, the virus was officially declared eradicated by the World Health Organization (WHO) in 1980. The former Soviet Union bioweapons program engineered a weaponized version of smallpox in the 1970s and 1980s.

Sneak and Peak: Sneak and peek warrants allow law enforcement officers to lawfully make surreptitious entries into areas where a reasonable expectation of privacy exists, search for items of evidence or contraband, and leave without making any seizures or giving concurrent notice of the search.

STAR program (Secure Trade in the APEC region): Program launched in 2002 whose objective is to focus on securing Asia-Pacific trade while protecting regional transportation networks. Specifically the program is designed to "enhance security while increasing trade by committing APEC economies to accelerate action on screening people and cargo for security before transit; increasing security on ships and airplanes when in route; and enhancing security in airports and seaports."

Strain: A genetic variation or subtype of any microorganism species. In pathogens, the strain can mean the difference between mild (or no) disease and severe, deadly virulence.

Strategic National Stockpile (SNS): Large-scale caches of antibiotics, medicines, vaccines, and other supplies capable of being rapidly deployed (within 12 hours) in the event of a major mass casualty event anywhere in the United States, and hypothetically capable of supplying antibiotics and other pharmaceuticals for hundreds of thousands of people.

Strategy: Ways or modalities by which we link capabilities or means we have or can generate to the ends, purposes, or objectives we seek. *Ends* are the goals sought. *Means* are the resources available to pursue the objectives. *Ways* are the concepts or methods for how one organizes and applies the resources. See also Carl von Clausewitz and Sun Tzu.

Substitutability: Concept associated with segments of national infrastructure that serve needs that can be met by assets available in other segments.

Sunset provisions: In public policy, a sunset provision or sunset clause is a provision in a statute or regulation that terminates or repeals all or portions of the law after a specific date, unless further legislative action is taken to extend it. Not all laws have sunset clauses. In such cases, the law goes on indefinitely.

Sun Tzu: Ancient Chinese philosopher of war who wrote *The Art of war*, considered by many to be a classic treatise on strategy. He argued a good military leader who can project an aura of strength can resolve a dispute without losing soldiers. He also articulated the need for soldiers to know themselves as much as the enemy they faced.

Target audience: People, aside from the victims, whom terrorists hope to inspire fear in through their actions.

Terrorism: Calculated events perpetrated by adversaries who seek strategically to attain particular objectives by such means. It is a rational, or purposive use, of the "irrational" or intimidating effects of violence. It is a tactic of political violence designed to intimidate or cause fear in an adversary.

Third wave of terrorism: Third of four waves of terrorism expounded on by David Rapoport. It is best exemplified by the Palestine Liberation Organization (PLO) in the late 1960s and through the 1970s. The terrorists in this wave were careful to use violence in a purposive way to achieve political goals and tended to stick with known methods. *See also* first wave of terrorism, second wave of terrorism, and fourth wave of terrorism.

Transgovernmentalism: Concept articulated by Anne-Marie Slaughter in which the component parts of states (whether judicial systems, legislatures, and bureaucracies) can make connections with their counterparts abroad and together develop mechanisms for governance in their sectors.

Transmission (of infectious agents): Any mechanism through which an infectious agent, such as a virus, is spread from a reservoir or source to a human being. Usually each type of infectious agent is spread by only one or a few of the different mechanisms of transmission. Types of transmission mechanisms include: (1) direct transmission to the body, via various possible routes (e.g., mucus membranes, sexual organs, mouth, nose, etc.); (2) indirect transmission, via vehicles (such as eating utensils, food, blood, etc.) and **vectors** or **hosts** (such as biting mosquitoes, flies, or other hosts); and (3) airborne transmission of suspended **aerosolized** particles, that usually infect via inhalation into the lungs.

Transnational: Relationships occurring across borders at nonexecutive levels of government, between subnational governments or government departments, and between private and non-governmental actors.

Trilateral countries: Australia, Austria, Belgium, Canada, the Czech Republic, Denmark, Estonia, Finland, France, Germany, Greece, Hong Kong, Hungary, Indonesia, Ireland, Italy, Japan, Malaysia, Mexico, the Netherlands, New Zealand, Norway, the People's Republic of China, the Philippines, Poland, Portugal, the Republic of Cyprus, the Republic of Korea, Singapore, Slovenia, Spain, Sweden, Taiwan, Thailand, the United Kingdom, and the United States.

Tsunami: Any unusual surges or waves of water that strike land, caused by a variety of underwater events, including earthquakes, landslides, volcanic eruptions, etc. Tsunamis following the December 2004 Great Sumatra Earthquake killed up to 280,000 people in south Asia and Africa.

Umma: The Muslim community.

Unconventional gas: Gas that is produced from coal (coalbed methane), shales, and tight sands. Gas hydrates are presently excluded from unconventional gas reserves estimates as they are currently nonproducible.

Unconventional oil: Oil that is more than 20.0 degrees API gravity, oil from coal and shale, bitumen, polar oil, and deepwater/ultra-deepwater oil, and liquids created from natural gas.

USA Patriot Act: *See* Patriot Act.

Vector: A carrier, usually an insect that transmits the disease-causing organisms from infected to noninfected individuals. Examples include mosquitoes carrying malaria and yellow fever virus, and ticks carrying Lyme disease or viral hemorrhagic fever-inducing viruses.

Virulence: A trait of a pathogen (germ) that enables it to cause disease; or the disease-causing ability of any microorganism. That is, the amount of harm (deaths and/or sickness, etc.) that a pathogen may or may not be able to inflict on an infected victim.

Virus: A microscopic parasitic organism, not visible under a normal light microscope, which depends on nutrients from another organism's living cells to metabolize and reproduce. Viruses generally have a simple construction, usually consisting of a strand of either DNA or RNA with a protein covering. From the Latin for "poison." *Examples* of infectious viral diseases include Ebola, influenza, hantavirus pulmonary syndrome, and HIV/AIDS.

Vulnerabilities: Those things potentially endangered by hazards. These include: population, critical infrastructure, residences, business/economy, sense of well-being and security, mental health, the environment, and animal populations.

War of ideas: Battle over ideals and principles and is a central element in any successful strategy of combat. Consists of waging a coordinated strategic campaign aimed at addressing root causes of grievances. The educational systems and media of societies are targeted in an effort to discredit extremism.

"War on Terror": Phrase used by George W. Bush in the aftermath of the September 11 attack to describe U.S. counterterrorism strategy.

Wassenaar Arrangement (officially The Wassenaar Arrangement on Export Controls for Conventional Arms and Dual-Use Goods and Technology): Arms control convention signed by forty countries whose goal is to "ensure responsible transfers of conventional arms and dual-use goods and technologies in furtherance of international and regional peace and security."

Weaponization of civilian assets: The process of modifying the structure of national critical infrastructure elements (e.g. aircrafts, chemical processing facilities) and using the resulting product as a weapon.

Weapons of mass destruction (WMD): Weapons that are capable of a high order of destruction and/or of being used in such a manner as to destroy large numbers of people. Generally considered to include chemical, biological, radiological, and nuclear weapons that are distinguishable from conventional weapons and explosives.

World Health Organization (WHO): Part of the United Nations system, located in Geneva, Switzerland, and established in 1946 to oversee and promote global health-related issues and to organize the world's nations toward self-reliance in health policy and implementation.

Zoonosis: Transmission to humans of a disease carried by an animal or insect.

Zoonotic disease: A particular human infection that is acquired, directly or indirectly, from animals, such as rats, mice, pigs, birds, dogs, cats, monkeys, bats, etc. Severe acute respiratory syndrome (SARS), first seen in 2003, is a recent example of a suspected zoonotic disease believed to have crossed the species barrier.

Index